GLOBALIZATION AND LITERARY STUDIES

This book provides a history of the way in which literature not only reflects but also actively shapes processes of globalization and our notions of global phenomena. It takes in a broad sweep of history, from antiquity through to the era of imperialism, to the present day. Whilst its primary focus is our own historical conjuncture, it looks at how earlier periods have shaped this by tracking key concepts that are imbricated with the concept of globalization, from translation to empire, to pandemics and environmental collapse. Drawing on these older themes and concerns, it then traces the germ of the relation between global phenomena and literary studies into the twentieth and twenty-first centuries, exploring key issues and frames of study such as contemporary slavery, the digital, world literature and the Anthropocene.

JOEL EVANS is Assistant Professor in Literature at the University of Nottingham. He is the author of *Conceptualising the Global in the Wake of the Postmodern: Literature, Culture, Theory* (2019).

CAMBRIDGE CRITICAL CONCEPTS

Cambridge Critical Concepts focuses on the important ideas animating twentieth- and twenty-first-century literary studies. Each concept addressed in the series has had a profound impact on literary studies, as well as on other disciplines, and already has a substantial critical bibliography surrounding it. This series captures the dynamic critical energies transmitted across twentieth- and twenty-first-century literary landscapes: the concepts critics bring to reading, interpretation and criticism. By addressing the origins, development and application of these ideas, the books collate and clarify how these particular concepts have developed, while also featuring fresh insights and establishing new lines of enquiry.

Cambridge Critical Concepts shifts the focus from period- or genre-based literary studies of key terms to the history and development of the terms themselves. Broad and detailed contributions cumulatively identify and investigate the various historical and cultural catalysts that made these critical concepts emerge as established twenty-first-century landmarks in the discipline. The level will be suitable for advanced undergraduates, graduates and specialists, as well as for those teaching outside their own research areas, and will have cross-disciplinary relevance for subjects such as history and philosophy.

Titles in the Series

Law and Literature
Edited by KIERAN DOLIN
University of Western Australia

Time and Literature
Edited by THOMAS M. ALLEN
University of Ottawa

The Global South and Literature
Edited by RUSSELL WEST-PAVLOV
University of Tübingen

Trauma and Literature
Edited by ROGER KURTZ
The College at Brockport, State University of New York

Food and Literature
Edited by GITANJALI SHAHANI
San Francisco State University

Animals, Animality, and Literature
Edited by BRUCE BOEHRER, MOLLY HAND AND BRIAN MASSUMI
Florida State University, University of Montreal

Terrorism and Literature
Edited by PETER HERMAN
San Diego State University

Climate and Literature
Edited by ADELINE JOHNS
University of Surrey

Orientalism and Literature
Edited by GEOFFREY NASH
SOAS, University of London

Decadence and Literature
Edited by JANE DESMARAIS AND DAVID WEIR
Goldsmiths, University of London and Hunter College

Affect and Literature
Edited by ALEX HOUEN
University of Cambridge

Sound and Literature
Edited by ANNA SNAITH
King's College London

Magical Realism and Literature
Edited by CHRISTOPHER WARNES AND KIM ANDERSON SASSER
University of Cambridge and Wheaton College, Illinois

Surrealism
Edited by NATALYA LUSTY
University of Melbourne

GLOBALIZATION AND LITERARY STUDIES

EDITED BY
JOEL EVANS
University of Nottingham

CAMBRIDGE
UNIVERSITY PRESS

University Printing House, Cambridge CB2 8BS, United Kingdom

One Liberty Plaza, 20th Floor, New York, NY 10006, USA

477 Williamstown Road, Port Melbourne, VIC 3207, Australia

314–321, 3rd Floor, Plot 3, Splendor Forum, Jasola District Centre, New Delhi – 110025, India

103 Penang Road, #05–06/07, Visioncrest Commercial, Singapore 238467

Cambridge University Press is part of the University of Cambridge.

It furthers the University's mission by disseminating knowledge in the pursuit of education, learning, and research at the highest international levels of excellence.

www.cambridge.org
Information on this title: www.cambridge.org/9781108840927
DOI: 10.1017/9781108887915

© Cambridge University Press 2022

This publication is in copyright. Subject to statutory exception and to the provisions of relevant collective licensing agreements, no reproduction of any part may take place without the written permission of Cambridge University Press.

First published 2022

Printed in the United Kingdom by TJ Books Limited, Padstow Cornwall

A catalogue record for this publication is available from the British Library.

Library of Congress Cataloging-in-Publication Data
NAMES: Evans, Joel, 1987– editor.
TITLE: Globalization and literary studies / edited by Joel Evans.
DESCRIPTION: Cambridge ; New York, NY : Cambridge University Press, 2022. | Includes bibliographical references and index.
IDENTIFIERS: LCCN 2021970025 | ISBN 9781108840927 (hardback) | ISBN 9781108887915 (ebook)
SUBJECTS: LCSH: Literature and globalization. | Globalization in literature. | Literature – History and criticism. | BISAC: LITERARY CRITICISM / Semiotics & Theory
CLASSIFICATION: LCC PN56.G55 G559 2022 | DDC 809–dc23/eng/20220202
LC record available at https://lccn.loc.gov/2021970025

ISBN 978-1-108-84092-7 Hardback

Cambridge University Press has no responsibility for the persistence or accuracy of URLs for external or third-party internet websites referred to in this publication and does not guarantee that any content on such websites is, or will remain, accurate or appropriate.

Contents

List of Figures	*page* ix
List of Tables	x
List of Contributors	xi
Acknowledgements	xiv
Introduction Joel Evans	1

PART I ORIGINS — 19

1. The Ecology of Globalization: Environmental Catastrophe and the History of Literature — 21
   Walter Cohen

2. Forms of Premodern Literary Circulation — 35
   Alexander Beecroft

3. The End of History: Literature, Eschatology and Its Legacies — 51
   Joel Evans

4. Translation: Print Culture and Internationalism — 67
   Mary Helen McMurran

5. Empire: The Nineteenth-Century Global Novel in English — 80
   Elleke Boehmer and Dominic Davies

PART II DEVELOPMENT — 95

6. Joseph Conrad, the Global and the Sea — 97
   Michael Greaney

7. Mutual Equality: Modernism and Globalization — 110
   Paul Stasi

viii *Contents*

8	Edward Said: Literature and the World *Conor McCarthy*	126
9	The New McWorld Order: Postmodernism and Corporate Globalization *Simon Malpas*	144
10	Pharmakon, Difference and the Arche-Digital *Claire Colebrook*	159
11	Time–Space Compression: The Long View *Mark Currie*	178
12	The Matter of Blackness in World Literature *Joseph H. Jackson*	195
13	World-Systems, Literature and Geoculture *Matthew Eatough*	210
14	World Author: On Exploding Canons and Writing towards More Equitable Literary Futures *Rebecca Braun*	226

PART III APPLICATION   245

15	The Globalization of the Enclave *Matthew Hart*	247
16	Geopolitics and the Novel: The Case of the Mediterranean Noir *Caren Irr*	262
17	Spy Fiction in the Age of the Global *Maria Christou*	277
18	The Twenty-First-Century Global Slave Narrative Trade *Laura T. Murphy*	294
19	Planetary Poetics *Christian Moraru*	305
20	Addressing Globalization in the Anthropocene *Sam Solnick*	318

References 334
Index 362

Figures

1 Statue of Goethe on display in Frankfurt
  Airport's Goethe Bar. *page* 226
2 The 'Verlagscollage'. 237

Tables

1	Climate change, 3300 BCE–400 CE	*page* 23
2	Epidemics and climate change, 150–1560 CE	26
3	Climate change, 1560–2020 CE	31

Contributors

ALEXANDER BEECROFT is Jessie Chapman Alcorn Memorial Professor of Foreign Languages and Professor of Classics and Comparative Literature at the University of South Carolina. He is the author of, among other works, *An Ecology of World Literature: From Antiquity to the Present Day* (2015).

ELLEKE BOEHMER is Professor of World Literature in the English faculty, Oxford, and Director of the Oxford Centre for Life-Writing at Wolfson College, Oxford. His recent work includes *Postcolonial Poetics* (2018) and *To the Volcano* (2019).

REBECCA BRAUN is Professor and Executive Dean in the College of Arts, Social Sciences and Celtic Studies at The National University of Ireland, Galway. She is the author of, amongst other works, *Authors and the World: Literary Authorship in Modern Germany* (2022).

MARIA CHRISTOU is Presidential Fellow in Modern and Contemporary Literature at the University of Manchester. She is the author of, among other works, *Eating Otherwise: The Philosophy of Food in Twentieth-Century Literature* (2017).

WALTER COHEN is Professor of English at the University of Michigan and is the author, most recently, of *A History of European Literature: The West and the World from Antiquity to the Present* (2017).

CLAIRE COLEBROOK is Edwin Erle Sparks Professor of English, Philosophy and Women's and Gender Studies at Penn State University. Her most recent book (co-authored with Tom Cohen and J. Hillis Miller) is *Twilight of the Anthropocene Idols* (2016).

MARK CURRIE is Professor of Contemporary Literature at Queen Mary University of London. His books include *About Time* (2007) and *The*

Unexpected (2013), and he is currently writing about the concepts of contingency and uncertainty in literature and culture.

DOMINIC DAVIES is Senior Lecturer in English at City, University of London. He is currently writing a book entitled *The Weight of World Literature*.

MATTHEW EATOUGH is Assistant Professor in Literature at Baruch College, City University New York. He is the assistant editor of *The Oxford Handbook of Global Modernisms* (2012) and the author of recent and forthcoming articles in *Modern Language Quarterly*, *Literature and Medicine*, *Twentieth-Century Literature* and *Safund*.

JOEL EVANS is Assistant Professor in Literature at the University of Nottingham. He is the author of, among other works, *Conceptualising the Global in the Wake of the Postmodern: Literature, Culture, Theory* (2019).

MICHAEL GREANEY is Senior Lecturer in the Department of English and Creative Writing at Lancaster University. He is the author of, among other works, *Sleep and the Novel: Fictions of Somnolence from Jane Austen to the Present* (2018).

MATTHEW HART is the author of *Extraterritorial: A Political Geography of Contemporary Fiction* (2020). He is Associate Professor and Director of Graduate Studies in the Department of English and Comparative Literature at Columbia University.

CAREN IRR is Professor of English at Brandeis University. She is the author of, among other works, *Toward the Geopolitical Novel: U.S. Fiction in the Twenty-First Century* (2014).

JOSEPH H. JACKSON is Assistant Professor in Twentieth-Century and Contemporary English Literature at the University of Nottingham. He is the author of, among other works, *Writing Black Scotland* (2020).

CONOR MCCARTHY teaches English literature and intellectual history at Maynooth University, Ireland. He has published *The Cambridge Introduction to Edward Said* (2010) and edited *The Revolutionary and Anti-Imperialist Writings of James Connolly 1893–1916* (2016).

MARY HELEN MCMURRAN teaches at the University of Western Ontario, where she specializes in eighteenth-century British literature. She is the author of, among other works, *The Spread of Novels: Translation and Prose Fiction in the Eighteenth Century* (2009).

List of Contributors

SIMON MALPAS lectures in English Literature at the University of Edinburgh. He is the author of, among other works, *Thomas Pynchon* (2013).

CHRISTIAN MORARU is Class of 1949 Distinguished Professor in the Humanities and Professor of English at the University of North Carolina, Greensboro. He has authored and co-edited books such as *Reading for the Planet: Toward a Geomethodology* (2015) and *Theory in the 'Post' Era: A Vocabulary for the Twenty-First-Century Conceptual Commons* (2021).

LAURA T. MURPHY is Professor of Human Rights and Contemporary Slavery at Sheffield Hallam University. She is the author of, among other works, *The New Slave Narrative: The Battle Over Representations of Contemporary Slavery* (2019).

SAM SOLNICK is Senior Lecturer in English Literature at the University of Liverpool. He is the author of, among other works, *Poetry and the Anthropocene: Ecology, Biology and Technology in Contemporary British and Irish Poetry* (2018).

PAUL STASI teaches twentieth-century anglophone literature at the State University of New York, Albany. He is the author of, among other works, *Modernism, Imperialism and the Historical Sense* (2012).

Acknowledgements

Thanks are due to Ray Ryan for suggesting this project in the first place and for having the patience to see it through. Thanks also to Rebecca Spence for reading some of the manuscript in its early stages and to Chris Griffin for assisting me with referencing, style and so on. Special thanks are due to Maria, my wife, who has read parts of this manuscript and who also cared for me and our daughter during a long period of illness I went through whilst this book was in preparation. Thanks go to my parents also for caring for us during this period.

Introduction
Globalization and Literary Studies
Joel Evans

What seemed until recently to be an enduring, albeit damaged system of global state-capitalism now increasingly appears at best volatile and at worst at the point of disintegration. It would seem odd, then, at this moment, to publish a book on globalization and literary studies. Surely, there are new paradigms, new contexts, and new forms to be analysed in a world that is now beholden to a host of new nationalisms set against the backdrop of a world-system in a state of managed decline. These are, of course, pressing issues, and this book does not shy away from addressing them and their relation to literary production and its theorization. In other words, a portion of this volume's remit will be to track what from one perspective is the phenomenon of economic-political globalization receding, to think what this means for literary studies, and to assess what new forms might emerge as a result. But this is only a small part of the story of globalization and the literary forms which we might in one way or another associate with this. The other part of the story is much more expansive and will involve us in a moment thinking about questions of periodization, critical method and conceptual definition.

In effect, this is another way of saying that the writings presented here seek to survey the history of globalization and its relation to literary studies in the widest historical sense possible. This will entail looking at periods in which globalization in the usual sense of the word – at least from the vantage points of the political and the economic – seems to have morphed or altered. But, as we will see too, this sense of alteration derives not only from the varieties of different meanings ascribed to the word globalization when placed in historical context, but also its range of conceptual kith and kin, from imperialism and globalism, through to world-systems, and on to that much broader category of the global itself. Summarized thus far, though, are in fact two of this volume's core contributions: firstly, its examination, in each chapter, of the phenomenon of globalization alongside, and as congruent with, the history of literary production; and secondly, the way in which it reaches back historically more than any other project on the topic.[1]

It would seem apt, then, to start by defining this slippery term – globalization – before proceeding to note how we might think about it in relation to literary production, and literary studies more broadly. If we want to make a general statement on periodization, we should bear in mind that there are at least two globalizations from this perspective, and as articulated in this book. Firstly, there is what we might call Globalization: a distinct phase in world history that kicks off fully in the late 1980s – the period in which the term was coined – and describes a perceived waning of the power and efficacy of the nation-state in the face of global phenomena, predominantly of the financial variety, but also of the cultural and technological variety.[2] Secondly, there is globalization, the less official, lower-case version, which involves all sorts of periods in world history whereby a polity exceeding the nation or region is instantiated via cultural, economic, military, organic or whatever other means. This is where the term becomes more readily substitutable with other terms such as those listed above (and others), even though the more clearly demarcated usage does overlap significantly with these and other terms also. Indeed, it is of course the case that we only call these usually earlier forms of globalization by this name at all due to its prevalence as a way of describing contemporary conditions. One can see this as either an ideological manoeuvre, whereby the past is coloured by our own skewed perception of the present, or as a paradigm shift. It is probably both. To put it differently, if the discourse on G/globalization occasionally obscures our ability to think about global capitalism and the conditions this engenders clearly, it also, at the same time, opens new avenues for thinking about this same system that may have previously seemed arcane or overly abstract.

Of course, any complex account of what the official Globalization is beyond discourse and ideology will need to include not just our now-disintegrating economic system but also some other more concrete factors. And so whilst there are various conceptual accoutrements – from the supposed erasure of borders stemming from free trade, to the apparent shrinking of the globe which arises via both advanced transportation systems and telecommunications networks[3] – that get placed around the main concept, we ought to identify three key factors that drive the efficacy of the latter. The first is the one we have touched on already: the emergence of a globe-encompassing form of capitalism in the wake of the collapse of the Soviet Union. The second is the form this capitalism takes, which is a neoliberal one (neoliberalism being quintessentially 'global' in vision and practice, despite recent nationalist inflections of this, which are themselves a symptom of the damaged global system to which we have already referred).[4] And the third is the emergence of a worldwide digital infrastructure in the guise of the internet.[5] All three of these factors emerge in the 1980s, and therefore offer not only a compelling material underpinning for the notion of Globalization – both as a state of things and an ongoing process – but offer a defined way of periodizing it. It is perhaps key to note that none of these factors is set to vanish any time soon, and it is only neoliberalism that would appear to be acquiring some kind of nationalist inflection. For better or worse, then, our horizon remains global, and the interlinked underpinnings of Globalization continue at an albeit modified pace.

It is these three factors that also frequently determine what then gets defined as globalization in the unofficial sense. As we will see throughout the book, the word can be used, for example, in its technological sense to describe the emergence of worldwide systems of infrastructure under empire; in its general sense to describe global systems of trade in the late nineteenth and early twentieth centuries; or in the more specific sense (as in the case of neoliberalism) to describe the conditions of imperialism in the era just referred to. And alongside this, the concept can be used as a lens through which to observe the dynamics and movements of labour, the worldwide transmission and suppression of disease, and the often-disastrous effects in the modifications of weather systems. This form of globalization has affinities with a sub-species of the genre, in which the globalization of culture in the guise of standardization, translation or circulation becomes an issue, and here we begin to approach the other side of this book's dual focus, which is the literary. The triptych of standardization, translation and circulation will also involve us witnessing a more direct divergence from globalization (of culture or whatever else) per se and delving into the theory of world-systems. Such theoretical frames are presented here not only due to their overlapping concerns with the relation between literary production and its global resonances, but also as an illustration of the twin dominance of these two related approaches. In other words, readings of literature focussed on world-systems are gradually becoming a dominant method of analysis at a scale beyond the nation-state, even though globalization still offers a not insignificant, and more encompassing frame for this. This book tries to take account of this, whilst at the same time highlighting overlaps between the two fields, flagging up other relevant (in some cases emergent) fields – from Actor Network

Theory (ANT) to planetary studies, to studies of new slave narratives – and showing where one theoretical standpoint might appear more useful than another.

Origins

One example of the overlap between world-literature studies and studies framed by a more general notion of globalization comes in the first two chapters of the book. A look at these will allow us to begin setting out the volume's approach to the literary, whilst also drawing attention to its scope. Our first chapter sees Walter Cohen tracing a 5,000-year history (3000 BCE–present day) of the relation between global environmental catastrophe and literary production. Here, we see the complex inter-relation between disease, climate change and literature, the ways in which the global reach of the first two hampers the global reach of the latter, and the way in which new forms eventually arise from such a process. This is globalization in its unofficial, process-oriented sense, then, but it is also a way of thinking about the globalization of literature itself. Something similar is under way in Alexander Beecroft's chapter, which also traces a long history of the development and circulation of literary forms. We see, for example, and amongst other things, how the *Pañcatantra*, a group of beast fables first composed around 300 CE in Sanskrit, offers a weak model of global circulation, whereby, over centuries, the tales circulate and mutate across Eurafrasia up until around 1260. For Beecroft, this is an example of a literary world-system, but one can nevertheless see a similar dynamic at work as in the first chapter. Both approaches focus on global circulation, and both are concerned with how literature constitutes a form of globalization or world-system itself.

These two chapters form part of a section entitled 'Origins', where we attempt to trace some of the earliest manifestations of literary globalization, and for a significant part offer something approximating the kind of long histories already outlined. In this section, the book opens up new dialogues and raises new questions for the broad field of global literary studies. But it also sets out the general framework for approaching the relation between globalization (and its related themes and concepts) and literature (and literary studies more broadly). To restate this in simple terms, the collected writings here seek to demonstrate how the literary has actively shaped, defined and been a part of G/globalization, rather than simply representing or being affected by it. Thus, in the two chapters just outlined, we see how literature constitutes a (global) system of circulation itself, with all sorts of permutations and anomalies. But we will see other ways in which this broad focus plays out, by tracing theoretical underpinnings, literary figurations and further systems of circulation.

'Origins' proceeds along a similar route in Chapter 3, but from a slightly different entry point. It is here that this book's broad coverage of literary studies begins to make itself felt, as Joel Evans thinks about the notion of the end of history, and its eschatological inflections, via the work of the philologist Erich Auerbach. Looking at Auerbach's body of work allows us, again, to produce a long history of the interaction between literature and globalization, which is made possible in part by the sheer scope of this writer's work. As we will see, if the end of history in its eschatological sense has always had a global dimension, this is one with various twists and turns, from the religious to the secular and on into our own rather more ambivalent era. But what Auerbach's work also makes clear is that the literary is in a sense the progenitor of eschatological worldviews, a role which it relinquishes with the advent of modernity, leaving critical discourse to pick up with it left off. Alongside this, Chapter 3 also traces how Auerbach's view of literary production fits in with an emergent concept of early Globalization once his work touches on the early twentieth century. The task then becomes to think through how the relation Auerbach articulates here might apply to our own era, which seems at once ready to leave the whole idea of eschatology behind, and yet is still strangely preoccupied with it.

Chapter 4 continues the long history model pursued thus far, in this case by thinking through the complexities of literary translation at an international level. As Mary Helen McMurran points out, world-literature studies has to an extent failed to take into account colonial and imperialist dynamics when thinking through the politics of circulation, but it has also failed to think through what translation actually means in these and other contexts. The global circulation and translation of texts in Renaissance Europe, colonial translations in North India and Arabic translations of European literature in the nineteenth century all serve to demonstrate the ways in which translation itself is far from a simple process of transferring from one language to another; indeed, it would be more accurate in these circumstances to say that texts are adapted, rendered, repurposed and reprinted. Such processes draw our attention to the fact that texts, in the way they circulate globally, do not operate in anything like the way in which an axiomatic understanding of globalization as a standardizing force suggests. McMurran theorizes this dynamic through recourse to

Actor Network Theory, constructing a theory of translation which makes visible multiple actors and spheres of influence within overarching imperial contexts.

The topic of colonialism is picked up once again in Chapter 5, in this instance via the global dimensions of literary figuration itself. In particular, we are concerned here with Dickens's *Dombey and Son* (1948) and Olive Schreiner's *The Story of an African Farm* (1870). Elleke Boehmer and Dominic Davies provide a reading of these two texts which, in turn, gives us an insight into two poles of a colonial world-system: the metropolitan centre and the southern periphery. What Boehmer and Davies seek to demonstrate here is the varied way in which texts which are apparently about close-knit domestic life nevertheless register global, colonial dynamics. In the tradition of Said and Spivak, in other words, this chapter maps the ways in which literature obliquely registers the broad expanse of empire. It is here that these texts' figurative qualities become important, and from a novel angle. For if they are concerned at one level with depicting the infrastructure of empire, which makes possible a leap from the contained space of the domestic scene to the global space of empire, then they are also in some way part of the infrastructure of empire itself. The nineteenth-century novel, as Boehmer and Davies put it, lays 'out tracks that expanded its readers' spatial imaginaries from national to global scales', a quality which has both a critical and a justificatory edge.

Developments

When it doesn't rub up against the twentieth and twenty-first centuries, then, the 'Origins' section traces lower-case globalization from all sorts of different, historical angles, including modes of actual circulation, translation and contagion, alongside literary figuration, exegesis and critique. We see in these chapters the germ of what will become literature's role within an era of full-blown Globalization, which is to say that what are emergent or weak global trends both become dominant ones and take on a life of their own once we reach the twentieth century. This, then, is what the next section of the book – 'Developments' – seeks to chart, and it does this by looking at some of the key conceptual building blocks and themes of Globalization and its specific relationship with the literary, from prototypical forms within the late imperial era, to the postmodern's relation to world markets, to the relationship between deconstruction and digital culture.

The first two chapters trace the varying ways in which a budding and then established modernist aesthetic tackles the topic of the global against a backdrop of imperialism. This gives us an opportunity, then, to think through the literary aspect of what has been seen as a first go, or trial-run of the Globalization of more recent years, the former being made possible by a now global system of trade and finance, an earlier instantiation of the telecommunications network, and innovations in worldwide transport. But the crucial difference in this version of Globalization, and as already spelled out, is its intimate connection with imperialist practice and ideology, and the two chapters here seek to think this through in some detail.

As Michael Greaney points out in Chapter 6, it has become almost a commonplace to describe Joseph Conrad as the first, truly global writer, something which touches on both Conrad's own, varied national allegiances, but also the expansive geographical scope deployed throughout his fictions. Greaney proceeds then to dissect a whole series of contradictions and vacillations in Conrad's work which take place within its figuration of the global, imperialist world-system. The first of these is that whilst Conrad is obsessed with mapping and discovery, he also loves the idea of unmapped territories free from the Western gaze. But this is complicated by the fact that the very idea of 'unmapped', or blank territory is of course itself a thoroughly imperialist idea; it presumes that places only exist once they are gazed on by a Western observer. Typically, Conrad here seems both to play into the imperial ideologeme in question and denounce it. Other contradictions, as Greaney points out, abound in Conrad's work: *Heart of Darkness* (1899) offers at once an antidote to imperialist homogenization through a modernist aesthetic of emptiness and ineffability, and an erasure of indigenous culture; the novels that deal with the sea and maritime industry foreground the sense of both interpersonal connection and dislocation characteristic to narratives of globalization more broadly; and the sea itself in Conrad's writing is something which is both singular and plural, a multiplicity that gets everywhere and eats away at human frontiers and lines of demarcation. If Conrad is a writer of early Globalization, then it seems safe to say that in Greaney's account of this he is so in a thoroughly dialectical sense.

One other way of thinking about the Conradian dialectic is to think of it as a kind of image, which again draws us back to modernist aesthetics. In some ways, Conrad's writing produces a more distant iteration of Ezra Pound's concept of the image as 'an intellectual and emotional complex', which in turn gives a 'sense of freedom from time limits and space'

(Pound 1968b: 4). Pound's notion of the image is what Paul Stasi begins with in Chapter 7, via a reading of Claude McKay's poem 'The Harlem Dancer'. For Stasi, Mckay reinvents the modernist image on the basis of spatial relations inherent in early Globalization; we find here a complex which blends together the experience of Harlem and of the Caribbean, and which therefore taps into all sorts of broader concerns which would appear to offer a glimpse of the way in which one might transcend the fundamental opposition between nationalism and imperialism of this period. Indeed, it is just this conceptual knot – that is, the dynamic between reactionary nationalism and imperialist expansion so characteristic of this late stage of modernity – that modernist writers from McKay to Pound to Joyce have tried to untie in a variety of ways. A picture therefore emerges of the modernist attitude toward Globalization in its prototypical form as one which tries to find a way to resist this, but at the same seeks to engage at the level of totality in an admittedly partial, or fragmented way.

In Chapter 8, we return to the focus on critical discourse, but with a more theoretical-biographical emphasis on a figure who perhaps has done more than any other critic and theorist to emphasize a global perspective, particularly with reference to (early and late) imperialist culture: Edward Said. Conor McCarthy here provides us with a breakdown of the various ways in which Said's work has taken into account the global, or world-perspective in literary studies, from his engagement with figures like Auerbach and the philological tradition more broadly (which itself also involves entering into the more expansive terrain of humanism) to his more well-known works on orientalism and imperialism. But McCarthy also traces the germ of a global or worldly emphasis in Said's early work on Conrad; we see this, for example, in Said's mapping of the tendency toward authority, or a will to power, in Conrad's work and the way in which this is always doubled by a form of molestation or fallibility. Conor illustrates this via Conrad's *Heart of Darkness* which both expresses a will to colonization and a critique of this, a double movement which underpins so many of the other contradictions identified in the chapter on Conrad described above, and is shot through with geopolitical resonances. This in turn allows us to observe the trace of the geopolitical in Said's early work, which then leads up to the explicitly imperialist and orientalist frames he tackles later in his career. According to McCarthy, this work in general not only offers a way of reading the literary at the level of the world itself, but also offers some stark lessons for those who wish to engage with the notion of Globalization, not least due to Said's critical position on the precise meaning of the term.

Introduction 9

Chapter 9 then takes us away from earlier forms and their relation to a prototypical Globalization and on to postmodernism and its relation to a now fully established Globalization, with all the hallmarks set out at the beginning of this introduction. Simon Malpas traces the relation here between postmodern literary culture and a new phase in global capitalism through the lens of the concept of the 'McWorld', which designates a then emergent sense of global, cultural homogenization. What this then allows Malpas to do is think through the ways in which the literature of the 1980s and 1990s has responded to and transformed key conceptual frameworks which cohere around the notion of a homogenized, corporatized world-system, an idea that fiction itself has helped form. The first of these is Fredric Jameson's notion of postmodernist art forms being intimately bound up with a multinational form of capitalism that is in some way always beyond our perceptual reach. For Jameson, the solution to such a problem lies in a new form of cognitive mapping which would enable us to re-orient ourselves within a new global, networked horizon (Jameson; 1991: 51); for Malpas, one can observe this kind of mapping already at work at an aesthetic level in Caryl Churchill's *Serious Money* (1987). Martin Amis's *Money* (1984), however, offers a rather depthless exposé of commercial culture which finds affinity with Jean Baudrillard's writings on hyperreality. And then there is Jean-François Lyotard's notion of a postmodern art form that offers a critical edge and an antidote to the totalizing qualities of the world-market, as opposed to a readily decodable, realist rendering of it. For Malpas, Bret Easton Ellis's *American Psycho* (1991) fits into this model. Malpas thus provides a kind of taxonomy of the various ways in which literary culture responds to and transcends global corporatism and homogenization, and he ends by demonstrating how literature moved on from this concern in the wake of the 1980s.

If knowledge of the globe can be at once redemptive and something we need to escape from in the postmodern moment, this is in a sense something which is raised to the level of a philosophical principle in poststructuralist thought. This is what Claire Colebrook sets out to explore in Chapter 10, arguing that what she calls globalism – in thought and practice – is always at once 'an opening to the infinite *and* an articulation of a specific relation through which the infinite is inscribed'. One can flesh out the nature of this double movement via three of the core concepts of deconstruction: difference, pharmacology and arche-writing. Social media, and digital culture more broadly, is one example in-practice of the way in which contemporary society is both in thrall to a vulgar variety of particularism via the various and distinct life-style choices and other modes of individualism encouraged by this and is part of a global unity of difference (the world wide web). What better way to think this dynamic, then, than via Derrida's (repurposed) concept of the trace, whereby each particularity opens out onto a stream of difference/deference. Indeed, the digital itself is of course simply another expression of what Derrida would have called (arche-) writing, which today has been made fully manifest through its global ubiquity. Globalism in its digital iteration is thus pharmacological, not only due to its associations with writing, but also because it poses both a solution to and is part of the problem of contemporary capitalism, or at least that which engenders its perpetuation; the digital presents both the possibility of an event which is at once universal and particular, and yet all too often ends up in difference which is co-opted and rendered inauthentic.

For the rest of the 'Developments' section, we return to this book's focus on providing histories of particular themes within the mesh of the relation between G/globalization and literary studies. Mark Currie kicks us off with this in Chapter 11 where we begin again in the 1980s with David Harvey's concept of time–space compression, which itself has become a key concept within Globalization studies and beyond. What Currie argues in this chapter is that the model of an elimination of temporal and spatial barriers that is so characteristic of classical theories of Globalization gives way in the twenty-first century to a sense of global, temporal contingency and uncertainty. In fact, contingency and uncertainty were already latent elements in Harvey's own theory; Currie teases these out, then, whilst also drawing out the complexities of the way in which Harvey views the relation between time–space compression and cultural production, along with thinking through how this might then relate to the era of full-blown contingency. What becomes clear here is that cultural forms, including literature, do not blankly register global developments and the ways these affect our sense of time and space; in fact, they actively shape and produce these. Currie demonstrates this by taking us back to a deconstructive view of cultural and media production, in this case via the work of Bernard Stiegler. What this cements is the notion that we ought not to expect literary texts to reflect either time–space compression, or new temporal contingencies, at least at the level of theme. Rather, we should seek to find new temporal articulations within formal qualities. Narrative tense offers a striking example, and Currie sets out some of the complexities of thinking this in relation to what we have just outlined.

Whilst the shrinking of space, so often figured as standardization, is characteristic of the experience of Globalization in its official sense, this of course does not mean that this phenomenon is absent from earlier attempts to figure the world in its totality. In Chapter 12, Joseph H. Jackson uncovers the central place that attempts to figure Blackness have within the history of an uneven world-system, the origins of which can be traced back to European colonialism. Taking Paul Gilroy's and Achille Mbembe's analyses of Blackness as models, Jackson shows how a vision of global Blackness, which unfolds both through diasporic and class relations, has been articulated in a range of anglophone and francophone literature. Global Blackness here is at once an articulation of a mass oppression brought about through the drawing together of global labour markets, and a symbol of potential liberation through the common link to a planetary cause. In its literary guise, an earlier modernist vision of Black planetarity conforms to, and actively shaped, this call to liberation. We see this in writers such as Aimé Césaire and Claude McKay. But we also see in these earlier visions a desire to survey what is a global, imperialistic system of labour from a Black perspective. This, then, is the negative side to Black planetarity and it is figured quite directly by writers such as Eric Walrond, or in a more complex, dialectical way in the work of Frantz Fanon. In the more contemporary world, we see what happens when this experience collides with Globalization properly speaking, in which the remnants of imperialism cohere into what Mbembe dubs 'the becoming black of the world' (2017: 5), whereby the conditions reserved for the colonial subject are extended to a burgeoning, generalized, global underclass. Jackson sets out against this backdrop to uncover the complex ways in which contemporary literature bears the weight of an earlier Black planetarity.

In Chapter 13, we return to a world-systems approach, and in particular to the notion of geoculture. As Matthew Eatough explains, the notion of geoculture in Immanuel Wallerstein's work is relatively under-theorized and doesn't really pertain directly to literary and broader forms of cultural production. Eatough thus sets out to think how we might expropriate the term for literary studies. In fact, there are two ways that this is, in a sense, already being done. The first is via what Eatough calls a phenomenological approach to texts, which involves thinking about the ways in which texts approach and render experiential life-worlds. The second is concerned with thinking at the level of the system, in this case what Eatough calls a genre-system. In this instance we are able to see how diverse genres as a whole map particular aspects of a world-system, to bring together a series of partial figurations and graft them into something resembling a figurative totality. Roberto Bolano's labyrinthine novel *2666* (2004) furnishes us with material to illustrate the first approach, and to think through in part how this might play out in a text that seeks to relate a broad swathe of our own current world-system. Eatough reaches back further to the early twentieth century, however, to give us an example of the second approach, which is illustrated via an overview of *fin-de-siècle* literary culture. This, in its various forms – from imperial romance and adventure to the detective story, and on to invasion narratives like *Dracula* (1897) and *War of the Worlds* (1897) – demonstrates the various takes that each genre provides of the world-system of the time. This then allows one to trace affinities with the broad expanse of the world-system itself, whilst articulating what the cultural content of this is, or in this case was.

If genre-systems offer a unique way of reading texts at the level of the world-system, then thinking through the lens of authorship offers another way of doing this. It is to this topic that Rebecca Braun turns in Chapter 14, developing an expansive concept of authorship and thinking through rigorously how this might link in with a global perspective. For Braun, it would be more accurate to think of the author as an 'originator', 'one whose overall agency is significantly relativized by that of [...] other agents, both people and things, influencing the real-world circumstances in which the work exists at any one point in time'. In an era of Globalization the agents can be multiple, and so Braun not only grounds her notion of the author and the world in Goethe's work on world literature, but also examines how Goethe himself has been subject to a system of world-authorship which mediates this originator's work. Mediation is thus a key term here, and the way different mediators or agents create an image of world-authorship is something that Braun tracks not just in relation to Goethe, but also the Rowohlt publishing house in 1960s Germany, and then on to Katja Petrowskaja's non-fiction work *Maybe Esther* (2014). Along the way, Braun identifies four core models of world-authorship, each of which have different implications and each of which can cross over with one another: the commemorative, the celebratory, the utopian and the satirical. This enables Braun to uncover the granular way in which texts are bound up with and mediated by different agents within late twentieth and early twenty-first century Globalization. As may be clear from the particular conceptual emphasis here, Braun grafts ANT onto her theory of world-authorship, and so we see in this chapter another way in which this broader paradigm (ANT) provides a lens through which to think how literary texts operate as part of global phenomena.

Applications

These last four expansive chapters end the 'Developments' section, and allow us to move on to the final section of the collection, which is entitled

'Applications'. This section reads literature alongside key, twenty-first century global issues and frames of analysis, from contemporary slavery to neo-feudalism and on to the Anthropocene. What the section also sets out to do is map some of the ways in which Globalization as an actual state of affairs and as a conceptual frame, is losing some of its efficacy.

Indeed, this last aspect of 'Applications' is something that we hit on straight away in Chapter 15, in which Matthew Hart explores how literature interacts and to an extent subverts a newly potent nationalism. Hart does this by looking at the brief history of the enclave narrative, from J. G. Ballard's work in the 1990s and early 2000s to Caryl Phillips's *A Distant Shore* (2003) and Ali Smith's seasonal quartet (2016–20). What Hart suggests, firstly, is that these narratives of the enclave are literary articulations of the parcelization of space in contemporary societies; all these texts, in other words, seek to render a situation in which the global super-rich wall themselves off from the world outside. As Hart shows, this parcelization is a phenomenon of Globalization itself, but it is also, to an extent, where the new forms of nationalism we encounter today originate. For Hart, though, literary renderings of the enclave offer more than just an exposé of the current situation. Whilst these texts do render these spaces visible, and allow us to reflect on global parcelization, they also provide a utopian or critical edge to this, and in this sense they also present us with ways of creatively resisting nativist reaction.

If nativism is one opposing tendency to be found within and running alongside our current world-system, there all also utopian tendencies to be found here which mirror the global expanse of capital. Caren Irr seeks to uncover such a dynamic in Chapter 16 via a wide-ranging reading of Mediterranean noir from the late twentieth century and into the twenty-first. First, Irr locates in this genre a preoccupation with corruption that is then shown to undergird multinational economics and politics. Indeed, this is a preoccupation which extends across a genre which takes in a whole section of the uneven, contemporary world-system, from France to Turkey to Lebanon. But, in writers such as Parker Bilal, Petros Markaris, Ahmed Ümit and Alex Mattich, Irr suggests that this attention to corruption and capital is doubled by an enduring vision of the sea as something utopian, or which poses an alternative to the negative vision of Globalization already outlined. This (albeit weak) utopianism has all sorts of variants, from the spiritual to the historical, but it does suggest as Irr argues both an enduring desire to pose an alternative to capitalist Globalization, and a proto-ecological inflection of the utopian. From this perspective, it is interesting to note that whilst the sea is seen as part and parcel of an earlier form of Globalization – say, in the novels of Conrad, as explored in Chapter 6 – it is here seen as something opposed to contemporary Globalization in its common or garden sense, offering in different ways an oblique escape route for perhiperalized areas of the world-system.

Chapter 17 continues in a similar vein in terms of its emphasis on genre – in this case spy fiction – but from the perspective of a single author: William Gibson. Gibson is of course crucial in the history of the discourse of Globalization itself, with his coining of the term cyberspace, and his narratives which seek to explore this. In this chapter, Maria Christou shows how Gibson continues to engage with the topic into the twenty-first century by completely reshaping spy fiction in the Blue Ant Trilogy, made up of *Pattern Recognition* (2003), *Spook Country* (2007), and *Zero History* (2010). If the traditional (fictional) spy is firmly associated with *national* politics, says Christou, Gibson unmoors this figure in these novels and places them within the context of global flows of capital, goods and information. The interest that this mode of fiction has had with totality (as pointed out by Fredric Jameson in particular – see Jameson 1991: 38) is here played out at an explicitly global level, rather than a national one which can be read as then speaking to a global context. But there is a strange anti-climatic tendency within this desire to map totality, with the novels foregrounding grand conspiracies that amount to trifles and master-plans that come to nothing. This tendency is attributable, Christou argues, to the removal of the state in these fictions as a guarantor of meaning. But it also draws our attention to the way in which Gibson's novels anticipate a new framework of power within the context of the emergent global configuration, which is most usefully characterized as neo-feudal.

One of the shockingly neglected aspects of the global flows of goods and labour in contemporary capitalism is the role that slavery continues to play in this. In Chapter 18 Laura T. Murphy provides an account of this by way of analysing the content and the politics surrounding contemporary, or 'new' slave narratives. As Murphy points out, these non-fictional accounts are concerned specifically with exposing current, actually-existing forms of slavery which form a crucial part of the global economy. Another key feature of these narratives is that they often draw our attention to the place of slavery within geopolitical flash points. Francis Bok's *My Escape from Slavery* (2003) offers a particularly striking example, with the book describing Bok's journey from slavery in Sudan in the late 1990s and early 2000s to eventual freedom in the United States. As Murphy points out, though, this slavery was in fact brought to fruition itself as a result of global struggle for oil supplies; the displacement and enslavement of Bok and his community occurs as a by-product of the drive to establish Western and Asian investment within Sudan, thus making it a part of the global oil trade. If the slave narrative thus forms an uneasy relationship with a globalized form of trade from this perspective, this is accentuated through the lack of reference to this dynamic in Bok's text, an aspect which has translated into greater marketability within a Western, and specifically anglophone context. As Murphy moves on to show, texts like Bok's in fact have a much deeper ideological function, and are often used as a tool to promote contemporary forms of imperialism, particularly within the United States.

We take a turn away from the explicitly geopolitical in Chapter 19 and move on to new theoretical ground within literary studies. Indeed, the next two chapters shift our attention again toward some of the ways in which we might challenge the frame and scale of readings structured around some of the core assumptions and grounding factors of Globalization. Christian Moraru does this in Chapter 19 by explicating what planetary studies is, how it differs from the notions of Globalization and the global, and how this then bears on the way in which we read contemporary literature. For Moraru both the concept of the globe and the planet offer particular takes on the world itself; they are ways, in other words, of altering our perception of this. If thinking in terms of the globe encourages a 'globalist' approach, tied to the current state of affairs, thinking at the level of the planet allows us to think how the world might be made differently. Instead of the expansive, totalizing view so often pursued by studies focussed around the notion of the global and of G/globalization, Moraru proposes that we attend to the particular ways in ways in which the world is made, and in which the planet refers to itself. This dynamic between the globe and the planet is in fact illustrated by Richard Powers's recent novel, *The Overstory* (2018), which tips the balance in favour of a planetary world-view which takes into account the mundane and particular, whilst linking it to an all-encompassing network of life. Moraru proceeds to demonstrate how the concept of the planetary applies and is re-worked in other examples of twenty-first-century literature.

Sam Solnick continues the emphasis on scale in Chapter 20, but in this case via a focus on poetry. As Solnick demonstrates, poetry offers a perspective on globalization through its different modes of address. By drawing on poetry that explicitly addresses environmental catastrophe within the contemporary world-system, Solnick demonstrates not only how address affects the scale at which we view or think the globe, but also the way in which this links in with key issues in the era of the Anthropocene. For example, by using an intimate mode of address which at points slips into the second-person plural, Kathy Jetn̄il-Kijiner's 'Dear Matafele Peinam' (2014) is able to link the fate of the peripheralized and ecologically precarious Marshall Islands to the fate of the world in general; geopolitics here is thus entwined with environmental foreboding. Juliana Spahr and Josuha Clover's *#Misanthropocene: 24 Theses* (2014), however, offers a much more general form of address by speaking to a 'you' that is characteristic of the degree of separation experienced when communicating to an online, 'global community'. By connecting the theme of the digital with world ecology, the poem foregrounds ways in which a general mode of address is at once conducive to action and a mitigation against this. Solnick moves on from this to think beyond this mode of address to one which addresses a planetary collectively, through reading Steven Collins' 'Almost Islands' (2013). For Solnick, what all these modes suggest is an effort on the behalf of the poet to engage in remaking a planetary future, and so this last chapter picks up in many ways on the issues raised in the one preceding it.

We thus end our history of the fate of G/globalization and its relationships with the literary where we started: with the prospect of environmental collapse. If the 'Applications' section treats highly contemporary global phenomena, then as with the rest of the volume it also demonstrates how literature both shapes these and proposes new frames of discourse and practice to transform them. What the historical aspect of this book ought to aide in doing is to think through how this shaping and framing has morphed and varied over time, something which is intimately bound up with the place within the world-system one inhabits. The hope is that, for example, by comparing the long history of literature's relationship with ecological collapse with its contemporary one, or by contrasting literary attitudes towards nationalism in the imperial era with nationalism in the contemporary era, or by comparing the postmodern figurations of a newly-emergent world-market with a contemporary rendering of planetary inter-relation, new dialogues can be spawned, and new ways of mapping the relationship between literature and global processes can be developed across a variety of modes of study, both within literary studies and beyond.

Notes

1 Most collections and books on the topic of the relation between literature and globalization focus on the way in which literature represents, or can be read within the context of, globalization, rather than viewing the two things as congruent or mutually affective phenomena. Similarly, most projects of this nature (but not all) are focussed on the 1980s onwards, or occasionally also with the

early twentieth century. The remit of the current volume, when each chapter is taken into account, stretches from ca. 3000 BCE to the present-day. For examples of the standard approach outlined, see Connell and Marsh; and Annesley. World-literature studies offers a much broader historical framework, and this volume draws on that, but puts an emphasis explicitly on *global* phenomena.

2 For similar, detailed accounts of this version of globalization see Robertson 1998; Bayart 2007; and Stiglitz 2002.

3 In fact, these are two of the most common ways of conceptualizing what globalization is, or the effects it has on our way of perceiving the world. See Robertson 1998: 8; and Beck 2000: 20, for examples.

4 For the extensive history on neoliberalism as global project, and as entrenched with a global vision, see Slobodian 2018.

5 For a similar account of the material underpinnings of Globalization as a discourse, see, for example, Balibar 2004: 105.

PART I

Origins

CHAPTER I

The Ecology of Globalization
Environmental Catastrophe and the History of Literature[*]
Walter Cohen

Today's crisis of global heating has triggered the sixth extinction (Kolbert 2009). The five predecessors, over the last half-billion years, each destroyed most species (Burgess et al. 2019; Grocholski 2019). All are succeeded by the triumph of previously marginal organisms – notably, mammals following the demise of dinosaurs 66 million years ago. Biological extinction provides an analogy for ecological catastrophe's impact on literacy and literature. But what if the analogy between those exogenously determined extinctions, on the one hand, and exogenously driven historical and literary-historical changes, on the other, turns out to be not an analogy at all but a local, human instance of the larger environmental embeddedness of our species an embeddedness in this sense no different from that of all other species that have ever existed on Earth? Ecological crises, always intertwined with technological, military, economic, social, political and ideological forces, initially curtail globalization, literacy and literature, and, consequently, literary globalization. But whenever environmentally induced population loss persists, it is followed by changes in literacy or literature, frequently including increased globalization. Such disasters undermine dominant literary modes and – even when they eradicate literacy (deMenocal 2001; Kaniewski et al. 2013; Kathayat et al. 2017) – thereby allow, though they do not directly cause, new forms to come to prominence in the ensuing more hospitable period. Literary innovation and geographical expansion often depend on the mass extinction of literary forms.[1]

Literacy and literature are thus shaped by recurrent alternation. Environmental catastrophe, perhaps aided by prior globalizing steps, strikes as cross-regional climate change, epidemic or geological disaster (Gaskill 2018: 38). The population declines, literacy and literature recede, globalization stalls and the old order is delegitimized. But when ecological conditions are again favourable, literacy and literature thrive, a new cultural age emerges and literary globalization advances. Here, globalization in general and literary globalization in particular are understood in similar terms. Both refer primarily to networks across cultures and secondarily to independent responses to the same ecological shock.

Demonstration of this repeating pattern across 5,000 years entails relative indifference to what might seem the strongest supporting evidence – explicit literary engagement with ecological ruin. This neglect is necessary because there is no correlation between the gravity of environmental devastation and the prominence of the literary response. Brief or local calamities can provoke influential meditation: flood, famine and plague in the Bible; the Athenian plague in Sophocles (Mitchell-Boyask 2007: 56–66) and Thucydides; earthquakes and volcanoes in Voltaire, Rousseau, Kleist, Byron, Mary Shelley and Leopardi (Bate 1996; Rigby 2014). Inversely, durable, widespread cataclysm may elicit little literary commentary: the plagues of Late Antiquity are a striking example. Second, and more important, environmental catastrophe's crucial effect on literature is not mimetic response. Instead, calamity opens the path to new literary eras – without, however, determining their innovations, which may ignore ecological tragedy.

The following discussion proceeds in three logical and chronological stages. The first, lasting almost four millennia, moves from the invention of literacy in the ancient Near East to the age of the classical empires. Climate change – aridity and global cooling – is the dominant ecological shock. In the ensuing 1,500 years, extending into early modernity, these disruptive forces, as well as devastating volcanic eruptions, often set the stage for a hitherto unknown scourge – the pandemic (cross-regional epidemic). Made possible for the first time by increasing globalization, it proves the key driver. Finally, beginning in the late sixteenth century, pandemics recede, at least in relative terms, owing to economic development, population growth, improved public health and medical advances. Climate change once again comes to the fore, first as global cooling and now as global heating. But in all three eras, ecological catastrophe is arguably the central force of creative destruction. By temporarily undermining literature in general and literary globalization in particular it ultimately enables literary innovation and its ever-increasing diffusion.

Since even these preliminary remarks raise methodological concerns, a few explanations are in order. First, though the causal categories may seem Procrustean, we will see that they at least indicate the kinds of evidence that would challenge them. Second, if the data seem to be cherry-picked, if few texts support the claims advanced here, it is worth determining if this indicates the power of these works or the weakness of the argument. Third, though there is the risk that correlations are here mistaken for causations, the claim is not that ecological calamity is a necessary or sufficient cause of literary expansion, but that expansion always follows such a calamity. Fourth, however, even if this conclusion is accepted, it is still difficult to distinguish between a *post hoc ergo propter hoc* argument and the one advanced here – that such cataclysms play a major, sometimes *the* major, part. The ensuing survey proceeds with these concerns in mind (Table 1).

Climate Change, 3300 BCE–400 CE

Table 1 *Climate change, 3300 BCE–400 CE*

Date	Events	Social and political effects	Literary effects
3500–3200 BCE	Relatively stable, cool weather		Proto-literacy 3300ff.: Sumerian, Egyptian
3200–2800 BCE	Extra cooling and aridity	Early dynastic state formation: Egypt; Ur; Indus civilization	
2800–2200 BCE	Warmer and wetter	Early dynastic Mesopotamia, then Akkadian Empire; Old Kingdom Egypt	2500: full literacy in Egypt, Mesopotamia, maybe Indus; early literature
2200–1900 BCE	Aridity: urban disease, war, famine, immigration	Collapse of Akkadian Empire; First Intermediate Egypt; end of Indus cities	End of Indus literacy
1900–1400 BCE	Stable climate, warmer and wetter	Neo-Sumerian Dynasty; Babylonian dynasties; Egyptian New Kingdom	Near Eastern literature: Egyptian, Sumerian, Akkadian, Hittite, etc.
1400–750 BCE, esp. 1200 BCE	Desiccation and cooling in Near East and China	End of Bronze Age in Mediterranean; imperial decline or collapse	End of Hittite, Ugaritic; Greek illiteracy Chinese writing 1200
750–550 BCE	End of climate crisis	Economic expansion in Mediterranean	Literature in Chinese, Hebrew, Greek
500 BCE–400 CE	Warmer, wetter	Iranian, Greek, Maurya, Han, Roman, Gupta Empires	Axial Age, Athens, Latin literature, late biblical, Chinese, Sanskrit

Source: Adapted primarily from Brooke (2014) and McMichael (2017), secondarily on Weiss (1993); McNeill (1998: 63–4, 79–81, 111–21, 125–7, 129–35, 137–41, 145–52); Davis (2000); deMenocal (2001); Freeman (2004: 23–32); Yancheva (2007); Parker (2014); and Kathayat (2017).

Note: Unshaded areas denote periods of literary advance, shaded ones eras of ecological crisis. The dates are often approximate.

Summarized in Table 1 is the relationship between ecology and ancient letters from the advent of literacy in Sumeria (ancient Mesopotamia, today's Iraq) to the classical empires. As the previous table note suggests, the alternation of shaded and unshaded rows (here and in subsequent tables) seeks to capture a pattern indicated earlier. Ecological catastrophe undermines literature and globalization alike. But in simultaneously undermining dominant cultural beliefs, it increases the possibility of the invention and cross-regional transmission of revolutionary new literary practices when environmental conditions once again prove more favourable. In any case, writing is perhaps globalized from the start, not in covering the whole world but in encompassing all extant literature in a single system, a single network (Cohen 2017: 20).[2] Its expansion is tied to the ecological oscillation just noted. The invention of literacy coincided with the relatively stable climate of the late fourth millennium BCE. Early Sumerian cuneiform arguably inspired the invention of Egyptian hieroglyphics, proto-Elamite (in today's Iran) and Indus Valley scripts (contemporary Pakistan). But from 3200 to 2800 BCE, reduced precipitation and consequent droughts destabilized Egypt and Mesopotamia. Partly in response, new states came to power (Brooke 2014: 165–212). Although initial literacy preceded the dry period, it 'is not so different from the Aztec codices that recorded ideas and that we categorize as non-writing' (Woods 2010: 20). Such 'writing' refers to, but does not render, speech. The missing features emerged in the third millennium, with the first literature in their wake – in a more hospitable climate (Woods 2010). Since the transition from referring to speech to rendering it is not inevitable, since it occurred in the Near East but not always elsewhere, perhaps this evolution requires an exogenous shock – here, the upheaval caused by late fourth-millennium aridity. Certainly, Sumerian was the key force behind Akkadian literacy (also Mesopotamia) in the mid-third millennium (see Tables 1–3).

Shortly before 2000 BCE, another stretch of cold and desiccation (Voosen 2018) may have impelled flight from the cities of northern South Asia for the countryside, thus ending the Indus civilization's writing (Brooke 2014: 295–6; Kathayat et al. 2017; Scheidel 2017: 278). In the Near East, a similar climate helps bring down the Akkadian Empire. The early second-millennium recovery includes literary achievement in Sumerian, Akkadian and Egyptian – in the latter two, the transition from oral to written form for many texts (Weiss et al. 1993; deMenocal 2001: 669–70; Freeman 2004: 53; Kubat 2011; Brooke 2014: 292–5; Marriner et al. 2017; Scheidel 2017: 280). What matters in this characteristic shift between crisis and revival is less the literary representation of calamity than the changes that calamity makes possible – the first evidence of a multilingual literary system. Sumerian and

Egyptian perhaps influence every other language of the first 2,000 years of writing – all from the Near East and contiguous regions. Texts from this period are extant in a dozen languages, literature in half that many. The independent emergence of Chinese literacy no later than the end of these two millennia represents both expansion and deglobalization. Expansion: writing thrives across a much wider geographical range. Deglobalization: written Chinese is almost certainly an independent invention; the world's writing systems are no longer part of a single network.

A final ancient, colder, dryer era from 1400 to 700 BCE helps end the Bronze Age in the Mediterranean and Near East. Literacy and literature are extinguished: Linear B, the initial vehicle of Greek writing; Hittite; Hurrian; Ugaritic (Kaniewski et al. 2013; Brooke 2014: 298–306; Marriner et al. 2017; Scheidel 2017: 270–4). This destruction once again opens the way to new literatures when the climate improves. The Phoenician alphabet, derived from Egyptian hieroglyphs, provides the model for two of the most influential writing systems of the last 3,000 years – Hebrew and Greek – beginning roughly in the eighth century BCE, drawing on prior Near Eastern literature (West 1997; Pritchard 2011) and sometimes rendering ecological catastrophe (Genesis 6–9, 37–50; Exodus 7–12; Homer 1962, Book 1). The earliest Chinese literature dates from the same era (Kaniewski et al. 2013; Brooke 2014: 298–306; Marriner et al. 2017; Scheidel 2017: 270–4). There, disruptive climate change leads, after the dynastic shift, not to a new literacy, followed rapidly by a new literature, as in Greek and Hebrew, but to the shift from literacy to literature, as in the Near East a millennium before.

The path, then, proceeds from ancient Near Eastern literature to some of the longest running and most consequential literatures. Hebrew remains geographically restricted; similarly, at this time, Chinese literacy covers little of today's country. But Greek settlements extend from Spain to Georgia, and from the Sea of Azov above the Black Sea in present-day Russia and Ukraine, to Egypt and Libya. By the sixth century BCE, literacy reaches from the Atlantic Ocean to the Arabian Sea, along with a separate development in China; literature from Greece to Mesopotamia, again with an independent Chinese presence. An 'oral' literary culture stretches from the North Atlantic to today's northwest China; material artefacts indicate ongoing cultural exchange across Afro-Eurasia. In addition, the earliest Mesoamerican writing – another expansion of literacy and counter to globalization – may be contemporaneous with, or even earlier than, the emergence of written Hebrew and alphabetical Greek (Rodríguez Martínez et al. 2006; Mann 2011).

The recovery from the late second-millennium collapse, characteristically aided by a prolonged favourable climate, ushers in the age of the classical empires. Starting with the Persians in the sixth century BCE, new regimes bind Eurasia and parts of Africa in unprecedented fashion. Persia influences leading theological, philosophical and literary movements – in Greek, Hebrew and South Asian languages, though not in Chinese. After Alexander vanquishes the country, the ensuing Hellenistic monarchies carry Greek culture to the Near East, Central Asia and India. Later, Rome, conqueror of Greece, brings this heritage westward – from North Africa to Britain. In the East, the Han extend Sinitic civilization well beyond previous bounds. And the Mauryas and later the Guptas unite much of South Asia. Their civilization reaches, first, present-day Sri Lanka, then – via Buddhism – South-east Asia and China. Moreover, the four transregional high-cultural languages – Greek, Chinese, Latin and Sanskrit – do not exist in splendid isolation. By the second century CE, a trans-Afro-Eurasian system connects the Atlantic to the Pacific, certainly in the visual arts, and possibly in letters as well.

Epidemics and Climate Change, 150–1560 CE

Table 2 *Epidemics and climate change, 150–1560 CE*

Date	Events	Social and political effects	Literary effects
161–322 CE	Epidemics (China: 160s, 310–322; Mediterranean: 165–180, Antonine Plague; 249–270, Cyprian Plague	Imperial, population decline – China: collapse; Rome: crisis. South Asia: population decline only	China: rural poetry, Buddhism; Rome: decline of Latin, rise of Christianity
400–900	Dark Age: cool Northern Hemisphere; dry South Asia; bubonic plague – Mediterranean: 541–750, Plague of Justinian; China: 610ff. Aridity: 750–900	Flat population; fall of Western, decline of Eastern Roman Empire seventh to eighth century: Tang Dynasty, Chinese influence on Japan; rise of Islam Maya collapse, fall of Tang	Western European literary backwardness Tang lyric; early Japanese literature; Arabic literature Maya literacy decline
900–1275	'Medieval' warming	European recovery; Song Dynasty growth	Romance and Persian literatures, Song culture, Arabic decline
1275–1450	Cooling (start of Little Ice Age), famine, Black Death	End of Western European serfdom, fall of Yuan Dynasty	Boccaccio, Petrarch; 15th c. literature of death

Table 2 (cont.)

Date	Events	Social and political effects	Literary effects
1450ff.			European Renaissance
1492ff.	American genocide		End of indigenous, rise of settler, literatures

In the climate-driven crises just reviewed, disease is secondary but probably ever-more important, with the growth of population, cities and inter-regional contact (McNeill 1998: 80–1). But pandemics *are* decisive in the next 1,500 years, both as effect and cause of expanded cross-cultural literary ties. Waves of mass devastation arise from contact among previously separated communities – successively, the plagues of Late Antiquity following the completion of the Silk Roads, the Black Death in the wake of the Mongol Empire, and the Native American genocide courtesy of Western European conquest of the Americas. These endeavours – trade, plunder, exploitation, religious conversion – allow microbes to reach vulnerable human populations. Endemic, manageable diseases become pandemics in a fresh locale. But here, too, in the aftermath of ecological disaster new connections emerge.

Three distinct visitations mark Late Antiquity – the Antonine Plague and its possibly linked Chinese analogue, the Plague of Cyprian and the Plague of Justinian. They contribute to the decline of the Roman Empire in the East and its fall in the West; to disunity in China; and to the triumph of Islam in much of Eurasia and North Africa. The half millennium beginning circa 400 returns to the intermittently harsher weather of the previous three millennia. From 3000 to 2000 BCE, the global population increases by 75 per cent. The same applies for 2000–1000 BCE. In the next 1,000 years, it more than doubles. But during the first millennium CE there is no change. From 200 to 900, the population may have dropped by almost 15 per cent – falling before the weather turns, primarily because of epidemics (Morabia 2009: 1364; Büntgen et al. 2011: 579–80; McCormick et al. 2012: 174, 203–5; Brooke 2014: 247, 259, 322–7).

For most of the last 4,000 years, Chinese dynasties fall following ecological disruption (Dian Zhang et al. 2005; David Zhang 2006; Z. Zhang 2010; Brooke 2014: 249, 252). An epidemic contributes to the Han collapse in 220 CE, coincident with a decline in 'the production of texts for social needs, such as commemorative inscription', and 'a striking increase in private texts including personal poetry' (Chang and Owen 2010: xxvii–xxviii, quote: xxx). In the West, the Antonine Plague and the Plague of Cyprian transform the Roman Empire and Roman literature alike (Duncan-Jones 1996: 115–18; Scheidel 2017: 326–30; McNeill and McNeill 2003, 78–81; Harper 2015). The last of the major Classical literary figures writing in Latin, as traditionally understood, is Apuleius (d. ca. 180). Surprisingly, with the empire still at its height, a distinguished tradition of four centuries fizzles out. The Antonine Plague marks that transition – back to Greek, the language of contemporary references to the epidemic (Littman and Littman 1973). More important is the new literary dispensation that triumphs following repeated catastrophes. Marginal through the third century, the Christian Bible then moves to the centre, not only in the original Greek but also in Latin, where it inspires a fresh start – with Ambrose, Jerome and Augustine. Similarly in China: Sanskrit Buddhist writings are imported before the late second-century epidemic but assume importance afterwards. In both locales, the new religion offers spiritual solace for widespread loss (McNeill 1998: 111–21, 125–7, 129–35, 137, 145–7; Brooke 2014: 346–7; Scheidel 2017: 333–4). Renewal requires a fresh impetus – from imported religions that unite vast areas of Eurasia.

Despite these plagues, environmental degradation (Hughes 1994: esp. 189–99) and other causes of collapse ('210' n.d.), the Eastern Roman Empire recovers. In the sixth century, the Eastern Emperor Justinian launches the reconquest of the former Western Empire. He retakes North Africa, most of Sicily and Italy, and sections of Spain – partly before and partly after the visitation of the disease named for him, the earliest epidemic definitively assigned to *Yersinia pestis*, the bubonic plague. Perhaps one-fourth to one-third of the Western Eurasian and Middle Eastern population perishes. The plague may have been aided by colder, dryer weather in the early sixth century, exacerbated by volcanic eruptions around 536 (McNeill 1998: 137–41, 147; Stathakopoulos 2007: 100; Morelli et al. 2010; Büntgen et al. 2011: 580; McCormick et al. 2012: 198, 205–6; Brooke 2014: 348–9; Harper 2015; Newfield 2016; Scheidel 2017: 319–26). Most historians emphasize the demographic consequences, with damage to agriculture, finance, and military power. The Lombards roll back Justinian's reconquest of Italy; Slavs and Avars occupy the Balkans. More important, the plague damages the Persian and Eastern Roman Empires. The rival powers are then further weakened by their wars of attrition against each other. Meanwhile, widespread flooding destroys Yemen, allowing Medina to emerge as Arabia's political centre. The triumph of Islam is aided by these developments. The Persian Empire falls to Arab armies, as do the Levant and North Africa – sections of the Eastern Roman Empire. Thus, the sixth-century ecological crisis helps reshape the Mediterranean world and the Near East, bringing antiquity to an end (Little 2007: 15–16; Brooke 2014: 348).

Byzantine Iconoclasm may partly respond to the plague's return in the 740s (Turner 1990). Crucially, the Eastern Empire's defeat in North Africa and the Levant sets the stage, in the post-disaster centuries of recovery, for a great era of Muslim literature – profoundly influential traditions from Spain to India. Farther east, the Tang Dynasty's reunification of China on a grand scale ushers in a major age of lyric poetry and the extension of Sinitic culture through Korea to Japan, for the first time. The Tang Dynasty and the Abbasid Caliphate develop various ties, and both have connections with South Asia. But a trans-Pacific cold, dry era in the eighth and ninth centuries contributes to both the decline of the Tang in China and the ruralization of the Maya, with a consequent sharp drop in Mesoamerican literacy (deMenocal 2001: 670; Yancheva et al. 2007; Brooke 2014: 355–8; Scheidel 2017: 274–8; Evans et al. 2018).

For almost four centuries, from around 900, Eurasia undergoes a mostly beneficial warming (Jones et al. 2001: 665; Büntgen et al. 2011: 580–1; David Zhang et al. 2011: 522; Brooke 2014: 358–60). Song Dynasty China experiences remarkable growth and innovation, including in literature. The simultaneous recovery of Western Europe eventually enables the rise of the Romance literary vernaculars. Their flagship genres, love lyric and romance, create a European literature in the strong sense – shared forms and themes – for the first time. But in the Arab-language world, global warming in an already hot region leads to aridity and political decline (Brown 2001; Issar and Zohar 2007: 193; David Zhang et al. 2011: 522; Kubat 2011; Butzer 2012). The corresponding eclipse of the classical age of Arabic literature may thus have an environmental dimension. But on the Caliphate's borders, outside this climate zone, Islamic letters thrive. The great period of Persian letters begins around 1000 CE. Its influence extends in space to South Asia, Central Asia, the Ottoman Empire, and probably Western Europe, and in time into the nineteenth century. In the same era (eleventh–twelfth centuries), Muslim Spain develops an important Arabic literature that in turn helps inspire distinguished Hebrew lyric there. The region is a key conduit through which Arabic, Greek, Persian and South Asian letters reach Western Europe. At least indirectly, Dante, Petrarch, Boccaccio, Chaucer, Shakespeare and Cervantes are heirs of these developments.

The path eastward also begins in South Asia, in this instance with Buddhist narratives. Sanskrit versions travel north and east via Iranian-language intermediaries, before arriving in China. Generic and linguistic shifts help give rise to the East Asian novel – notably, Murasaki's *Tale of Genji* (Japan) and, much later, Cao Xueqin and Gao E's *Story of the Stone* (China). As in the age of the classical empires, Old World globalization takes the form of a flattened 'T', running from India to the Iranian-language zone, and from the Atlantic to the Pacific.

This very connectedness helps pave the way for ecological catastrophe, however. Global cooling (the Little Ice Age) begins late in the thirteenth century, lasting into the late nineteenth. Western Europe suffers from crop failure, ruinous famine, and mass death early in the fourteenth century (Brooke 2014: 384–90). The weakened population may have proven especially susceptible to another bubonic plague pandemic, the Black Death, which devastates most of North Africa and Eurasia from the 1340s and intermittently for centuries thereafter. Elsewhere, the Tarim Basin (western China) becomes wetter after 1180, allowing the Mongols to move south and fuelling their conquest of most of Eurasia (Davis 2016: 42–3; but see Putnam 2016. The Black Death probably originates in China (Morelli et al. 2010): the bacterium hitches a ride with the invading armies.

Europe's population might have been cut in half between 1300 and 1430 (Scheidel 2017: 304). The multicontinental death toll from the late 1340s may have amounted to one-third of the population – at least 75 million people. In China, the Yuan (Mongols) are overthrown by the Ming. In Western Europe, reflections on the Black Death appear in Petrarch, Chaucer, and above all Boccaccio (Steel 1981). Yet these writers' full influence requires substantial delay – until a new model for literature is developed. The Classical revival of fifteenth-century Italy, along with the decline of vernacular literature, shows the way. Only in the sixteenth- and early seventeenth-century vernacular Renaissance do Petrarch's sonnets, Chaucer's narrative poetry, and Boccaccio's fiction have their major influence. Though environmental catastrophe delegitimizes dominant literary forms, up to a quarter of a millennium passes before adequate responses to the new conditions crystallize.

Finally, the European conquest of the Americas is intertwined with pandemics that dramatically reduce both the indigenous populations and anti-imperial resistance. Contact introduces pathogens previously unknown in the New World (Brynildsrud et al. 2018), producing a population loss of 50–60 million, or 90 per cent (Scheidel 2017; Lindo et al. 2018; Vågene et al. 2018; Koch et al. 2019). The Spanish destroy nearly all Mayan texts; writing in the language soon ceases. But the main story is the replacement of indigenous languages and literatures by Western European ones, with global consequences (Table 2).

Climate Change, 1560–2020 CE

Table 3 *Climate change, 1560–2020 CE*

Date	Events	Social and political effects	Literary effects
Late sixteenth to seventeenth century	Little Ice Age; return of plague	Crisis of the seventeenth century	Shakespeare, Hobbes, etc.
1700–1870	Little Ice Age slowly ends	European capitalism, industrialism, imperialism	Europe: Enlightenment, rise of novel
Late nineteenth century	El Niño; famine in India, China, Brazil	India: anticolonialism; China: republicanism	India: Tagore; China: vernacular, Lu Xun
1890s–1980	1918 flu pandemic; anthropogenic famines		Modernism, post-modernism
Late twentieth–twenty-first century	AIDS, pandemics, threat of nuclear war, global warming		Post-apocalyptic fiction

Although disease remains significant in the last half millennium, it is rarely the main exogenous influence on cultural change. The Little Ice Age reaches its nadir in the seventeenth century, when its plummeting temperatures are a major force behind the era's global crisis (Parker 2014: 3–109). Its causes remain elusive: intense volcanism, declining solar energy, soaring El Niño activity and repeated plague visitations (Miller et al. 2012; Davis 2018; Gaskill 2018). In addition, the huge death toll from Old World disease renders the Native American labour force incapable of farming previously cultivated land. The resulting reforestation removes carbon from the atmosphere, thus generating half the global cooling in the Northern hemisphere between 1560 and 1630 – enough to wreak agricultural havoc (Koch et al. 2019: 27–30) in an inadvertent, natural experiment in counteracting global warming (Conniff 2019). Harvests fail, famines proliferate, disease and death skyrocket and governments typically respond in predatory ways. Between 1600 and 1650, the global population remains unchanged. Only the period from 200 to 400 and the era of the Black Death are demographically worse: the population declines (deMenocal 2001; Jones et al. 2001; Brooke 2014: 259; Parker 2014: 3–25, 76–109). In China, the Ming are overthrown by the Qing (or Manchus); in Europe, civil and international war rule (Table 3).

The storm scenes of Shakespeare's *King Lear* (1605–1606) respond to an early stage of the crisis (Brooke 2014: 451–66; Parker 2014: 587–667). In the late seventeenth century, Milton's and Racine's Classicism marks the end of the age of tragedy and epic. But *Don Quixote*, a work contemporary with *King Lear*, arguably anticipates the crucial European literary development following the worst of the Little Ice Age, the modern novel. As we have seen in other times and places, the crucial impact of ecological catastrophe is located less in the individual text than in a two-stage process. The calamity undermines the old literary order, thereby allowing, when the climate recovers, the gradual emergence of a new dispensation typically tied to an expanded geographical range. Here, the Classical revival, a narrow European phenomenon, is superseded by a form of prose fiction, new at least in Europe, that eventually becomes the first genuinely global literary form, the central genre in the first genuinely global literary network.

The three centuries after seventeenth-century cooling rarely witness comparable calamities. In an era of increasing globalization, some governments get better at protecting their people, the world population grows in unprecedented fashion, and modern pandemics, though rivalling the most devastating disasters in human history, thus kill off an ever-declining percentage of humanity. The misnamed Spanish flu of 1918 causes 50–100 million deaths globally, 'only' 5 per cent of humanity. Perhaps partly for that reason, the flu's literary significance is hard to detect (Spinner 2017: 261–71). The same goes for HIV/AIDS, which by 2017 had killed 35 million people (WHO). Individual writers, even national literatures, may be significantly influenced, but a new literary era does not ensue.

On the other hand, famines – located in poorer countries, sometimes affected by the climate (notably El Niño) and always by political malfeasance – perhaps will prove more consequential. Late nineteenth-century incidences have deadly results in Brazil, India and China. Tens of millions perish (Davis 2000). In India the great age of famines begins before and continues after this period. It is driven by British rule and hence results from globalization. Over 30 million die in the last third of the eighteenth century, a catastrophe that wipes out perhaps one-third of Bengal's population and is followed by the early stirrings of the Bengali renaissance – probably the first major reception of modern European culture in non-European letters. The literary dimension of that renaissance begins after the suppression of the 1857–1858 Indian revolution. But only following the deaths of another 10–15 million famine victims during the 1860s and 1870s does it attain its literary highpoint, in the work of Tagore beginning in the 1890s, a decade of atypically slow population growth, partly because of 2 million more famine deaths ('Demographics of India'; Kaviraj 2003: 534–62). In China, Western imperialism plays a major role in the Great North China Famine of 1876–1879, when 10 million people die – one-tenth of the population in the afflicted provinces, one-third in the worst-hit area ('Northern Chinese Famine of 1876–1879'). Population growth slows (Demographics of China). The Qing Dynasty pays the price and is replaced by republicanism. A few years later, the New Culture and May 4th Movements stage a comparable literary shift, elevating the written vernacular above classical Chinese. Lu Xun is the central figure in a movement that leads to the international presence of Chinese literature.

But the last thirty years offer something new. Coincident with the fall of communism, unprecedented globalization has brought the existential threat of global heating (Wallace-Wells 2019). Today's post-apocalyptic ecological fiction overlaps with political dystopias, the post-apocalyptic nuclear-war novel, more general sci-fi, and the current ecological narrative concerned with actual environmental disasters. As befits its subject-matter, the genre of ecological fiction is increasingly global in production and consumption alike. Environmental doom is still cultivated above all in English, however. Because Atwood's celebrated *Handmaid's Tale* (1985) frontally attacks misogyny, critics usually fail to notice that the concluding 'Historical Notes' reveal the disappearance of Caucasians from Canada, thus reversing European genocide and connecting female fertility and women's rights to ecological disaster. The same goes for its sequel, *The Testaments* (2019). Fredric Jameson, sceptical of most recent historical fiction, invokes Mitchell's *Cloud Atlas* (2004) to argue that the successful historical novel must project itself into the future (Jameson 2013: 308–11). But the opposite claim might be more persuasive: to represent the future, one needs to be rooted in the past. *Cloud Atlas*'s multiple embedded narratives begin in the nineteenth century, move forward to the present and then to a calamitous future, before retracing their steps back to the nineteenth century, while ranging across the Polynesian South Pacific, continental Western Europe, California, the UK, post-apocalyptic Korea, and an even more post-apocalyptic Hawaii. Similarly, in Wallace's *Infinite Jest* (1996) formal complexity is combined with a setting in a recognizable (near) future marked by environmental toxicity. Post-apocalyptic ecological fiction thus thematically anticipates the world after environmental disaster.

We have seen this before, in what eventually become global phenomena, Buddhism and Christianity. The Christian Bible, including of course its eschatological dimension, is composed prior to the Late Antique plagues of the Mediterranean but acquires much of its force only in their wake. It is as if the religion required the *ex post facto* confirmation provided by ecological catastrophe to gain affective persuasiveness. The same goes for Dante's world of the dead, prior to the Black Death, and for *King Lear*'s adumbration of climatic apocalypse just before the worst of the Little Ice Age. These earlier texts are succeeded by environmental catastrophe in the short run and by recoveries in the long run connected to steps towards greater globalization. Even this steep price of progress is by no means assured for us. The vocation of post-apocalyptic fiction is to open the way to such advances but without paying the price.

Notes

[*] For their reading of and often critical comments on earlier versions of this article, I would like to thank Gregg Crane, Joel Evans, Marjorie Levinson, Perrin Selcer, Sharon O'Dair and the other members of a seminar on Marxism and Shakespeare at the Shakespeare Association of America Conference; Stefan Helgesson and his colleagues in the English Department at Stockholm University; and the faculty and doctoral students at Washington University in St Louis.

1 Limitations of space prevent an adequate account here of the arguments and evidence that might be adduced in support of the baldly stated claims of this chapter – a defect I hope to remedy in a longer study.

2 Cohen (2017) is also the source for most claims about literary globalization in the present chapter.

CHAPTER 2

Forms of Premodern Literary Circulation

Alexander Beecroft

One of the problems that both World Literature and world-systems theory seek to resolve is that of scale. 'What are the appropriate units to study if one wishes to describe this "difference" [the creation of the modern world] and account for it?' is the version of this question Immanuel Wallerstein turns to early in the introduction to the first volume of his *The Modern World-System* (2011: 3). The answer will, of course, turn out to be the world-system itself: an economic system of core and periphery that operates as a world (whether or not it covers the entire planet), in that it is larger than any juridically defined unit. This world-system is economic, not political, in structure, and the unique accomplishment, Wallerstein claims, of the modern world-system is that it has eliminated the middleman of empire, increasing the flow of wealth from periphery to core, from lower strata to upper strata, by reducing the necessary scale of political superstructure (Wallerstein 2011: 15–16).

The modern world-system is at once unique and not unique for Wallerstein – it is sufficiently unlike any of its predecessors, sufficiently *sui generis* that it is not possible to create laws to describe it (since methodologically one cannot create laws to explain a single instance) (Wallerstein 2011: 7). Yet there have been many other world-systems in history, albeit cases which always degenerated into empire: China, Persia, Rome (Wallerstein 2011: 16). By the twelfth century, Wallerstein argues, Eurasia contained many 'small worlds' – the Mediterranean, the Red Sea/Indian Ocean, the steppes with their Silk Road, China, and an incipient 'world' in the Baltic and north-western Europe – but it will only be after the European Age of Discovery and colonization, beginning around 1450, that a true world-system begins to take shape (Wallerstein 2011: 17).

The why and the how of the uniqueness of the modern world-system is a question for sociologists and economic historians, not for scholars of literature, but I will continue to pursue the analogy between systems of economic and of literary circulation a while longer. André Gunder Frank and Barry Gills argued for a world-system on Wallersteinian lines existing from the age of ancient Sumer and its trade with India (Frank and Gills 1993). More recently, Philippe Beaujard has re-examined the notion of a 5,000-year world-system, refocussing our attention on the Indian Ocean as the core of that system, with the Mediterranean and Europe as one of many peripheries, and noting the transmission across long distances not only of the familiar luxury goods of the silk and spice trades but also trade in commodities such as metals, lumber and grain (Beaujard 2019). Janet Abu-Lughod likewise provincialized Europe in her understanding of the world-system while arguing for very different dating, suggesting that the Mongol conquests in fact inaugurate a world-system (Abu-Lughod 1989). Abu-Lughod identifies a series of eight circuits which constituted for her an overlapping set of economic sub-systems, ensuring a regional density of exchange and permitting continuous economic contact across Eurasia without a high volume of truly long-distance trade. These circuits include, from west to east, the commercial and manufacturing centres of France, Flanders and Italy; the Mediterranean; the Silk Road; the Persian Gulf; the Red Sea; the Arabian Sea; the Bay of Bengal; and the East and South China Seas. Cities at the intersections of these circuits, from Venice, Alexandria and Constantinople to Baghdad, Calicut and Hangzhou, profited immensely from their capacity to link vast territories in each direction (Abu-Lughod 1989: 32–8).

To some extent, these methodological quarrels are as much about terminology as anything else. Each of these scholars agrees, for example, that the Silk Road was an economically significant network of exchange, with their differences being more about the comparability of that network to the global economy of the sixteenth – or twenty-first – century, and about which regions acted as cores and peripheries at which times. The incipient world-systems that, for Wallerstein, degenerate into mere empire become, for Frank, Beaujard and others, world-systems in their own right, and the 'small worlds' which Wallerstein sees in the twelfth century, unlinked by his Eurocentric world-system, are, for Abu-Lughod, linked instead as circuits within the world-system she sees as created by the *Pax Mongolica*. But these definitional disputes have real consequences if we return to Wallerstein's question about the appropriate unit (one might also say scale) of study. A study of the world economy focussed on the Baltic, say, as an appropriate unit of study will almost inevitably downplay or misrepresent out-of-network exchanges with more distant lands, while a focus on the largest-scale networks may render invisible more local exchanges that were orders of magnitude denser, and therefore more significant to the economic lives of those in the region.

Refocussing for a moment on the scale of the emergent nation-state, but in a comparative context, James C. Scott has used the heterogeneity and asymmetry of landscape and its consequences for transport to explain the premodern South-east Asian state, and the kinds of economic life that held it together (Scott 2009: 50–63).[1] Large fertile plains in the valleys of great rivers provided the space within which rice-based agriculture could take place, and grain crops had the great advantage, for tax purposes, of being easily measured and hard to conceal. But the trade in that commodity agriculture was only viable over short land distances (and longer distances by river, but with an enormous differential between upstream and downstream travel). Smaller, high-value products from the hill country surrounding the plains could be exchanged with hill-country residents, but they could not be integrated into the state, because their products (whether root crops or the mineral or vegetal resources of their region) were not easily measured, surveyed and therefore managed by a centralized state. Long-distance trade in such products could, by contrast, be regulated, if it could be made to flow through certain ports or towns. Hill country, therefore, provided an escape valve for the more highly regulated lives of valley farmers, while the various effects of geography structured state and economic space, and both facilitated and limited exchange of goods.

Do these observations about premodern forms of economic circulation help us to answer questions about literary circulation, and particularly, perhaps, the question of the appropriate object of study for literary history? If, like Wallerstein, we are sceptical of the value of the nation-state or its precursors as the appropriate scale on which to study literary history, we might be tempted to develop parallel notions of the literary system. But how can we talk about literary circulation before modernity? As with material goods, literary texts have long circulated across considerable distances, and in what follows I will offer a model which looks not unlike that proposed by Janet Abu-Lughod for the economic world-system. I will suggest a large-scale, weaker form of circulation, operating across the whole of Eurafrasia by the Mongol era but mostly restricted to easily transported units of literature such as animal fables arranged in frame tales. Meanwhile, thicker and denser nodes of circulation exist in narrower spaces, like the circuits of trade sketched by Abu-Lughod. These nodes are characterized by deeper kinds of literary circulation, such as the traffic in literary form, requiring thicker connections between regions and deeper awareness of each other's cultures. These nodes are by no means mutually exclusive, and it is in fact their overlapping through specific languages and centres that allows for that broader if weaker circulation across the whole of the pre-Columbian 'globe'.

The Beast Fable

First, a look at that broad and weak global circulation of narrative. The same beast-fable stories show up in ancient Egyptian texts and in Sanskrit, though we are unable to determine which direction such stories moved. Later, there is reason to think that there was a traffic between Egyptian prose fiction and the ancient Greek novel, both of which were prominent in Alexandria in overlapping time periods, though again the details of transmission aren't always clear. Through the reception of the (prose) novel of ancient Greece in the verse novels of Byzantium, we can trace one of the origins of the romances of medieval Europe, and ultimately of the European novel, demonstrating a continuous, if slender, thread of narrative fiction extending over the past 4,000 years.[2]

The circulation of more specific texts can sometimes be traced in more detail. A case in point is the *Pañcatantra*, a collection of interlaced beast fables, with a frame narrative establishing the collection as a sort of mirror for princes and featuring a conversation between two learned jackals, probably composed in Sanskrit somewhere around 300 CE (Olivelle 1999: xii–xiii). A delightful Persian legend preserved in the epic the *Shahnameh* tells us of a doctor named Burzōy who went from Persia to India in around 550 in search of a potion that would raise the dead. After a year of futile ethnopharmacology, Burzōy discovers that the potion is in fact the *Pañcatantra*. The king, zealously protecting this precious text, prohibits the physician from taking a copy of the book, but Burzōy manages to read a chapter a day of the original manuscript, later noting down in his diary the stories he had read. On his return to Persia, Burzōy arranges to have the whole text translated into Persian (Blois 1990). This version, which would have been in the Middle Persian language, no longer survives, but, we're told, it was translated into Arabic by the bureaucrat and scholar Ibn al-Muqaffaʿ (who died between 756 and 759), himself of Persian origin. This new Arabic version bore the title *Kalīla wa Dimna*, names given to the jackals in the Persian translation. The Persian text alters the introduction to the whole text, so that it no longer refers to a prince and his three sons but rather to a merchant and his three sons. The Arabic translation, additionally, inserts Burzōy's own adventures as still another layer.

This Arabic translation by Ibn al-Muqaffaʿ does not survive either but is said to be the basis for later Arabic versions of *Kalīla wa Dimna* which do survive, as well as a translation into Syriac. Somewhere around 1080, an Antiochene scholar and doctor named Symeon Seth translated the Arabic text into Greek for the Byzantine court of Michael VII Doukas, changing the names of the jackals to the more Hellenic Stephanites and Ichnelates (Mullett 2017). In 1251, the future King Alfonso XII of Castile commissioned a translation into the Spanish of his time (the *Calila e Dimna*), which had a major influence on other Iberian frame tales of the period.[3] Somewhere around 1200 the otherwise unknown Rabbi Joel translated the Arabic into Hebrew, which formed the basis in turn for a Latin translation by a John of Capua in the 1260s or so. That Latin version, finally, would lead to translations in all the major languages of Europe. The tales of the *Pañcatantra*, meanwhile, had travelled east as well as west, along with the Sanskrit language and Hindu and Buddhist religious traditions, leading to versions in Javanese and Thai comparable in age to the European translations (Venkatasubbia 1966). Through their parallel use in the *Jataka* story collection in the Buddhist canon, many of these stories made a separate journey north to China, Japan and Korea as well.

We can construct similar journeys, in comparable detail, for other texts as well, such as the *Alexander Romance* (Selden 2012) and the story taken from Buddhist scripture that becomes the tale of the Christian saints *Barlaam and Josaphat* in medieval Europe (Almond 1987). The case of the *Pañcatantra* is exemplary enough. We can see that each node of translation requires relatively little infrastructure: at a minimum, one or more bilingual individuals able to read the source text and to compose the target text, and ideally some leisure within which the translation can happen, or else a sponsor to pay for it. But we can also see that this translation need not be exact, for frame narratives and tale collections in particular. The story of Burzōy's translation of the *Pañcatantra* (from which all other Western translations ultimately depend until direct translation from Sanskrit becomes possible), while fanciful in its details, offers a model for a kind of inexact, rough translation that might be ruinous to a work of poetry, but which could create valuable and entertaining (if not always terribly accurately translated) works of prose literature. As we trace the transmission of the *Pañcatantra*, we see also that fables get added and deleted, frames expanded, contracted, reshaped and repurposed, to suit local contexts. It has been argued, for example, that either the Arabic and Persian translators of the text were anxious to suppress altogether the notion that this text was a form of political critique, or alternatively that these translators retained that critique while rendering it more oblique. Texts can even switch religions with disconcerting ease, as was the case with Buddha/Barlaam. It seems, in other words, that these sorts of fables gathered together in a frame narrative are ideal works for long-distance translation. The artistry of the tale is only weakly connected with its diction, syntax and style; the content of each individual element can be altered, as can the arrangement of elements.

Clearly, short prose narratives, or at least their plots, can travel far and wide and endure over long periods of time, and they do sketch out a pan-Eurasian (maybe even in some cases a pan-Eurafrasian) sphere of circulation for texts well before modernity, much in the same way that a pan-Eurasian or pan-Eurafrasian market existed for certain kinds of luxury goods. With material objects, the objects which travelled the greatest distances were often those which combined low mass and volume with high cash value: perfume and incense; precious gems; luxurious fabrics. The stories which travelled the furthest seem to share a very different set of features: easily translated or assimilated from one language to another; built out of small, substitutable building blocks; universal in their meaning or capable of multiple readings. Beast fables don't depend heavily on the finer points of diction, metre or rhyme to make their impact. They generally contain within them all the information necessary for their interpretation, freeing them from the cultural or ecological specificities of their point of origin. At other times, stories can be redeployed for new purposes, as mirrors for princes become entertainment for children, and Buddhist parables become Christian stories.

Similarly, we have observed that some goods were shipped great distances even at considerable cost if they filled a genuine need. The textual equivalent here might be religious scriptures and works seen as having practical scientific value. Such works travelled far indeed, often undergoing costly and time-consuming processes of careful translation, as we've seen with some of the vast translation projects of ancient times: that of the Buddhist canon in China (Zürcher 2007); of the Septuagint Greek version of the Hebrew Bible (Aejmelaeus 2007); of Greek scientific and philosophical works into Arabic (Gutas 2012). When they did not experience translation, they commanded formidable feats of language learning from those who wished to engage with the texts in question. To consider an admittedly extreme case, the sacred texts of the Manicheans are known to have circulated in Fujian province in China in the seventeenth century, written in Sogdian Persian and transcribed painfully into Chinese characters, even though the religion had faded away long ago in its Mesopotamian heartland (Lieu 2012).

Is all of Eurafrasia, then, one single literary space from ancient times onwards, a vast world-system across which texts have always circulated with great freedom – a textual precursor to the modern world economy of Wallerstein? I would argue rather for a model similar to that proposed by Janet Abu-Lughod for pre-Mongol times, when a handful of circuits defined the general reach of trade within regions of Eurafrasia, with only a limited number of goods, as we've seen, travelling beyond one circuit into another. In the case of literature, I have argued that these partially overlapping spaces were (at least by the pre-Mongol era discussed by Abu-Lughod) defined in part by the cosmopolitan literary language at the heart of each regional system: Greek, Latin, Persian, Arabic, Sanskrit, Classical Chinese.[4] Other distinctions accompany this affiliation with a cosmopolitan language. There is typically a greater volume of translation from the cosmopolitan language into the other languages of its ecological system – and that translation is often more comprehensive and systematic than the more sporadic and capricious patterns of translation between systems.[5]

The *Qasida* and the Sonnet

Another, particularly telling, index of the tight integration of a literary system is the borrowing of a literary form, especially a poetic form. Bound as they frequently are to the specifics of a source language, and also at times to the specifics of that culture, poetic forms such as the Greek lyric poem (famously adapted into Latin by Horace), the sonnet or the Arabic *qasida*, don't always lend themselves well or easily to use in another language, and so the migration of a literary form across a linguistic boundary speaks to a particularly dense network of circulation between source and target language – and to the high value attached to literary materials from the source language. The phenomena which organize poetic forms – pitch and stress accents, vowel quantities, alliteration, rhyme, parallelism and so on – operate differently in different languages, so that a kind of linguistic patterning that poses an interesting formal constraint to poets in one language might impose an almost insuperable obstacle to writing in another and might be trivially easy in a third. Poets, accordingly, do not lightly adopt poetic forms from other languages if they do not have a compelling reason to do so. Sometimes, as with twentieth-century anglophone uses of *haiku* or the *ghazal*, for example, that adoption might be motivated by the desire to experiment, or by the unexpected pleasures of a new poetic form.[6] More often, perhaps, poetic forms are adopted into a target language primarily because of the prestige of the source language, whether it is a regionally important cosmopolitan language or a privileged vernacular. Borrowings of poetic form, then, can act as an index of the relation of a given language to its literary neighbours, and they can therefore also be the mark of a family of vernacular and other languages possessing a shared relationship to a cosmopolitan model.

In the remainder of this chapter, I will sketch out briefly how two poetic forms have travelled, demonstrating how these travels help to define systems of literary circulation. My first example is the Arabic poetic form the *qasida* (plural *qasa'id*), occasionally translated as 'ode', though the vagueness of that word for most modern English speakers matches only in part the broad range of content found in the *qasida*. There are a number of possible metres for each verse (*bayt*), each of which involves a fixed pattern of syllables ending in consonants and others ending in vowels, with other flexible syllables within the verse, and a second half of each verse which nearly repeats the first half, but with a minor variation. Every verse ends with the same rhyme syllable, and in addition the two halves of the first verse each end with this rhyme sound. The *qasida* typically runs to between 30 and 100 verses and falls into three sections, though either of the first two can be omitted or greatly abridged. First comes the *nasib*, or erotic prelude, in which the poet typically views with sorrow the traces of an old encampment which remind him of the woman he loved there, along with nostalgic reflections on the home he left behind, the campfire lit by the beloved, sleepless nights spent stargazing and so on. Next is the *takhallus*, or 'disengagement' section of the poem, where the poet removes himself thematically from the erotic nostalgia he began with and begins to move towards his main theme. But this disengagement is often a literal journey as well, a journey on camel or sometimes horseback, with careful descriptions of the poet's steed and of other desert animals and landscapes. Finally, the poet arrives at his main theme, the *gharad*, which might be love, praise or blame for a prominent individual (the praise motivated by loyalty or cash, the blame direct or indirect), self-praise, lament, wisdom or description.

The *qasida* is thus a multifarious poetic form, not totally fixed either in form or in content, but operating within a limited range of possible variation for both. It is the first poetic form to develop in pre-Islamic Arabic poetry, being extant from at least 500 CE, and it has continued to have high prestige in Arabic poetry ever since, even though many of the specifics of theme quickly grew alien to poets who adapted both to city life and to Islam – later Arab poets grew reluctant, for example, to lavish descriptive attention on the camel, which they are no longer expected to possess. Other poetic forms derive from the *qasida*, notably the *ghazal*, originally a love poem following the metrical and rhyme expectations of the *qasida* in shorter format.

Islam famously spread rapidly, so that within little more than a century after the death of Muhammad there were Muslims everywhere from Spain to Central Asia, and at least some knowledge of Arabic spread wherever the faith did. But given the culturally specific content of the *qasida*, it is not surprising that it was some time before the first *qasa'id* were written in languages other than Arabic. It is perhaps to be expected that the first language into which the *qasida* was exported was Persian – Persian literature had a long and glorious history prior to the Arabic conquest, but the rise of Islam and the consequent near-total collapse of Zoroastrianism in its nation of origin led to substantial loss of textual material in the early centuries of the new religion, to the abandonment of old literary forms and to a search for new forms, especially as the Abbasid Caliphate grew weaker in the Persian east, and new Perso-Islamic kingdoms emerged there. A legend accounts for the first *qasida* to be composed in Persian in very much these terms: we're told that the Saffarid ruler Ya'qub ibn Lais was unable to understand Arabic *qasa'id* composed for his victories in 867 CE, and so his court poet, Muhammad b. Vasif, composed equivalent poems for the king in Persian. This charming poetic myth hints at the diglossia that will follow classical Persian literature in this period: Persian poets of the *qasida* were expected to be able to compose poems in Arabic as well, with an increasingly cosmopolitan Persian literature complementing rather than substituting for Arabic. The two were also held to have different strengths and flavours, such that the Persian *qasida* was conventionally understood to replace the crude and desolate desert encampment of the Arabic *nasib* with an elegant garden scene, and the hopeless passion of the Arabic poem with a more courtly love in the Persian (Meisami 2014: 40). The first great poet of the *qasida* in Persian (and indeed the first great poet in the modern Persian language) was the poet Rudaki (880–941), famously active at the court of the Samanid ruler Nasr b. Ahmad II (r. 914–943) – tradition tells us that Rudaki was richly rewarded for composing a poem which encouraged the ruler to return from his summer capital of Herat to his permanent capital at Bukhara. From that moment forward, the *qasida*, specifically in the form of praise poem for the king, becomes an indispensable element of classical Persian poetry, taking on board the quantitative metrics of Arabic poetry as well as the diction of the Arabic poetic tradition. The production of Arabic-style praise poetry in Persian had, presumably, a kind of performative effect beyond its content, emphasizing the worldly nature of the ruler whose praises are sung in Arabic and in Persian alike.

Perhaps more surprisingly, the next literary language to adopt the *qasida* was Hebrew. In an episode redolent of the cosmopolitan world of early

Islam, a young Jewish scholar named Dunash ben Labrat, born in Fez in Morocco and of partly Berber origin, travelled before 940 CE to Baghdad, where he studied under the greatest Jewish scholar of the time, Sa'adia Gaon. While studying in Baghdad, Dunash worked out a complex strategy for fitting Hebrew words into Arabic quantitative verse. These efforts were little appreciated by his teacher, but later, as he settles in Cordoba in Spain (already a great centre of Arabo-Islamic learning), his adaptations of the *qasida* to the Hebrew language gained an audience (Cole 2009: 23). As it evolves in Spain and elsewhere, the Hebrew *qasida* is a brilliant synthesis of the Arabic form and its traditions with biblical Hebrew language and ethos. Arabic themes of panegyric and of desert life are entwined with a mystical relationship to the god of the Israelites, and descriptions of male beauty make the handsome subject at once a gazelle and a hero of biblical history. Dunash and his Hebrew *qasida* do not mark quite the beginning of medieval Hebrew literature, but they do cast that literature into its enduring form. And here, of course, is the reason why Jewish poets of this period wrote *qasa'id* in Hebrew: from a desire to renew that language as a vehicle for literature, one still steeped in the Jewish faith but no longer restricted to the poetic forms of the Hebrew Bible. The cultural prestige of Arabic as not only a religious language but also a literary one made it the natural source for new literary forms to be explored in Hebrew.

The *qasida* continues to spread, at least in Arabic and Persian, so that by the late twelfth century we hear of the poet Ibrahim al-Kanemi (d. 1212/1213) composing Arabic-language *qasa'id* in the state of Kanem near Lake Chad (Hunwick 1996: 83–4), and of Persian-language poems in the genre being composed in eleventh-century Lahore, four thousand miles to the north-east (Shackle 1996: 208). But after Persian and Hebrew, there is a gap of some time before we are aware of another literary language adopting the *qasida*. We see the *qasida* in Ottoman Turkish from the time of Necatî (d. 1509), that is, after the establishment of the Ottoman court in Istanbul, and the beginnings of an Ottoman literary tradition intimately engaged with its Arabic and Persian precursors (Andrews 1996). Poems known as *qasa'id* were produced in Urdu in the late seventeenth century, while the true master of the classical Urdu *qasida* was Mirza Muhammad Rafi Sauda (1713–1781), and many of the major Urdu works in the form were created at the eighteenth-century Muslim courts in Delhi, Lucknow and Hyderabad, coming under increasing British influence at this time (Shackle 1996: 219). In both cases, the early *qasida* can be difficult to distinguish from the *ghazal*, since even in Arabic and Persian the distinction is more thematic than metrical, though of course the self-identification by poets of their works as one form or another is a meaningful act whether or not those works fully fit the source-language expectations for the form.

The *qasida* spread beyond these languages of great world empires. The eminent Kurdish poet Melayê Cizîrî (1570–1620) composed numerous poems in the form, mostly on the theme of love, both secular and Sufi spiritual (Shakely 1996). The *qasida* in Pashto (the language of eastern Iranian origin spoken in Afghanistan) has a short but distinguished history, notably including the poet Kushhal Khan Khatak (1613–1688), who left fifty-nine *qasa'id* on a wide range of themes, from his religious faith to sexual desire, from boasts of his military and poetic prowess to falconry, though in the case of Pashto the very different structure of the language (including clusters of three or more consonants) forced the early abandonment of Arabic quantitative metres. The circulation of the *qasida*, then, at least in premodern contexts, seems to take one of two forms: in cases (such as Persian and Ottoman Turkish) where Islamic rulers sought to articulate and aestheticize their rule in such a way as to lay claim to universal power, they used Arabic poetic forms such as the *qasida*, using the resources of their existing cosmopolitan language to begin building the cosmopolitan status of their own language (Pollock 2006: 117). In these languages, the *qasida* was imported principally as a kind of praise poem. But the form was imported into other, vernacular, languages with no pretensions to universal rule – languages such as Hebrew, Kurdish and Pashto – and there it served a much broader function, filling out the wide range of thematic content found in the pre-Islamic Arabic *qasida*, but notably tending to exclude praise of the ruler, the cosmopolitan function par excellence. Wherever the *qasida* crossed linguistic borders, it did so in contexts of rich and sustained intercultural engagement, often though not always assured by the Islamic faith, but always thanks to speakers of the target language with deep knowledge of the literary culture of the source language.

Among the territories in which the *qasida*, and its monothematic (and typically erotic) offshoot the *ghazal*, were composed was Sicily, that Mediterranean land contested by Normans, Byzantines, Arabs and others. The Sicilian *qasida* was an Arabic-language form, though it did not always have Arabic or Islamic rulers as its theme. During the era of Norman rule, we know of a number of *qasa'id*, for example, composed in honour of Roger II (r. 1130–1156) (Mallette 2011: 98–101). A comparatively short time later, a Sicilian poet, Giacomo da Lentini (1210–1260), appears to have invented the sonnet. Given that the erotic and intellectual content of the sonnet and of the *ghazal* in particular can certainly overlap, and given that they are rhyming poems of comparable length, it has proved tempting to many scholars to imagine that the sonnet emerges directly from the ashes of Arabic poetry on Sicily, though as Karla Mallette and others have shown there is no evidence that the one form derives from the other (Mallette 2011: 76). Tellingly, while the Sicilian pioneers of the sonnet do explicitly link their work to previous Romance vernacular poetry in Occitan, they do not (as Hebrew and Persian poets do) identify themselves as working within an Arabic-inspired lineage; none ever uses the word *qasida*, or any transliterated variant, to refer to his poem. The non-avowal of any connection between the origins of the sonnet and Arabic poetry is, in its own way, a definitive statement, at least about affiliational aspirations.

The fourteen-line sonnet, with its complex rhyming patterns and division into octet and sestet, lent itself extremely well to intellectualized musings on love, and in that guise it circulated in Italy – we know of about a thousand sonnets written in various registers of Italian by 1300. The poets of the *dolce stil nuovo* of the early fourteenth century (most famously, of course, Dante) develop the sonnet further, and the canonicity of the form is further enshrined by Petrarch (1304–1374), who uses the form for the vast majority of his long cycle of poems on his obsessively celebrated Laura. Interestingly, while it will take some time for the sonnet form to be composed away from Italian soil, it is a multilingual form almost from the beginning within Italy itself, with sonnets written not only in Hebrew, Latin and Occitan but also with the existence of the so-called sonnet *bilinguis* or *semilitteratus*, respectively composed in two vernaculars, or composed in the vernacular and in Latin. Trilingual sonnets, in French, Italian and Latin, are not unheard of (Duso 2004: xv–xvi). While there is a received narrative about the circulation of the sonnet (moving from Italy to Spain, thence to France and England), there is also a rich multilingual history of the sonnet *within* late medieval Italy, and we cannot have an accurate understanding of the circulation of the sonnet without taking that local multilingualism into account.

Hebrew is again the most striking case in point, where the poet Immanuel of Rome (1260–1330) appears to have been composing sonnets before Petrarch's birth, even using a form of the Italian hendecasyllabic line (Bregman and Brener 1991). The early history of the Hebrew sonnet escaped the notice of earlier scholars of Petrarchism (and not entirely unreasonably, since clearly Immanuel of Rome was not a Petrarchan poet, even if he was a sonneteer), but we should not be surprised that a small but tenacious diasporic linguistic community, eager at various points in its long history to revitalize its literary language, should have been a comparatively early adopter of both the sonnet and the *qasida*. Admittedly, the first flowering of the Hebrew sonnet dies out with Immanuel himself, and yet (as Dvora Bregman points out) even the *revival* of the Hebrew sonnet, with Yosef Tzarfati (d. 1527) and his friend Moshe ben Yoav, is still earlier than the first adoptions of the form in most other major European languages.

The sonnet's second linguistic move, into Latin, remains little discussed, whether by national-literature oriented scholars of Petrarchism (used to thinking in terms of national literatures, and thus to not looking at the Latin literature of early modernity) or by scholars of Neo-Latin itself, who tend to focus on the use of ancient poetic forms by modern poets, rather than on the unusual importation of vernacular poetic forms into Latin. But beginning in the fourteenth century, a small number of minor Italian writers composed sonnets in Latin, as well as multilingual sonnets partly in Latin, a tradition which continued throughout at least the seventeenth century (Duso 2004). It might not seem surprising to a modern reader that early modern poets should choose to adapt one of the most prominent of modern poetic forms for use in Latin but given the enormous cultural prestige of poetry in Classical Latin, and the powerful desire to emulate this work whenever writing in Latin (or indeed in the vernacular), the existence of the Latin sonnet is in fact a little unexpected. The phenomenon is little studied (major recent handbooks of Neo-Latin literature do not address the Latin sonnet (Knight 2018), nor does a recent collection of essays on Neo-Latin and vernacular literatures (Deneire 2014)) apart from the recent study by Elena Maria Duso cited above. Duso identifies two major categories of Latin sonnets in the early years of the form (late thirteenth to early fourteenth centuries): the Latin sonnets of the Veneto, which fit Latin vocabulary to the accentual metres of Italian poetry and whose Christian themes lend themselves to a heavily liturgical diction; and those of Humanist Tuscany and Bologna, with classical literary allusions and diction that either aims at the classical or that is deliberately inauthentic, with, respectively, erotic or parodic themes (Duso 2004: xl). Later in the fifteenth and sixteenth centuries, as the Humanist rediscovery of the Classics progresses, Latin sonneteers will adapt the form to classical Latin metres. Some will use hexameter or elegiac couplets, and these hyper-classicizing sonnets also usually avoid rhyme, while the majority will retain an eleven-syllable line but organize that line according to vowel quantity rather than stress accent (Duso 2004: xli). As with Hebrew, a rich and diverse strain of Latin or partly Latin sonnet writing is developing in Italy before the poetic form's first overseas journeys.

It is perhaps less startling that the sonnet should travel into Occitan without leaving Italy. Poets at the Norman court in Sicily had certainly been familiar with troubadour poetry in Occitan, and the ethos of that poetry must surely have been an influence on the sonnet's origins there, while the influence of Occitan poetry on Dante and his generation remained strong (cf. the discussion of the *langue d'oc* in *De vulgari eloquentia*, as one of the three main divisions of modern Romance speech, along with French and Italian, and the numinous appearance of Arnault Daniel in the *Purgatorio*). We know that several Italian poets of the fourteenth century composed sonnets in Occitan, before the form spread back to the homelands of that language (Bec 1994). Three such poems survive. The first, by Paolo Lanfranchi of Pistoia, was composed in 1284 to commemorate Peter III of Aragon's intervention in the War of the Sicilian Vespers. In this case, the identity of the *laudandus* is probably explanation enough of the choice of language. The other two Occitan sonnets from Italy are by Dante de Maiano, correspondent and older contemporary of that more famous Dante; both poems are elegant renditions of the traditional torments of love familiar both from the Italian sonnet and from troubadour poetry (Kleinhenz 1998). There is no obvious reason why the poet chose to compose these two poems in Occitan when the rest of his *oeuvre* is in Italian – other than, of course, the general multilingual vernacularity of the era. The sonnet never fully took root in Occitan poetry, and the general decline of the language at the expense of French contributed to the ongoing obscurity of the Occitan sonnet. Nonetheless, it seems worth dwelling on the fact that the sonnet had already enjoyed a rich and multilingual existence in at least three languages before it was first used outside Italy. In each of these cases, of course, the sonnet writers in question were fully fluent in the source literary tradition of Italian, perhaps more so than in their target languages, and thus mark less a process of transculturation than the normal practices of a translingual culture.

The sonnet's first adventures past the shores of Italy, and its entry therefore into a broader literary history and circulation, were in modern Spain. There are a few Catalan adaptations of Petrarchan poems from the late fourteenth and early fifteenth centuries, but these adaptations do not carry across the poetic form of the sonnet. This happens for the first time (that we can confirm) in the mid-fifteenth century, with the forty-two sonnets 'made in the Italian manner' by the Spanish Marquis de Santillana (1444), though as Ernest Wilkins rather loftily observes (Wilkins 1950: 333), '[t]he Marquis, however, poet though he proved himself in other writings, did not, in these sonnets, attain either smoothness of form or distinction in content; and they did not serve to establish a Petrarchistic tradition in Spain'. That tradition, in Spain and elsewhere, would begin properly after the strenuous efforts of Pietro Bembo (1470–1547) at reasserting Petrarch's canonical status, during the age of Renaissance Humanism, which otherwise tended to relegate vernacular developments to the margins.

Thereafter, the sonnet would spread swiftly, and enduringly, across the major European languages, finding early gifted exponents in Spanish with Juan Boscán (d. 1542) and Garcilaso de la Vega (1503–1536); Portuguese with Camões (1547–1580); French with Clement Marot (1496–1544); English with Wyatt (1503–1542) and Surrey (1517–1547); and German with Opitz (1597–1639) (Wilkins 1950). Less globally famous, but roughly contemporaneously, poets composed sonnets in Dutch, Croatian, Polish, Cypriot Greek and doubtless other languages not noted by Wilkins. The sonnet, interestingly, shows more formal flexibility from language to language than did the early *qasida*: several languages replace the hendecasyllabic line of the Italian sonnet with a locally favoured metre (the French *alexendrin*, the English iambic pentameter), while rhyme-challenged English even opens up the rhyme scheme of the Petrarchan sonnet, ultimately converting the octave and sestet format to a series of three quatrains and a couplet. But in each of these cases, the writers who imported the Italian sonnet into their native vernaculars had long been accustomed to recognize Italy as the source of a prestige vernacular culture (and, to be sure, of the cosmopolitan culture of Latin which lay beneath all European literature in the period). Contacts among the Western and Central European languages in which sonnets emerged were rich, complex and multilateral, and they took place in multiple vernaculars as well as in Latin itself.

Both the *qasida* and the sonnet, then, seem to define meaningful spaces of literary circulation. The *qasida* helps to define an Islamic-ruled literary space (which includes many non-Islamic subjects, notably Jews and Hindus). The *qasida* also identifies Arabic and later Persian (and still later Ottoman Turkish) as parallel cosmopolitan languages for this region, used by speakers of a wide range of spoken languages as a privileged form of literary expression. Only gradually do other languages make use of the privileged form of the *qasida*, and generally without its panegyric functions. Audiences in this cultural circuit knew the *qasida* as a cosmopolitan-language literary form long before they felt comfortable importing it into their own languages.

The sonnet, by contrast, moved within Western Europe, a literary circuit with a flatter hierarchy, where a sole surviving cosmopolitan language (Latin) was gradually being reserved for more and more selective purposes;

where a range of vernaculars had cultural status, notably Dante's trio of French, Occitan and Italian, but where that very multiplicity of vernaculars led for a significant time to their specialization along generic lines (as Dante himself noted). In an environment where works in Latin circulated in multiple directions across a politically multipolar world, and where multiple vernaculars served discrete literary functions, the translation of a genre from one language to another happened more quickly as a kind of polyglot play than as a means for *arriviste* vernaculars to acquire cultural capital. The environment in which that happened – the era in which sonnets began to proliferate in Portuguese and Dutch and English – was an era in which a larger and larger number of literary vernaculars began to compete in Europe, and with that increase, arguably, came the tendency to reserve each vernacular for national rather than generic use. Still, the fact that the *qasida* and the sonnet both circulated in large but mostly non-overlapping circles (at least prior to the twentieth century) helps to sketch out large literary spaces of rich and complex circulation, much larger than the nation-state, yet smaller than the world, or even than Eurafrasia. The tracing of such spaces and their evolutions is in its infancy, and the preliminary observations possible are merely tentative, but a fuller understanding of these premodern literary circulations would illuminate much, including more modern forms of circulation.

Notes

1 For a distinctive, yet related, perspective on this comparison, see Lieberman (2009).
2 I discuss this history in more detail, with references, in Beecroft (2018).
3 See Chapter 3 of Wacks (2007).
4 See, for example, Chapters 3 and 4 of Beecroft (2015).
5 As an example of 'sporadic and capricious' translation from one literary system to another, one might look at the translation of Chinese works into European languages around 1800. The works translated included a number of highly canonical texts (notably Confucius's *Analects*) and a number of pragmatic texts around areas of specialized interest such as silk-making. But they also included several novels, and not those that would later become canonical in China itself, but rather fairly everyday works such as that novel read by Goethe, in whose discussion he first invokes the term *Weltliteratur*. For a catalogue of early translations from Chinese into European languages, see Wylie (1964).
6 See Kawano (1983) and Goodyear (2000).

CHAPTER 3

The End of History
Literature, Eschatology and Its Legacies

Joel Evans

At least since the beginnings of Christianity, history has been conceived of as linear and its end has always been obliquely in sight. For almost two thousand years, an eschatological concept of history, based on the Jewish and Christian sacred texts, reigned supreme, at least in the areas of the globe in which they had been established. This concept dictated that time followed a linear progression toward the world-beyond, which would ideally be one of salvation. The world would not end with the end of history, but earthly history, with all its evils and struggles, would come to an end. The end of history is thus also an end to human subjugation, or, put positively, a tale of human liberation through the divine. As Jacob Taubes and others have pointed out, around the 1600s we begin to see a secularization of this vision of the end of history, one which finds its fulfilment in figures such as Hegel and Marx (see Taubes 2009: 125–31; and Löwith 1949: 18–19). History and its end become, in this secularized, philosophical model, tethered to the development of the human exclusively; any appeal towards an absolute, guiding principle is to be found solely within the domain of the development of humanity itself. Modernity, in other words, maintains an eschatological world view, but in a wholly secular sense, and the emphasis on progress during the latter part of this period is merely one of the most obvious symptoms of this disposition. Liberation henceforth becomes earthly and is a matter of attaining self-consciousness, freedom and equality.

In some ways, we remain within this secular paradigm. In others, as we will see, it would seem we have abandoned it. The question thus remains open as to whether secularism will fully hatch, and the eschatological shell with which we have been left will now be discarded in favour of some new way of constructing time altogether.

The case for the continuance of the secular eschatological model entails treading a well-worn path and has in fact been part and parcel of the theory of globalization pretty much since its inception. Let us briefly run through it. The most famous, contemporary articulation of the model is to be found in Francis Fukuyama's variant of secular eschatology, first advanced in 1989 in an article entitled 'The End of History?', and shortly thereafter in a book of the same name (Fukuyama 1989, 1992). In these, Fukuyama argues that history has already come to an end, in the sense that the global struggle for domination between communist states and capitalist states had ended when the Cold War did (1992: 287–99). Fukuyama derives the mechanics of his argument from Alexandre Kojève, who posited, via a reading of Hegel, that all history is the history of the struggle for recognition between 'warlike Masters and working Slaves' (Kojève 1969: 43). Once this struggle had ended, according to Kojève, history – in its universal sense – would have ended too. Oddly enough, for Kojève the end of history was observable in *both* the Soviet Union and Communist China, and the United States. These represented for him a continuation of the spirit of 'Robespierrian Bonapartism', which, supposedly, had put an end to the conflict between masters and slaves. Kojève naively, or perhaps just flippantly, views the United States as a 'classless society' in which everyone can 'from now on appropriate for themselves what seems good to them without thereby working more than their heart dictates'. In this regard, China and Russia at the time appear merely as 'Americans who are still poor' (Kojève 1969: 160–1). Fukuyama, meanwhile, and as already mentioned, pegs things rather later (and more neatly), with the advent of a pretty much all-encompassing, global form of capitalism. The struggle between master and bondsman in the Fukuyamian model, in other words, is transposed onto geopolitical struggle between states; history thus comes to an end, and the globe is all but unified, with the triumph of what Fukuyama called liberalism – or what we might call more precisely the liberal capitalist state – and the extension of this as a model for all other states.[1]

Some of the basic bones of Fukuyama's argument became, and in many ways still are, a staple of thought in Western, or core, states, on both the left and the right; some significant changes (touched on below) have occurred in the last few years, but most people have accepted that global, inter-state capitalism – in its narrower, liberal guise, or as such – has won out, and that there is currently no viable, or at least no potent, alternative to this system.[2] But (as suggested above) there is also a sense in which we are moving away from this logic, something which will allow us in a moment to make part of the case for the end of secular eschatology.

It is worth mentioning first, however, that the other part of this case pops up in an intellectual sense around the same time as (if not a bit before) Fukuyama's own suggestion that history has ended. After all, the postmodern scepticism towards history and progress in a sense already marks an end to the end of history. This is perhaps an additional reason why for some decades human liberation has seemed out of reach, even as an idea: an incredulity towards the grand narratives of history has largely gone hand in hand with an incredulity towards the idea of (a final) human emancipation, and we may well posit that this is because these two things have been so closely linked throughout history. On the more positive view, however, it may just be that the postmodern is the era in which liberation is no longer tied to transcendence of any kind. As Antonio Negri has suggested, in the postmodern era, human emancipation no longer comes under the remit of God, or indeed any other transcendent force, but is instead part of an ontologically 'constituent process', a 'commonality that precedes and forms the condition of every resistance and every decision': 'it is not to God but to the plural and articulated ensemble of relations, of communication, of the formative processes of meaning that we answer; it is not to a limiting measure, but to an explosion of values, to a measureless excess of potentiality, that we remit ourselves'. Even time itself 'is no longer what modern eschatology wanted it to be', as, 'in the postmodern, time is an intensity, and every instant is eternal, charged with responsibility and constituent potentiality' (Negri 2010: 38).

To add to this, there are now a series of rather more concrete factors that are eroding the efficacy of the Fukuyamian end of history thesis. Climate and ecological collapse, and the corollary threat of extinction, seem increasingly unavoidable without transitioning (at a minimum) to some new, less growth-oriented order of things, whilst the rise in commons-oriented technologies signals a potential lacuna, or at the very least a fundamental transformation, in the extraction of value, surplus or otherwise.[3] Consider also the damage the (neo)liberal capitalist state has inflicted on itself in recent years (the stand-out here being the 2008 crash), and the various oppositions on the left and right that have sprung up against it in the arena of representative politics, and we have a clear indication that the end of history, at least in the Fukuyamian sense, is receding rapidly.[4] These issues are, as hinted, of a different order than that of the postmodern; they are all, as it were, global problems which require one to think at the level of totality, but which nevertheless question the totalizing system of global capitalism which once seemed, at least to some, to have brought us to a terminus. Of course, these problems do not preclude the concept of the end of history being articulated in some other guise. But they do suggest a decoupling of this from any stable foundation, with no other forthcoming.

We have come a long way, then, from the origin of the end of history in religious narrative. The rest of this chapter will seek to delineate the evolution of the eschatological model from a specifically *literary* angle. In the main, we will do this by looking at one of the unsung proponents of a literary end of history, Erich Auerbach (1892–1957). Reading Auerbach's philological writings from the early to mid-twentieth century gives us an opportunity to trace a version of this mode of thinking that precedes those of Kojève and Fukuyama. If the end of history seems to be coming to an end today, then attending to earlier versions of this will not only give us further clues as to how it breaks down but also point us to ways in which it ends up persisting. Further, it will allow us not only to examine the literary *origins* of the matter in hand but also to trace the vicissitudes of this idea from the point of view of literary form and content. In other words, we will see how the eschatological model develops on what is in fact its home terrain, alongside evaluating the consequences this has for how we think about narrative itself. Like Fukuyama's idea of the end of history, Auerbach's too is one which is elevated to a global scale, and so we will find a concrete connection here between an analysis of literary texts and a vision of an earlier form of globalization than our own. Part of the task here, then, will be to situate this within other patterns of thought of the time which envisage this early form of globalization. But this will also allow us, briefly, to consider how Auerbach's conclusions bear on our own era, and how this then maps onto the broader outline of the fate of eschatological thinking outlined above.

Figura

Auerbach allows us to flesh out the first, religious phase of the evolution outlined above through his examinations of the etymology of the Latin word *figura*, how this came to be adopted in early Christian theology and was then later developed into a way of seeing in European literature more generally. *Figura*, Auerbach tells us, originally meant 'plastic form' and was used to express 'something living and dynamic, incomplete and playful' (Auerbach 1984: 11–12). Varro and Cicero are key examples here, in that they allow the word to take the place of the Greek *schēma* (the 'perceptual shape', as opposed to the classical form or idea) but still retain its plastic signification.[5] Thus, *figura* comes to designate an outward, defined shape – distinct from the ideal, or real – which is at the same time malleable, as in the case, to take another example, of Lucretius's images of things – or film images – which are 'peeled off the surface of objects' (Lucretius: 95).

These, as Auerbach informs us, 'are designated by Lucretius as "*simulacra, imagines, effigies* and sometimes *figurae*"' (1984: 17). The development of this word continues along similar lines in pagan antiquity though a venerable series of divergent authors, including Ovid, Vitruvius and Quintilian.

A dramatic turn in the signification of *figura* takes place, however, with the advent of Christian antiquity and the writings of the church fathers. Tertullian, the initiator of this turn according to Auerbach, uses *figura* to describe a 'prophetic event foreshadowing things to come'. Auerbach's example here is Tertullian's reading of Joshua in the Old Testament, who is read as a kind of cipher for Jesus himself, not least because these two names are one in Ancient Greek (Ιησούς). The story of Joshua is a figurative one for Tertullian not only because of name resemblance but also because, as Auerbach puts it, 'just as Joshua and not Moses led the people of Israel into the promised land of Palestine, so the grace of Jesus, and not the Jewish law, leads the "second people" into the promised land of eternal beautitude'. *Figura*, in this sense, not only refers to a prophetic event, but it is also 'something real and historical which announces something else real and historical' (1984: 29). Joshua–Jesus is in fact part of a whole series of people and instances that Tertullian designates as figural, thereby forming a tradition of interpretation which permeates the Christian tradition. We find a more complex version of this in St Augustine, which throughout the 'fourth and following centuries' is recurrently 'employed in sermons and religious instruction' (1984: 43–4). Augustine employs the word *figura* in a number of different instances, all contributing to his overall view of the Old Testament as, in Auerbach's words, a 'pure phenomenal prophecy' (1984: 39). But, largely in his sermons, Augustine clearly marks out another temporal order: that of salvation, which is figured by removing 'the concrete event [of the Gospels], completely preserved as it is, from time and transpos[ing] it into a perspective of eternity' (1984: 43). As in Tertullian, the real-world event comes to signal another event in the future, which itself will eventually bear us off into the land of milk and honey, after the end of earthly history. The appropriateness of the word *figura* to designate these temporal twists and turns of an overall, mapped-out and essential trajectory can be seen in its origins as the sign of plastic form; indeed, as Auerbach points out, this is likely the very reason it persisted as a way of describing the phenomenal-eternal prophecy, combining as it does 'the creative, formative principle, the change amid the enduring essence, the shades of meaning between copy and archetype' (1984: 49).

What we can glean from all this (despite the fact that Auerbach does not explicate it himself) is that *figura* is a fundamental building block of the eschatological world view; it bolsters and brings to the fore an already existing Christian view of the end of history. All the versions of eschatology surveyed in the introduction to this chapter owe a debt to this exegetical mode of reading. Figural readings are thus at one with eschatological temporality; they provide a concrete instance of the way in which a group of texts' (the Old Testament and the Gospels) form and content can both be read in relation to a vision of global history and be said to be at the origin of this vision itself.

Auerbach himself continues to trace this way of constructing textual time on into medieval literature, and in particular to Dante. Far from being abstracted from earthly experience, Dante's *Divine Comedy*, we are told, clarifies this by providing a figural take on history. By showing his characters as already subjected to the end times, or the final judgement, Dante actually 'captures the fullest intensity of their individual earthly-historical being and identifies it with the ultimate state of things' (1984: 71). But figural literature and interpretation supposedly end with the advent of the secular world, just as religious eschatology does. The genre that takes over, at least in Auerbach's model of literary history, is realism, and it is to the account of this that we will have to turn in order to continue fleshing out the literary story of eschatology.

A Common Life of Mankind on Earth

In his magnum opus *Mimesis: The Representation of Reality in Western Literature* (1946), Auerbach argues that realism is just one instance in literary history under which the Ancient doctrine of strict levels of style is overridden. The Gospels provide another instance of this. Here, everyday, humble characters are opened up to the revolutionary, profoundly historical experience of the divine: the treatment of the 'common people' collides with the lofty religious drama (Auerbach 2003: 42–3). Or, in medieval literary production, Dante's *Divine Comedy* offers a prime example of the subversion of levels of style, in that we are presented with a 'mixture of sublimity and triviality which, measured by the standards of antiquity, is monstrous' (2003: 184). But whilst both of these circumventions of style involve an explicitly religious aspect, realism, for Auerbach, treats everyday characters and circumstances as being part of world-revolutionary events in a secular way. In other words, if the first two circumventions coincide with the era of (classic) figural representation, realism takes place outside this aesthetic and conceptual mode. From this angle, then, it would initially appear that Auerbach locates the same basic secular model of human history and eschatology in literature as had people such as Taubes in philosophy and the likes of Hegel and Marx. The germ of this model is to be found in the way Auerbach approaches realist literary production, but we will not get a full view of the eschatological aspect until he turns to the then-budding modernist experiment. And it is here too that we can identify an unexpected development in the story of literary eschatology, one that the secular nature of realism initially obscures.

There are two further key aspects of Auerbach's account of realism in *Mimesis* other than its circumvention of levels of style. The first is the way in which the realist novel seeks to embed individual experience within a social *milieu*. Such is the case in works by authors such as Stendhal and Balzac, whom Auerbach addresses directly. Here, the destiny of human beings is shown to be linked to 'a defined historical and social setting' which appears wholly necessary, 'a total atmosphere which envelops all its several *milieux* [sic.]' (2003: 473). There is, in other words, no outside, transcendent force which determines the fate of the social and the historical in the realist novel. The second key aspect is what Auerbach describes as 'the embedding of random persons and events in the general course of contemporary history' (2003: 491). Nothing is pre-figured about the moment being treated, and the persons who take part in the action of the novel could have been drawn from any part of the social *milieu*. Thus, human development in the realist novel is ultimately secular and contingent; the march of history is tied only to the development of human forces themselves, whether these are revolutionary or everyday forces, or both. There is no pre-ordained sequence of time or events that needs to be followed to trace human history, and the style via which this is conveyed is non-hierarchical, treating the everyday in such a way that is incomprehensible when viewed through the lens of fixed orders of style.

These conditions are only intensified in the modernist text. Virginia Woolf's multi-perspective novel *To the Lighthouse* (1927) is the most striking example, an extract from which Auerbach uses at the start of the final chapter of *Mimesis*. Here, 'the writer as narrator of objective facts has completely vanished', and we are left in a situation whereby there 'seems to be no viewpoint at all outside the novel from which the people and events within it are observed, any more than there seems to be an objective reality apart from what is the consciousness of the characters' (Auerbach 2003: 534). Instead of focussing solely on this turn toward interiority, however, Auerbach hones in here on the way in which this general trend – which we can see novels such as Hamson's *Pan* and Joyce's *Ulysses* as being a part of – might be justified or explained by broader historical circumstances.

Here, the emphasis is on 'the widening of man's horizon' and the 'increase of his experience, knowledge, ideas, and possible forms of existence' which accelerated rapidly during the decades of the First World War and after (Auerbach 2003: 550). As Auerbach elaborates, 'the spread of publicity and the crowding of mankind on a shrinking globe sharpened awareness of the differences in ways of life and attitudes', and this can be seen as a, if not *the*, motivating factor for the multiple perspective narrative, shorn as it is of a single, unified mode of narration (Auerbach 2003).

The random moment is again a key feature in the modernist text. By placing characters in such situations, the flattening out of style is both accentuated and taken to its ultimate logic: 'the more numerous, varied, and simple the people appear as subjects of such random moments', says Auerbach, 'the more effectively must what they have in common shine forth'. The chapter that deals with Woolf ends with the following summary, which brings together the textual and actual phenomena Auerbach had been delineating throughout the chapter:

> The strata of societies and their different ways of life have become inextricably mingled. There are no longer even exotic peoples. A century ago ... Corsicans or Spaniards were still exotic; today the term would be quite unsuitable for Pearl Buck's Chinese peasants. Beneath the conflicts, and also through them, an economic and cultural levelling process is taking place. It is still a long way to a common life of mankind on earth, but the goal begins to be visible. And it is most concretely visible now in the unprejudiced, precise, interior and exterior representation of the random moment in the lives of different people. (Auerbach 2003: 552)

This seems utopian from the point of view of our own circumstances, let alone those in which Auerbach found himself in the 1940s, as an exile from Germany temporarily living in Turkey.[6] 'A common life of mankind on earth': this, in essence, is the utopian proposition, or slogan here, and whilst it seeks to bring together all the stylistic and thematic features of the modernist movement (which is clearly here a descendant of the realist mode), it also has more than a touch of political-eschatological thinking about it. For what Auerbach is proposing that Woolf and others pre-figure – through their use of random moments and multi-perspective narration – is a global, secular unification or levelling based on what humankind holds in common. Wittingly or not, then, Auerbach excavates here a *figural* role for literary engagement, albeit a secular, contingent one. Crucially, though, it is no longer literature *itself* that is figural here, in the way that it had been with Dante or the books of the Christian holy texts: rather, the literary text requires a reader (in this case Auerbach) to articulate a *potential* figural role or vocation. Nothing in the text itself that is being examined anticipates an event that later takes place, or one that is destined to take place (and even if it did, this is not what is held to be important). Rather, it is the reader of the text that looks for patterns, links these with historical phenomena and seeks to find an eschatological meaning.

It should be clear, then, that whilst literature itself does have some resonance with the turn towards secular eschatology in this account, this is ultimately residual. Instead, Auerbach's approach suggests that it now falls to the *critic* to extrapolate a potentially emancipatory vision on the basis of literary form and content; utopian or otherwise, the end point in human history becomes a wholly extra-textual affair in this instance.

We might note here that, from the point of view of utopia, Fredric Jameson's work is surely the most prominent example of this way of doing criticism in our own era. For as Jameson has consistently argued, texts have both an ideological and a utopian function, whether this is to be found in so-called high or low culture. As he puts it,

> to reawaken, in the midst of a privatised and psychologising society, obsessed with commodities and bombarded by the ideological slogans of big business, some sense of the ineradicable drive towards collectivity that can be detected, no matter how faintly or feebly, in the most degraded works of mass culture just as surely as in the classics of modernism – is surely an indispensable precondition of any meaningful Marxist intervention in culture. (Jameson 1979: 148)[7]

Crucially, the utopian quality of the cultural text for Jameson is an 'underlying impulse', one which is 'distorted and repressed' (1979: 148). It is the task of the critic to draw out a text's utopian aspect, which in turn offers a vision of potential human liberation. Whilst he is not alluding to a global form of collectivity in the remarks above, Jameson's general emphasis on utopian collective forms finds a counterpart in Auerbach's common life of mankind on Earth. Both suggest different ways in which a utopian meaning can be produced from cultural texts, even if the latter are not overtly suggestive of this.

Aside from global or more discrete utopian and eschatological imaginaries, literary and cultural studies in general remain in thrall to the paradigm above, albeit the more negative (ideological) one that Jameson outlines. In seeking to find underlying, repressed or ideological meanings in texts, we always in some way remain within a hermeneutic mode that focusses on the gaps or absent-presences of the text. What the (Western) critic in the modern hermeneutic mode does, then, is re-inscribe a largely secular system of significance and meaningfulness, which draws together the various elements of cultural production which lack political commitment under a common cause.

Auerbach and Jameson, from this perspective, are just two notable parts of a vast system of criticism which generates extra-textual meaning. This may or may not be eschatological in orientation, but evidently it has a quasi-religious disposition in an analogous way to the secular forms of eschatology that sprang up in the nineteenth century. Of course, in recent years there has been a renewed commitment to abandoning the hermeneutic mode, but that is a discussion for another day.

Bringing the discussion back to Auerbach's historical schema in particular, the final thing to add in relation to the treatment of modernism here is that, in the disappearance of an *overt* figural disposition (secular or otherwise) in literature, we see that – at the very least with modernism, but to an extent with realism also – there has been a constituent version of human time and interactions long before people such as Negri saw this appearing in the postmodern more broadly. The modernist preoccupation with time as duration, multiplicity and intensity appears here in full relief as an antidote to any eschatological frame of thought, and in turn any figure of time or social relations that appeals to the transcendent. The standing of the modernist (and perhaps the realist) literary text, then, is almost in opposition to those texts which seek to read modernism (or realism) itself, such as Auerbach's or Jameson's, by the latter's very admission.

In later years, Auerbach would begin to articulate the end point he had sketched out in *Mimesis* with much less of a utopian flourish. In the preface to *Literary Language and Its Public in Late Antiquity and in the Middle Ages* (1958), he takes a somewhat neutral stance, which is nevertheless tinged with a kind of localized millenarianism: 'European civilization is approaching the term of its existence; its history as a distinct entity would seem to be at an end, for already it is beginning to be engulfed in another, more comprehensive unity'. Through philological enquiry, Auerbach says, we can survey what is still a recent civilizational phenomenon in the process of passing away (Auerbach 1965: 6). What we have here, then, is a vision of all-encompassing or global cultural unity – the corollary of the common life of mankind on Earth – that has been intermingled with a (perhaps slightly mournful) picture of the waning of a distinctly European culture.

This complex idea acquires its full force in a now well-known essay originally published in 1952, entitled 'Philology and *Weltliteratur*'. Here, Auerbach opens with the assumption that 'human life is becoming standardized', a phenomenon that can be observed not only through geopolitical interactions but also through literary expression and modes of thought:

'all human activity', he says, 'is being concentrated either into European-American or into Russian-Bolshevist patterns'. Despite the perceived severity of differences in these two patterns, for Auerbach they don't amount to much. This means that, if such trends were to continue, we would have to get used to 'a standardized world, to a single literary culture, and perhaps even a single literary language'. World literature (*Weltliteratur*) as an intercourse between the cultures of the family of nations would disappear, and we would be left merely with 'what is generically common'. In other words, 'the notion of *Weltliteratur* would at once be realised and destroyed' (Auerbach 1969: 2–3). Left without their customary vocation, the task of the philologist in this situation would become the study of the history of culture so as to orient the human within both a view of the totality of human endeavours and the 'progression of events in general'. This is put in somewhat Hegelian terms, which are of course also indebted to the philological method as such: what ought to be the object of study is 'the inner history of the last thousand years', which is itself 'the history of mankind achieving self-expression' (Auerbach 1969: 5). Auerbach then proceeds to outline his philological method, its limitations and its potentialities. But what is clear here is that philology is envisaged as a kind of antidote to a situation in which 'our earth grows closer and closer together' (Auerbach 1969: 16), rather than something that attempts merely to register the signs of this.

The other name for this drawing closer together is, as we have just seen, generic commonality, which functions as an equivalent of the notion of a European civilization at its terminus, or the more utopian-edged 'common life of mankind on earth'. In all cases, this is a fundamentally secular, literary eschatology, which almost by default involves a vision of the fate of the entire globe. It is telling that, in the land of generic commonality (which is to come), the task of philology is merely to look back in the knowledge that nothing new can occur. Again, this is quite literally a vision of the end of history. Of course, Auerbach's own proclamation on the slip towards standardization contradicts itself, as this is in fact an instance of looking into the future, from a philological standpoint. Again, then, the notion of a future generic commonality is an eschatologically inflected viewpoint that takes place outside the bounds of the literary or cultural text and is based rather on observations formed from studying in the broad field of philological enquiry. If critical enquiry offers a solution to the problem of global standardization, then this is, at least in part, a solution to a self-created problem, to an imagined, extra-textual horizon.

In sum – and before moving on to the final part of this chapter – Auerbach's work might initially seem to offer a route to tracing an emergent secularization of eschatological thinking in literature. But, in fact, things are more complex: the figural has all but vanished from literary production itself, and this is something that started properly with the realist aesthetic. But, instead of disappearing completely, figural representation becomes the task of the critic. If, in other words, the end of history remains an issue in Auerbach's account of the development of literary forms, this is so because he articulates this himself, because philology (akin to philosophy) becomes the primary vehicle for such proclamations.

Early to Late Globalization

Auerbach's vision of a common life of mankind on Earth, the terminus of European civilization and a coming generic commonality all point towards an awareness of an increasingly interconnected globe, so we might situate his thought within this growing feeling of the time more generally. From one perspective, *Mimesis* and other works seem to fall outside what is seen by some as an earlier phase of globalization, which comes to an end around the beginning of the First World War. But, from another perspective, Auerbach's work is part of an emergent and ongoing strain of thought which follows on from the earlier phase just alluded to and seeks to think through the implications of interrelated economic and social systems, media and network technologies.[8] The catalyst for these strains of thought in either case is surely the imperial manifestation of capitalism, even though Auerbach doesn't really interrogate this in any substantial sense. In what follows, then, we will put the argument forward for this second perspective, before moving on to address briefly the fate of globalization and the end of history in the contemporary world, and the ways in which Auerbach's analyses, and their broader resonances, might be useful still today.

Keynes's famous evocation of the possibilities open to an inhabitant of London prior to the First World War is emblematic of both the nexus of capital, transport networks and telecommunications cohering to foster a global world-system going into the twentieth century, and the perception of the globe drawing closer together during this period. As he puts it,

> the inhabitant of London could order by telephone, sipping his morning tea in bed, the various products of the whole earth, in such quantity as he may see fit, and reasonably expect their early delivery upon his doorstep; he could at the same moment and by the same means adventure his wealth in the natural resources and new enterprises of any quarter of the world, and share, without exertion or even trouble, in their prospective fruits and advantages. (Keynes 1920: 9)

This is followed by a long list of similar things one could do, and a final statement which is somewhat enlightening for our purposes: Keynes's imaginary, or exemplary, inhabitant, as he puts it, 'regarded this state of affairs as normal, certain, and permanent, except in the direction of further improvement, and any deviation from it as aberrant, scandalous and avoidable' (Keynes 1920: 8). Keynes thus sets out here what many have designated as the first stage, or at least 'the "belle epoque" of early globalization' (Pike and Winseck 2008: 28), which then fizzles out during a long period of all-out war, and, we might add, the break-up of empires.[9] What is key here also is that Keynes evokes again a feeling that history has ended, that no radically new world-system could conceivably be brought into being. This, of course, resonates quite strongly with what Fukuyama and others would come to articulate explicitly – albeit more abstractly – in the 1990s.

One ought to tread carefully here, but from a certain perspective Auerbach's own work is an example of the way in which this logic is developed in a more conceptual, or philosophically oriented, vein during the period of world war, which is to say that it is a kind of continuation of the phenomenon described by Keynes, albeit with a rather different focus. I will attempt to explain how and why shortly, but let us first look back to Auerbach's eschatological vision, and in turn to some of the ideas with which it might have similarities.

Auerbach finds in Woolf and others random moments of consciousness which for him herald a new form of global interconnection. The projection that Auerbach thus makes is one founded along idealist lines: it is these spots of conscious and unconscious impressions that give us a glimpse of the common life of mankind on Earth. We do not have to make a huge leap to then link this with Auerbach's own vision of the role of philology. If this is to make use of, in the Spitzerian sense, 'the power bestowed on the human mind of investigating the human mind', then in Auerbach's case, this power has been extended to be able to read the mind of the world (Spitzer 2016: 24). As Auerbach puts it himself in 'Philology and *Weltliteratur*', 'we must return, in admittedly altered circumstances, to the knowledge that prenational medieval culture already possessed: that the spirit [*Geist*] is not national' (Auerbach 1969: 17). Thus, the common life of mankind on Earth and generic commonality both suggest a convergence at the level of spirit, marking them out as idealist visions of the global.

From this point of view, Auerbach's notion of a coming together of humanity is rather similar to H. G. Wells's notion of the world brain, articulated in a series of essays and lectures between 1936 and 1938. Here, Wells continues his interest in global polities – or 'the world-state' – by putting forward a notion of a 'Permanent World Encyclopaedia', which miraculously seems to offer an anticipation of (a version of) the internet of today.[10] Wells viewed this as a site of information that was constantly being updated on a global scale, made possible through developments in media and telecommunications technologies. The World Encyclopaedia would serve to 'pull the world of the mind together' and offer a corrective to the slide towards nationalism that was beginning to make itself felt all the more keenly (Wells 2016a: 42; Wells 2016b: 75). Or, later on, there is Pierre Tielhard de Chardin's 1955 notion of the omega point, or super brain, both of which signify a coming together at the level of consciousness on a planetary scale, again as a result of advances in telecommunications technology and the increasing complexification of (global) human relations (Chardin 1965a: 162; Chardin 1965b: 111–16). All three of these visions pose a global unity of mind, and they are no doubt traceable back to Hegel and his own notion of Absolute Spirit at the end of history. But, in the case of Auerbach, Wells and De Chardin, it is media technology and – less explicitly – a particular type of world-system that catalyses this coming together of the globe. From this point of view too, these writers represent a continuation of the notion that Keynes had put forward some decades earlier, but in an abstract, conceptual sense. Again, then, this is a continuation of the eschatologically inflected view of the interconnection of humankind, albeit from a slightly different angle.

What might this tell us about the intersection between the discourse of globalization and the end of history narrative today? The answer, perhaps, is that despite peaks and troughs in imperialist and free-trade ventures, the broad narrative, and its conceptual underpinnings or flourishings, manages to hum along relatively smoothly. The various technological networks which were once part and parcel of an integrated world-system become the dominant emblems of an eschatologically inflected world view. The infrastructure of integrated global capitalism thus remains symbolically resonant in what is otherwise a disintegrated, nationalistic version of that same overarching system. The broad outline of a potential end to eschatological thinking provided at the start of this chapter, then, might well be correct, but this does not preclude there being a long last breath of this way of thinking at the same time.

Thus, from the vantage point of our own era of emergent nationalism and disintegration, we might well expect to continue seeing variants of the end of history thesis for some time into the twenty-first century, which emphasize the infrastructural remnants of an integrated world-system. The contemporary core-state visions of disembodied, often hive-like, networked forms of consciousness residing eternally in cyberspace are particularly prominent examples of this, which have surely gained vastly more attention than Wells's encyclopaedia or Auerbach's generic commonality did at the time. The so-called singularity – popularized by the likes of Ray Kurzweil and Yuval Noah Harari – is one apt example of this complex of ideas (see Kurzweil 2009; Harari 2014: 110–12). But, perhaps significantly, this new variant of eschatological thinking finds its way into literary, filmic and televisual narrative in a quite explicit sense. Films and TV series such as *Her* (2013), *Chappie* (2014) and *Black Mirror* (2011–present) all popularize a vision of an eternal form of consciousness that can either be generated from or uploaded to the global network. There are various iterations of this idea in literary production also, some of which emphasize forms of network consciousness directly, whilst others take this on as a more tacit theme. But, in either case, we can observe the phenomenon in novels such as Don Delillo's *Cosmopolis* (2003) and *Zero K* (2016), Charles Stross's *Accelerando* (2006), Douglas Coupland's *Generation A* (2009) and *Player One* (2010), and Ali Smith's *How to Be Both* (2014). It may well be that an analysis of these narratives and other works would serve as a starting point in tracing a re-emergence of eschatological forms in narrative as well as outside this, one which heralds a movement away from the postmodern and the literary vision of time and social relations fully and first established in modernism. But this ought always to come with the proviso that the end of history thesis is now truly on its last legs, that the crises of global capitalism and looming extinction threaten to make what is a recurrent thought-figure simply an idle musing.

Notes

1. On the limitations of Fukuyama's geopolitical focus, see Eliot, who points out that Fukuyama excludes 'intra-capitalist contradictions from his panorama' (2008: 54).
2. Amongst others, Slavoj Žižek has been fond of making this point (see, for example, Žižek 2006: 301). Mark Fisher's influential *Capitalist Realism* (2009) also puts forward the case (see Fisher 2008: 6–7). From a more conservative perspective, Peter Sloterdijk has been a prominent proponent of this position (see Sloterdijk 2014: 191).
3. On this first point, see, for example, Klein (2015: 64–95) and Pettifor (2019). On the latter point, see Hardt and Negri (2004: xv–xvi) and Wark (2019: 39–59).
4. Fukuyama has himself found various cracks in his own edifice, which are largely based on more small-scale threats to the liberal-democratic, capitalist state. Most recently, he has argued that, with the election of Trump in the United States and the United Kingdom vote to withdraw from the European Union, (a vaguely defined) 'populism' has taken over. The '"democratic" part of liberal democracy is … now rising up and taking revenge on the "liberal" part' (2016: 2). This marks an interesting shift away from Fukuyama's customary focus on geopolitics.

5 Schēma (σχῆμα), in other words, stands opposed to *eidos* (εἶδος) and *morphē* (μορφή), the latter two words being used in reference to forms or ideas in Platonic and Aristotelian philosophy.
6 On this, see Konuk (2010: 1–19).
7 See also Jameson (1981: 296).
8 We have already explored some of Auerbach's remarks on this topic, but consider, in addition to this, the claim that 'the widening of man's horizon, and the increase of his experiences, knowledge, ideas, and possible forms of existence', is part of a slow process that explodes at the beginning of the twentieth century. In this case, 'the spread of publicity and the crowding of mankind on a shrinking globe sharpened awareness of the differences in ways of life and attitudes, and mobilized the interests and forms of existence which the new changes either furthered or threatened. In all parts of the world crises of adjustment arose; they increased in number and coalesced' (Auerbach 2003: 549–50).
9 On this, and the explicit link with Keynes's famous passage, see also Müller and Tworek (2015).
10 For a non-fictional take by Wells on the possibility of a new world polity, see Wells (1928); for a fictional take, see Wells (2005).

CHAPTER 4

Translation
Print Culture and Internationalism
Mary Helen McMurran

'Most literature circulates in the world in translation', David Damrosch writes, as if acknowledging a simple, self-evident truth (2009: 65). Translation may be an indispensable instrument of world literature and perhaps '*the* craft of world literature', but there is little consensus about the significance of its role (d'Haen 2012; Harrison 2014: 411). For some, translation represents a net gain for world literature through the progressive exchange of literary art and, ultimately, the potential to fulfil the ideal of *Weltliteratur*. Others lament the losses in translation induced by globalization: the over-representation of English as the source language of translations and the under-circulation and consequent repression of the mass of the world's languages and literatures (Apter 2013; Hegelsson 2018). The canon of world literature, as Harish Trivedi argues, consists exclusively of literary works translated into English, which prevents the vast majority of literature in Indian languages, among others, from entering these honoured ranks (Trivedi 2019). Translation into English is not necessarily an advantage in India, however, as Trivedi explains, since Indian writers and literary critics have shown little interest in the idea of world literature. At the same time, many Indian writers effectively bypass the restrictive and homogenizing global anglophone literary market by writing in English for local consumption. If the discourse of world literature has not taken account of its colonial and neo-colonial formulation, the discourse of translation as gain or loss – as liberatory circulation or as a cautionary tale of flattened differences – fails to capture the less systematic intersections of translation with the literatures of the globe.

Recent studies of translation and globalization are questioning assumptions about its operations and meanings, and the very terms on which translation's relation to world literature is conceived. This chapter aims to fortify the current challenge to familiar models of literary translation, not least by drawing on examples from diverse spatio-temporal zones: Western European literary translations during the Renaissance, colonial translations in North India and Arabic translations of European literature in the nineteenth century. Opening up literary studies to translation shows that rather than conveying belated, second acts of prime literary works, translation is deeply embedded in literatures. As its fundamental role comes to light, so does translation's daunting and irreducible complexity. No two translations have ever looked exactly alike nor ever will: a single text's basic lexical and syntactic units present innumerable possibilities when put in another idiom. Likewise, any single translation alters its source text and enacts alterations in the network of language, literature and culture that it enters. Compared with modern modes, early modern literary translations are non-linear transfers; texts are rendered, reprinted, retranslated or adapted in unregulated ways, and an uptick of translations of disparate literatures and languages due to imperial expansion proliferates these complications.

To do justice to these complexities, we can begin by understanding translation not as a product, but as mediations enabled by agents, and as itself an agent in the connectivity of literatures. This view borrows from Bruno Latour's Actor Network Theory (ANT), which as Rita Felski explains in her essay on ANT and translation studies, emphasizes 'connection as co-creation rather than as limit or constraint' (Felski 2016: 750). ANT thus provides an escape from two common but unreconciled positions about literary translation: first, that literary art's power and presence is unique and therefore untranslatable, which emphasizes an intrinsic loss in translation; and second, that translation is a reflection of larger concerns, and thus a function of some extrinsic force, generally that of uneven distributions of economic power. In ANT, the aesthetic qualities of power and presence are not attenuated by translation and instead are 'made possible by its relations' (Felski 2016: 750); similarly, translation is not merely 'a vehicle of homogenization or false equivalence, echoing, in its imposition of sameness, the logic of capitalist globalization' (Felski 2016: 752). Rather, translation is characterized as vibrant, 'associated with unpredictability, ambiguity, impurity, and increase in "noise"' (Felski 2016: 752).

In ANT no actor in the ensemble is unimportant. In the case of translation specifically, human agents such as writers, translators and editors play significant roles, but agents may also be non-humans. Most important for present purposes are three non-human agents that are as significant to the process as writers and translators: first, the material book, which alters the perception of a literary text in translation in ways the printer and publisher do not always control; second, the abstract notion of world literature, which exceeds any one writer's conception, and which takes part in transforming the relation of translation and literature. A third actor, often overlooked, is the term 'translation' itself. European vernaculars adopt the Latin *transferre/translatus* or 'transfer', from a multiplicity of Latin terms for translating. As a result, English and Romance languages not only conceptualize the activity of translating as the direct motion of a single entity from one point to another, but this term's function as a category enables the universalization of translation theory. Just as world literature can only be fully globalized by undertaking a critique of its narrowed compass, so, too, multiple agents of translation, including the idea of translation itself, ought to undergo re-examination.

The Print Networks of Renaissance Translation

During the Renaissance, translations circulated in Western Europe as printed books for the first time. From the fifteenth century onward, the innovative technology of the printing press, which Elizabeth Eisenstein depicts as an agent of change, also enacted change in literary translation. William Caxton, who chose the literary translation *Recuyell of the Historyes of Troye* (Bruges 1473) to be the first printed book in English, published many translations, mostly from French, that amounted to three quarters of his catalogue. In her study of English Renaissance textuality and translation, A. E. B. Coldiron explains that Caxton's translations, which use Continental goods and modes of book production, transmitted script to print in a 'complex "translation" – translation of content, forms, materials, and design' (Coldiron 2015: 37–8). In addition, many Renaissance scholars noted that the boost in printed translations from Latin into vernaculars and between European vernaculars meant that 'the line of transmission was not always simple and clear' (Barker and Hosington 2013: xx). Coldiron describes a pattern in which printed and reprinted translations defy simple, direct lines from source to target. These 'catenary' transfers may be concentrated or dilated over time. A second pattern is 'radiant': the same text is translated into several languages by the same printer within a short span of time. The radiant pattern, more common on the Continent, relied on an abundance of material resources including sets of type in many languages as well as significant numbers of translators and correctors needed for these different configurations (Coldiron 2015: 20–3).

Perhaps the most fitting emblem of the networked agents of print, vernacular, literature and translation in early modern Europe is the multilingual book. Typically, these editions combine language instruction with exposure to foreign literature. Such editions, printed in two or more languages, fill a need but also activate the demand for competence in languages at a time when they are learned primarily in a written medium. Guyda Armstrong traces some examples, including *The pretie and wittie historie of Arnalt & Lucenda*, a romance written by the Castilian Spanish author Diego de San Pedro, first printed in 1491 (Armstrong 2015). It was published in parallel columnar texts of Italian and English by Claude Hollyband in 1575, but Hollyband borrowed a previously published bilingual Italian–French edition and inserted a new English translation of *Arnalt & Lucenda* for the French one. These parallel texts effectively encoded the kinship and diversity of European languages by printing them in tandem using different typefaces – blackletter type for English text and italic for Italian-language text. Multilingual mise-en-page enables the visualization of simultaneously equivalent and non-equivalent languages. Rather than a representation of existing bonds between languages, this print phenomenon invites the reader's engagement in interpretive comparison, which in itself is a rudimentary form of translation. In *The Poet's Tongues*, Leonard Forster defines the Baroque poet's transition from a classical education to writing in one's own vernacular as marked by the desire to acquire 'abundant linguistic equipment' (Armstrong 2015: 28). Because literary language in particular offers diverse established formulae, translating literary works as a part of language instruction helped the writer garner these formulae. Spanish romances printed on the Continent in bilingual Spanish–French formats, and then used by English readers in the sixteenth century (with French as the best intermediary language), functioned in this way: they spark the infusion and transmutation of foreign words and rhetoric to effect new literary styles (Taylor 2013). The multiple agents of Renaissance vernacular translation interact such that a rendered text is rarely a simple transfer, but because the scale of Renaissance European print culture was relatively small, their complexity maintains a high degree of transparency.

Imperial Translation and Orientalism

These features of Renaissance translation were slowly but indelibly altered with the expansion of European empires. At first, translation networks operated largely unchanged, but literary content began to be globalized. For example, Richard Fanshawe's translation of the great Portuguese epic of Vasco da Gama's voyage to India, Luis de Camões' *Os Lusíadas*, the first in English, extended multilingual, instruction-based vernacular translation to world literature. Fanshawe, a seventeenth-century diplomat, translator and royalist poet, is said to have used Manuel de Faria y Sousa's *Lusíadas Comentadas*, a Spanish translation, as the source for his translation instead of the original Portuguese. Yet Fanshawe's translation uses Sousa only as 'an auxiliary tool in his translation, making use of its copious notes and critical paratexts, while focussing his translating efforts on the original Portuguese text, itself included in Sousa's edition' (Garcia 2017: 15). Fanshawe acquired reading knowledge of Portuguese with the aid of Spanish, but also relied on his expertise in Latin to enable translation, as evinced by his Latin version of Camões's text and his renderings from Spanish into Latin. The use of intermediaries 'does not necessarily imply a greater distance between original and final translation', in the case of *The Lusiads*, but rather the persistent overlap of European languages and literary activities, not least because of easy access to printed works in multiple languages (Garcia 2017: 15). As in the previous century, translator-writers such as Fanshawe, author-editor-commentators such as Sousa, editor-printers and other hyphenated actors prolonged these entanglements.

European literary representations of empire such as Camões's world epic circulated in European languages, but conquest and settlement across the globe also causes the efflorescence of literary translations from diverse languages, some in unknown scripts, some from oral languages – all of which are novel to Europeans. If print technology combines with habits of Latin-language education to energize the relations of European vernacular languages and literatures, imperial translation cannot sustain this relative stability. One sign of Europeans' consciousness of dislocation is the spike in literary pseudo-translation. Many fictional works which purport to be from distant places in the East are local productions. For example, the *Continuation of Letters Written by a Turkish Spy* (1718) pretends to be from Arabic originally, then translated into Italian and from Italian into English, but in fact it is composed in English by Daniel Defoe. The book begs the question not only of its origins as an oriental narrative but also of what constitutes an original text. It may not be a translation in the strict sense, but Defoe's work is derivative of a foreign source since it adapts the previously published *Letters of a Turkish Spy* (Defoe 1694), written by Giovanni Marana, an Italian refugee at the French court. The first volume of this original *Letters of a Turkish Spy* is composed by Marana in both French and Italian and translated into English, but the source of the subsequent volumes in English remains unverified. The English translation nonetheless becomes the source of a translation into French (Ballaster 2005; Aravamudan 2009). Faux translations enact both the concealments and the hyper-visibility of literary translation in the period. They also reveal the heightened agency of print in translating networks, not least because the title page and prefatory texts, which are the primary sources of information for readers, sow confusion over the distinctions between originals and translations.

An exemplary case of these and corresponding cultural occlusions and distortions in global translation is the first English version of a Chinese novel. The original is from the Qing period in China, mid-seventeenth century, and was translated by James Wilkinson, an employee of the East India Company. He makes a manuscript translation of the novel, probably for the purposes of learning Chinese, but it may have been completed by his Portuguese tutor and done with the aid of a Portuguese translation of the story (Fan 1946). Thomas Percy, an Anglican bishop and editor-compiler who knew no Chinese, publishes Wilkinson's manuscript as *Hau kiou chooan or the pleasing history* (1761). He introduces it to readers as a printed edition of an anonymous manuscript, and neither Wilkinson's nor Percy's name appears in the printed book. It is quickly presumed to be a pseudo-translation, and Percy is at pains to correct this impression in his new preface to the subsequent 1774 edition.

Percy's four-volume *Hau kiou chooan* is a significant literary event, not only because it suggests how difficult it is for readers to discern a translation from a pseudo-translation or adaptation, but because the book does not merely print Wilkinson's manuscript. It contains a long introductory preface; explanatory footnotes taken from European travel and missionary sources regarding politics, religion, manners and the material culture of China; and a bibliography. These features of the printed text perform an excess of mediation by the receiver culture while deracinating the original from its own cultural context in the Qing period and its role in Chinese literary canons. The Chinese narrative is a type of 'scholar-beauty romance' in which the male protagonist of the scholar-official class and a 'sheltered daughter of nobility' – both models of rectitude and Confucian morality – unite despite obstacles (Cheung 2003: 31). The English edition, however, paints a picture of Chinese civilization. This literary form of ethnographic imperialism also motivates the addition of a collection of literary specimens of Chinese literature to the edition: the outline of a Chinese play, 'a collection of Chinese proverbs' and 'fragments of Chinese poetry', much of which is taken from the French Jesuit collector of missionary accounts from China, Jean-Baptiste Du Halde. A year later, Percy follows this edition with two volumes of *Miscellaneous Pieces Relating to the Chinese* (1762). The novel is translated again from the original Chinese in 1829 by Sir John Davis of Royal Asiatic Society and re-entitled *The Fortunate*

Union. It features a title page with parallel English and Chinese in place of Percy's transliterated title, but the more erudite orientalist retranslation also enforces a new domestication of the text by anglicizing Chinese terms and culturally specific references in place of explanatory footnotes (St André 2003).

Percy's *Hau kiou chooan*, which becomes the source for German and French translations, is symptomatic of European transformations of an Asian source at a time when there are very few translations of other works of Chinese literature in which to situate it. It ironically exemplifies the interference of many European agents – translators, editors, influential readers, the design of the printed book – when it makes the remarkable leap from the happenstance acquisition of Wilkinson's instructional exercise to world literature. In the period between these two orientalist versions of *Hau kiou chooan*, the book famously receives the attention of Johann Wolfgang von Goethe. In his characteristic enthusiasm for affinities, Goethe makes the kind of ethnographic comparisons that Percy's edition proffers: the Chinese 'think, act, and feel almost exactly like us', but what they do is more 'pure and decorous' (Goethe 2014: 18). These remarks, from a conversation recounted later by Eckermann, also include Goethe's comparison of *Hau kiou chooan* to his own novel *Hermann and Dorothea* as well as to Samuel Richardson's acclaimed novels of virtue from the mid-eighteenth century. From these comparisons, Goethe projects an imminent age of world literature. Goethe is not the first to use the term world literature, nor does he systematically develop it, but he launches it into European discourse definitively in the 1820s (Pizer 2006). His formalist comparisons may signal a world literature built on robust literary internationalization, but when he also excludes some literatures as inferior while extolling the superiority of the ancient Greeks, world literature is commandeered by a prescriptive literary aesthetics that universalizes the parochial in place of discovering global literature.

World literature can be seen, then, as an unworldly contraction: European values and literary forms are imposed in translations from the East. Similarly, Europeans' exportation of literary works throughout their empires by way of colonial translations can be seen as part of the attempt to dominate, restructure and establish cultural and literary authority over the orient (Said 1979). Edward Said's orientalism is a dyadic model in which Western discourse consolidates imperial power and management. The oriental tale, its paradigmatic form, begins trending in Europe with Antoine Galland's version of the *Thousand and One Nights* (taken from Arabic and Persian sources), as a popular fictional type, made and remade in multiple European languages. It undergoes an unexpected transfer to colonial North India as an element in John Gilchrist's plan for imperial education at Fort William College in early nineteenth-century Calcutta. As Maryam Khan explains, Gilchrist shifts from instruction in classical languages to the region's vernaculars, but Urdu and Hindi, are 'artificially crafted' languages invented by imperial administrators to divide Muslims and Hindus (Khan 2017: 30). Key to this project is Gilchrist's importation of the oriental tale style familiar to Europeans. The simple style and moral of the oriental tale, lacks resemblance to any native fictional forms, such that when it was adapted into Urdu and Hindi, it 'reordered extant notions of literariness and language in North India', for English-speakers and for natives to whom it circulated (30). Francesca Orsini notes, however, that printing presses at Fort William College not only forwarded the agenda of language division, but 'several of the texts produced at the college were printed in both Urdu and Hindi scripts, implying that they were in fact mutually intelligible in terms of language and subject matter' (Orsini 2019: 74). Orientalism in imperialist North India serves the regulation and authorization of literary language and genres, but as in other translation networks, unforeseen counter-effects fall within the larger ambit. Because imperial translation involves networks of agents whose intentions may be visible, but not determining, the pathways and effects of transfer are not as predictable as the power relations which underpin them.

Arabophone Literary Translation

In the European imaginary, the oriental tale and, indeed, the origins of fiction itself stem from the Arabic-speaking East even as orientalism becomes mobile and translative in ways that complicate its trajectory. What happens when the route is reversed in the nineteenth century and Arabic translators render European fiction? European texts are not merely accepted as canonical, but as with *Robinson Crusoe*, for example, an 1835 Arabic version nativizes its vocabulary and asserts its place in a culturally diverse Ottoman Empire, effectively disrupting the novel's intended use by missionaries to enforce a global Christian dialect (Johnson 2021). The 'print public sphere' of the nineteenth- and early twentieth-century Arab Enlightenment or *Nahḍa* performs these and other conscious mediations of non-Arabic literature. Arabic translators highlight 'discrepancies between languages as differences that are impossible to resolve' even when they undertake to harmonize linguistic differences (Johnson 2021: 5). Unlike Western European literary translation, Arabic literary culture's circumscriptions of the foreign do not emanate from a collective ideology and geographical centre. Arabophone literary translation, taking place at a time of globally connected trade, transportation and technology, necessarily defies simple routes or means of transfer, not least because the language, literature and publishing centres are dispersed throughout the Middle East in cities such as Beirut and Cairo, in the Western metropoles, and in the Americas, Iran and South Asia.

Such decentralized views of translation networks supersede frameworks that attempt a comprehensive account of translation and world literature in the global power structure. Immanuel Wallerstein's world-system theory, which he traces back to the beginnings of empire in the sixteenth century, describes global circulation from the core to semi-periphery to periphery, driven by imperialism and capitalism. Applying Wallerstein's cartography to translation, original literature from the metropolitan core provides a majority of sources transferred to a semi-periphery, and belatedly to the periphery – all with a formal solidity that reinforces the source (Moretti 1991; Heilbron 1999; Beecroft 2008). In place of these conduits of political and economic control, translation is better described as dynamic assemblies, unfixed and without stable termination points, so that translation is not merely a vehicle of transfer: it plays an active role in the formation of literatures in the world.

Two recent studies grounded in an Actor Network Theory of literary translation help draw out some of the implications of the shift from world-system theory to ANT. In *Literary Translation and the Making of Originals*, Karen Emmerich argues that translation is not the unique manipulation of a literary work inflicted on an otherwise stable source but instead continues a process of textual iteration already at work in an original composition (Emmerich 2017). The argument echoes Lawrence Venuti's criticism of translation as merely 'the reproduction or transfer of an invariant' source and his related argument for the translator's agency in 'an interpretive act' free from any assumptions about the singularity and integrity of that which is transported (Venuti 2019: 1–2). Emmerich furthers this distinction between transfer and interpretation to argue that the original, which itself may be altered in its different editions, is just as derivative as a translation. Therefore, 'a particular text becomes an "original" only when another derivative text comes along to *make* it so' (Emmerich 2017: 13–14). A different kind of study also clarifies translation's role as a maker of literature. Part of a larger project called 'prismatic translation', this digital humanities initiative uses big data to analyse textual and lexical aspects of the entirety of the versions of *Jane Eyre* across the globe from inception to the present. The 'relationship between texts that get called "translations" and those that get called "sources" is a matter of "interactive discovery and co-creation"' (Reynolds 2020: 3). Thus, *Jane Eyre* is not simply an individual entity authored by Charlotte Bronte with unfettered aesthetic autonomy, but the sum of translations of *Jane Eyre*. Translation, not least in a global context where innumerable agents intentionally and unintentionally refract the process, ultimately redefines the very ontology of a literary work. Translation de-thrones the primacy of the original, and likewise, it redefines its own ontology by sharing in the original entity.

Reconsidering 'Translation' and Its Translations

As in most discussions, the term 'translation' has been used throughout this chapter in two ways. First, it designates a single rendering of a text, that is, an individual translation, even though any single translation involves multiple actors and outcomes. Second, translation designates a category or class of individual translations. As a category, the term suggests commonalities and a nature uniting the individuals. To understand translation as a co-creative actor implies this latter, abstract usage: translation has a nature – one that now looks different from the traditional view that translation is a kind of representation, or object of transfer, or even interpretation. This shift in ontology demonstrates that the question of the nature of translation continues to animate the links between individual translations and the category. Yet this equivocation has beset translation since the Renaissance, when vernaculars appropriate and later standardize this one term for a variety of concepts around translating. One result is that the analysis of any specific translated work mobilizes the universalizing discourse of translation theory, not least because most discussions reach beyond a specific instance to the general category to explore its significance. This ambiguity is peculiar, however, to European languages. In many non-Western languages, as David Bellos points out, the term does not carry this dual weight of individual and class. Thus, discussions of translation as a category become discussions of the 'European questions of the "the true nature of translation"' (Bellos 2011: 25).

Few scholars have thoroughly investigated the equivocation of 'translation' and its active role in the network of translation within and outside Europe. The term's etymology is too often an obligatory trope instead of an investigation of its derivation from the Latin *transferre* and its past participle *translatus*. Nor has there been intensive study of how translation became the single word for the ancient idiom's great stock of expressions for translating: *aemulari* [rival], *convertere* [to cause to revolve, rotate], *exponere* [to bring out into the open], *effingere* [shape, mould], *explicare* [to free from fold, unfold, straighten out], *exprimere* [to squeeze or press, elicit, extort], *interpretare* [give an account of], *mutare* [give and receive, exchange], *ponere* [to place, set], *reddere* [give back, restore], *traducere* [to bring over or across], *transferre* [to carry from one place to another], *vertere* [to cause to spin, revolve] (McElduff 2013: 189). In the first monolingual English dictionary, 'translation' is 'a carrying ouer', an anglicization of Latin, and used for physicalized transfers such as that of bishoprics, or in an astronomical sense to signify a lighter planet separating from a weightier one, as well as for translating languages (Cawdrey 1617). Because early lexicographers recycle word lists and definitions from Latin dictionaries, this 'free coinage' of English words precipitates the arrival in English of 'translate', but also alternatives such as interpret, render, expound and paraphrase (Starnes 1937: 18). The definitions of interpret and expound, like translate, apply to discourse generally as well as to putting one language into another (Hexham 1647–1648; Kersey 1702). When such terms specifically indicate the operations of translation, they do not suggest a complete and mirror-like image of an original, but rough or fuzzy translating. Title pages of seventeenth-century literary translations are accordingly heterogeneous: the original is 'Englished', or 'done out of' some other language, 'altered' from its source, a 'version', a 'paraphrase'. The modern notion of 'translation' as faithful rendition is not yet secure when Samuel Johnson's authoritative *Dictionary of the English Language* (Johnson 1755) is published. Johnson reiterates the Latin meaning in the first definition of translate – 'transport, remove' – and 'to interpret in another language' appears as the fifth definition. This flexible vocabulary and the rich metaphorical discourse of translation linger, but by the end of the eighteenth century, 'translation' is four times more likely to appear on a title page of a literary text than 'version', and ten times more likely than 'paraphrase' (ECCO).

The libertine translators of the later seventeenth century appear to keep translation open and unconfined as the dictionary definitions suggest. In a curious twist, they pose as creative agents in the transmission of literary texts and demonize other translators as slavish or pedantic by emphasizing the limitations of the term translation. Abraham Cowley famously writes in the preface to his translation of the *Pindaric Odes* (Cowley 1694) that he does not abide by the term translation: 'It does not at all trouble me that the *Grammarians* perhaps will not suffer this libertine way of rendering foreign Authors, to be called *Translation*; for I am not so much enamored of the *Name Translator*, as not to wish rather to be *Something Better* though it want yet a *Name*' (Cowley 1694: n.p.). A dispute erupts between libertine and faithful translation, but the seemingly conventional arguments about fidelity and treachery point as much to a discomfort around the term *translation*. The poet and translator Katherine Philips disparages the libertines in a letter from the early 1660s: 'I cannot but be surprised at the great Liberty they have taken in adding, omitting and altering the original as they please themselves. This I take to be a liberty not pardonable in Translation and unbecoming the Modesty of that Attempt' (Phillips 1705: 179). Philips's defence of the translator's duty seems to polarize translation practices, but the last part of her thought, 'not pardonable *in Translation* and unbecoming the Modesty of *that* Attempt' is, like Cowley's remark, an observation on vocabulary. She does not imply that freedoms are necessarily offensive per se, only that freely rendered work is not properly understood by the term 'translation'. With its etymological allusion to direct transfer, the *translation* is suited to fidelity, but other kinds of translation, however normativized, lack names. As the word takes hold in European languages, it becomes an agent of categorization, at once more constrained and yet less settled about what the essence or nature of the category may be.

Many non-Western languages, meanwhile, do not have a single, equivalent term for translation but rather a set of related terms and metaphors. In a brief survey of the term in several languages around the world, Maria Tymoczko writes that the Sanskrit *rupantar* means 'change in form', but *anuvad* or 'speaking after, following' can also be used for translation. The latter comes from a word that originally refers to ritually exact discursive repetitions associated with incantation. The words for translation in the African language Igbo include *tapia* from *ta* 'to tell, narrate' and *kowa* from *ko* 'narrate, talk about' and *wa*, 'break in pieces' (Tymoczko 2007: 69–70). In Japanese, there is no one term akin to 'translation' but many different compound words, each of which designates some aspect of the circumstance or approach to translating, including words for direct translation and one for a looser translation (Bellos 2011: 22–3). Martha Cheung writes that the word for translation, 'fanyi', in modern Chinese comes from various early Chinese metaphors. She explains that 'yi' means transmitting 'the words of the tribes in the four directions' but considers other terms – 'ji', 'xiang', 'Didi' – as a 'network of inter-related meanings' for translating (Cheung 2005: 36). Joseph Allen remarks on the role of translation in early China: 'There is not one mention of "translation" (at least in terms now recognized) in the standard pre-Han classics (*Shijing, Shu jing, Yijing*) or the early Confucian canon (*Chunqiu, Lunyu, Mengzi, Sunzi*), nor is there any mention in the core Daoist texts (*Zhuangzi, Laozi*)' (Allen 2019: 122). Indeed, before substantial contact with Europeans, mercantile and diplomatic translation notwithstanding, translation in literature, religion and philosophy is not a relevant consideration but is instead 'inattentive, angst-free' (Allen 2019: 123). It is likely that the dominance of European languages and discourse, with their equivocation of the individual translation with translation as a category, imposes an object that appears universal, but which in fact is not discoverable globally.

World literature may need translation, but the early history of print translation across the globe suggests the need to reconfigure our understanding of this relationship. Modern translation imposes isolations and restrictions: monolingual readers expect translations to provide them with replicas of foreign sources. In earlier periods, literary translation is a ubiquitous and co-creative agent in the connectivity of languages and literatures. The very word 'translation' plays an important role as an unnecessarily limiting construction on this cooperation. Concealing its own equivocations, and becoming a recursive but universalizing discourse, European terms and the resulting ideas of translation become a corpus of theory that has historically hampered our idea of what it means to translate across the world. Apprehending its co-productive role can help refashion translation's worldly endeavour. In this light, world literature may begin as a European construction, but as in the Arabic arena or in India, literature's transformations in translation suggest another way towards world literature, one which attends to the complex and unexpected moves in its networks of agents.

CHAPTER 5

Empire
The Nineteenth-Century Global Novel in English

Elleke Boehmer and Dominic Davies

In his 1883 series of lectures, *The Expansion of England*, the Victorian historian John Seeley famously observed that Britain had 'conquered and peopled half the world in a fit of absence of mind' (1971: 12). This suggestion, that the British Empire was somehow stumbled upon and incidentally conceived, underpins the long-held assumption that nineteenth-century literature was only ever concerned within a narrowly defined British framework. By addressing matters such as industrialization, the growth of cities or the woman question as if these matters took the dimensions exclusively of the proverbial 'small island' of Britain, Seeley concealed a vast history of global and globalizing entanglements that imperial Britain played a crucial role in building – from the very beginning of the nineteenth century and, indeed, before then, too.

This chapter will address the integral role that literary writing in English, and especially the realist novel, played in imaginatively shaping, structuring and on occasion obscuring processes of nineteenth-century globalization, for which empire was the constitutive ground. We will observe how the novel composed what Raymond Williams called 'structures of feeling' that combined together human relationships and their wider contexts in communicable ways even when, as here, those contexts extended beyond the nation and took on global dimensions (Williams 1973: 158). Throughout, globalization will be taken as the incremental and unequal incorporation of non-capitalist regions of the world into the rising capitalist economies of Europe and then North America, a process accompanied by the uneven imposition of cultural, technological and infrastructural influence (Wallerstein 1996). We proceed in this chapter on the conviction that imperialism was an essential aspect of globalization through the long nineteenth century, redistributing wealth unevenly and restructuring the global economy in favour of imperial power. Globalization and empire were therefore folded into one another, taking on different features at their geographic and economic cores and peripheral edges. To capture two contrasting yet interestingly complementary views of this system, we therefore take our illustrative examples in this chapter from, on the one hand, Charles Dickens's writing from the heart of empire in London, and, on the other, from the South African Olive Schreiner's work set in – and mostly written from – zones of economic extraction.

Advocating for his vision of a newly global England, Seeley was reiterating the politician Charles Dilke's earlier call for a 'Greater Britain' (1868): a racialized geographical vision of an expanded anglophone 'white man's world' in which 'domestic Britons', as well as those scattered across dominions, colonies, mandates and protectorates, would learn to 'narrate their own lives as imperial men, women, and children' (Boehmer 1998: 112–19; Schwarz 2011: 10). Though so differently located, Dickens and Schreiner were part of that expanding world and narrated its lives. While for Dilke 'the difficulties that impede progress to universal dominion of the English people lie in the conflict with the cheaper races' (Dilke 2009: 406), for the later Seeley the English people's racial exclusivity was more self-evident and clearly expressed throughout the settler colonies, which included South Africa. As he noted, the 'enormous Indian population does not make part of Greater Britain in the same sense as those ten millions of Englishmen who live outside of the British Islands' (Seeley 1971: 11). Like other imperial ideologues, Seeley's views were simultaneously expansionist and segregationist, his slippage between the terms 'England' and 'Britain' betraying a distinct colonizing disposition also towards Scotland and, more especially, Ireland. These men viewed an expanded Britain on which 'the sun never set' as at once a global and a supra-national entity, even while also always placing it within a meticulously mythologized nationalist frame – a frame that Dickens and Schreiner in their different ways both accepted and interrogated.

Already at this relatively early stage, therefore, the paradoxical axes of globalization and nationalism were thrown into stark relief: on the one hand, their commodity flows and fluid trade routes; on the other, their restrictive border regimes and unequal citizenship rights. In the twenty-first century, the violent rhythms of this globalized dispensation unmistakably persist in hyper-nationalist imaginaries and their all-too-real regimes of border walls and immigration quotas. We need only replace Dilke's 'Greater Britain' with the 'Global Britain' of Dominic Raab, Priti Patel and other Conservative Party authors of *Britannia Unchained* (see Kwarteng et al. 2012) to see the continued resonance of the nineteenth century's imperial globalism.[1] To this we might add the persistent faith in a global Commonwealth still built on unequal postcolonial relations (see Hirsch 2019), or a continuing obsession with whiteness as a structuring concept of global space (see Shilliam 2018).

The morphing of 'Greater' into 'Global Britain' is a firm reminder that the British Empire was always a global, world-enveloping project, something both Dickens and Schreiner perceived. The 'dishonesty' of this project, to use the late-Victorian author Robert Louis Stevenson's word, was sustained by many forms of nineteenth-century writing but also in some remarkable instances exposed – as in Stevenson himself or his contemporary Joseph Conrad. Centred in India, Britain's 'second empire' – its colonization of North America had been the first (see Bayly 1989) – was thus mobilized, maintained and defended through the medium of a vast body of written documentation. From official memos and bureaucratic reports, through to diaries, letters and memoirs, as well as of course imaginative fiction, 'literature, broadly defined, underpinned efforts to interpret other lands, offering home audiences a way of thinking about exploration, Western conquest, national valour, new colonial acquisitions' (Boehmer 2005: 15). The global influence of empire was understood through these books and associated documents, and these in many ways came to constitute it. The colonies were in this sense textual creations, albeit bearing violently material effects.

It is true, of course, that to a great extent the nineteenth-century novel coded colonial and global experience obliquely – seemingly at an angle, or in encrypted ways. Its spatial logic was typically focussed on delimited and circumscribed spaces. Yet, with a slight change of tack, it becomes possible to see that the imaginative world of the nineteenth-century novel in English almost always had global designs. It was engaged in the cartographic visualization of global space, strikingly drawing on empire for the means whereby plot – both literary and national – might be moved forwards. For example, in his field-shifting reading of Jane Austen's *Mansfield Park* (1814), Edward Said revealed the extent to which 'Thomas Bertram's slave plantation in Antigua is mysteriously necessary to the poise and the beauty of Mansfield Park, a place described in moral and aesthetic terms well before the scramble for Africa, or before the age of empire officially began' (Said 1993: 59). With this analysis, Said developed his influential practice of 'contrapuntal reading' (66): an approach to literary texts that reassessed 'passing references' to sugar plantations and colonial outposts not as inconsequential cues or incidental coordinates, but as enriching points of analysis that illuminated for readers the truly global remit of the nineteenth-century novel.

Inspired by Jean Rhys's novel *Wide Sargasso Sea*, a 1966 rewriting of Charlotte Brontë's *Jane Eyre* (1847), Said's colleague Gayatri Spivak engaged in a related postcolonial project to demonstrate the extent to which canonized novels, though seemingly confined to 'the domestic inscription of space', were in fact predicated on the 'axiomatics of imperialism' (Spivak 1985: 246–7). As Said and Spivak both showed, these works' settings and plots, characters and action, were all impinged upon by the global economies of slavery and trade. Since their much-cited interventions, a significant body of critical literature has reassessed the realist novel in terms of its world-spanning imperial machinations, also emphasizing the role played by the material book in the formation of an imperial – and so we would add global – commons (Burton and Hofmeyr 2014).

In this chapter, we build on the work of these critics to explore the imaginative work undertaken by the mainstream literary novel in nineteenth-century processes of globalization. We focus our argument on two contrasting novels that critically register and respond to diametrically different geographies of globalization's socio-economic upheaval: in the northern imperial metropolis, Dickens's *Dombey and Son* (1848), and at its far southern periphery, Schreiner's *The Story of an African Farm* (1883, hereafter *African Farm*). Reading these novels comparatively, we demonstrate the extent to which the nineteenth-century novel in English built stories that functioned as imaginative endorsements of empire or, more rarely, as unsettling critiques of it. In both cases, these stories worked as a kind of infrastructure, laying out tracks that expanded its readers' spatial imaginaries from national to global scales, even while, as for Seeley and Dilke, they sometimes also conflated those scales to equate nation and world. The term infrastructure here emphasizes the extent to which novelistic narrative impacted global, colonial and postcolonial geographies in physical as well as imaginative ways (see Boehmer and Davies 2018). For, as Said pithily reminds us, the 'actual possession of land is what empire in the final analysis is all about' (Said 1993: 78); the stories built to regulate, administer, constrain and confine that land, along with the vast oceanic spaces that connected it, were crucially circulated via the global novel written in English.

From Dickens to Schreiner: Building Stories of Globalization

Published at mid-century, Charles Dickens's 1848 novel, *Dombey and Son*, describes a London riven with infrastructural tumult:

The first shock of a great earthquake had, just at that period, rent the whole neighbourhood to its centre. Traces of its course were visible on every side. Houses were knocked down; streets broken through and stopped; deep pits and trenches dug in the ground; enormous heaps of earth and clay thrown up; buildings that were undermined and shaking, propped by great beams of wood. … Everywhere were bridges that led nowhere; thoroughfares that were wholly impassable; Babel towers of chimneys, wanting half their height; temporary wooden houses and enclosures, in the most unlikely situations; carcasses of ragged tenements, and fragments of unfinished walls and arches, and piles of scaffolding, and wildernesses of bricks, and giant forms of cranes, and tripods straddling above nothing. … mounds of ashes blocked up rights of way, and wholly changed the law and custom of the neighbourhood.

In short, the yet unfinished and unopened Railroad was in progress; and, from the very core of all this dire disorder, trailed smoothly away, upon its mighty course of civilisation and improvement. (Dickens 2008: 68)

In this vivid description, repeated semi-colons fragment the paragraph into disjointed lines. The short declarative sentences capture the disarrayed urban landscape, repeating the uneven rhythms of the city's 'creative destruction' (Harvey 2012: 16). Only the train, carrying stories of 'civilisation and improvement', releases the paragraph from its stuttering construction into a sentence that trails 'smoothly away' (Dickens 2008: 68). Here we catch Dickens in the act of building stories, and national ones at that, drawing Britain into what would soon become a newly connected 'infrastructure state' (Guldi 2012). As Franco Moretti argues in his *Atlas of the European Novel, 1800–1900*, 'state-building requires streamlining', and 'the style of nineteenth-century novels – informal, impersonal, "common" – contributes to this centralization more than any other discourse' (Moretti 1991: 45). Dickens is *building* stories, certainly, but these are also *stories of building*, and he implies intimate connections between two. He grapples here for a language that might, like the train he describes, encase and smooth over the contortions of global capital that were rupturing his familiarly local borough of Camden.

Contrasting markedly with the hyper-activity of Dickens's mid-century London, far from his vantage point at the very heart of empire, is the setting of Olive Schreiner's *African Farm*: a novel written through the 1870s in the vast expanse of the Karoo semi-desert in the South African Cape and finished before the author made the 'voyage in' to London in the early 1880s. Situated at the very edge of the globalizing economy, *African Farm* supplies a more critical account of the waste and destruction that, with colonial expansion, such processes wrought. For the critic Jed Esty, *African*

Farm describes 'the failure of development in both characterological and geopolitical registers' (Esty 2012: 71), a failure that seeps even into its narrative syntax. The opening paragraphs, which give a wide-angle lens onto the solitary farm and capture the layered age of the African Earth, describes a sleepy setting, not a hive of activity. The 'zinc roof of the great, open waggon house, [and] the roofs of the outbuildings that jutted from its side' are rubbed to a 'burnished silver' by the light of the full moon (Schreiner 2003: 47). Yet the 'solemn monotony' Schreiner describes is a temporality inextricably connected to the infrastructural earthquake of Dickens's London, indexing globalization's patchwork of extraction, investment, construction and destruction, as it teeters between competing economic zones.

Schreiner made clear in her preface to the second edition of *African Farm* that hers was not a story of romance and adventure. These, she argued, were 'best written in Piccadilly or in the Strand' where 'the gifts of the creative imagination, untrammelled by contact with any fact, may spread their wings' (Schreiner 2003: 42). Schreiner realized that to capture the dislocation of an underdeveloped economy, another form of writing was required. While the hodgepodge of styles and forms of which *African Farm* is comprised suggest the failure of her project, that Schreiner cannot quite see her way towards a new colonial realism is, we argue, significant. The novel's mosaic of broken and unfinished pieces, variously cartographic and allegorical, is a significant correlate for the uneven terrain of globalization that surreptitiously – and sometimes shockingly – impacts upon her Southern African world.

In contrast to the spare economy of Schreiner's narrative, the plunder of globalization is up front in *Dombey and Son*, ornamenting London's concrete surfaces. The offices of the novel's titular shipping firm are 'ten minutes' walk' from the Royal Exchange and the Bank of England, financial institutions functioning both as 'the clearing house of the world economy' and as symbolic edifices of the empire in 'the public imagination' (Black 1999: 96). They are, moreover, 'just around the corner' from the 'rich East India House', a building described by Dickens as 'teeming with suggestions of precocious stuffs and stones, tiers, elephants, howdahs, hookahs, umbrellas, palm trees, palanquins, and gorgeous princes of a brown complexion sitting on carpets with their slippers very much turned up at the toes' (Dickens 2008: 36). The expansive circuitry of shipping lanes that funnels these orientalized commodities into the city provides an irreducibly global backdrop to its local fabric:

> Anywhere in the immediate vicinity [of East India House] there might be seen pictures of ships speeding away full sail to all parts of the world;

outfitting warehouses ready to pack off anybody anywhere, fully equipped in half an hour; and little timber midshipmen in obsolete naval uniforms, eternally employed outside the shop doors of nautical instrument-makers in taking observations of the hackney carriages. (Dickens 2008: 36)

For Jeff Nunokawa (1995: 141), in *Dombey and Son* 'capital is exhibition', functioning as 'sign' rather than 'substance' and coded on exoticist and orientalist vectors. Certainly, the framed 'pictures' of ships, 'precocious stuffs' and 'little' shipbuilders render the oceanic space beyond London as smooth and abstract ('anybody anywhere'), especially when read against the rigorously physical description of railway construction in Camden. The speeding ships evoke the smooth flows of the rapidly globalizing economy that project the brutal violence of empire and conquest far beyond the edges of its aesthetic 'picture' frame. And yet, when taken as a whole, the novel involves London's infrastructural upheaval in this broader circuitry, gesturing to the entangled connections between floating commodities, exoticist discourses and the radical restructuring of local space.

The African farm of Schreiner's novel is drained of such imperial splendour, described only as 'a place to eat in, to sleep in, not to be happy in' (Schreiner 2003: 65). Otto, a colonial German and owner of the farm, has only a 'little dingy room, with its worm-eaten rafters and mud floor, and broken white-washed walls' (65). His possessions are minimal, too: 'a little bookshelf with its well-worn books', 'a string of onions' hanging from the rafters and 'in the corner, a heap of filled and empty grain bags'. But even in this scene of frontier scarcity and impoverishment, there are clues that register the presence of the globalizing economy – peripheral privations on which the imperial centre's wealth depends. The grain is of course exported from the farm to feed expanding colonial cities and passing imperial armies. Otto's bed is 'covered by a patchwork quilt of faded red lions', a symbol evoking the Royal Standard with its connotations of British mettle and pluck, recognized across the empire, though fading here on the frontier. Finally, the only item adorning the wall of Otto's hut is 'a map of South Germany, with a red line drawn through it to show where the German had wandered' (65). While Schreiner explains the map in no greater detail, we can imagine the line connecting Europe to the tip of Southern Africa, perhaps overland, though more likely by the sea routes that expand beyond the London of *Dombey and Son*. Penned just two years before the Berlin Convention of 1885, Schreiner also codes a sideways reference to Britain's imperial competition with Germany, conjuring a globalized world in which power dynamics were tipping towards Central Europe.

Astronomical Ambitions, Knowable Communities

Dombey and Son and *African Farm*'s vision of globalization is irreducibly at once imperial and colonial (see Young 2018). Throughout his novels, as we've begun to see, Dickens organizes the world along narrative and infrastructural tracks that extend outwards as 'tentacles of progress' (see Headrick 1988). By contrast, Schreiner approaches these 'tentacles' at their outer edge, where they touch South Africa's diamond and later gold mines to suck resources from the colonial landscape. In the case of both writers, economic and imaginative geographies set up networked trade along uneven and unequal axes, directing wealth (and people, as we will later see) towards the metropolitan core.

Schreiner's African moon silvers the landscape in ways at once phantasmic and excessive: the 'weird and almost oppressive beauty' of the all-pervading 'white light' is evocative of the precious minerals and metals at that time being discovered beneath the 'ironstones' of South Africa. Diamond motifs are threaded throughout the novel, often connected to the exchange of women and land as property in marriage. Yet the uncanny white light at the same time suggests that this surfeit of mineral wealth, even as it draws the speculators of many nations to the country and to the farm, is superficial and unreal. Though such wealth drives the empire, it has deadening and ghostly effects that find their way into the plot, as they also do in several other key Victorian fictions of this period, from Anthony Trollope's *The Eustace Diamonds* (1871–1873) and George Eliot's *Daniel Deronda* (1876) to H. Rider Haggard's *King Solomon's Mines* (1885).

Similarly, in *Dombey and Son*, the 'heavens' perform symbolic work:

> The earth was made for Dombey and Son to trade in, and the sun and moon were made to give them light. Rivers and seas were formed to float their ships; rainbows gave them promise of fair weather; winds blew for or against their enterprises; stars and planets circled in their orbits, to preserve inviolate a system of which they were the centre. (Dickens 2008: 2)

The use of climactic and astronomical metaphors to describe the winds and light of capital flow again points to the global horizons of *Dombey and Son*'s London. Like many of his contemporaries, Dickens in this and many other passages inserts the 'knowable community' of his native London, to use Raymond Williams's phrase, into a much wider cosmological map.

For Williams, writing in *The Country and the City* (1973), Dickens's 'genius' lay in his ability to reconcile the social upheaval of the industrializing metropolis with the novel's compulsion to produce such a 'knowable community' – 'to show people and their relationships in essentially knowable and communicable ways' (Williams 1973: 165). Dickens achieved this, Williams continues, by constructing 'structures of feeling' that were able to take nations and seas in their scope (158). Reading these same passages from *Dombey and Son*, Williams points to the newly global 'way of seeing' that Dickens cultivated through his descriptive gaze (161; see also Grossman 2012: 92). Importantly, the networks of nineteenth-century globalization are not simply reflected in the tangled relationships of Dickens's major novels but were themselves imaginatively fostered and shaped by his writing.

Though Schreiner's world is the ostensibly limited and easily knowable community of the provincial farm, nonetheless that community is refracted into the wider world through various peculiar motifs. In the second half of the book, after Otto has left the farm, he is replaced by another labourer, an effeminate frontiersman named Gregory Rose. Rose's home, not unlike Otto's before it, is 'a little square daub-and-wattle building, far out in the "karroo", two miles from the homestead' (Schreiner 2003: 171). Again, the narrative rhythm of this landscape is one of 'dreary monotony', conspicuously contrasting with the creative destruction of Dickens's imperial London. To ward off homesickness – Schreiner notes his 'depressing circumstances', presumably both economic and emotional – Rose has covered 'the whitewashed walls' of his new home 'profusely … with pasted-on prints cut from the *Illustrated London News*' (171). Alone in the Karroo, in a zone of economic underdevelopment, Rose wallpapers the single building to which he has access in stories and pictures referencing the wider empire and globe. While he may not be able to reinsert himself into that wider network economically, the proliferation of stories and their accompanying images imaginatively render that community knowable and habitable to him. In this we find another clear instance of a novel as defined by Williams attending 'to "the close living substance" of the local while simultaneously tracing the "occluded relationships" – the vast transnational economic pressures, the labor and commodity dynamics – that invisibly shape the local' (Nixon 2011: 45; see also Williams 1983: 238).

Though *Dombey and Son* at first appears to soften its global horizon into a smooth oceanic space easily traversed by trading ships, on closer inspection the full turbulence of those 'occluded relationships' comes through, built into the entangled narrative coincidences of the stories. In one particularly compelling motif that repeats throughout *Dombey and Son*, the tumult of globalization 'surfaces' with the image of the shipwreck, which has echoes in later novels such as *Bleak House* (see Buzard 2018: 521–2). Early on in chapter 13, Mr Dombey sends his employee, Walter Gay, 'to fill a junior station in the counting-house at Barbados' (187). After his departure,

Walter's ship quickly disappears at sea, where he remains missing for much of the novel, until his return in chapter 49. Understandably, then, when Dombey's neglected daughter Florence sets out to visit the City of London in pursuit of news of Walter, her attention is drawn to the pictures of 'dangerous seas, where fragments of great wrecks were drifting, perhaps, and helpless men were rocked upon them into a sleep as deep as the unfathomable waters' (344). Here, the calm waters 'formed to float [Dombey's] ships' are suddenly transformed into an unsteady and deathly terrain. Florence sees not 'pictures of ships speeding away full sail to all parts of the world' (36), but 'prints of vessels fighting with the rolling waves', framed images that fill 'her with alarm' (344). Globalization rocks the narrative of *Dombey and Son*, both at home and abroad, altering the material fabric of the imperial metropolis and re-plotting its story frames along oceanic axes.

Carceral Archipelagos: Dickens's Duress, Schreiner's Schisms

In his global history of the nineteenth century, Jürgen Osterhammel (2014: 19) reminds us that fiction writers such as Dickens and Schreiner were the first sociologists. They drew on the same methods of abstracted ordering, logical progression and feigned empiricism that underpinned other contemporaneous genres, from the burgeoning shelves of travel writing to the pseudo-scientific manifestos of early race theorists. When Benedict Anderson influentially highlighted the role played by print culture in facilitating a national community that imagined itself bound to the borders of a geographic territory, he also emphasized, as did Williams, this role of the novel in building stories of national proportion. Novels allowed individuals to see themselves as part of a far larger 'knowable community', Dickens's 'popular serialised novels' themselves appearing as an important footnote to Anderson's argument (Dickens 2008: 35, n.61).

However, as Deirdre David, among others, has observed (David 2005: 86), the mid-century middle classes, while devouring novels with their newspapers, were also acclimatizing to a *global* as well as national consciousness. They were already subject to a barrage of world-spanning stories that – much like Schreiner's *African Farm* – migrated inwards from imperial outposts. They sent letters to and from family members who were traversing the globe as missionaries and colonial officials and their wives. Settler emigration to the colonies across the English-speaking world was supported by a vast outpouring of writing (see Shaikh 2018). The iron girders of railways, the mappable lines of shipping routes and the sentences of the realist novel all together played symbiotic roles in recasting the globe as a habitable and familiar space (Davies 2017: 21). Again like the railways, novels circulated far beyond Britain in a way that filled colonial libraries, train compartments and hill stations across the empire, leading the imaginations of readers 'along parallel grooves' (Boehmer 2008: 52). Indeed, as Priya Joshi (2002) shows, the global sale of British novels overseas had come by the end of the nineteenth century to underwrite the profits of London-based publishers. Dickens's novels, like Trollope's, were published across the globe, beginning in Australasia as early as 1838 (Gagnier 2018: 727–8). The Victorian novel can thus be thought of 'as a technology that functions like a railway or a canal' (Murray 2008: 12), sewing itself and its readers firmly into the irrevocably global metabolism of Britain's industrializing economy, while also imaginatively enabling it.

The realist novel in this sense allowed writers to investigate new 'infrastructures of feeling' – to extend Williams's phrase – that were global and even planetary not only in their reach, but in their most basic constitution. Schreiner's novel was enmeshed in these structures, strongly indebted to the work of thinkers such as John Stuart Mill and Herbert Spencer, while also troubling, through its proto-modernist, 'underdeveloped' form, some of the more imperialistic and racialized strands of their arguments. In this way the nineteenth-century global novel did not just map global space but produced it as well, even when it did so, as for *African Farm*, through schismatic spatial imaginaries. It cultivated a certain optic, a way of seeing society that allowed its readers to narrate themselves into a supra-national terrain, sometimes smoothly, as with Dickens's train, or in a juddering wreck, like the ships of *Dombey and Son*'s storms. Physical infrastructures such as railways, steamships and telegraphs were of course central to this shift, yet the nineteenth-century novel worked in similar ways, as an imaginative infrastructure with extraordinary resilience.

The imperial historian Ann Laura Stoler uses the term 'duress' to capture this infrastructural and imaginative endurance (Stoler 2016: 7), emphasizing the constraints through which imperial histories continue to impact upon contemporary global mobilities. To capture this, Stoler revives Michel Foucault's notion of the 'carceral archipelago' (Foucault 1995: 314), unfolding his cartography of the European prison system across a broader imperial terrain to encompass the 'penal colonies, settler colonies, [and] detention camps' that have shaped global space as a network of restrictions (Anderson 2000; Stoler 2016: 75). As we have already seen, for Dickens and Schreiner, along with many other Victorian novelists, the globalized story-worlds of nineteenth-century literature are never simply about capital flows. These novelists were just as preoccupied with rising economic inequalities, the traffic in human bodies, and the infrastructures of incarceration and the expanding penitentiary system that regulated the movement of those bodies across the globe (see Schwan 2012).

In *Dickens and Empire*, Grace Moore points out that the exiling of 'problematic characters to distant dominions was certainly, in the early novels, an expedient means of providing the conventional "happy ending" demanded by readers and the marketplace' (Moore 2016: 12–13). For example, the villain Jack Maldon is dismissed to India in *David Copperfield* (1850), while in the same novel Mr Micawber and his family 'abandon' the 'luxuries of the old country' for a frontier 'life afloat, in the bush' of Australia (Dickens 1990: 677) – where, it is essential to remember, massacres committed against Indigenous populations were brutally under way (Allam and Evershed 2019). Elsewhere, in *Hard Times* (1854), Tom Gradgrind is shuttled off 'to North or South America, or any distant part of the world to which he could be the most speedily and privately dispatched' (Dickens 2001: 211). This plot strategy is repeated by several of Dickens's contemporaries, most notably Elizabeth Gaskell in both *Mary Barton* (1848) and *Cranford* (1853) (see David 2005: 87), creating an extended cast of exiled literary characters that also begins to explain where the intrusive young men of Schreiner's *African Farm* might have come from.

These examples show how the nineteenth-century novel's expansive story-worlds envisioned a form of globalization predicated not on smooth flows, open borders or even free trade, but rather on a deeply selective regime of mobility and immobility. Through their strategic mapping of distant horizons these novels normalized an emerging global infrastructure that channelled the often politically disenfranchised – whether criminal, or simply poor – into far-flung repositories. There, already inhabited territories were transformed through dispossession and often genocide into holding pens that alleviated, if only temporarily, social upheaval in the metropolitan centre. It was hardly a case of Seeley's 'fit of absence of mind'.

Yet such expulsions from Britain out across the empire were not without consequence for the metropolitan centre. Dickens entertains across many of his novels a fascination with the émigré's – or rather, the colonist's – counter-figure: 'the returned exile' (Moore 2016: 13). Moore reads the haunting presence of innumerable returnees across Dickens's novels, from *Nicholas Nickleby* (1838) and *Oliver Twist* (1839) to *The Old Curiosity Shop* (1840) and *David Copperfield* (1850), as 'demonstrative of the shortcomings of emigration as a viable remedy for the evils of poverty' (2016: 13). In *Dombey and Son*, when Walter Gay – compulsorily exiled by Dombey, with no say in his supposed 'mobility' – does eventually return, he assumes a peculiarly ghostly form, Florence at first spying 'the shadow of a man upon the wall close to her' (730). A ghost of globalization haunts the novel, a spectrality that beckons readers to conceive of space not only along formal imperial connections but also across multiple informal economic ties that took in swathes of South America, the Middle East, China and of course America as well.

Both Dickens and Schreiner are also keenly aware of the violence under way in settler colonial spaces. As the Native American scholar Gerald Vizenor points out in his extended reading of Dickens's *American Notes for General Circulation* (1842), there is a 'sense of adventure, to be sure, but at a literary distance' (Vizenor 1998: 77). For Vizenor, Dickens draws Indigenous figures as absent even when they are technically present in the lines of the writing: 'the presence of natives' is reduced to little more than 'a romantic soliloquy of their absence' (77). We find this in Dickens's novels, and again, in *Dombey and Son*, where Dombey's 'native' servant is violently wrenched away from a named indigenous geography. This character is 'a dark servant of the Major's who Miss Tox was quite content to classify as a "native", without connecting him with any geographical idea whatever' (Dickens 2008: 98); he has 'no particular name, but answered to any vituperative epithet' (290). This erasure couples the nineteenth-century novel in English to settler colonial and imperial narratives elsewhere that considered huge swathes of global space as *terra nullius*, and thus open to annexation and plunder.

The 'legal fiction' of *terra nullius* functioned alongside the extensive fictions of both the realist novel and the nation-state to diminish Indigenous people's 'ontological relationship to land' in a number of settler contexts, from Australia to Canada and elsewhere (Moreton-Robinson 2015:15). While in *African Farm* Schreiner never quite writes the voices of the Indigenous directly, her novel does insist on their lingering and felt presence, and their verbal dexterity. The presence of the Indigenous inhabitants of the Karroo, where Schreiner's fictional homestead is built, is acknowledged through 'some Bushmen-paintings', the 'red and black pigments' of which have 'been preserved through long years' (Schreiner 2003: 55). As Bart Moore-Gilbert (2003: 96) and Deborah Shapple (2004: 114) point out, this is both a potentially disruptive allusion to a 'suppressed pre-colonial history', while also an erasure of that history from 'the present narrative moment'. For Davies (2017: 143), it is significant that these paintings are made 'to speak' by Schreiner's male protagonist, Waldo, who gives voice to them during a conversation about Napoleon Bonaparte's early nineteenth-century imperialist ambitions (and which are coded throughout as allegorical of Britain's own slightly later, though equally aggressive, expansions). Indeed, Waldo interrupts this celebratory discussion of Napoleon as 'the greatest man who ever lived' by insisting on the presence of the distinct geological formations and the art of the Indigenous with which they are marked: 'If *they* could talk, if *they* could tell us now!' he says, placing his hand directly onto the rock (Schreiner 2003: 58, 60). The partially silenced yet still insistent Indigenous presence disrupts the narrative temporalities of Schreiner's novel, as in Dickens, stilting the imperial rhetoric of progress and the forces of global modernity it helped enable.

Conclusion: At Once Imperial and Global

The narrative structures of the nineteenth-century novel in English helped to mould and support the British imperial vision. As we have demonstrated with the examples of Dickens and Schreiner writing from their northern and southern vantage points, Victorian novels laid down structures of feeling and regimes of economic possibility that were at once national and global in their reach. They also exposed the underlying contradictions of the key myths of empire, such as the claim that global hegemony was justified by 'English' moral fitness, or that imperial profit depended on hard work and self-discipline. Most dramatically, Magwitch, arguably Dickens's most prominent colonial character and Pip's benefactor in *Great Expectations*, demonstrates throughout that novel that middle-class aspirations are 'sponsored by the very antithesis of middle-class virtues: criminal cash laundered in the colonies' (Joshi 2011: 264–5). And Schreiner's misfit characters, such as Waldo and Otto, similarly expose the unequal and exploitative axes of the globalizing economy.

But perhaps the most significant contribution made by the global novel in English is its formal diagnosis of empire and globalization, of the steep hierarchies of economic disparity on which they were, and continue to be, built. These novelistic visions go beyond mapping for their readers a simple dichotomy of city and country, as Williams defined it, and rather draw out a patch-worked terrain of unequally interdependent, and most definitely global, spaces.

Note

1 The title of this volume is crudely taken from the eighteenth-century patriotic anthem 'Rule Britannia', the lyrics of which refer to the Atlantic slave trade and the integral role played by Britain's engagement in it.

PART II

Development

CHAPTER 6

Joseph Conrad, the Global and the Sea

Michael Greaney

It has become a critical commonplace to describe Józef Teodor Konrad Korzeniowski (1857–1924), or, to use the pen name under which he became a major modernist writer, Joseph Conrad, as the first truly 'global' writer. 'Conrad wouldn't have known the word "globalization"', writes the historian Maya Jasanoff in an important recent study, 'but ... he embodied it' (Jasanoff 2017: 7). She further argues that Conrad's major fictional works, such as *Heart of Darkness* (1899), *Nostromo* (1904), *The Secret Agent* (1907) and *Under Western Eyes* (1911), provide a 'history of globalization from the inside out' (Jasanoff 2017: 9). Nor is Jasanoff the only reader to hail Conrad as a novelist of globalization *avant la lettre*. For Terry Collits, Conrad's depictions of cross-cultural and transnational experience foreshadow what a twenty-first-century reader would recognize as the 'wall-to-wall internationalist arrangements' of the contemporary world (Collits 2007: 172). Richard Niland, likewise, describes Conrad's 'global consciousness' as both a product of and a reflection on a new world-system (Niland 2017: 156). If we need a literary mascot for globalization, it seems that we can do a lot worse than point to Conrad. How did this come about?

The notion that Conrad is somehow synonymous with globalization has a twofold origin: it can be traced back both to the extraordinary geographical displacements of his life and to the lavishly varied and far-flung settings of his work. He was born in what was then a Russian-ruled area of Polish Ukraine and lived for a time in northern Russia when his father, the writer and activist Apollo Korzeniowski, was exiled to Vologda for patriotic conspiracy. He subsequently moved from Chernihiv to Lwów to Cracow, always in the shadow of Czarist autocracy (indeed, Conrad would not be formally released from Russian subjecthood until he was in his early thirties). At the age of sixteen he relocated to Marseille, which became his home for a number of years but also the base for a number of sea voyages to the Caribbean. In 1878 he obtained a berth as an apprentice on a British steamer, and so began a career in the British Merchant Service that would take him to Australia, the Mediterranean, Singapore, India, Java, Borneo, Siam, Mauritius, the Congo and Canada. During this time, he rose up the ranks, passing his master mariner's examination in November 1886, just three months after he was naturalized as a British subject – though in a sense, by then, he was already a citizen of the world. If Conrad's story had ended there, it would have been remarkable enough, but it was followed by an astonishingly unexpected literary career in which this trilingual Polish expatriate reinvented himself as an experimental novelist whose work is variously set in France, Belgium, Spain, Italy, Switzerland, Russia, West Africa, the Caribbean, Latin America, Siam and the Dutch East Indies. To anyone whose sense of the spatial possibilities of English fiction has been shaped by the work of, say, Jane Austen – whose most richly imagined heroine has never seen the sea – the fiction of Conrad stands as a breathtakingly wide-ranging example of an 'extra-territorial' writing that ranges beyond national and linguistic boundaries.

Sailors and Globe-Trotters

The engine of globalization, in Conrad's lifetime, was the steam engine. His literary career is the record of a time when, thanks in no small part to the new dominance of steam, the sea becomes a routinely navigable set of trade routes that connect the great European imperial powers to a network of colonies, outposts and local power bases. Not that Conrad was an enthusiast for this potent new technology; rather, his fiction seems reluctantly to harness the power of steam even as it gazes with lingering nostalgia back an at earlier, wind-powered age of seafaring, whose simplicity and elegance have been sacrificed to the sheer size and brutal mechanical power of the vessels that now traverse the globe. 'If I only live long enough', he writes in his memoir *A Personal Record* (1912), 'I shall become a bizarre relic of a dead barbarism, a sort of monstrous antiquity, the only seaman of the dark ages who had never gone into steam – not really' (Conrad 2008: 105). Conrad's resistance to steam as the dominant maritime technology is motivated by more than simple nostalgia for the age of sail. It also marks a certain resistance to what steam represents – a technology that promises to make the world smaller by granting unprecedentedly reliable access to all corners of the globe. The steam engine is what powers nineteenth-century globalization on a seemingly irresistible journey towards homogeneity in which all places and all cultures become one place, one culture – but the emphasis in Conrad's writings is repeatedly on the complex, intractable heterogeneity of the new global landscape. The climactic and tragic events of *Lord Jim* (1900), for example, are a tale of sacrifice, heroism and pathos that plays out 'three hundred miles beyond the end of telegraph cables and mail-boat lines' (Conrad 2012: 212). Conrad was fond of the notion that some spaces have not yet been infiltrated and annexed by Western technologies of travel and communication, and to a certain extent the very textures of his fiction – with their notorious narrative indeterminacy and linguistic complexity – work against the mechanisms of speedy, efficient and reliable interconnectedness that now criss-cross the globe. Though his writings are alive to the thrill of geographic discovery, he frequently objects to the notion that all cultures are now available as a spectacle to a privileged Western gaze. A notable symptom of his resistance to the homogenization of global space is his obvious animosity to a new category of person who emerges in his lifetime: the globe-trotter. Referring to a long-haul traveller, usually white, male and European, for whom intercontinental travel is a matter of pleasure rather than business, 'globe-trotter' was coined in the second half of the nineteenth century – the earliest use of the term recorded by the *Oxford English Dictionary* is from 1873. Conrad took a generally dim view of the facile worldliness exhibited by this new breed of traveller who believes that the world can now be frictionlessly circumnavigated for pleasure. When the term is used in his fiction, it is done so with pointed disdain. 'A sailor isn't a globe-trotter', says Captain Charlie Marlow (Conrad 1923: 30), the seasoned seafarer and enigmatic raconteur who functions as Conrad's Anglo-Saxon alter ego in a number of texts. As Donovan has argued, Conrad views long-haul tourism, a privileged Western cultural practice that emerges in the late nineteenth century, as a simulacrum of the kind of authentic voyaging that is practised by Marlow and other traditional seafarers (Donovan 2005: 80–91). In *Lord Jim*, when Marlow catches sight of a group of 'well-groomed male globe-trotters' swapping jovial stories about bazaars in Cairo over coffee and cigars, he views these itinerant masculine storytellers as 'infinitely remote' – they are, in other words, the alter egos of Conrad's alter ego (Conrad 2012: 70).

Map-Gazing and Empire-Building

The familiar but 'infinitely remote' figure of the globe-trotter is Conrad's bête noire because he represents a facile consumerist chapter in the otherwise inspiring history of geographical discovery. Conrad's geographical enthusiasms are most fully articulated in his late essay 'The Romance of Travel' (1924), which was commissioned by the editor and encyclopaedist Sir John Hammerton (1871–1949) as an introduction for his six-volume geographical reference work, *Countries of the World*. Later reprinted as 'Geography and Some Explorers' in *Last Essays*, this piece provides a playfully speculative mediation on the history of geographical thought in the context of Conrad's lifelong addiction to 'map-gazing' and his lingering resentment at the schoolteachers who sucked the joy and glamour out of his youthful enthusiasm for cartography (Conrad 2010: 11). Reflecting fondly on the 'fabulous' prehistory of modern geography, when unknown regions were populated with monsters and marvels, the essay invites us to cast our minds back to 'the medieval mind playing in its ponderous, childish way with the problems of our earth's shape, its size, its character, its products, its inhabitants' (Conrad 2010: 4). These 'problems', as they are called, haven't gone away. The twentieth and twenty-first centuries have their own models for thinking about the earth's shape, size, character, products and inhabitants – and concepts such as the 'global' and 'globalization' now dominate such thinking. Reading 'Geography and Some Explorers' in the twenty-first century, we can begin to see how Conrad uses the history of geography to trace the emergence of a modern sense of the global. Crucial to his narrative in this essay is the transition between the 'geography fabulous' of the medieval imagination, which populated unknown regions with monsters and marvels, and the 'geography militant' of the great age of exploration, which sought to bring all unexplored territory under the purview of a rational cartographical gaze. Dominating this essay is the author's personal Valhalla of heroic male seafarers (Vasco Nuñez de Balboa, Abel Tasman, James Cook, Sir John Franklin, Mungo Park, Heinrich Barth, David Livingstone), all of whom are associated with some form of breakthrough – the glimpsing of the Pacific, the discovery of the antipodes, polar exploration, the mapping of the African interior – that enabled us to envision the world as a coherent, self-contained, navigable entity that is at long last susceptible to comprehensive cartographical representation.

Conrad further points out that for all its aggressive rationalism, geography militant was in thrall to the fantasy of the *Terra Australis Incognita* – a vast undiscovered land mass in the Southern hemisphere whose conjectured existence spoke of the extraordinary resilience of all the spatial fantasies that the science of modern cartography has supposedly dispelled. Part of Conrad sympathizes with this lingering strain of fantastical world-building in the sober discourse of Enlightenment map-making. For him, the expansion of geography's remit is experienced as a somewhat demoralizing trade-off between knowledge and mystery. The globe is being filled up, blank spaces are being filled in, the world is becoming less mysterious, and the job of the writer is to inflect all the excitements of geographical discovery with a measuredly poignant sense of loss and disappointment as glamorously unknown regions of the earth are steadily converted by map-makers into drearily unenigmatic cartographical space on our 'much surveyed earth' (Conrad 2010: 68). Conrad once ruefully declared that we are now inhabitants of an 'explored earth in which the latitudes and longitudes having been recorded once for all have become things of no importance, in the sense that they can no longer appeal to the spirit of adventure' (Conrad 2010: 68). His darkly ironic political novel *The Secret Agent* might be read as a disturbing attempt to recover some sort of imaginative 'importance' for these abstract cartographical markers. The political atrocity around which the novel revolves is an attack on the Greenwich Observatory – or, symbolically, an attack on the Greenwich Meridian, Longitude Zero, the imaginary line from which every place on Earth can be mapped and measured. The terrorist strike in this novel is horribly botched, but it could never have 'worked' in the first place – it is, from the outset, a kind of mad category error, one that dreams of exploding the new official geometry of time and space that emerged in the nineteenth century with Greenwich as its symbolic headquarters.

It goes without saying that Conrad's evocations of a golden age of geographical discovery, in which pioneering Europeans continually stumbled upon seemingly 'unknown' corners of the Earth, are shot through with imperial ideology. The notion of 'discovery', in such a context, rests on the assumption that a given territory was somehow 'undiscovered' – even somehow 'unreal' – until a European adventurer clapped eyes on it. Often, this Eurocentric world view is compounded in Conrad's fiction by one of the narrative scenarios that he revisits through his literary career. This particular scenario, which haunts his representation of African and Asian territories, is one in which, in the most seemingly far-flung recesses of the globe, up the furthest reaches of a river or in the very depths of a jungle, what we find is, of all things – a white man. This white man could be a washed-up underachiever escaping his past (Kaspar Almayer in *Almayer's Folly* [1895]; Peter Willems in *An Outcast of the Islands* [1896]); or he could be a local potentate, a de facto ruler, whether benign ('Tuan' Jim in *Lord Jim*) or megalomaniacal (Mr Kurtz in *Heart of Darkness*), who has parlayed his whiteness into political status and authority. The ubiquity of the white European male in Conrad's non-European landscapes is symptomatic of the way in which colonial male subjectivity seems to find itself wherever it looks – it visits exotic new places only to discover, in a moment of narcissistic serendipity, that it was always already there. One corollary of this scenario is that these 'exotic' scenes of colonial (self-)discovery often cease to exist, or at least cease to matter, once the white man is no longer there. It is certainly worth noting how frequently Conrad represents Africa and Asia as places where white European men go to die. As well as Kurtz, Jim and Almayer, we might add the names of Kayerts and Carlier in 'An Outpost of Progress' (1896), Martin Decoud in *Nostromo* and Axel Heyst in *Victory* (1915) to the grim roll call of Conrad heroes who make a fatal one-way journey to the global south. It is often the case in these narratives that, as the hero expires, so too does the text's interest in the place where they met their end. Kurtz's death in *Heart of Darkness* spells the end of Marlow's active involvement in Africa, just as Jim's death draws a line under Marlow's sustained interest in the fate of Patusan. In both cases, it as though the global south, as a place with its own complex histories, becomes primarily a trope or prism through which to examine European subjectivity *in extremis* and an 'exotic' graveyard for European ambitions.

However, despite the unmistakeably Eurocentric position from which he writes, Conrad is under no illusions about what motivates European voyages of territorial expansion. Particularly memorable in this regard is the damning verdict on the European presence in Africa that he delivers in 'Geography and Some Explorers': 'the vilest scramble for loot that ever disfigured the history of human conscience and geographical exploration. What an end to the idealized realities of a boy's daydreams!' (Conrad 2010: 14). This is a stirring denunciation of the appalling crimes that have been committed in the name of civilization and progress, but it is one that perhaps too easily insulates supposedly 'innocent' boyish daydreams of exploration from the atrocities that they lead to, as though the vile scramble for loot has no relation at all to the desires and ambitions in which it originates.

Though Conrad seems eager to keep the 'innocent' activities of map-making and map-reading separate from the squalid business of imperial conquest and exploitation, the style and texture of his writing show that the two cannot be neatly differentiated. He writes in an era of territorial expansion, when territories across the globe are 'welcomed' onto European-authored maps of a new world-picture, surrendering their political and cultural autonomy and regarded as *tabulae rasae* on which imperial ideology can inscribe its own fantasies of authority and control. Which is to say that the map, as much of Conrad's writings implicitly acknowledge and as readers such as Robert Hampson have shown, is a technology of power that passes itself off as a 'neutral' pictorial record of the physical and political landscapes of the world we inhabit (Hampson 2005). Alongside

Conrad's predilection for maps is a powerful vein of what we might call anti-cartographical thinking – and nowhere is this tension more sharply perceptible than in his most controversial work, *Heart of Darkness*.

It is in some ways fitting that the author of *Heart of Darkness*, a text that is notorious for its at times overwrought language of emptiness, lack, hollowness, non-presence and ineffability, should have been thrilled as a child by images of cartographical absence. For him, nothing is more exciting than the discovery of the undiscovered – the discovery of absence. The pristine emptiness of an as-yet-unmapped African interior has the young Conrad, already a cartographical enthusiast, drooling over 'exciting spaces of white paper. Regions unknown!' (Conrad 2010: 12). These mesmerizing empty spaces provoke a paradoxical double response in Conrad's imagination. When he confronts geographical emptiness, he has the cartographer's impulse to fill it in with legible text; but his writing is also animated by a more subtle ambition, which is to find ways of representing absence and emptiness on their own elusive terms. In pursuit of the latter ambition, he evolves a new and recognizably modernist aesthetic of emptiness, deferral and absence in which his narrative discourse dwells on what it can't report about a given region of experience. Nowhere does Conrad's language wrestle with its own limitations more conspicuously – and notoriously – than in Marlow's report of his experiences in Africa, a serpentine and tortuously indirect travelogue that abounds in talk of the *incomprehensible, indefinable, inscrutable, impenetrable, insoluble, inconceivable, unspeakable, incalculable* and *inexplicable*. Conrad's alter ego is an explorer who repeatedly discovers the undiscoverability of Africa, in a negative language of cognitive and linguistic failure. This language is profoundly double-edged. On the one hand, in confessing the limits of its own power to grasp the otherness of African landscapes, languages, cultures and histories, *Heart of Darkness* delivers a pre-emptive antidote to the notion of globalization as an irresistible march towards homogenization. On the other hand, the notion of Africa as a kind of continent-wide aporia seems to collude all too readily with an imperial logic of silence and erasure, one that denies Indigenous people any say in defining their own histories and geographies.

When Chinua Achebe (1930–2013), in what is probably the most famous and frequently quoted modern reading of the text, described *Heart of Darkness* as a racist work, he inaugurated a new era of Conrad studies in which the author's representations of non-Western people, cultures and spaces have been subjected to forensic critique (1990). Achebe's reading provides a valuable corrective to a universalizing interpretation of *Heart of Darkness* as a disturbing glimpse into the violence that lies just below the surface 'veneer' of civilization. Such a reading, even though it is one that the text itself might seem to endorse, is all too indifferent to the cultural specificity of Conrad's writing. Few intelligible words are spoken by African people in *Heart of Darkness*, and their bodies, lives and histories are primarily presented as an 'exotic' backdrop to the story of a fateful encounter between two European men. Numerous critics, including Edward Said, Frances Singh, Benita Parry and Cedric Watts, have weighed in on this debate, and it is probably fair to say that the controversy over Conrad's relationship with imperialism and xenophobia has acquired something like a permanently unresolved status. Once upon a time, *Heart of Darkness* was a canonical text that became controversial; now, it is canonical *because* of the controversy. Nor is the controversy likely to evaporate anytime soon. There can't be many people who read *Heart of Darkness* and decide that imperialism is a good thing and that we need more of it, but Achebe's intervention nevertheless underscores the text's very obvious limitations as a representation of non-European people, culture and history. The novella is not so much an informative 'image of Africa' as a snapshot of distinctly European fears, desires and prejudices that are projected onto the so-called Dark Continent, whose position in *Heart of Darkness* is as a tantalizing silhouette of everything the text can't talk about.

Modernism at Sea

The sea represents a different kind of absence for Conrad. For him, the waters of the globe might be said to represent everything that is unthought or repressed in the land-obsessed discourses of geography. He comments with some bemusement in 'Geography and Some Explorers' on the acute reluctance with which the European cartographical imagination came round to the fact that 'there was much more water than land on this globe' (Conrad 2010: 6). The great anti-climax of the era of geography militant, in other words, was that its grand quest for Terra Australis Incognita eventuated simply in the discovery of more and more water. To the geographical imagination, this represented a kind of non-discovery, a fruitless encounter with huge tracts of emptiness or nothingness, as though the ocean, to the cartographical gaze, can never be anything more than the disappointing absence of land. Conrad, by contrast, responds to the sea in extraordinarily complex, vivid and varied ways. Although it would be an exaggeration to say that Conrad discovered the sea for literary fiction, we can certainly say that his writings – from 'Typhoon' and *The Nigger of* the 'Narcissus' to 'The Secret Sharer' (1910) and *The Shadow-Line* (1917) – rediscover the sea and its meanings for modernity in its imperial heyday.

As is well known, Conrad was never happy about being classified as a primarily maritime writer. Towards the end of his career, he was still energetically fulminating about the 'infernal tale of ships' that continued to dog his reputation, lamenting the fact that 'Spinner of sea-yarns – master mariner – seaman writer' (Karl and Davies 2007: 130) were still the terms in which his writerly identity was marketed. We can sympathize here with the stylist's lament – to be better known for one's subject matter than for the innovative manner in which it is handled – but there is something curiously disingenuous about Conrad's insistence that the sea was as secondary and incidental to his art as drawing rooms were to Thackeray's. Sailors, seascapes and ships are so pervasive in his fiction that his political novel *Under Western Eyes*, in which the action is divided between St Petersburg and Geneva, stands out in the Conrad oeuvre as the only one of his major works to be a genuinely landlocked text; elsewhere in his writings, we are never far from the sea. For all his protestations to the contrary, it is tempting to think of Conrad's narrative imagination as in some sense a maritime imagination – one, indeed, that in discovering and envisioning the sea for literary fiction obsessively revisits and works through a subliminal double entendre between *sea* and *see*.

How, exactly, does Conrad see the sea? In 1906 he published a memoir entitled *The Mirror of the Sea*, and his fiction spends a long time gazing into this mirror. Conrad is prone to regard the ocean as 'hallowed ground', as an 'unchangeable' space whose timeless, elemental existence provides both a refuge from the vicissitudes of history and an arena in which human resourcefulness discovers its own true stuff in a clarifying ordeal of wind and water (Conrad 2010: 14). One quality that Conrad seems ready to attribute to the sea is the capacity to transcend difference, as, for example, when the variegated and fractious crew of the *Narcissus* are knitted together by their ordeal at sea into a seamlessly coherent microcommunity, a waterborne *Gemeinschaft* that provides a utopian alternative to the alienated, atomized social worlds of the modern nation-state. You don't have to spend much time on land in Conrad's fiction – whether in the soulless Geneva of *Under Western Eyes* or the dank, labyrinthine London of *The Secret Agent* – to feel the attractions of such an idealized maritime community. The sea, in such a context, functions as a seemingly contentless border or frame between the self-contained communal world of the ship and the wider network of social and economic entanglements from which the narrative has strategically isolated that vessel and its crew. Conrad's sea thus plays a double role, as Fredric Jameson puts it, as 'both a strategy of containment and a place of real business' (Jameson 1981: 210). Which is to say that the sea provides its own sealed narrative worlds, microcosms of the wider human community that are as aesthetically self-contained in their own way as the country house or the desert island, which let us inspect human relationships and interactions in an unusually 'pure' form, isolated from extraneous secondary factors. But this picturesque extra-economic status is something of a mirage, for the sea is also an inescapably economic space, a trade route that connects nations and economies in a new worldwide economic system. Or, to put it another way, the sea in Conrad is purifying but it is never pure.

There can be a distinctly nostalgic flavour to Conrad's seascapes. A defining characteristic of his maritime writings is an attachment to the idea of what the sea *was*. Globalization, so the saying goes, makes the world a smaller place – and the sea, in the discourse of Conrad's fiction, reminds us of its vastness at a time when efforts were being made to cut it down to size. Nowhere is this official 'shrinking' of the globe better exemplified than in the opening in 1869 of the Suez Canal to provide a shipping lane between the Red Sea and the Mediterranean, thus removing the need for ships bound from Europe to Asia (or vice versa) to negotiate the notoriously difficult 'Cape Route' around the southern tip of Africa. Opened in 1914, the Panama Canal would in turn create a navigable connection between the Atlantic and Pacific oceans. Literary responses to these shortcuts between continents and hemispheres have varied enormously. Walt Whitman (1819–1892), in his euphoric poem 'Passage to India' (1871), greets the Suez Canal as the harbinger of a new sense of worldwide community and interconnectedness. Rather more ambivalent was E. M. Forster (1879–1970), who repurposed Whitman's phrase as the title of his classic novel of vexed Anglo-Indian friendship, *A Passage to India* (1924). Conrad, meanwhile, is openly scathing in his description of the Suez Canal as that 'dismal but profitable ditch' (Conrad 2016: 12). If the canal is at all valuable to Conrad, it is only because of the nostalgia it provokes for the time when it wasn't there.

If the nostalgic Conrad wants to evoke a sea we can no longer see, there is also a sceptical Conrad who wants to define the sea as that which by its very nature defeats visual mastery. One of the recurring tropes of his fiction is the figure of the sailor who is plunged into darkness, whether it's the circle of amateur yachtsmen who comprise the audience for Marlow's nocturnal tale in *Heart of Darkness*, the captain with failing eyesight in 'The End of the Tether' (1902) or the sailors in 'Typhoon' who cannot make one another out as they stagger on a pitching deck during a ferocious storm. In this way, Conrad's fiction negotiates a new and uncanny phenomenology of globalization whose weird reversals of near and far are such that you might experience a new sense of systemic interconnectedness with people halfway round the world even as you are barely able to discern the person next to you. At vertiginous moments such as these, the sea is a dark mirror in which we catch sight not just of ourselves but of our weirdly decentred positions in a new global economic system.

Darkness, disorientation and vertigo are central to the experience of the storms at sea that are evoked in some of Conrad's most memorably sustained set pieces of descriptive writing. Violent maritime weather is something that he evokes with particular gusto in *The Nigger of the 'Narcissus'*, the story of a sailing vessel battered by the elements en route from Bombay to London, and in 'Typhoon', a novella about a steamer running into a tropical storm en route from Britain to Fu-Chau on the south China coast. The surging energy and unpredictable violence of these storms convert the smooth reflective surface of the 'mirror of the sea' – a mirror in which the crew of the *Narcissus* might be tempted narcissistically to adore themselves – into something rough, turbulent and pitilessly indifferent to human desires and designs. The point about the sea in these texts is that it gets everywhere. No longer a mirror or frame to the action, it inundates and overwhelms human-made structures. The experience of being soaked, supersaturated or engulfed by what otherwise might seem like a picturesque backdrop is a chastening and indeed character-forming ordeal for the seafarers in these tales. As the *Narcissus* emerges from ferocious weather around the Cape of Good Hope, it is a slimy, dripping and sodden environment in which seawater has infiltrated not just the ship but every nook and cranny of the sailors' intimate lives. Streams of water trickle out their chests. Their beds and bedding are waterlogged. A stray boot is full of dirty water. One revealing linguistic symptom of the unmanageable plurality and pervasiveness of the sea in this text is the narrator's habit of pivoting from referencing the *sea* to referencing the *seas*: 'The sea on deck, and the seas on every side of her, mingled together in a deafening roar' (Conrad 2017: 88). The sea is both a single and a plural entity, one that confronts us with multiple versions of itself, resists any easy opposition between singularity and multiplicity, and overwhelms human-made frontiers between sea and non-sea. Such frontiers, as the sailors who mop the decks and work the pumps will know better than anyone, are a function of frantic labour rather than of boundaries enshrined in and respected by nature. In a nautical culture where timetables are subdivided into a cycle of 'watches',

Conrad's writing is always on the lookout for opportunities to convert the sea – an empty cartographic space that lets us criss-cross the globe – into something stubbornly or even violently resistant to human purposes.

One of the ways in which the sea resists human purposes in Conrad is its refusal to be contained by its own official boundaries. To a certain extent this is also true of the discourses and narratives of the sea as they permeate Conrad's writings. Even when his stories are not waterborne they are nearly always maritime-adjacent, and it would probably be more accurate to designate Conrad a 'land-and-sea' novelist rather than a 'sea novelist' *tout court*. His imagination is dependably stirred by those liminal spaces where land and water confront and interact with one another – ports, harbours, dockyards, loading stations and estuaries. In the imaginative cartographies of his fiction, the variously glamorous and seedy transitional spaces between land and water seem to give rise to new kinds of subjectivity. We tend to side-line the fact that the swaggeringly charismatic Nostromo is a dock hand, just as the facts of Jim's day job schmoozing with recently disembarked sailors would count among the more forgettable aspects of the career of this flawed idealist and would-be adventurer. Nevertheless, the jobs that at least partly define Jim and Nostromo only exist because of the economic needs and demands created by the threshold between land and sea. In different ways these heroes are tasked with managing this interface, and in different ways they come to embody and internalize a conflict in Conrad between the glamorously heroic associations of the sea and its status as just another workplace dominated by the dull grind of economic necessity.

Shipwrecked

We often think of Conrad as a writer who uses his seafaring narratives to grant a British readership access to 'exotic' and far-flung territories in South East Asia or Latin America; however, one of his most distinctive achievements is not the discovery of the exotic but rather what we might call the exoticization of the ordinary. No Conrad narrative does this more poignantly than his short story 'Amy Foster' (1904), the tragic narrative of a Polish shipwreck survivor washed up on the shores of southeast England where he is met with hostility and incomprehension among a largely narrow-minded and suspicious community. For the hapless Yanko Goorall, Kent is a veritable terra incognita, an alien landscape populated by cruel, unsympathetic strangers: 'There was nothing here the same as in his country! The earth and the water were different … The very grass was different, and the trees' (Conrad 1924: 129). Exploring the otherness of England through the eyes of a vulnerable, sympathetic outsider, 'Amy Foster' might be said to invent for modern literature a figure who would become better known as the stateless person, *sans-papiers* or asylum seeker – a displaced person for whom doubleness, liminality and in-betweenness are experienced as ordeal rather than privilege. In this sad story of cultural incomprehension, 'Amy Foster' is eloquent on its hero's linguistic isolation. Disorientated by an illness that will eventually end his life, Yanko desperately endeavours to communicate in his native tongue with his wife Amy, but she greets his words with fearful incomprehension. If any obituary for Yanko were ever to be written, it might say that the language barrier, as much as the fever, was the cause of death.

Yanko Goorall could not have written 'Amy Foster', and the dialectical truth of the story lies in the tension between Conrad's status as the purveyor of a new modernist *écriture* that traverses the old national boundaries, and the ordeal of its tongue-tied hero, who tragically falls foul of those very boundaries, a victim of the frontiers of language and culture that his creator so acrobatically leap-frogged. A salutary reminder that there is all the difference between living in a global world and living in a world without borders, 'Amy Foster' shows that Conrad could hardly be described as a naive cheerleader for the emerging globalization that shaped his life and literary career. Rather, as Jasanoff puts it, he experiences globalization from the 'inside' as the very condition of possibility for his writing, one that profoundly shapes the ideological content and linguistic form of his literary output. Globalization produced the writer 'Joseph Conrad', and his writings have in turn given us a potent language in which to inscribe our mental maps of a modern globalized world. Whether we still want to speak this language, with its unsettling mixture of cognitive scepticism and unexamined Eurocentrism, is of course another matter. There could be a point where Conrad seems as remote from us as the globe-trotters in *Lord Jim* seem from Marlow. But for all its problems and contradictions, the fictional language that the author himself nicknamed 'Conradese' (Karl and Davies 1983: 109) remains one of the most resonantly powerful idioms in which a globalized world has told the stories of its past, present and possible futures.

CHAPTER 7

Mutual Equality
Modernism and Globalization
Paul Stasi

In 1917, Claude McKay, a Jamaican immigrant who had recently relocated to Harlem, published a sonnet entitled 'The Harlem Dancer', which I will quote in full:

> Applauding youths laughed with young prostitutes
> And watched her perfect, half-clothed body sway;
> Her voice was like the sound of blended flutes
> Blown by black players upon a picnic day.
> She sang and danced on gracefully and calm,
> The light gauze hanging loose about her form;
> To me she seemed a proudly-swaying palm
> Grown lovelier for passing through a storm.
> Upon her swarthy neck black, shiny curls
> Profusely fell; and, tossing coins in praise,
> The wine-flushed, bold-eyed boys, and even the girls,
> Devoured her with their eager, passionate gaze;
> But, looking at her falsely-smiling face
> I knew her self was not in that strange place.   (McKay 2008: 172)

Depicting an aesthetically compelling dance taking place in less-than-ideal circumstances, this poem touches on a set of themes central to modernism generally, and to the Harlem Renaissance more specifically, and in doing so transforms them. The standard modernist opposition between high and mass culture is here united in an art object – the woman's dance – only to be separated out as the responses of two distinct audiences. Artistry persists, McKay suggests, even in a relatively debased form, as the speaker finds a beauty that eludes the devouring eyes of the rest of the dance's wine-flushed onlookers. The poem thus captures the dilemma of the Black artist at the time of the Harlem Renaissance, a moment of cultural flourishing that nevertheless required the patronage of white publishers and audiences. Could the Black artist produce authentic cultural work under such conditions? The poem seems to answer affirmatively.

In doing so, however, it discloses a second set of concerns central to the theme of globalization. For in transcoding the woman's performance as the 'sound of blended flutes / Blown by black players upon a picnic day', McKay also shifts her location in lines that provide the grounds for the connection he feels. Understood as a 'proudly-swaying palm', the dancer becomes a migrant like McKay, 'her self' alienated in the 'strange place' that is Harlem. As important as the theme is the formal strategy by which it is conveyed. Harlem opens up to the Caribbean through that 'swift perception of relations' Ezra Pound took to be the hallmark of artistic genius, embodied in one of modernist poetry's most tried and true techniques: the image (Pound 1968a: 158).[1] Here is Pound's canonical definition: 'An "Image" is that which presents an intellectual and emotional complex in an instant of time … It is the presentation of such a "complex" instantaneously which gives that sense of sudden liberation; that sense of freedom from time limits and space' (Pound 1968b: 4). McKay's image certainly presents 'an intellectual and emotional complex in an instant of time', but it's not quite right to see it as a 'liberation' from 'time limits and space'. Rather, McKay here frees himself from one space only to enforce the parameters of another. National space opens up, in 'The Harlem Dancer', to the world beyond it.

In discussing modernism and globalization, then, I would like to begin with a few central premises. First, modernism registered, to an unprecedented degree, in both formal and thematic terms, an early moment of what we have now come to call globalization. Second, globalization, then and, indeed, now, has to be thought of in relation to the structures of global capital, which, in the modernist period, was typically described as imperialism. Third, one of modernism's defining conditions was the mass migration that results from the increased connection of disparate parts of the world through globalization. And finally, what an earlier criticism understood as modernist internationalism, which has been recently re-baptized as cosmopolitanism, represents both the ways in which modernism has been shaped by globalization and also the ways in which it can be understood to resist it. It is this simultaneous resistance and complicity – registered most obviously in modernism's consistent critique of both capitalism and nationalism, articulated on both its left and right wings – that is of relevance to the discussion of globalization today. For the modernist critique of globalization typically refuses what Ezra Pound disdainfully called the 'yelp of nationalism' (Pound 1973: 189). It thus separates out what we might call economic from cultural globalization, even while registering their complicity, and in doing so untangles a persistent – and reactionary – conceptual knot, one that continues to plague us today in the Trump/Brexit era. 'The Harlem Dancer', for instance, makes no mention of the nation; rather it testifies to the haunting presence of one region – the Caribbean – within another: Harlem.

This movement is central to modernist literature, which is filled with texts that continually establish the presence of other worlds lodged within their more immediate locales. Pound's *Cantos* is perhaps the clearest example of a work that wishes to include the entire globe, moving from Italy to Greece to America to China as it tries to gather up all the cultural practices Pound found of value in the centuries preceding what he considered a debased modern era. James Joyce's Dublin is determined by the presence of the two masters – one British and one Italian – that its colonized subjects must serve, as well as the Odyssean parallel that structures their wanderings, a dramatic representation of the way a colonized people's daily reality is determined by forces outside their immediate horizon. *The Waste Land*, too, discloses the presence within the financial centre of its 'Unreal city' of the 'Falling towers' of various empires, as well as the parched and barren Ganga, whose contemporary famines were the direct result of England's imperial control (Eliot 1963: 61, 67). Joseph Conrad's Marlow, deep in his African journey, thinks of the 'knitting old woman' – 'a most improper person to be sitting at the other end of this affair' – while mistaking the 'beat of a drum for the beating of my heart' (Conrad 1988: 64). At the text's end he will substitute Kurtz's dying words – 'The horror! The horror!' – for the name of Kurtz's intended, in a drawing room whose piano represents the civilized transformation of the ivory whose extraction called forth or revealed – Conrad is not quite sure which – the most primitive instincts of that product of all Europe (69). And here is Virginia Woolf in *Jacob's Room*, describing her titular character's daily routine:

> Then, sometimes a game of chess; or pictures in Bond Street, or a long way home to take the air with Bonamy on his arm, meditatively marching, head thrown back, the world a spectacle, the early moon above the steeples coming in for praise, the sea-gulls flying high, Nelson on his column surveying the horizon, and the world our ship. (Woolf 2008: 121)

If Jacob is characteristically confident of his abilities – proclaiming to his friend Bonamy, for instance, that 'we are the only people in the world who know what the Greeks mean' despite barely muddling through a play or two – that confidence emerges from a national space that conceives of itself in imperial terms: the world as the determining horizon of Jacob's personality (Woolf 2008: 102).

The most immediate thing to observe about all these instances is that the theme of globalization, in the modernist period, is at one and the same time the theme of imperialism. Indeed, as Frederic Jameson has argued, the discourse of the period – embodied in both V. I. Lenin's *Imperialism* and the work of J. A. Hobson on which he drew – favoured the word empire, and it did so primarily to name inter-imperialist rivalry, the scramble for Africa, rather than the relation between centre and periphery. Thus, in *Howard's End*, the chief opposition is between the English and the Germans, although Jameson detects the presence of empire in the Great North Road. 'It is Empire which stretches the roads out to infinity', Jameson writes, 'beyond the bounds and borders of the national state' (Jameson 2007: 162). We could extend the claim to Dorothy Richardson's *Pilgrimage*. Its first volume, *Pointed Roofs*, published in 1917, barely mentions empire at all but, like *Howard's End*, is deeply invested in outlining the distinctions between the Germans and the English. Volume 2 even teases us with an imperial image of otherness – its first line is 'A swarthy turbaned face shone at Miriam from a tapestry screen' – before resolving that otherness into the distinction between the 'horrid' suburban world of North London and the heroine's more cultured life in London proper (Richardson 1979: 189). When 'a significant structural segment of the economic system as a whole is now located elsewhere', Jameson concludes, it becomes impossible 'to grasp the way the system functions as a whole' (Jameson 2007: 157). Modernist texts thus found textual analogues for the imperialism they were not quite able to cognize.

Jameson's essay, originally published in 1990, was a watershed in modernist studies, marking the first serious attempt to think about how the structures of empire might have conditioned the *form* of even those modernist works that do not directly address the colonies, or do so only in abbreviated ways.[2] And yet if Jameson's argument emphasizes the inability of the modernist work to grasp this totality – a reason for modernism's characteristic emphasis on fragmentation and the intensities of a subjective perception that refuses omniscience – a range of other critics have shown how modernist works register the gradual irruption of the colonial other into the previously hermetically sealed national space. Modernist primitivism – Picasso's African masks, for instance – is only the most obvious manifestation of this phenomenon. Indeed, it is possible to imagine the entire assault on traditional representation as part and parcel of an emergent awareness of an imperial other, a sense that perhaps Western traditions could not be taken for the stable universals a more confident nineteenth century had imagined them to be.

Here is Joe Cleary describing the relationship between the modernist novel and its realist predecessors:

> The European classical bourgeois realist novel had produced and nourished a consistent sense of 'the real' only by foreclosing its optic on the world beyond Europe and by largely repressing the business of imperialism; what had been repressed returned to Europe in the twentieth century in the form of calamitous interimperial rivalry, fascism, and race theory and contributed as such to the destruction of Europe and of the literary world it had long dominated. (Cleary 2012: 260)

Modernism, Cleary continues,

> might today be described less as the antithesis of realism than as a term for a wide variety of literary experiments that collectively registered the beginning of the dissolution of the old Paris-centered literary world-system and that sought to bring into being either radical new types of literature or radical new roles for literature, and in effect therefore to inaugurate some new literary dispensation or world-system in place of the old. (Cleary 2012: 261)

Modernism, in other words, represents a new kind of realism, not only in its fidelity to the stream of consciousness or the vicissitudes of our emotional and affective life, but also in its awareness of the totality of an increasingly global economic system, an awareness that has important consequences for artistic representation. On the one hand, as Cleary suggests, this totality fractures the secure frame of the nation-state which underpinned the nineteenth-century novel, itself a vehicle for national consciousness, as Benedict Anderson, among others, has so eloquently described. Take for instance George Eliot's *Middlemarch* (1871–1872), whose 'study of provincial life' (the novel's subtitle) is largely concerned with the ways in which a small community of diverse individuals is able to perceive the web of social relations that bind them, all against the steady backdrop of railroads and parliamentary reform that will more securely link the provincial town to national centres of power. This depiction of the national story can be profitably contrasted to Conrad's *Nostromo*, which narrates independence in a fragmented style that consistently undermines the very themes of solidarity and unity that so concern Eliot. For Conrad, his fictional Central American nation can only be a pale imitation of the heroic endeavours of Garibaldi, representing a fundamental reversal of Anderson's reading of the centrality of creole nationalisms to the very concept of the nation.[3] At the same time, however, Conrad's depiction of what we might call the constitutive incoherence of independence in the periphery anticipates the theme of a wide range of postcolonial novels – we can think of V. S. Naipaul's *The Mimic Men*, whose similarly fictional island nation, Isabella, takes its name from Conrad's novel – that demonstrate the ways in which formal political independence is hampered by continued economic dependence. Nationalism falters in the face of economic globalization. Given the tight link scholars have seen between the nation and the novel-form, it is no surprise to find that globalization transforms the novel's structures. Indeed, this destruction of traditional forms is one of the only real points of unity among the diverse works we tend to name as modernist.[4]

On the other hand, modernist texts, as I have already suggested, are often haunted by the presence of these other worlds. They not only transform the means of representation, then, due to the presence of the imperial other, but they explicitly thematize the rupture in representation that results from this presence. Globalization, that is to say, produces a particular structure of feeling within modernist texts: the presence of things that are not immediately present. Consider, in this light, the following lines from *The Waste Land*:

> The river bears no empty bottles, sandwich papers,
> Silk handkerchiefs, cardboard boxes, cigarette ends
> Or other testimony of summer nights.   (Eliot 1963: 60)

Given the specificity of Eliot's line – its enumeration of precisely those things that are absent – it is nearly impossible not to immediately populate the scene with those absent objects. And this play between presence and absence is constitutive of the entire poem: its desolate waste land is brimming with cultural material. If one of its speakers laments 'I can connect / Nothing with nothing', the poem, nevertheless, connects these materials to one another, even if it often seems uncertain of the efficacy of such a gesture (Eliot 1963: 64).

Henry James, too, writes consistently of absent things that nevertheless determine present consciousness, not just in his famous ghost stories, but in works such as 'The Beast in the Jungle', where the main character's entire life is determined by his sense that some un-named, indeed un-nameable, event will someday transform it. The irony of the story, of course, is that this event is precisely the sense he has of its possibility. In waiting his entire life for the event to occur, he ends up wasting it. The great event, then, is simply the transformation of anticipation into retrospect, which is to say the inevitable result of an ageing that is precisely not the singular event he was anticipating. That this entire drama is conceived in the language of an

H. R. Haggard novel is not only the wry joke James plays on his theme, but a further sign that this particular structure has something to do with Europe's relationship to its imperial others.

We can observe two important points, then, about the persistence of this formal relationship within modernism. The first is that the theme of imperialism in the period does, in a refracted way, register the dependence of the centre on its periphery, with the consequence that we might continue to name this imperialism, rather than the more neutral term globalization, in order to better capture the power dynamics involved.[5] Indeed, it is possible to argue that the accumulation of cultural capital that characterizes modernism – the way its works depend not only on the realist structures that they critique but also on the cultural allusions which are laced through many of its most prominent instances – is itself dependent on the accumulation of money capital that occurs in metropolitan centres. This accumulation, in turn, draws the collection of immigrants and transplants which, as Raymond Williams argued, were the main practitioners of literary modernism. Their relationship to the national traditions they entered was often a mediated one, which is perhaps why Eliot – an American born in St Louis, who converted to British citizenship in 1927 – would describe tradition, in 'Tradition and the Individual Talent', as something that 'cannot be inherited, and if you want it you must obtain it by great labour' (Eliot 1964: 4).

For Williams, what is unique about modernism is the 'new and specific location of the artists and intellectuals of this movement within the changing cultural milieu of the metropolis' (Williams 2007: 44). These metropolitan cities – centres of the 'new imperialism, which offered themselves as transnational capitals of an art without frontiers' (34) – provided a 'magnetic concentration of wealth and power ... and the simultaneous cosmopolitan access to a wide variety of subordinate cultures' (Williams 2007: 44). The openness of such a metropolitan centre allowed a set of dissident bourgeois cultural practices to find locations in ways that would have been impossible in more traditional social organizations. The result was the presence of 'a very mixed population, from a variety of social and cultural origins', with important aesthetic consequences:

> Liberated or breaking from their national or provincial cultures, placed in quite new relations to those other native languages or native visual traditions, encountering meanwhile a novel and dynamic common environment from which many of the older forms were obviously distant, the artists and writers and thinkers of this phase found the only community available to them: a community of the medium; of their own practices. Thus language

Mutual Equality: Modernism and Globalization

was perceived quite differently. It was no longer, in the old sense, customary and naturalized, but in many ways arbitrary and conventional. To the immigrants especially ... language was more evident as a medium ... than as social custom. (Williams 2007: 45–6)

Williams here, in his characteristically offhand manner, dramatically rewrites the theme of modernization as the story of mass migration, even as he locates the aesthetic transformations of modernist works – often described in autonomous terms – within a clear social formation. In doing so, he transforms our understanding of another central coordinate of modernism: its relationship to modernity.

That modernism is tied to modernity is, by this point, a truism, enshrined in the title of the period's flagship journal *Modernism/modernity*, and providing the justification for the expansion that has characterized modernist studies since the 1990s.[6] Thinking of modernity in terms of a mass migration attendant upon imperialism allows us, however, greater historical specificity. For as Jameson has argued, there is a singular modernity.[7] And if that modernity takes shape in different places in distinct ways, that difference needs to be thought through colonialism, which Ashish Nandy once named the 'armed version' of modernity itself (Nandy 1983: xiv).

Underpinning both terms is the development of global capital, the unifying force behind Jameson's singular modernity, whose uneven development produces a striated world that is one but unequal. Reading modernity as imperialism highlights the economic underpinnings of the modernist moment: an overaccumulation of capital that sought an outlet in colonial territories, which in turn provided the spur for capital's perpetually primitive accumulation. I have said that modernism was united primarily by what it rejected; one of the main things it rejected was capitalism. Cleary is again helpful:

> Whether written from the right, the center, or the left, most of the great modernist epics are animated by a pronounced hostility to twentieth-century capitalism and by a drive to totalization registered in compositional processes manifestly different from either nineteenth-century classical realism or late twentieth-century postmodernism. (Cleary 2012: 260)

At the same time, modernism is clearly conditioned by the world economic structure that is its largest social condition, as Cleary's 'drive to totality' suggests. *The Cantos*, for instance, is inconceivable without the increased connection among nations facilitated by global capital, a connection Pound himself, who always argued for the deep relationship between artistic and economic structures, would have readily acknowledged. And this economic structure is behind the mass migrations Williams names as the social ground for modernism's dissident attacks on bourgeois life, migrations that were not always voluntary. The cosmopolitan artists of the metropolitan centres find their political analogues in the stateless peoples created across Europe after the First World War.

We can return, in this context, to McKay, whose 1929 novel *Banjo* depicts a group of diasporic Africans living 'a story without a plot' on the coast of the Mediterranean, that 'gorgeous bowl of blue water unrestingly agitated by the great commerce of all the continents' (McKay 1970: 66). Defined by their opposition to capitalism – their resistance to work is one with the novel's resistance to development – the characters nevertheless are brought together by its structures. Ray – a writer who is, in various ways, a stand-in for McKay – elaborates:

> [In the port he could meet] picturesque proletarians from far waters whose names were warm with romance: the Caribbean, the Gulf of Guinea, the Persian Gulf, the Bay of Bengal, the China Seas, the Indian Archipelago. And, oh, the earthy mingled smells of the docks! Grain from Canada, rice from India, rubber from the Congo, tea from China, brown sugar from Cuba, bananas from Guinea, lumber from the Soudan, coffee from Brazil, skins from the Argentine, palm-oil from Nigeria, pimento from Jamaica, wool from Australia, oranges from Spain and oranges from Jerusalem … the fine harvest of all the lands of the earth. (McKay 1970: 67)

Along with this harvest comes the characters of the novel itself: 'In no other port had [Ray] ever seen congregated such a picturesque variety of Negroes. Negroes speaking the civilized tongues, Negroes speaking all the African dialects, black Negroes, brown Negroes, yellow Negroes. It was as if every country of the world where Negroes lived had sent representatives drifting in to Marseilles' (McKay 1970: 68). Diaspora, in *Banjo*, is a condition of global capital, which brings people to the port of Marseilles as easily as it does raw materials and commodities. Once again, we see how capitalism creates the very pockets of bohemian life which then resist its structures; the primary interests of the 'beach boys' of Marseilles are music and drinking.

It would be a mistake to read this complicity as capitulation, for the fact that the work of art bears the mark of its conditioning ground is not only a sign that it contains those ideologies it might oppose. Its social location is also the condition of whatever efficacy the work of art might actually have. Only works that are conditioned by global capital can help us understand how it works. And this is a lesson consistently presented to us in modernist works.

Nowhere is this clearer than in Joyce's *Portrait of the Artist as a Young Man*, where Joyce relentlessly demonstrates his protagonist Stephen Dedalus's conditioning by a social order he attempts to escape. Stephen wishes to fly by the nets of 'nationality, language, religion' in order to express himself in 'unfettered freedom' (Joyce 1964: 203, 246). These lines are often taken quite seriously, but it is worth pondering how someone who imagines himself to be a writer might free himself from language. Furthermore, as Joyce shows time and again, that language is laced with others' meanings. This is abundantly clear in Stephen's conversation with the English Dean of Studies, where Stephen realizes that 'the language in which we are speaking is his before it is mine' (Joyce 1964: 189). And it's clear in the unbidden thoughts which occur to him in the lecture hall, as he scorns the 'voice, the accent, the mind' that mark a fellow student as from Belfast and, by association, instrumental in his educational aims, Protestant in his religion and British in his national allegiances (Joyce 1964: 193). 'That thought', Stephen thinks 'is not mine' (Joyce 1964: 193).

More painfully for Stephen, the world also inhabits his aesthetic doctrine, which turns on a notion of autonomy that its form more or less negates. 'An esthetic image', Stephen tells us in the final chapter of *Portrait*, 'is presented to us either in space or in time... [it] is first luminously apprehended as selfbounded and selfcontained upon the immeasurable background of space and time which it is not. You apprehend it as *one* thing. You see it as one whole. You apprehend its wholeness' (Joyce 1964: 212). Stephen's theory is, as he himself admits, borrowed from Aquinas, the first sign that it is dependent on the world around him. But it also sounds suspiciously like the commodity form, which similarly presents itself to us, in Marx's famous formulation, as self-bounded and self-contained, shorn of the social labour that is, nevertheless, at its core. When we recall that the doctrine of the autonomy of the work of art originates precisely at the moment when patronage ends – when, that is to say, the work of art enters the marketplace – we can see the social grounds for understanding the two as constitutive of one another. In *Stephen Hero*, Joyce's first draft of the novel, Stephen will refer to this moment as the work of art's epiphany, explicitly drawing on the religious structures he seeks to overcome. And if that wasn't enough, Joyce continually interrupts Stephen's intellectual abstractions with the reality of his poverty-stricken environment, women begging for money, lice crawling along his neck. The point, however, is not to critique Stephen for his complicity with his social order, but to show the impossibility of the 'unfettered freedom' which he desires, to show, in other words, how it is his social order itself which conditions his desire to flee its conditioning force. The work of art, as Joyce's own works continually suggest, is entirely embedded in its social context.

Modernist cosmopolitanism, then, is conditioned by the economic structures of globalization, but if globalization tends, through the commodity form, towards homogeneous, socially distinct forms of labour, and if, further, it does so in the name of empire, modernism moves in a different direction. I have already suggested how *The Cantos* can best be understood as an alternative to globalization. What is more striking, perhaps, is that Pound – despite his consistent and relentless anti-Semitism – was also a sharp and consistent critic of nationalism. The 1917 essay 'Provincialism the Enemy', from which the line quoted above about the 'yelp of nationality' comes, defines its titular concept as both 'An ignorance of the manners, customs and nature of people living outside one's own village, parish, or nation' and 'A desire to coerce others into uniformity' (Pound 1973: 190, 189). Similarly, he rejected the 'crime' of teaching courses in American literature by asserting that 'You might as well give courses in "American chemistry"' (Pound 1973: 218). Eliot, too, spoke, in 'Tradition and the Individual Talent', of the 'mind of Europe' (Eliot 1964: 6). This has seemed restrictive to many, but it is nevertheless a resistance to understanding literature in nationalist terms, and the structure Eliot outlines – where the intervention of a new work alters the previously existing tradition – clearly allows for revisionary works of postcolonial critique, perhaps one reason for the surprising affinity writers such as Kamau Brathwaite and Derek Walcott felt for the Anglican conservative.[8]

It would be easy to associate the critique of nationalism with globalization. Indeed, in contemporary discourse the two are often conflated: nationalists oppose globalization. And I do mean to suggest that modernist internationalism is conditioned by global economic structures. However, we must be careful in distinguishing the rhetoric of nationalist resistance to globalization with the reality of the world economic market. For what nationalists consistently object to is not globalization *tout court*, but rather the mass migration that comes with it. Modernist anti-Semitism, then, shares something of this particular structure of feeling: happily welcoming some migrants while viciously rejecting others. In this context, *Banjo* is exemplary, clearly registering the conditioning power of globalization on culture but also, explicitly, in the movements of people. Pound's *Cantos*, Eliot's *Waste Land* – cultural materials circulate in these texts but in ways that tend to obscure their personal or individual origins. *Banjo*, by contrast, highlights this connection, producing something like a pro-immigration critique of global capital.

Mutual Equality: Modernism and Globalization

No text of modernism more clearly illustrates these dynamics than Joyce's *Ulysses*, which interweaves the themes of nationalism, imperialism, migration and globalization in its depiction of a single day in early twentieth-century Dublin. Joyce's hero is, of course, Leopold Bloom, an Irish Jew whose father immigrated from Hungary, married to Molly Bloom, born on the Rock of Gibraltar, and of dubious parentage. His two central characters, then, could be considered immigrants, and the Odyssean parallel only underlines their cosmopolitan character. Furthermore, the novel is famously obscure about Molly's origins. She may have a Jewish mother. Her father is meant to be an Irish soldier, but the details she offers do not line up with available historical facts. As one might expect, this has produced a wide range of critical commentary, trying to locate the origin of these errors. Their origin matters less than the obscurity itself. Nevertheless, the citizens of Dublin consider Molly to be Irish even if they are often uncertain about Bloom's status, a fact that illustrates the fabricated nature of the nationalist imaginary. Indeed, Joyce's text highlights Bloom's outsider status with two key instances of anti-Semitism that occur just prior to his entrance in the text. The first comes from Haines, the Englishman who has come to Ireland to collect specimens of its folklore, including, perhaps, some of Stephen's own witticisms. 'Would I make money by it', Stephen tactlessly asks him, and in doing so highlights the economic motive cloaked under Haines's more seemingly innocent cultural interests (Joyce 1990: 16). 'I don't want to see my country fall into the hands of German jews either', Haines tells Stephen. 'That's our national problem, I'm afraid, just now' (Joyce 1990: 21). Similarly, Mr Deasy, the Ulster headmaster of Stephen's school, declares that 'England is in the hand of the jews' who 'are the sign of the nation's decay' (Joyce 1990: 33). Seemingly unsatisfied with this remark, he chases Stephen down to tell him a 'joke':

> —I just wanted to say, he said. Ireland, they say, has the honour of being the only country which never persecuted the jews. Do you know that? No. And do you know why?
> He frowned sternly on the bright air.
> —Why, sir? Stephen asked, beginning to smile.
> —Because she never let them in, Mr Deasy said solemnly. (Joyce 1990: 36)

Anti-Semitism, however, is not confined to the English or those in Ireland who are identified with them but is also the provenance of the single-minded Citizen who dominates the 'Cyclops' chapter. The Citizen is a caricature of Irish nationalism, loudly complaining about the 'births and death in the Irish all for Ireland Independent' because the names aren't

Irish enough and reciting endless lists of Irish accomplishments with dubious historical grounds (Joyce 1990: 298). His worst insults are reserved for Bloom, whose presence goads him into increasingly direct statements of hostility. 'We want no more strangers in our house', he begins, before directly contradicting Mr Deasy: 'The strangers, says the citizen. Our own fault. We let them come in. We brought them. The adulteress and her paramour brought the Saxon robbers here' (Joyce 1990: 322, 323). 'A dishonoured wife', he concludes in lines that resonate painfully with Bloom's domestic tragedy, since his wife, Molly, is cheating on him this very day, 'that's what's the cause of all our misfortunes' (Joyce 1990: 324).

Bloom counters the Citizen's rancour with a critique of 'persecution ... perpetuating national hatred among nations', that, under question, leads to his blundered definition of the nation as either 'the same people living in the same place' or 'also living in different places' (Joyce 1990: 331). This incoherence is, of course, not only Bloom's but is endemic to the very concept of the nation-state itself, which seeks to conflate geographical territory with biological origin. What Bloom is most clear about, however, is his own nationality. Pressed by the Citizen to name his nation, Bloom does not hesitate: 'Ireland, says Bloom. I was born here. Ireland' (Joyce 1990: 331). Joyce's point couldn't be clearer: though Jewish, Bloom is no less Irish than anyone else. Nevertheless, he is subject throughout the day to a series of what we would now call micro-aggressions – asked in 'Hades' for his 'Christian name', or told in 'Aelous' that William Brayden looks like '*Our* savior' – in addition to the more violent rhetoric of the Citizen described above (Joyce 1990: 111, 117, emphasis mine). Joyce, in other words, associates anti-Semitism with both English imperialism and the Irish nationalism that would oppose it, while also showing how it operates in more everyday discourse, emphasizing, once again, how his subjects are conditioned by the social world around them, even when it concerns ideologies to which they are not explicitly aligned. Making his modern-day Odysseus Jewish, Joyce levels a powerful critique of the anti-Semitic blindness of his supposedly cosmopolitan compatriots.

More to the point, Joyce illustrates the absurdity of an anti-immigration discourse that fetishizes purity, conceiving of the nation through domestic metaphors that emphasize individual agency. Mr Deasy and the Citizen are united on this point.[9] They differ on whether 'we let them in' or not, but their language couldn't be clearer: immigration is conceived here as hospitality, a metaphor that conjures individual agency out of large historical forces, drawing clear boundary lines where none exist. This agency is, in part, a screen for a more deeply rooted misogyny. If the

Citizen blames a 'dishonoured wife' for all our misfortunes, Mr Deasy similarly claims that 'a faithless wife first brought the strangers to our shore' (Joyce 1990: 34–5). Colonialism itself seems to have been caused by female promiscuity.

Joyce, however, in one of his rare public statements about politics, rejected these claims. Speaking in cosmopolitan Trieste, in Italian, he articulated a vision of the nation that is still, sadly, relevant:

> Our civilization is a vast fabric, in which the most diverse elements are mingled ... In such a fabric, it is useless to look for a thread that may have remained pure and virgin without having undergone the influence of a neighboring thread. What race, of what language ... can boast of being pure today. (Joyce 1989, 165–6)

Joyce's language is precise: 'pure and virgin'. Nationality, in its demand for purity, leads almost directly to patriarchal control.[10] Bloom, the Jew let in to both the nation and to Molly's bed, is, by contrast, the 'new womanly man', presenting, all at once, an image that resists the patriarchy, misogyny and nationalism of both the Citizen and Mr Deasy and the violence upon which these concepts rest (Joyce 1990: 493). There is no slaying of the suitors here. Bloom is not only the 'unconquered hero' but he is unconquering (Joyce 1990: 264). To compel Molly's obedience would be to use force, 'the very opposite of that that is really life', which Bloom quickly defines as 'Love' (Joyce 1990: 333). Intertwining the domestic with the imperial, Joyce shows the impossibility of any clean separation between the two; we are conditioned by our social order even in our most intimate relations. The familial metaphor, then, is retained, even as its terms are reversed, the rejection of control in the private sphere becoming a metaphor for its rejection in the public.

Joyce, through the figure of Bloom, rejects force as much as he rejects the twin forces of imperialism and nationalism, their drives for racial purity and the patriarchal control that is its direct result. Joyce's world is mongrel, which is to say, defined by a migration that his text welcomes. If our contemporary world seems to offer only the intolerable opposition between, on the one hand, a neoliberal global order or, on the other, a xenophobic nationalist response, Joyce articulates a different vision: a critique of empire that resists the yelp of nationality, a vision of the global built, in Bloom's words, 'not on mutual superiority but on mutual equality' (Joyce 1990: 643). Provincialism is, indeed, the enemy, as Pound's essay suggests, a point with which all the writers I've addressed here would agree. In highlighting this element of modernism, rather than its more reactionary strands, I have tried to illustrate how the contradictions of any historical moment open themselves up to transformations that are impossible to predict. It is perhaps this particular structure of feeling – at the root of the unprecedented aesthetic innovation of the modernist era and tied to cultural displacements of all sorts – that we are in most need of today.

Notes

1 Pound is quoting Aristotle, with whom he agrees.
2 Edward Said had made a similar point, though he did not follow it up in any systematic way, when he described 'the crisis of modernism, which foundered on or was frozen in contemplative irony for various reasons, of which one was the disturbing appearance in Europe of various Others, whose provenance was the imperial domain. In the works of Eliot, Conrad, Mann, Proust, Woolf, Pound, Lawrence, Joyce and Forster, alterity and difference are systematically associated with strangers, who, whether women, natives or sexual eccentrics, erupt into vision, there to challenge and resist settled metropolitan histories, forms, modes of thought' (Said 1989: 222). Jameson's essay was followed by the 2000 edited collection *Modernism and Empire*, another landmark in the secondary literature which helped establish empire as the central topic it has since become. Nevertheless, in 2007, Richard Begam and Michael Valdez Moses could still bemoan the fact that 'few studies have provided a sustained and comprehensive account of the relation of modernism to colonialism' (2).
3 In *Imagined Communities*, a text central to the study of nationalism, Anderson asks the momentous question: 'why was it precisely *creole* communities [in the "New World"] that developed so early conceptions of their nation-ness—*well before most of Europe?*' (2006: 50). The answer lies, in part, in the ways in which imperial control tended to unify territories more rapidly than if they had been left to their own devices.
4 Perry Anderson, whose review of Marshal Berman's *All That Is Solid Melts Into Air* provides what is still the best reading of the historical conjuncture that produced modernism, makes this point succinctly: 'Without the common adversary of official academicism [in its promotion of traditional forms], the wide span of new aesthetic practices have little or no unity' (1991: 105).
5 This distinction is common in the literature on globalization. John Smith (2016), along with James Petras and Henry Veltmeyer (2001), provide helpful articulations of this point.
6 This expansion was famously described by Douglas Mao and Rebecca Walkowitz in 'The New Modernist Studies' as having 'temporal, spatial and vertical' dimensions, the latter referring to the loss of a sharp boundary between high and low cultural objects (2009: 737). The fullest realization of this expansion can be seen in Susan Stanford Freidman's *Planetary Modernisms*, where 'Every modernity has its distinct modernism' (53).

7 Critiquing the theory of 'alternative modernities', Jameson claims that 'the standardization projected by capitalist globalization in this third or late stage of the system casts considerable doubt on all these pious hopes for cultural variety in a future world colonized by a universal market order', a point he then clarifies in an important footnote: 'The position here (and many of us believe that it was that of Marx, and that "England" was itself only one of those paths and not the normative model) is that all paths to capitalism are unique and "exceptional", contingent and determined by a unique national situation' (Jameson 2002: 12–13; 218, ft 12).

8 Charles W. Pollard's *New World Modernisms* is the definitive account of this influence (2004).

9 The common ground between imperialism and the nationalism that has become a staple of postcolonial critique. An early articulation of this point is found in Partha Chatterjee's ground-breaking *Nationalist Thought and the Colonial World: A Derivative Discourse* (1993).

10 Thus Stephen, walking along Sandymount Strand, thinks of the 'Danevikings', who arrived in Ireland centuries before the British (Joyce 1990, 45).

CHAPTER 8

Edward Said
Literature and the World

Conor McCarthy

'Globalization' was not a term much used, if at all, by Edward Said. Yet the Palestinian-American critic's life and work developed in a manner which could be said both to illustrate and to dramatize globalization. Said's work on orientalism is famous, of course, and for many reasons. But he was highly productive and prolific in other related (or sometimes unrelated, at least apparently) fields or subfields – literary theory, writing about classical music, arguing the cause of Palestine, writing about literature and empire. This chapter will argue that Said can offer globalization studies a particularly striking example and angle, one which is predicated partly on his seeming hostility or recalcitrance vis-à-vis the terminology of 'globalization'. We shall see that Said had a strong sense of what we might call 'the global' which he derived from sources sharply at variance with modern sociological, economic or political-scientific visions of globalization. This perspective comes from cultural and philosophical resources of a very particular kind.

Beginnings

It's sometimes forgotten, or too easily passed over, that Said's disciplinary formation was in comparative literature. Further, he entered this field at a particularly crucial time in its development: the early Cold War. Said was an undergraduate student at Princeton University in the early 1950s and embarked on his doctoral work at Harvard University in 1958. His primary supervisor was Harry Levin, a major American critic who contributed significant work on English Renaissance drama, on nineteenth-century French realism, and one of the earliest monographs on James Joyce. At Princeton, Said had encountered the regnant American New Criticism in its most eccentric and individualized form in the person and work of R. P. Blackmur. At Harvard, in his doctoral research, he turned away from the New Criticism to European phenomenology and existentialism – specifically the work of the Geneva School. Thus equipped, yet already standing apart from the critical orthodoxy, he produced his foundational study of Joseph Conrad – the greatest writer (though not yet fully recognized at the time) in English on empire and its discontents (Said 1966).

But Said produced other work shortly after his Conrad book (published in 1966), and this other work displays him starting to elaborate not only the kind of criticism for which he would become famous but also the intellectual territory he would make his own. These other early works – important essays on Giambattista Vico and Erich Auerbach – show Said studying and mining the tradition of Romance philology, which would be one of the great constants of his career. By 'philology', we mean that precursor to modern literary studies which is the study of the history of languages and literature, paying equal attention to textual criticism (the history of variants of texts), linguistics (the technical workings of language) and literary criticism (the aesthetic analysis of texts). Philology was the predominant mode of academic study of texts in the nineteenth century, associated particularly with the German tradition running from the Romantics (such as the Schlegel brothers and Herder) to Nietzsche.

When Said's small book *Humanism and Democratic Criticism* was published posthumously in 2004, many readers were startled at the stress it put on philology (Said 2004). Philology appeared to be unfashionably antiquarian and far from the avant-garde criticism – inflected with Western Marxism, structuralism and poststructuralism – with which Said had apparently associated himself in books such as *Orientalism* and *Culture and Imperialism*. He was reckoned to have been influenced primarily by thinkers such as Michel Foucault, Theodor Adorno and Antonio Gramsci. The crucial point to be made here is that Said was indeed influenced by these writers, but he never left behind or abandoned or belittled the tradition of philology – especially Romance philology, concerned as it is with the linguistic and cultural heritage of the Christian Latin world – which marked American comparative literature so profoundly in the early years of his intellectual formation. On the contrary: the real basis of Said's criticism lay in his powerful and repeated efforts to reconcile the older model of scholarship with the new.

In his memoir, *Out of Place* (2000), Said mentions his graduate studies only briefly. He suggests that the studies required of him in the Harvard programme were mostly dull and conformist: 'Conventional history and a dry formalism ruled the literary faculty … [M]y own intellectual discoveries were made outside what the regimen required.' Said's work fell rather under the spell of these more unorthodox influences: 'The most important events for me, as the Middle East drifted further and further from my consciousness ... were such things as Vico's *New Science*, Lukacs's *History and Class Consciousness*, Sartre, Heidegger, Merleau-Ponty, all of whom shaped my dissertation on Conrad' (Said 1999: 290).

Said drew various lessons and influences from these early readings. His reading of Conrad and of the Polish writer's 'mind', as dramatized in his letters and short fiction and as illuminated by phenomenological and existentialist theory, gave Said a model of intellectual consciousness which would stay with him throughout his career. Lukacs provided Said with a vision of intellectual insurrection which also shaped much of his work, from *Beginnings* up to the focus on 'late style'. But one might argue that it was Vico who was the most profound influence. We must note also that Vico was as much a philologist as a philosopher, and this goes to the root of Said's self-making early in his career. Vico's greatest reader and commentator in the 1950s, perhaps both in Europe and in America, was Erich Auerbach. Auerbach, who was teaching at Yale University by the early 1950s, stood along with Leo Spitzer and Ernst Robert Curtius as the acme of a model of both philology and comparative literature which motivated Said from the start. It is this model, derived from Vico and Auerbach, which reappears in his writing in the posthumous *Humanism and Democratic Criticism*, reminding us that this was his guiding star all along.

What I wish to show here, then, is that Said was equipped from the start of his career with an idea of 'the global', but not under that name. He might have referred to 'the worldly', or to 'secular criticism'. Or he might take his cue from Johann Wilhelm von Goethe's famous idea of '*Weltliteratur*'. I will elaborate on this, of course, but I wish to state my suggestion baldly – that Said offers us in his criticism, funnelled through influences such as Conrad, Vico and Auerbach, a version – highly literary and culturalist – of 'globalization' which he derives from the disciplines of comparative literature and Romance philology, as well as from his reading of the great novelist of empire. This is a model of 'globalization' which runs athwart contemporary social scientific theorizations, and as such it is possessed both of strengths and weaknesses, but it may offer a critical angle nevertheless.

Said and Conrad

Conrad was important to Said in many ways. He recognized in the Pole-turned-Englishman an exile, like himself. He recognized a writer with a profoundly alienated relationship to place, language and identity: 'No-one could represent the fate of lostness and disorientation better than [Conrad] did, and no-one was more ironic about the effort of trying to replace that condition with new arrangements and accommodations' (Said 2000: 6). As I've already suggested, Said developed, in and through his early reading of Conrad, a model of the intellectual or writerly subject, which he described at one point as follows:

> We have a sense of ourselves within us (intelligible); when put into practice (empirical), this sense is modified; and when put within the framework of the society in which we live, it becomes further modified (acquired). As a result of the interplay between the individual and the world, we endow ourselves with a sense of ethical and psychological self-location … which in most cases stays with us all our lives. (Said 1966: 108–9)

It is this sense of self-location which Said is referring to when in the mid-1970s he writes a classic essay entitled 'The Text, the World, the Critic' (later the lead essay of the collection *The World, the Text, and the Critic*) (Said 1984: 31–53). That essay is notable for its location of the critic and the text not simply vis-à-vis a tradition or a temporal inheritance, but in relation to 'the world', a geographical framework. Of course, Said used the term 'the world' in a variety of ways, including the idea that criticism and texts are events which take place in the everyday 'world' of work, commerce, institutions and politics, and also that criticism is properly a 'worldly' activity, as much at home on the street, as it were, as in the seminar room, and not some hermetic or esoteric practice. But it's important also that we note the frequency of spatial or geographical metaphors in Said's writing. This would become very obvious with late career work such as *Culture and Imperialism*, where representations of space and territory – whether in Austen, Verdi or Yeats – are chief among the tell-tale signs by which Said would read imperial contexts back into work which often seems to deny such connections (Said 1993). But much earlier in his career, Said was setting out his own idea of criticism or 'critical consciousness' as predicated on worldliness, adjacency, affiliation and situatedness. If Said is customarily seen as a scholar deeply concerned with the *historical* contexts of literature and criticism, then we must immediately note also that he evinces an equally strong sense of the *geography* of literature and critique.

Said's idea of 'the world', then, undoubtedly had a geopolitical aspect. At the same time as he formulated the process of intellection or cerebration in the terms of worldly self-location just cited, Said noted a complex interplay in Conrad and in Conrad's characters between power or confidence or discipline – what Said called 'authority' – and the opposite of those qualities – fallibility, transgression, resistance – which Said termed 'molestation'. The conflict of authority and molestation would remain a root motif of Said's criticism throughout his career (Said 1975: 83–4).

We can dramatize these concepts particularly vividly in two closely related passages of one of Conrad's most famous works, *Heart of Darkness*. First, Marlow describes his youthful hope of exploration:

> Now when I was a little chap I had a passion for maps. I would look for hours at South America, or Africa, or Australia, and lose myself in all the glories of exploration. At that time there were many blank spaces on the earth, and when I saw one that looked particularly inviting on a map (but they all look that) I would put my finger on it and say, 'When I grow up I will go there'. (Conrad 2007: 281–2)

We see in this dramatization the linkage between the will to knowledge and the will to power, and then we realize that both knowledge and power are also metaphorically dependent on geography: the ability to penetrate a literary or political problem is, for Said, directly analogous to the ability and the will to penetrate a territory. The child Marlow expresses an interest in the 'blank spaces on the earth'; the mature Marlow will go there, in an act at once cognitive and speculative, and acquisitive. When the mature Marlow does 'go there', he finds something different:

> The conquest of the earth, which mostly means the taking it away from those who have a different complexion or slightly flatter noses than ourselves, is not a pretty thing when you look into it too much. What redeems it is the idea only. An idea at the back of it; not a sentimental pretence but an idea; and an unselfish belief in the idea – something you can set up, and bow down before, and offer a sacrifice to. (Conrad 2007: 503)

Here, Conrad suggests that the conquest of the earth is an act of cynical theft and even rapacity. It can be redeemed by an 'idea' to which one offers 'unselfish belief'. Yet this idea, which is the root of a kind of secular religion, is to be worshipped and that worship can be glossed in 'primitive' terms (as an idol) as much as in putatively civilized terms. Conrad is hinting that European conquest and control of the earth partakes as much of barbarous regression as it does of the *mission civilizatrice*. Here, therefore, an assertion of power admits its weakness even in its own enunciation. It is this doubled or ambivalent sense of power and its limitations or inner corruption, authority and molestation, high ideals and 'material interests', that Said brings to the discipline of comparative literature.

Said, Vico and Auerbach

To a considerable extent, Said encountered Vico and Auerbach together. Vico, as we've said, found maybe his greatest twentieth-century avatar in Auerbach, who noted that the lonely Neapolitan rhetorician and legal scholar anticipated the historicism of Herder and his generation by half a century, and in a situation of extraordinary intellectual isolation. Auerbach translated *The New Science* into German, and often referred to Vico in his writings. His most extended treatments come in the essay 'Vico and Aesthetic Historism', and in the introduction to *Literary Language and Its Public in Late Latin Antiquity and in the Middle Ages,* 'Introduction: Purpose and Method' (later echoed in Said's *Beginnings: Intention and Method*) (Auerbach 1965; Auerbach 1984: 183–200).

In 'Vico and Aesthetic Historism', Auerbach points out what he considers to be the notable strengths of Vico, most of which would find their way to influencing Said. He notes the importance of historism (or, as we'd say, historicism), whether Vico's or Herder's, as a reaction against and implicit critique of Enlightenment universalism. Where even the French philosophes such as Diderot or Voltaire predicated their ideas on an absolute concept of human nature, historicism suggested that human nature was context-dependent. Whether that humanity was 'primitive' (as thought by Rousseau) or rationalist (Descartes), the French Enlightenment saw it as universal. For such thought, the historical variety of human experiences and institutions was evidence of their unreliable character. Historicism as we now recognize it was created by the German Romantics. Their concept of the 'folk genius' led to their fascination with their own 'primitive' past and with 'primitive' peoples and cultures in their own time. But they also saw history not as a mere chain of exterior events but rather as a slow, organic and evolutionary process – the working out of the Divine will in the natural world. The sheer variety of iterations of this process – looked at both temporally and spatially, diachronically and synchronically – was a testament to the power and fertility of God.

J. W. Goethe, F. H. Jacobi and J. G. Hamann read Vico but did not fully understand him. Herder may have read him in translation but nowhere mentions his work. Yet the lonely Neapolitan philosopher and philologist anticipated the Romantics by half a century. In *The New Science* (1744), Vico invented our modern historical understanding. Well before the German Romantics, he focussed on the 'genius' of a people, suggesting that classical epic literature, such as the work of Homer, was not the product of one person but an assemblage of ideas, motifs and forms from various sources: the product of a culture. Vico's most fundamental idea was his epistemology, which related knowledge and creation: the world of nature, made by God, could only really be understood by God; but the 'world of nations', the world of history, made by human beings, was the province of human knowledge (Vico 2002: 39). Therefore, all of human experience was to be found in the potentialities of the human mind, and the human mind could penetrate any or all human experience. This idea, a version of what became known in the German tradition as *'verstehen'*, the empathic understanding of human action and culture, makes Vico arguably the first anthropologist.

Much more than Herder and the Romantics, Vico was interested in the postulation of a grand scheme of historical stages. His vision of primitives was of giants, yet they were imbued with a poetic and mythical sense of themselves. Their lives, he wrote, were 'a severe poem' (Vico 2002: 71). Like Herder, Vico saw the ancients as irrational, poetic and imaginative. Later stages in history were marked by forms of class struggle and increasing rationalism. Where Herder and his confederates were fascinated by the individual cases or cultural events their method illuminated, Vico was more interested in his overall architecture – a stageist model of human development, where specific instances were of interest primarily as types or as illustrations of the theory.

Auerbach took several things from Vico. Principally, he notes Vico's 'magical formalism' in his study of primitive societies – Vico's stress on mythic institutions and also on the poetic nature of man. Auerbach also points to Vico's theory of cognition as primarily historical – the entire development of human history is contained in the human mind, and to the extent that we can penetrate and intuit the human mind, it is knowable to scholars by a process of research and re-evocation. This process of re-evocation must be both analytical and synthetic. It produces an idea of a *Geist* (or what we'd now call, with Fredric Jameson, a 'cultural dominant' – a kind of world view or general framework which encompasses all forms of human (representational) activity in a given place and era) (Jameson 1991: 3). By this theory, Vico 'created the principle of historical understanding, entirely unknown to his contemporaries' (Auerbach 1984: 197). Stemming from this, Vico created the concept of the historical nature of man – he came to see human nature and human history as synonymous. As against all the (neo-classical) formulations of an absolute and invariant 'human nature', Vico saw human nature as a function of history – the distinction between human nature and human history disappears and Vico says that human history is a permanent Platonic state. Divinity makes human nature change from period to period, and in each period, institutions emerge which match exactly the human nature of that period.

For Said, Vico offers additional intellectual and political resources. Unlike the German tradition, especially once it reaches figures such as Hegel and Fichte, Vico's thought does not point to cultural nationalism or the justification of the state. Furthermore, in a way that caught the eye of James Joyce, Vico's model of history was of cycles and spirals, as against a grandly unfolding linear metanarrative. One hundred and fifty years before Nietzsche and 250 years before Foucault, Vico's historicist contextualizing was an anti-essentialist and proto-genealogical mode of investigation which spoke clearly to Said. In his essay 'Vico: Autodidact and Humanist', originally published in 1967 and then reworked as the conclusion to *Beginnings*, Said lists themes or approaches he takes from the Italian: an interest in beginnings, as against origins; the combination of intellectual work and a commitment to collectivity; an interest in lateral or adjacent (affiliative) relationships in intellectual and creative work, as against linear, dynastic (filiative) ones; and beginning in writing as inaugurating a new order (Said 1975: 357). Said then reads *The New Science* side by side with Vico's *Autobiography*, and the result is a model of the study of intellect and cerebration which is at once attentive to contradiction and complexity and also highly reflective on its own historical and spatial situatedness. Vico, in other words, gives Said a way of historicizing the model of intellectual subjectivity he developed while studying Conrad. But Vico's reflexiveness also allows Said to mobilize the traditions of philology and humanism, while at the same time developing a powerful critique of those same traditions. Thus, he says, humanism turns into its own critique.

Said and Auerbach

Said absorbed Vico through Auerbach, the most famous of the great *philologen* who survived into the twentieth century. Along with his peers, friends and sometime rivals Karl Vossler, Leo Spitzer and Ernst Robert Curtius, Auerbach is generally accepted as embodying the intellectual values of Romance philology at its peak and conclusion. His masterpiece, *Mimesis* (1946), remains one of the most admired single-volume histories of European literature ever written. In translating Auerbach's late but programmatic essay 'Philology and *Weltliteratur*' in 1969, Said was asserting himself as Auerbach's inheritor while also declaring an agenda for the future. Auerbach's essay was first published in 1953, and it is characterized both by a sense of a great scholar standing at the pinnacle of his career and of that career within an intellectual tradition, and by a sense of the end of that career and of that tradition. Auerbach himself died only four years after the essay's publication (Auerbach 1969: 1–17).

Auerbach's essay title conjoins two themes which were crucial to him and to Said. *Weltliteratur* was a term coined in 1827 by Goethe and used increasingly thereafter to refer not merely to some idea of great books from around the globe, but rather to what Edward and Maire Said call in the introduction to their translation 'universal literature, or literature which expresses *Humanitat*, humanity … [which is] literature's ultimate purpose' ('Philology and *Weltliteratur*, p. 1). Goethean *Weltliteratur* transcended national literatures while continuing to recognize their specific natures. For Goethe, according to the Saids, *Weltliteratur* was to be seen as a 'concert', a unified, internally varied but mutually sustaining movement of all writing produced by man about man. A quarter century after his translation of Auerbach, Said put the matter in similar terms: a vision arose in the eighteenth century, particularly in the pre-imperial German lands, of human culture and especially literary culture as a 'marvellous, almost symphonic whole' which could be studied as the historical and secular expression of humanity (Said 1993: 50–1). This reminds us that the idea of world literature was formulated at approximately the same time as the emergence of German historicism and philology and also at the time of a particular conception of humanity and humanism.

This pairing or intersection of *Weltliteratur* and philology represents a problematic that concerned Said in much of his critical writing after 1969 – the fate of the idea of *Weltliteratur* in the contemporary moment, and the fate of the intellectual tradition represented by the lineage running from Wolf to Auerbach and Spitzer. Much of Said's energy and erudition, as displayed in his major works – *Beginnings* (1975), *Orientalism* (1978), *The Question of Palestine* (1979), *The World, the Text, and the Critic* (1983) and *Culture and Imperialism* (1993) – can be seen as concerned with the effort to critique the Romance philological tradition but also and at the same time to update it, modernize it and radicalize it. Said was identified with the explication of and advocacy for the then-new French 'theory' of the 1960s and 1970s, but in the excitement that greeted his career-making books (*Beginnings, Orientalism*), his simultaneous invocation of the older philology was mostly overlooked. Another way to put this is to see that even as Said helped to introduce the new French anti-humanism (of Barthes, Foucault and Derrida) to anglophone audiences, he remained deeply committed to the worldly humanism of the Romance philological tradition. To this extent, Said's 'return to philology', announced in *Humanism and*

Democratic Criticism, can be seen as merely the resurgence of a 'ground bass' which had always been fundamental to his work (Said 2000: 555).

The linkage that Said makes between philology, *Weltliteratur* and historicism is foundational for his project. For Said realizes, as did Auerbach, that no matter how ambitious or erudite the vision of a worldly cultural concert, it would always be made from a specific perspective. For the tradition of which Auerbach and Spitzer and Curtius were the inheritors, that world was 'Romania' or the European world of Christian Latinity. Auerbach certainly saw himself as providing – in *Mimesis* – a vision of a coherent European culture at its culmination but also at its limit point, both geographically and historically. Writing outside of Europe – Auerbach famously composed *Mimesis* in Istanbul, a Jewish exile from Nazi Germany – while that continent and civilization tore itself apart, Auerbach made what Said called an act of 'cultural, even civilizational, survival' (Said 1984: 6). In the decade between the writing of *Mimesis* (1942–1945) and the publication of 'Philologie und *Weltliteratur*', Auerbach realized not only that European culture had been catastrophically damaged by war and genocide but also that capitalist modernity itself would both realize the Goethean ideal and cancel it, at one and the same time.

Said looked at this metanarrative in two primary ways. First, he injected the Conradian theme of authority and its molestations into the historicist vision and the philological method. This is the burden of *Orientalism* – the incriminating shared origins of philology, historicism and *Weltliteratur* in the will to power, the dubious affiliation of those great humanist projects with the European effort to create knowledge and hence power over the 'Orient', whether in Ernest Renan or in Gustave Flaubert.

Yet the second way that Said looked at this Auerbachian narrative was to see that the Romance philological tradition furnished him with a model of 'the world' long before the term 'globalization' came into its present use, and it was from the foundation offered by this tradition that Said can be understood as offering an analysis of and also a rebuke to the concept of globalization today. So, we'd have to start off by saying that Said's idea of 'the world' is wrapped up with Enlightenment concepts of the universal and the human also, and it is expressed in literature and language.

Timothy Brennan, Said's biographer and one of his best readers, has pointed this out in several important essays. Said's authority or intellectual capital was 'always ultimately literary', Brennan argues, and this must be remembered when considering the full range of disciplines in which Said intervened or from which he borrowed (Brennan 2004: 23). For Brennan, Said 'sought to author not only a body of written texts, but also a life-model of intellectual conduct', and 'his redefinition of comparative literature performed the instigating function for the larger enterprise' (Brennan 2004: 24). Said's career and *oeuvre*, that is, can be understood as the project of forming a certain kind of intellectual performance. The stage and context for this was the discipline of comparative literature.

Said, Comparative Literature and Philology

Comparative literature, as Said entered it in the 1950s and 1960s in America, at Harvard and then at Columbia University, was in a transitional phase. A wave of European refugee scholars had marked it or established themselves as its leaders – Spitzer and Auerbach but also René Wellek, Roman Jakobson, Paul de Man and Theodor Adorno. The later, primarily French, structuralist and post-structuralist wave had not yet come. In American literary scholarship itself, the conservative neo-Kantian New Criticism was dominant, apart from the occasional exceptional figure such as Northrop Frye. The elite American universities in the 1950s were, with these stellar European additions, still largely conservative bastions of WASP privilege. The United States had arrived at the end of the Second World War in a position of unparalleled global military and economic dominance; outside the universities was a largely conformist society which understood itself to be locked into a profound ideological contest with the new Communist enemy.

In this world, Said arrived as an outsider, albeit one equipped with a heavily British and European education. But his alienation was not initially one driven by a sense of Palestinian or even Arab national identity. That did not come until the 1967 war and its aftermath. Imre Saluzinsky, in his interview with Said in the 1980s, noted that his persona was rather 'urbane and assimilated', and the facts of Said's assimilation to the United States are often overlooked in the emphasis so often paid to his Palestinian patrimony (Saluzinsky 2004). Said famously and repeatedly drew lessons for criticism from the facts of exile, but his sense of exile is too often simply seen as exile from Palestine. Less frequently understood is his doubled sense of being at home in and yet marginal to the United States. The exile's condition, for Said, is not only or merely a matter of geographical alienation. Conrad was an exile, of course, and as early as *Beginnings*, Said referred to the intellectual as 'a wanderer, going from place to place for his material, but remaining a man essentially between homes … Such notions as "exteriority" and "in-betweenness" … do not refer to a sort of fellow-travelling critical eclecticism. Rather, they describe a transformation that has taken place in the working reality of the self-conscious writer' (Said 1975: 8–9). But it was the translation of 'Philology and *Weltliteratur*' that gave Said the formulation to which he turned most frequently. Auerbach concludes that essay with lines from Hugo of St Victor's *Didascalicon*:

> The man who finds his homeland sweet is still a tender beginner; he to whom every soil is as his native one is already strong; but he is perfect to whom the entire world is as a foreign land. (Auerbach 1969: 17)

Said repeatedly invoked these lines. But he would have agreed with Auerbach's gloss: 'Hugo intended these lines for one whose aim is to free himself from a love of the world. But it is a good way also for one who wishes to earn a proper love for the world (Auerbach 1969: 17). By the time we reach the long Introduction to his last great volume of essays, Said simply offers the pairing 'criticism and exile', a binary pair, each inhering in the other. Across his career, his wish was to place himself within the tradition of philology and *Weltliteratur*, but at the same time to manifest his alienation from it. 'One must have tradition in oneself', Adorno wrote in *Minima Moralia*, 'in order to hate it properly' (Adorno 1974: 56). For Said, the idea of a humanism pitted against itself was an exemplum of the critical act. In 1982, we find him writing of the professional description 'humanist' thus: 'a description for which I have contradictory feelings of affection and revulsion' (Said 2000: 118). Said self-consciously performed a European philological humanism which was alienated from itself both temporally and spatially, and which turned upon itself critically: a humanism belated or asynchronous in relation to its context; a humanism brought to fertile crisis by his immanent analysis of its contradictions; a humanism deconstructed by his transplanting it to the non-European world; a humanism which in his hands reveals its imbrication with its own Eurocentrism, class prejudice, masculinism; and a humanism shown its own passive acceptance of its 'humane marginality' as created by modern institutions of political and economic power.

The haunting and beautiful lines from Hugo of St Victor perform various functions for Said. They introduce the idea of the 'world'. They predicate on exile and alienation the development of the 'perfect' man. With Auerbach's reading, we get the additional sense that truly to love the world is to accept a critical-exilic distance from it. Said's project in philology and in *Weltliteratur* was to inject this critical distance, to take the worldliness of 'world literature' or 'universal literature' and to press it to its limits. Combining this with the spatial perspectivism and sense of location of the writing subject he developed in his study of Conrad, Said was equipped to provide a formidable immanent critique of the putatively universalizing European humanist tradition, in its name and with its own materials.

That sense of limits is already present in Auerbach's essay. He writes at a moment when he feels that Goethe's concept will imminently be both realized and cancelled. Writing in the early 1950s, Auerbach has a strong sense of the overdetermination of his context. Less than a decade earlier, the world and Europe in particular had been engulfed in a catastrophic total war, which had witnessed destruction and suffering on a scale without precedent, including the nearly successful industrial genocide of a people. Now that same world was split politically between the polarizing zones of control of two superpowers, whose confrontation threatened renewed conflict. Not merely this, but older supra-national political structures – the old colonial empires – were now tottering, their once world-defining rivalries giving way to the ideological opposition between the superpowers. And underlining all this was the wider and deeper sense that the socio-economic forces of modernity – capitalist commodification, reification, urbanization, the massification of culture and education – were colluding to produce a world which was characterized as much by an increasingly bland homogeneity as by an increasingly riven difference.

As much as his turn to phenomenological criticism (most overtly evidenced in the Conrad book), Said's abiding interest in philology must be seen as stemming from his efforts to steer a path independent of the intensely formalist and ahistorical New Criticism which dominated American English departments in the 1950s at the start of his career, and the reified and emasculated 'theory' which dominated American English and comparative literature departments by the end of his career in the 1990s. Philological humanism, of the kind Said identified in Vico and Auerbach, was far from being some kind of dusty antiquarianism but the space and form for intellectual adventure. Philological humanism was for Said precisely a mechanism to steer between the Scylla of mere formalism and the Charybdis of technocratic 'theory'. But it was also a framework, as Brennan points out, within which Said made himself into the kind of intellectual he became (2004).

The sheer range of Auerbach (and Curtius and Spitzer) licenced in Said a similar purview. In the great *philologen*, range was a form of rigour – it was about as far from *belle-lettristic* amateurism or dilettantism as could be imagined. But so also with Said. The author of only one conventional single-author study, Said brought 'generalism' to a particular height and focus. Many critics have noticed the rough parallelism between *Mimesis* and *Orientalism*. Sometimes – as in Aijaz Ahmad – the comparison is made only to denigrate both Said and Auerbach (Ahmad 1992). But the comparison is apt insofar as it focusses on particular shared features of the two books: not only the epic span but also the breach of professional boundaries and codes, the injection of a very personal stake into the books' respective narratives, their self-consciousness as books shaped by exile, and their status as books made in the context of war and global conflict. Auerbach produced *Mimesis* in exile in Istanbul, and he noted at the book's end that it was shaped by its circumstances of production – his lack of a European library, his lack of contact with current scholarship, and his strong sense of offering a picture of European literary culture at both its culmination and its likely ending in totalitarianism, genocide and war. But Auerbach regarded those 'lacks' as the enabling conditions of his work – without conventional German scholarly resources he was freed to write as he did. Detached from Europe, he saw it more clearly. And in roughly similar ways, Said's book, after all, transgresses many disciplinary borders; it was produced by an 'Oriental' writing from within the West but against the West, a Conradian 'secret sharer' disinterring the affiliations with power of monuments of European humanism; it was written by a Palestinian exile; and it was produced at the end of the great wave of post-1945 decolonization. Even more, as a Palestinian, Said wrote as a victim, arguably, of the last European colonizing project, which has outlived him, continuing to this day.

Said, Philology and 'Theory'

Comparative literature departments in the United States in the 1960s and 1970s were crucial reception and mediation points for 'theory'. Said stood as both an insider and an outsider in such places. He drove a radicalization of the study of 'world literature' and 'comparative literature', helping the transformation of both into 'postcolonial literature'. Yet Said never described himself as a 'postcolonial critic'. It was not just that his concerns and interests were larger than a mere academic field, or that he had his own descriptions for what he did – most obviously 'secular criticism' or 'worldly criticism'. It was also the case that he was determined to achieve a mixing or meeting of what Brennan calls 'a demotic and popular instinct' with serious scholarship (Brennan 2004: 26). Advocating the 'worldliness' of criticism, Said rejected New Critical formalism and the faux radicalism of 'theory'. Poised between Romance philology and deconstruction, Said equipped himself to criticize and transcend both. This is made obvious in the title of *Humanism and Democratic Criticism*. Humanism and democracy are revealed as closely related or even as aspects of each other. Criticism is, in the Enlightenment manner, seen as a democratic activity or as an activity conducive to democracy. But the book also advocates a 'return to philology' as the intellectual mode of that critical democracy. Once again, this Saidian 'philology' is not intended to be some musty practice of arcana, but a criticism that combines what Foucault called 'relentless erudition' with accessibility, refined reading with street-fighting polemic (Foucault 1977: 140).

Said opens *Humanism and Democratic Criticism* with a survey of what 'humanism' has meant in the United States hitherto. He notes the long-time domination of 'the humanities' by largely conservative, highly Eurocentric or even WASP Eliotian values and canons in literature, and how this version of humanism – typified in more recent times by the fierce rear-guard polemics of writers such as Allan Bloom and Alvin Kiernan – had begun to break down during and since the 1960s.[1] The liberal movements of that period – the civil rights movements, the women's movements, the vast expansion in the student body in American higher education, the anti-war campaigns – had eventually found voice inside the academy itself and produced new, expanded or radicalized visions of 'the humanities', as the culture of non-European immigrants, or black people, or of women were accorded new respect, and new models of critique and scholarship were produced out of that effort. Said's own *Orientalism* partook of – was a major statement of – that spirit. Consequently, for Said, any idea of 'American humanism' or 'American national culture' must take cognizance of two facts, in particular: first, the extraordinary power of the United States as the last global superpower; and second, the sense that the United States, as a vast society predicated from its earliest moment on immigration (forced and voluntary), contains communities from all over the world. To put the matter bluntly, even crudely: the United States bestrides the world, while also and at the same time containing the world. When Said quotes Fanon's famous remark that, in the colonies, the 'artificial sentinel' of 'the Greco-Latin pedestal' crumbles to dust, he is implying a critique both of American culture as colonial in its origins, and of American cultural intervention in the globalized world it has made in its own image as imperialist in its current character (Fanon 1967: 36).

For Said, the position of the critical intellectual in the Atlantic West generally and in the United States in particular is one where a properly 'worldly' analysis must recognize, along with Immanuel Wallerstein, the Eurocentric origins of the social science and humanities disciplines as we find them constituted today (Said 2004: 53). Furthermore, the strongly identitarian character of these disciplines must also be noted and critiqued. Against such compromising forces, Said argues for 'a *modernist* theory and practice of reading and interpreting the part to the whole in such a way as neither to deny the specificity of the individual experience in and of an aesthetic work nor to rule out the validity of a projected, putative, or implied sense of the whole' (2004: 55–6).

In a characteristic move, Said moves on immediately to point out that the philological tradition encompasses thinkers as different as Vico and Nietzsche, but also is to be found outside European culture, including in the 'Arabic-Islamic tradition' that shaped him, numbering figures such as Khalil ibn Ahmad and Sibawayh (2004: 58). These traditions of reading, reception, attentiveness to language – all must take account of the 'secularity' or 'worldliness' of intellectual activity (2004: 61). All such interpretative activity is both geographically and historically located, at the point of its production and at that of its reception. Said here enunciates an updated historicism which reflexively takes its place and time of production into its own practice.

This critical activity is not one performed alone, but rather as part of what Stanley Fish has famously called an 'interpretive community' (1980: 147–74). Fish here alludes to the fact that a given reader is never isolated from a wider discourse or structure of hermeneutical attitudes and structures. Said, again, illustrates this point using examples from the Arabic tradition: Qu'ranic interpretation is always hedged by the sense that the sacred text was delivered, in one event, to the Prophet, as a perfectly realized form. Yet we as reader-inheritors must read the text again and try to understand it again. We do this in the knowledge of 'the presence of others ... a community of witnesses, whose availability to the contemporary reader is retained in the form of a chain, each witness depending in some degree on an earlier one' (Said 2004: 68). This system of interconnected readings, called '*isnad*' in Arabic, is counterpoised with that mode of subjective interpretation, that 'component of personal commitment and extraordinary effort' dubbed '*ijtihad*' (Said 2004: 68). It was entirely characteristic of Said's project that no sooner had he articulated the theory of the critic as standing between 'culture and system' or self-locating between a hermeneutic 'tradition' and an act of individual interpretation (the vision of European thinkers from Eliot to Gadamer), than he found a rich analogous and parallel intellectual tradition and procedure stemming from Islamic scholarship.

For Said, this careful, detailed analytical and historical work in language amounts to a resistance to what he reckons are 'the dehumanising forces of globalization, neoliberal values, economic greed ... as well as imperialist ambition' (Said 2004: 71). At stake is not merely an elitist defence of traditional high culture, but, for Said (with Auerbach and Vico behind him), a stubborn, willed and recalcitrant reiteration of what it is to be human. Such is the urgency of Said's understanding that he quite openly pitches the values and practice of a radicalized critical humanism against what he sees as the technocratic and reifying tendencies within the processes of globalization. The implication is that the formidable erudition and linguistic sensitivity of the *philolog* can be pressed into service to analyse, critique and dismantle the forms of commodified information and knowledge that circulate in a 'globalized' world (Said 2004: 73). We may pause at this apparently jarring juxtaposition, and then we remember that this is exactly what Said did in *Orientalism*, in *The Question of Palestine* and in *Covering Islam*. Particularly in *Orientalism* but in fact in all three books, Said deployed a critic's sensitivity to the dense reticulations of language, to prise open a gap between political language and its objects, and to reveal discourses which purport to produce truth (of 'the Orient', 'Islam', 'terrorism', and here 'globalization', 'free markets', 'the international community') as modes of both accumulation and displacement — accumulation of capital, power, political legitimacy; and displacement of people, other conceptual systems, earlier legitimacy.

For Said, such analysis is fundamental to humanism's activity and mission. Against the grand visions implicit (or indeed explicit) in models of globalization, Said argues, we must insert the idea of the human into or between those large concepts: 'the leap to mobilized collective selves — without careful transition or deliberate reflection or with only unmediated assertion — ... [proves] to be more destructive than anything they are supposedly defending'.

> Those transitionless leaps are the ones to be looked at very hard and very severely. They lead to what Lukacs used to call totalities, unknowable existentially but powerfully mobilizing. They possess great force exactly because they are corporate and can stand in unjustifiably for action that is supposed to be careful, measured and humane. (Said 2004: 80)

Rather than risk mere 'humane marginality', which is all too often the fate of academic humanism, Said boldly wagers the cultural capital of the critic in the battle outside the seminar room and beyond the university. His worldly humanism urgently asserts the moral and political imperative not just to examine a great novel or epic poem for its dramatization of the struggle for human freedom or justice, but to realize that the academic setting and the academic interpretation sits in some loose but dynamic and important dialectical relationship with the 'world' outside (Said 2004: 78). Quoting Pierre Bourdieu, Said suggests that we pursue 'para-doxical' thought – cutting equally against fine sentiments and common sense, subjecting the relation between social space and physical space to rigorous examination. A worldly humanism wedges open the space between words and concepts, and the terrains of their deployment, manipulation, appropriation, reception and interpretation. In this way, a Saidian humanism has much to add to theorizations of the global.

Note

1 On this, see Bloom (1987); Kiernan (1990).

CHAPTER 9

The New McWorld Order
Postmodernism and Corporate Globalization
Simon Malpas

The emergence of postmodernism as a topic of general cultural debate in the 1980s and 1990s coincided with, and responded to, a significant transformation in global economics. During those decades, a model of globalization emerged that saw it as a process through which new forms of international capitalism were developing that threatened to invade not just the governmental traditions of the nations of the world but all aspects of cultural and social interaction. This globalization was perceived, in other words, as more than simply a means of expanding established national markets along new international lines; rather, the move to late-phase capitalism heralded a radical political shift into an entirely new supra-national global culture. The term used by many to identify this culture was 'postmodernism'. In the words of Marxist critic Fredric Jameson, postmodernist culture developed as the 'cultural logic of late capitalism': postmodernism must be understood, he asserts, as a cultural product of the revolution happening in globalizing capitalism in the final decades of the twentieth century.[1]

The aim of this chapter is to introduce some of the most influential accounts from that time of what these transformations might mean for theories of globalization and postmodernism, and to examine the ways in which some key literary texts of the period responded to the changes taking place. Focussing on the 1980s and 1990s, it will examine the means by which theorists and authors engaged with the perception that a 'New World Order' was establishing itself and transforming the globe.

Globalization and the 'Cultural Logic of Late Capitalism'

The form of globalization most frequently invoked in the postmodern theory of the period rests on a specific and limited definition of the term, and one explicitly focussed on its impact on the developed world. It is labelled as 'globalism' by sociologist Ulrich Beck in his influential book *What Is Globalization?* This mode of globalization, Beck argues, presents 'the view that the world market eliminates or supplants political action – that is, the ideology of rule by the world market, the ideology of neo-liberalism. It proceeds monocausally and economistically, reducing the multi-dimensionality of globalization to a single, economic dimension.... If it mentions at all the other dimensions of globalization – ecology, culture, politics, civil society – it does so only by placing them under the sway of the world-market system'; and, as a result of this, he argues, 'the ideological core of globalism is that a basic difference of ... modernity is hereby liquidated, that is, the difference between politics and economics' (Beck 2000: 9). The claim about a loss of political agency in this 'globalism' is contentious, but it was certainly a charge that was levelled at the time by both supporters and critics of the new economic systems and the concomitant postmodernist culture.[2] Beck's model does, though, identify a central premise of the postmodern analysis of multinational capitalism in its account of nation-states coming to function in the same manner as, and having an equivalent legal status to, commercial companies: the collapse of politics into economics marks the reduction of the nation-state to the status of a geographically limited company. Beck is not alone in proposing this model: by the close of the twentieth century, social, cultural and political commentators were increasingly identifying the success or failure of a nation-state in terms of its capacity to function effectively in an ever more interconnected, pervasive and dominant world market.

This image of the state as a company recurs frequently in the literature and culture of the period and is perhaps captured most succinctly in a speech from the 1987 film *Wall Street* in which an anti-hero 'corporate raider' named Gordon Gecko, played by Michael Douglas, addresses the shareholders of Teldar Paper, a company he is seeking to buy, with a celebration of the power of financial self-interest: 'Greed, for lack of a better word, is good; greed is right; greed works; greed clarifies, cuts through, and captures the essence of the evolutionary spirit ... and greed, you mark my words, will not only save Teldar Paper but that other malfunctioning corporation called the USA'. Economic thinking that equates the state with a failing company in the rhetoric of Gecko and his real-world stockbroker followers who saw themselves, to use a name borrowed from Tom Wolfe's satirical novel, as 'Masters of the Universe' reduces all values to finance and sees the state's role dwindle to being little more than a facilitator for the increasing profits of the private companies and shareholders located within its borders (Wolfe 1988). While *Wall Street* and *Bonfire of the Vanities* present critical accounts of the 'greed is good' culture of the 1980s, both were also identified by commentators at the time as celebrating the economic transformations taking place, especially in the United States.

Iain Banks's novel *The Business* from 1999 explores this tension between a private corporation and a nation-state in more global terms. It depicts the machinations of a company, called simply 'The Business', whose origins 'predate the Christian church, but not the Roman Empire ... which, at one point – technically, at any rate – [it] owned', as it seeks to buy up the government of a small country in order to take its seat at the United Nations and put itself on a par with the nations of the world (Banks 1999: 37). The precise nature of the business that The Business conducts is never made clear, although over the course of its history it appears to have had a hand in many of the most significant economic, political and social movements that have shaped the contemporary world, and it continues to have interests in most sectors of the economy. The Business demands loyalty from its members after the manner of a state: those becoming managers must renounce prior religious and national interests and devote themselves exclusively to the good of the firm. The protagonist Kate, an up-and-coming executive, is sent to the small Himalayan country of Thulahn to act as an ambassador (while being pressured into a quasi-dynastic marriage with its crown prince) and secure the country and its UN seat for the company. The novel charts the machinations occurring within the company's management as various factions compete to profit from the acquisition of the country. These political intrigues, and the celebrations of fashion, wealth and conspicuous consumption that accompany them, are contrasted vividly with the celebrations of traditional community within Thulahn; and the narrative follows Kate's increasingly sceptical questioning of the values of the corporate system she represents. The novel's contrasts between the corruption of the Western corporate world and an idealized third-world community certainly romanticizes the latter in a manner that limits the scope of its political critique, but the image it develops of an interconnected world of transnational corporate interest vividly captures the perceived reach of multinational business power at the end of the century.

The rapid development of the new forms of global capitalism practised by emerging corporate giants with international reach engendered, according to Jameson, a sense that significant changes were occurring in the economies of both developed and developing nations: 'new forms of business organization (multinationals, transnationals) beyond the monopoly stage but, above all, a vision of a world capitalist system fundamentally distinct from the older imperialism' (Jameson 1991: 117). While companies continued to be registered in and to sell their produce to Western states, and those states came under increasing pressure to deregulate their markets and open their borders to trade, production and manufacturing were 'offshored' to developing nations with larger exploitable workforces that were cheaper and had less access to employment rights. The outcome of this in the West was, according to Beck, 'capitalism without work': the focus of political and economic analysis of contemporary society moves from traditional and broadly Marxist notions based on the means and relations of production to the postmodern exploration of the interactions and techniques of consumption and the culture that accompanies it.

Globalized postmodern culture emerges from and reacts to this transformed transnational capitalism. For the Western consumer, the new economic forms produced, in the words of political scientist Benjamin R. Barber, a vision of a 'cosmopolitan future': a 'future in shimmering pastels, a busy portrait of onrushing economic, technological and ecological forces that demand integration and uniformity and that mesmerise peoples everywhere with fast music, fast computers, and fast food – MTV, Macintosh, and McDonald's – pressing nations into one homogenous global theme park, one McWorld tied together by communications, information, entertainment, and commerce' (Barber 1995: 4).[3] The globalized culture of this 'world capitalist system' was transforming into what postmodern theorist Jean Baudrillard identified as a 'consumer society': a society in which the 'circulation, purchase, sale, appropriation of differentiated goods and signs/objects today constitute our language, our code, the code by which the entire society *communicates* and converses' (Baudrillard 1998: 79). This 'shimmering pastel' consumer culture as the 'code by which the entire society *communicates*' was quickly identified as an essential basis of the art, literature and culture of postmodernism.

The French philosopher Jean-François Lyotard opens his essay 'An Answer to the Question: What Is the Postmodern?' with an account of the cultural experience lying at the heart of this consumer McWorld:

> Eclecticism is the degree zero of contemporary general culture: you listen to reggae; you watch a western; you eat McDonald's at midday and local cuisine at night; you wear Paris perfume in Tokyo and dress retro in Hong Kong; knowledge is the stuff of tv gameshows .... Together, artist, gallery owner, critic, and public indulge one another in the Anything Goes – it is time to relax .... [T]his realism of Anything Goes is the realism of money .... This realism accommodates every tendency just as capitalism accommodates every need – so long as these tendencies and needs have buying power. (Lyotard 1992: 8)

What Lyotard depicts here as the new globalized realism of 'Anything Goes' is the superficial uniformity presented by Barber combined with Baudrillard's insistence on consumption as constituting our social code: the 'mesmerising' fluidity of a culture that breaks down all distances and borders in eclectic fusions of what might once have appeared as discrete languages, traditions and identities but have by now become the mere 'lifestyle choices' of the global postmodern consumer. The single rule that governs such culture is, according to Lyotard, the rule of the 'realism of money': 'anything goes' as long as it sells; or, to put it even more brutally, contemporary reality is a function of exchangeability, of 'buying power'.

Postmodern Capitalism, Culture and Critique: Jameson, Baudrillard and Lyotard

Throughout the 1980s and 1990s, the three theorists whose definitions of postmodernism proved most influential and far-reaching in terms of their analyses of the impact of late capitalism on globalized culture were Jameson, Baudrillard and Lyotard. Each challenges the marketization of culture that they identify as essential to postmodernity, albeit in quite different ways, and their three versions of resistance provide helpful models for exploring literature's potential to respond to corporate globalism.

For Jameson, because postmodernism is the 'cultural logic' of contemporary capitalism, 'every position on postmodernism in culture ... is also at one and the same time, and *necessarily*, an implicitly or explicitly political stance on the nature of multinational capitalism today' (Jameson 1991: 3). In a series of striking examples in the opening chapters of *Postmodernism*, Jameson explores the ways postmodern culture generates a 'schizophrenic intensity' of experience that eliminates any possibility of objectivity: things, commodities, brands to be purchased and the potential lifestyles associated with them, 'come before the subject with heightened intensity, bearing a mysterious charge of affect, here described in negative terms of anxiety and loss of reality, but which one could just as well imagine in the positive terms of euphoria, a high, an intoxicatory or hallucinogenic intensity' that produce, in short, a 'new depthlessness' for experience (27–2). This leads to a 'loss of cognitive distance' in the ubiquity and immediacy of postmodern consumer culture that makes modern modes of objective critique challenging (Jameson 1991: 51). *Postmodernism* argues that if an artistic or philosophical challenge to late capitalism is to be mounted and traditional forms of political activism are to retain their value in the contemporary world, criticism must break down the hallucinations conjured by contemporary marketing and find ways to reoccupy the forms of agency that stood at the core of modern critique: 'the practical reconquest of a sense of place and the construction or reconstruction of an articulated ensemble which can be retained in memory and which the individual can map and remap along the moments of mobile alternative trajectories' (51). To this end, Jameson proposes a mode of analysis that will enable the subject to reorientate her or himself by means of a process he calls 'cognitive mapping': adopting a 'critical distance' able to generate a 'situational representation' from the mass of images and commodities that make up the experience of everyday life in order to make apparent the 'vaster and properly unrepresentable totality which is the ensemble of society's structures as a whole' (51). In short, a coherent political response to the postmodern superstructure of our late capitalist world must, for Jameson, begin with a critical reorientation of experience that will provide a solid ground for critique and enable a revivification of the modern political categories global capitalism has sought to leave behind.

Caryl Churchill's 1987 play *Serious Money* provides a helpful example of what the cognitive 'situational representation' that Jameson is suggesting might actually entail. The play satirizes the so-called Big Bang moment when the London stock market was deregulated in 1986, which opened up what had been a gentlemanly old-boys network to the cut-throat vigour of a new class of international speculators. The play does this by distancing the audience from these events, creating a dialogue between past and present that focusses attention on both the political continuities with the past and that which is radically new. It opens with a scene from Thomas Shadwell's 1692 play *The Volunteers* that sent up the new-fangled 'stock-jobbers' of the seventeenth century, and this has the effect of providing a historical context for the play's contemporary world to reflect. The present-day action emerges out of this as the scene fades into the 1980s with an incessant ringing of telephones and the overlapping, shouted financial-jargon-laden speech of the contemporary commodities exchanges (much of which audiences found just as incomprehensible as they did the archaic Restoration period-specific references in Shadwell's play). As it develops, the play reinvents the stage techniques of Restoration theatre – rhyming couplets, musical interludes, asides and in-jokes with the audience – to defamiliarize and estrange the contemporary commercial dialogue and provoke questions about the economic motivations and political ideas that underpin the action. Plotted around the investigation of the death of a trader involved in a major global deal, the links between physical violence and corporate finance, and the profound international impacts of financial decisions, explicitly demonstrate the global consequences of each share deal, marketing campaign and corporate acquisition. The play ends with a rousing chorus sung by the entire cast that extols the virtues of the new economics: 'Five more glorious years/We're crossing forbidden frontiers for five more glorious years/pissed and promiscuous, the money's ridiculous/send her victorious for five fucking morious/five more glorious years' (Churchill 1990: 309). *Serious Money*, employing theatrical techniques borrowed from Bertolt Brecht's epic theatre, distances the audience from identifying with the characters and presses them to question the political consequences of this celebration of the new markets. In doing so, it was one of the first pieces of literature to explore the reach and structure of the new market economy made possible by the deregulation of finance, and it helped Churchill stand out in the 1980s and 1990s as one of very few writers able to articulate a sophisticated critique of the new economic world order in the manner Jameson's theory suggests.

Jean Baudrillard's account of postmodern consumerism presents a culture that is even more all-encompassing in terms of its 'hallucinogenic intensity' than Jameson's as he rejects any hope of an alternative rational space in which 'critical distance' or political resistance is possible. The 'real world', according to Baudrillard, has ceased being a source of representational truth as 'reality' is transformed into an effect generated by the ubiquitous commercialism of global culture's signifying practices: 'There is no longer any critical and speculative distance between the real and the rational. There is no longer really even any projection of models in the real ... but an in-the-field, here-and-now transfiguration of the real into model. A fantastic short-circuit: the real is hyperrealised .... The hyperreal is the abolition of the real not by violent distinction, but by its assumption, elevation to the strength of the model' (Baudrillard 1983: 83–4). In Baudrillard's postmodern hyperreality, the combination of technological advances allowing ever more 'realistic' images and media with the commodification of identities in lifestyle advertising serves to market and monetize everyday experience in a manner that models 'the real' and 'the rational' as effects to be purchased for pleasure by the contemporary consumer. One's sense of self is thus, for Baudrillard, produced by the signs and symbols of fashion ubiquitously circulating in a culture that 'sets in place a whole array of sham objects, of characteristic signs of happiness, and then waits ... for happiness to alight' (Baudrillard 1998: 31). Failure to achieve this promised happiness is not an indication that such a goal might be unreal or unrealizable, but a goad towards further consumption, to that next commodity that one is seduced into believing will finally confer satisfaction. What Baudrillard calls 'the desert of the real itself' is, precisely, this absence lying beneath the infinitely seductive play of simulations in postmodern hyperreality (Baudrillard 1983: 1).

The most influential image of this transformation of the real occurs in his reading of Disneyland:

> Disneyland is there to conceal the fact that it is the 'real' country, all of the 'real' America, which *is* Disneyland .... Disneyland is presented as imaginary in order to make us believe that the rest is real, when in fact all of Los Angeles and the America surrounding it are no longer real, but of the order of the hyperreal and simulation. It is no longer a question of a false representation of reality (ideology), but of concealing the fact that the real is no longer real. (Baudrillard 1983: 25)

Disneyland is, in other words, 'a deterrence machine set up in order to rejuvenate in reverse the fiction of the real' (Baudrillard 1983: 25). Its function as 'hyperreal' and 'simulation' is not to provide a fantastical escape from the mundanity of day-to-day reality, but, rather, to mask the hyperreality of an everyday world that partakes in the exact same logics of image, desire and consumption that Disneyland projects as means of escape. To critique the unreality and fantasy wish-fulfilment of the consumer culture of postmodernism on the basis of a 'cognitive distance' that for critics such as Jameson rests on clear distinctions between reality and unreality is, according to Baudrillard, to be a dupe of simulation, to have missed the transformation into hyperreality that global society has undergone.

Martin Amis's 1984 novel *Money: A Suicide Note* builds a world that exhibits many of the structures of Baudrillard's postmodernism: the narrative depicts the precipitous decline of the first-person narrator John Self, a narcissistic misogynist obsessed with fashion, alcohol, pornography and wealth, as he fritters away and is swindled out of the money that has made him who he is. Contemplating his position, Self identifies a gap: 'Something is missing from the present too. Wouldn't you say? Mobile, spangled and glamorous, my life looks good – on paper, anyhow .... [But] I feel invaded, duped, fucked around. I hear strange voices and speak in strange tongues. I get thoughts that are way over my head. I feel violated' (Amis 1984: 66). Throughout the novel, Self strives to fill the perceived void, using the chief means at his disposal ('I've *got* money, plenty of it, I'm due to make lots more') to acquire increasingly superficial gratifications: 'Fast food, sex shows, space games, slot machines, video nasties, nude mags, drink, pubs, fighting, television, handjobs', and anything else on sale in the transatlantic culture he inhabits (Amis 1984: 66–7). Self is being played, manipulated and deceived not only by his nemesis, the financier Fielding Goodney, but by the whole culture in which he is financially and emotionally invested: focalized through Self's narcissism, *Money* draws readers into the simulations that make up his world in a stream of disturbing and ironic deflations of his attempts to assert control. There is no overtly articulated critique in the novel, even when the author inserts himself into the narrative as the erudite 'Martin Amis', and no alternative system is offered; instead, its potential critique comes through the alienating experience of occupying Self's deluded postmodern consciousness.

In contrast to Jameson's call to rediscover the cognitive distance necessary for a critique of depthless postmodern culture and Baudrillard's insistence on the inescapable hyperreality of contemporary existence, Jean-François Lyotard identifies a form of immanent postmodernist cultural disruption that occurs at moments where the consumer 'realism of Anything Goes' falls into self-contradiction. This insistence on an intrinsic disruptive potential within postmodern culture is central to Lyotard's work: his diagnosis of a 'postmodern condition' generated by contemporary capitalist society is supplemented by an interpretation of postmodern*ism* as a critical mode of artistic engagement that challenges the status quo.

Lyotard's account of contemporary society is set out most clearly in *The Postmodern Condition: A Report on Knowledge*, which examines 'the condition of knowledge in the most highly developed societies' by analysing the ways in which such societies value scientific research (1984: xxiii). He argues that, unlike modern models that see rationality, research and education as valuable in themselves, knowledge has come to be treated in contemporary capitalism as just another commodity to be exchanged on the global markets. This commercialization marks a point of transformation from an Enlightenment world in which the pursuit of knowledge was either perceived as intrinsically valuable or valued as a means of emancipating humanity from superstition and suffering. In contrast to such ideals, Lyotard describes postmodern knowledge as fragmented and incapable of finding legitimacy in any greater historical, scientific, theological or political account of collective human progress, evolution or destiny. And this forms the basis of his definition of the postmodern as a condition of 'incredulity toward metanarratives': a world where larger collective goals and aspirations ('metanarratives') have been replaced by short-term commercial imperatives of minimizing costs and maximizing profits. 'In matters of social justice and scientific truth alike', Lyotard asserts, knowledge's value 'is based on its optimising the system's performance – efficiency', and the criteria for success are simple: 'be operational ... or disappear' (Lyotard

1984: xxiv). This operational imperative not only defines the values of scientific research but also, according to *The Postmodern Condition*, structures all interactions in the contemporary world: the postmodern is a condition in which the capitalist operational imperative has spread to every aspect of social existence, and the narratives that held traditional societies together are being made to 'disappear'.

He identifies the culture that accompanies this shift as the realism of 'Anything Goes', and its role is to depict the world in an operationally efficient manner so that a consumer can 'decode images and sequences rapidly', from a 'point of view that would give [them] a recognisable meaning' and thus 'protect [their] consciousness from doubt' (Lyotard 1992: 5–6). This realism 'works' because it is simple to consume: it gives the audience the world they expect, sets it out according to conventions that are immediately decodable, and its messages fall quickly into line with familiar and established beliefs. This is, at the same time, Jameson's intoxicating depthlessness and Baudrillard's hyperreality: the simplicity and obviousness of the meaning behind the realist spectacle makes consumption instantaneous and avoids difficulty or doubt.

What Lyotard defines as critical postmodernist art and literature disrupts this realism from within by 'presenting the existence of something unpresentable. Showing that there is something we can conceive of that we can neither see nor show' (1992: 11). This critical moment does not emerge from outside realism to depict an alternative 'better' reality but, rather, 'invokes the unpresentable in presentation itself': it 'refuses the consensus of taste permitting a common experience of nostalgia for the impossible, and inquires into new presentations – not to take pleasure in them, but to better produce the feeling that there is something unpresentable', and, in so doing, wages 'a war on [the] totality' presented by the all-encompassing realism of global consumer culture (Lyotard 1992: 15–16).[4] In other words, for Lyotard, postmodernism offers a moment of critical disruption in the totalizing global marketplace where rationality itself has been co-opted to the operational imperative.

An example of a literary exploration of the postmodern idea of eclectic consumption as the foundational code of contemporary cultural identity and its immanent disruption through formal textual experimentation occurs in the novels of Bret Easton Ellis, particularly in his controversial 1991 text *American Psycho*. The novel follows Patrick Bateman, a Manhattan investment banker and serial killer (and the immediacy of the present-tense first-person narrative voice strongly suggests a parallel between these occupations) who exists in a hypercompetitive culture obsessed with appearance, fashion and the status that being up-to-the-minute brings. The narrative style captures the consumerist depthlessness of its world: characters are interchangeable, frequently interchanged and mistaken for one another, and the focus on designer labels and product descriptions as stand-ins for personal identity is obsessive. A typical scene-setting passage reads: 'He's wearing a linen suit by Canali Milano, a cotton shirt by Ike Behar, a silk tie by Bill Blass and cap-toed leather lace-ups from Brooks Brothers. I'm wearing a lightweight linen suit with pleated trousers, a cotton shirt, a dotted silk tie, all by Valentino Couture, and perforated cap-toe leather shoes by Allen-Edmonds' (Ellis 1991: 29). The name-checking and flatness of this prose solicits identification from readers who have no other access to the novel's world than identification with the values embodied by consumption. This language, the 'realism' of consumerism, is presented as the totality of lived experience and depicts the protagonist's descent into violence as inevitable and without need for any alteration of tone or focus. Episodes of murder, rape and dismemberment occur in the same lexicon as commodity descriptions: they are logical continuations of Bateman's fashion obsessions and are depicted as necessary extensions of his world view. Like *Money*, *American Psycho* presents no objective narrative critique of its protagonist. However, its form disturbs identification and response in a way that is absent from Amis's novel: as the violence increases, the question of whether the events described happen in the novel's real world or are merely impotent fantasies of power projected by the narrator's juvenile egotism is impossible to answer. The status of the action, its meaning, is thus disrupted by the narration: the true nature of Bateman's reactions to the realism of the consumer culture he inhabits, which might be sadistic violence or ineffectual fantasy, is unpresentable within the narrative form, and this problem of presentation leaves readers with unanswerable and troubling questions about the political consequences of the world views the novel presents.

A New McWorld Order: New Economies, New Threats and New Resistances

The theories of late capitalist culture, postmodernism and the potential for critical analysis focus explicitly on the experience of culture on the part of the Western consumer, but their implications for ideas of globalization reach much further, especially in relation to the idea of a New World Order that marked the end of the Cold War. The fall of the Berlin Wall on 9 November 1989 was quickly hailed by many in the West as the moment that victory over the Soviet Union had been achieved, the Cold War was won and communism ceased to be a viable alternative to capitalism. This post-Cold War era was defined by both Soviet Premier Mikhail Gorbachev and US President George H. W. Bush, albeit with different resonances, as marking a New World Order. In a speech made on 11 September 1990 that committed US troops to overturn Saddam Hussein's invasion of Kuwait, Bush claimed:

> A new partnership of nations has begun, and we stand today at a unique and extraordinary moment. The crisis in the Persian Gulf, as grave as it is, also offers a rare opportunity to move toward an historic period of cooperation. Out of these troubled times, our ... objective—a new world order—can emerge: A new era—freer from the threat of terror, stronger in the pursuit of justice and more secure in the quest for peace. An era in which the nations of the world, east and west, north and south, can prosper and live in harmony. (Bush 1990)

The date of this speech and its invocation of freedom from terror would prove deeply ironic, but it set the tone for a decade-long drive to bring what many in the West saw as the benefits of 'free-market democracy' (usually with emphasis on the first term) to the whole world. For a thinker such as Francis Fukuyama, this moment marked 'the end of history' as the new order would make possible 'the limitless accumulation of wealth, and this the satisfaction of an ever-expanding set of human desires' in a 'process [that] guarantees an increasing homogenisation of all human societies, regardless of their origins or cultural inheritances', as it is 'a universal evolution in the direction of capitalism' (Fukuyama 1992: xiv–xv). While Fukuyama's jubilant celebration of 'limitless accumulation' was quickly challenged as politically and philosophically naive, it captured a sense of the potential global expansion being pursued by governments and companies during the decade.

In contrast to this vision of a rejuvenated *Pax Americana* in which the joys of the free market would spread seamlessly across the globe, economic deregulation was experienced by many in both the developing world and the West as the loss of financial security and self-determination.[5] As Beck describes it, '[h]igh unemployment in the so-called Third World and post-Communist Europe forces the governments there to pursue an export-oriented economic policy, at the price of poor social and environmental standards. With low wages, often pitiful working conditions and "no-union" zones, these countries compete for foreign capital both with one another and with rich Western countries'; and, because standards and wages in these countries could always undercut the West, the last decades of the century saw a rapid process of 'offshoring' as manufacturing and industry moved away from regulation, taking the jobs with them and *'redistributing unemployment'* in the West to replace full-time work with 'new hybrids of employment and unemployment (short-time contracts, "junk jobs", part-time work, etc.)' (Beck 2000: 59, 119). In short, for many in both the West and the developing world, the job was becoming a 'McJob': short-term, shorn of employment rights or benefits, and with little prospect of promotion or progress in multinational companies no longer regulated by national governments. As tax rates were reduced and revenues fell, national regulations were removed to open borders for trade by global corporations, and the power and reach of international economic bodies such as the World Bank and International Monetary Fund increased, the nation-state, which had functioned as the cornerstone of modern political organization, began to lose its power, sovereignty and ability to confer a sense of collective identity for its citizens.

Two plays by Scottish playwright David Greig, *Europe* (1994) and *The Cosmonaut's Last Message to the Woman He Once Loved in the Former Soviet Union* (1999), explore this impact of the New World Order on identity. *Europe* depicts events in a small Central European town whose station no longer has trains stopping as it has ceased to be a border between states. Along with the loss of its major industry and its border-town status comes a crisis of identity for a community that saw itself as 'famous for our soup, for our factory which makes lightbulbs and for being on the border' but now feels forgotten in a changing world (Greig 2002: 5). The arrival of a pair of refugees stirs up conflict between those who yearn to travel themselves, escaping their dying town, and others who see immigration as a further threat to their already collapsing identity. The play depicts the erosion of hope that comes with the stagnation of a community bypassed by the new cultural and financial realities of a globalized, economically borderless world, the retreat into racist nationalism by those who feel excluded and left behind, and the violence aimed at anyone perceived as different or foreign that this engenders. *Cosmonaut's Last Message* tells a related tale from a different perspective and introduces an array of diverse but linked characters, including two cosmonauts orbiting the earth in a capsule that is cut off by its malfunctioning radio and has been forgotten amidst the chaos surrounding the collapse of the Soviet Union, the emigrant daughter of one of them who has come to Britain in search of money and finds work as an erotic dancer, a middle-aged civil servant who feels lost in the new world and terrified of his neighbours, a representative of the World Bank who sees his job as being 'a bulwark against the flood' of 'violence, atrocity and injustice' into which the world is sinking, and a UFO researcher whose attempts to contact the unresponsive and unknown satellite he has spotted end in failure. The play explores the impossibility of communication in a world where the links of tradition (family, community, nation) are breaking down and depicts a range of the forms of alienation generated by contemporary global life.

In contrast to the texts discussed earlier, the protagonists of these plays are not the traders, brokers, financiers and other Masters of the Universe who drive economic globalization, but, rather, those at the margins of this world who find themselves excluded from the delights of postmodern consumption promised by the New World Order. Greig's plays adopt some of the formal techniques deployed in *Serious Money*, particularly the fragmented action, choric presentations of community and narrative discontinuities, although there is less sense of a defined Marxist/Brechtian framework to contextualize the action that underlies Churchill's play and provides Jameson's sense of the critical distance necessary for critique. In these terms, even if not in their modes of presentation, the plays' explorations of globalization from the perspectives of those marginalized by the great narratives of the period place them closer to the disruptive aesthetics of Lyotard's postmodernism: a New World Order vitiated by the disorder of, as Zygmunt Bauman put it in 1998, 'the indeterminate, unruly and self-propelled character of world affairs; the absence of a centre, of a controlling desk, of a board of directors, of a managerial office' (Bauman 1998: 59). If both plays offer some optimism about the potential for discovering new modes of human community, this is very much a community that will be scraped together from the scraps of an out-of-control global system from which the plays' characters find themselves excluded and displaced.

Eleven years to the day after Bush's 'New World Order' speech, Islamist terrorists hijacked planes and crashed them into the twin towers of the World Trade Center in an event that radically transformed the senses of globalization and nation underpinning the postmodern culture of the previous decades. That one of the targets chosen for attack was a symbol of the new global capitalism is not coincidental: to return to Benjamin Barber's central opposition in his analysis of the post-Cold-War world, the vision of a new McWorld was suddenly shattered by Jihad. This attack and the subsequent 'War on Terror' gave rise to a conflict that superficially appeared to straightforwardly pit the Western 'universalism of the profit motive (and its accompanying politics of commodities)' against 'the parochialism of ethnic identity (and its accompanying politics of resentment)' of Islamist terrorism, but which actually led to a reaffirmation of traditional national power through the mobilization of militaries, re-establishment of state borders, curtailment of domestic civil liberties with statues such as the USA PATRIOT Act and its equivalents in other countries, and the assertion of nations' rights to undertake unilateral action without sanction from the United Nations (Barber 1995: 219–20). Although the new global economics remained a driving force of development, the reassertion of state power and national identity challenged the satirical play of postmodern culture and literature with calls for a new sincerity, a new realism and an end to postmodern culture's 'age of irony' (Rosenblatt 2001: 79).

Notes

1 See Jameson (1991) for the most thorough and far-reaching discussion of this idea.
2 See, for two examples, Callinicos (1989) and Norris (1992), both of which attack postmodern theory for what they perceive to be its failure to adequately mobilize political opposition to the New World Order of contemporary neoliberal politics and economics.
3 Although this chapter focusses predominantly on the 'McWorld' side of Barber's opposition, the simultaneous rise of Jihadist politics, a 'retribalisation of large swathes of humankind by war and bloodshed' that rejects 'every kind of interdependence, every kind of artificial social cooperation and mutuality', and even 'modernity itself' (Barber 1995: 4), is crucial to understanding the transformation of globalization at the turn of the millennium.
4 The aesthetic form Lyotard bases this argument on is the 'sublime', which his work explores in detail. For more on this, see Malpas (2003: 33–50, 87–102).
5 See Muravchick (1991: 23) for a contemporary assertion of this idea.

CHAPTER 10

Pharmakon, Difference and the Arche-Digital
Claire Colebrook

One way to think about globalism, especially in the twenty-first century, is as a doubled or contrary movement. The idea of the globe allows any single perception, experience or event to be thought of in terms of its own difference, opening every particularity to what is not yet present. The more I become aware of the other cultures that exist beyond my own milieu, the more sense I have of my own distinction. This is not only true of comparative and world literatures, and of the modern projects of anthropology and cultural difference, but it marks the very possibility of both the humanities and the sciences in the contemporary West. The globe, and globalism as a historical trajectory, is an expansive movement that ruptures every closed world. Alexandre Koyré has defined modernity as the shift from the closed world to the infinite universe: rather than simply accepting the truth and immediacy of one's own existence, modern science seeks the truth of every possible world (Koyré 1968). The experience and meaning of truth is *what would be true* for any subject whatsoever. From scientific universalism to museums that catalogue each fragment of culture as an expression of a humanity that is given only through its variations, globalism appears as an opening to difference. Writing about Edmund Husserl's attempt to chart the history of truth without reducing truth to yet one more local and relative world view, Jacques Derrida referred to an opening to infinity that would increasingly preoccupy twentieth-century thought (Derrida 1989: 130). Although the pretension to 'pure truth' is manifestly philosophical, it also has a significant literary expression, ranging from John Milton's claim in *Areopagitica* that the circulation of texts would allow the truth to emerge, to William Wordsworth's sixth book of *The Prelude*, where the articulation of the sense of the eternal does not require a concrete and material archive but relies upon what is truly and silently human (Milton 1959; Wordsworth 1984: 464).

Without some sense of truth *in general*, every world would remain enclosed in the relativity of its own time and place; only a comportment towards the globe opens to the infinite. One might think of non-Western senses of a time beyond humanity, a dreaming or planetary consciousness, that opens the local to the eternal. John Carroll argued that it made sense to think of Western truth along these lines, as a 'dreaming' akin to Indigenous Australian culture's capacity to imagine its own world as a fragment of a time and space beyond the actual world (Carroll 2001). Every world, we might say, has its own globe, its own sense of the eternal. So, if globalism is a striving for the infinite, it also has the capacity to recognize a number of articulations of what exists beyond the world. This is globalism's contrary tendency: at once an opening to the infinite *and* an articulation of a specific relation through which the infinite is inscribed. In the modern West it has been mathematical and purely formal thought that signals a truth beyond finite perception. We might say that the truths of geometry transcend Euclid or any single geometer, and yet there must have been a Euclid (Derrida 1989: 72). One might think of this expansion and contraction, this double tendency of the global, in terms of analogue and digital differentiations; each space or world can be marked as distinct only with the recognition of its own singular mode of parsing difference, and yet that very recognition of different systems of difference requires translation into a unified, global and increasingly digital frame of reference.

This problem of the material genesis of the infinite, for both Husserl and Derrida, was a problem of writing and technics. Without some system for inscribing, systematizing, storing, remembering and stabilizing experience, there could be no sense of what would be true across time and cultures, no science in its broadest sense. Even relativism requires some general system – such as a language of anthropology – in which other cultures might be perceived as differing from each other. The aspiration to some sort of global comprehension is at once a transcendence of one's own world *and* a reduction of all worlds to what Derrida, again commenting on Husserl, would refer to as a silent presupposed 'we'. Here is Derrida, commenting on the ways in which a sense of global humanity is inextricably intertwined with language's very possibility. To speak is to intimate, and presuppose, a sense beyond oneself:

> The horizon of fellow mankind supposes the horizon of the world: it stands out and articulates its unity against the unity of the world. Of course, the world and fellow mankind here designate the all-inclusive, but infinitely open, unity of possible experiences and not this world right here, these fellow men right here, whose factuality for Husserl is never anything but a variable example. Consciousness of being-in-community in one and the same world establishes the possibility of a universal language. (Derrida 1989: 79)

If Derrida, following Husserl, argues that any truth requires some material articulation that, in turn, implies global recognition, we might also note that any recognized singularity or cultural particular also implies a generality of which it is a fragment. World literature, world music, fusion cuisine, foreign-language cinema, social media and protest movements such as Occupy Wall Street and #MeToo not only rely on the material substrata of exchange – from multinational corporations to the internet – but generate what we might think of as global digitality: some common horizon of culture that enables recognition. The sense of the globe is made possible by a single network of relations such that one can observe a Japanese tea ceremony, an Indigenous Australian corroboree and a concert performance of Berlioz's *Trojan*'s as expressions of culture, as articulations of who 'we' are. If YouTube and Penguin Classics give us a sense of the globe, they do so by way of a specific sense and mediation of 'culture'. The experience of difference is always relative and grounded on a capitalist axiomatic. Capitalist globalism, in which everything can be exchanged, is but one possible way in which an orientation towards other worlds becomes systemic and all-inclusive. In the twenty-first century, it is not only the rendering of everything into a commodity that marks global communication; communication itself – the flow of data – is inscribed into various forms of data analytics, which are in turn exchanged and commodified. Google's, Amazon's and Facebook's data-gathering ventures monetize our relations to commodities and to each other. What is being sold is part and parcel of the concretion of globalism: the relations we have to things are subsumed by a general and expansive system of data mining.

The very capacity to communicate with, view, read, visit, translate and listen to the globe as a whole is made possible by industries that gather data, capture and sell attention, and increasingly intensify the small differences of the private sphere for the sake of global profit. Jack Halberstam has recently commented on Facebook's 'custom' gender options, currently standing at fifty-eight if we include male and female (Halberstam 2018). The expansive and all-inclusive striving for recognition and difference is at the same time a taxonomy and contribution to the algorithms that now mediate our relations to ourselves and each other. In short, one might refuse the normality of white, Western heteronormativity, but in doing so you also contribute to the rendering axiomatic of minor differences. From the boom industries of Aboriginal Art and eco-friendly tourism to the pussy hats and gender non-conforming stickers and t-shirts you can buy on Amazon, it's apparent that difference sells, and that questioning difference sells even better. Globalism's exchange of ideas, images, tastes and affects opens the parochialism of the West to a constant stream of difference. And yet all these differences are contained within the sense of global unity and made possible by the *relative* system of global exchange. Globalism's differences are extensive rather than intensive; every difference adds to the richness of humankind (rather than disturbing the sense of 'the human'). Every Facebook gender category – you still have to choose one of the pre-listed terms – tracks and subsumes all variations.

What becomes apparent in the twenty-first century with global data gathering and surveillance becoming increasingly digitized and micropolitical – operating at ever finer and more nuanced levels of difference – is that the global subsumption of worlds is the condition for the possibility of recognizing difference. The relation between the local, singular and worldly versus the universal, abstract and global *is* a difference in kind, but it is a difference that we always encounter and assess through some system that renders all differences into variations of a global whole, as differences of degree.

In this respect, perhaps nothing is more appropriate than the term 'Anthropocene' to name the double-edged tendency of globalism: 'Anthropos' does not name the species as a stable entity within the world – some natural kind that we can gather together by way of an essence, common feature or family resemblance – but rather the historical event whereby the Earth appears as a living system, known as that which has been transformed by an agent whose effects are given *ex post facto*. The globe of the Anthropocene is given as an effect of a complex network of events, and in this respect it extends and intensifies the longer history of Western globalism whereby the globe is not the planet but the way in which the planet – as globe – is a figure deployed to imagine the unity of human existence. Globalism's 'anthropos' is *both* a geological event of naming, so that who 'we' are is not merely a futural ideal but also a retrospective recognition of what 'we' have done, *and* a performative articulation. The industries of globalism – from colonization to intensive agriculture – transform the planet and require that we think of a single humanity that now faces the problem of its possible non-being. Bruno Latour has argued that Koyré's modernity, which moved 'from the closed world to the infinite universe', needs to return to the Earth. Latour's insistence that we think of ourselves as 'Earthbound' is a rearticulation, rather than a rejection, of globalism; it generates a single humanity unified not so much by abstract truth as by a common experience of having nowhere else to go:

> Suddenly we have to pull back on our imaginary voyages; Galileo's expanding universe is as if suspended, its forward motion interrupted. Koyré's title

has to be read in the opposite direction from now on: 'Returning from the infinite universe to the closed and limited cosmos'. (Latour 2017: 80)

If globalism was once an orientation to an ideal of truth in general, it is now for Latour a recognition of the multiple modes of existence that compose a unity given only in its common boundedness to the Earth. The twenty-first century is poised between these two motions of globalism, at once a recognition of the distinct modes of existence that diversify humanity *and* the sense that this difference is what unites us all. One might think of the global moment of the Anthropocene as the recognition of what Derrida has referred to as the necessary impossibility of the 'end of man'. 'Man' is that being who cannot be fixed by any determined essence or predicate, and who constantly gives himself his own end, always oriented beyond mere existence (Derrida 1969). At the same time, every attempt to bring all essentialisms, parochialisms or chauvinisms to an end – ending any fixed concept of 'man' – reinstalls a proper 'end'. Man's proper being is that he has no fixed property. Any attempt to consider who we are beyond any particular culture is necessary if we are to confront the common predicament and responsibility of the present; and yet that very striving for global horizons – beyond 'man' – reinscribes a specific ideal of 'the human' (usually Western, capitalist, individualist and hyper-consuming) as a silent presupposed 'we'. I can only recognize others *as others* within some comparative sense of who 'we' are, all the while maintaining the ideal that 'we' are irreducible to our actual modes of difference. The global is always inscribed from within some worldly system and yet always transcending its own articulated limits; the recognition of the rich analogue difference of worlds requires the digital capacity to translate those differences into some global system of exchange.

What appears to be a perhaps simple opposition between the immediate and rich differences of worlds versus the disenchanted, systematized and digitalized globe is both important and impossible. In the twenty-first century there is perhaps more urgency than ever to think beyond global humanism, and to acknowledge those other modes of existence that bear the burden of globalism's harms. Without the sense that 'anthropos' does not include us all, there could be neither a future of imagining another mode of existence nor a just present. And yet any event of recognition tends to be recuperated cynically as a way in which 'anthropos' might live on. Indigenous ways of living are admired or co-opted as alternatives, but usually as alternatives *for us*. 'We' turn to non-Western ways of being – from Buddhism to yoga – to regain a more authentic and implicitly more properly human existence (Irigaray 2003; Wallace 2009). In this respect, it is perhaps best to think of global difference not so much as a single system, and especially not as the single system of human recognition or even capitalism, but instead as a dynamic relation between the analogue and the digital, between emerging new differences that are inevitably translated into differences for 'us', always with minor mutations of who 'we' take ourselves to be. There could not be the Western vogue for yoga, world music and the authentic without global systems of exchange; and yet every new fashion for the authentic both reinforces the sense of 'the human' while nevertheless introducing inflections. At what point, we might ask, do differences that are extensive – merely adding to the sense of human complexity – become intensive, introducing a disruption of global systems that would constitute a genuine event? To date, the history of globalism has been remarkably resilient in rendering differences into variations of 'the human'.

Posthumanism as Humanism

What becomes increasingly apparent in the twenty-first century is that the inescapable condition of globalism at a political and economic level is accompanied by a no less intractable humanism, even – and especially – when forms of post-humanism return us all to one interconnected mesh or web of life. Here, again, we confront globalism's double tendency: the attachment to individualism, interiority, privacy and one's own unique sexuality may be modern and Western, but attempts to think beyond the self and beyond the human frequently extend, rather than fracture, globalism's impossible humanism. As an example, we might think of the valiant attempt to refer to one's self as 'non-binary', which is in part a different way of thinking about what it means to be a subject outside the system of gender recognition; it's not just another category, but a marking that refuses a certain mode of category. That same inflection – or attempt to think difference *differently* and outside sexual difference – becomes one of Facebook's alternative gender categories.

It might appear that we have entered an age where planetary concerns supplant those of globalism. The fate of life as such might seem to be a more urgent problem than the different and uneven ways in which humans are able to live. Rather than an enclosed globalism, the twenty-first century might need to confront forces beyond political relations among humans. This outwards move towards the planetary and inhuman is both theoretical and political. In theory, we might think of the new materialisms, speculative realisms, vitalisms and naturalisms that situate the globe within a planetary system that cannot be contained within human agency. Forms of bio-deconstruction (Vitale 2018) and eco-deconstruction (Fritsch, Lynes and Wood 2018) locate the differential movement of inscriptive systems in life itself. What appears to be global and human – the opening of any particular identity to an expansive and open futurity – marks life as such. What makes any event possible is also what exposes that same event to dissolution and indifference. Globalism in its imperialist, Enlightenment and capitalist forms was the assumption that all human others were, deep down, just like me; but that global subsumption of alterity, or the digitalization of the whole, would also be ruptured in its repetitions, open to what Karen Barad has referred to as a 'queerness' in nature itself (Barad 2018), or what Francesco Vitale has referred to as bio-deconstruction such that 'life itself' already bears the tendency to open beyond itself. The globe unfolds from the figure of man, both conceptually and materially; 'man' is that being who is always more than his nature, and yet always capable of recognizing himself in all others. That same oscillation of expansion and contraction that typifies humanist globalism becomes more apparent in twenty-first-century movements beyond 'the human'. There can be no sense, desire, anticipation or imagination of the universal without the various technologies (from writing to the internet) that orient experience beyond itself to the worldwide web of life. The same can be said for the planetary, where various forms of attunement, connection and sympathy for inhuman life draw upon the very inscriptive and global systems they seek to surpass. Globalism may operate as a single system of exchange and equivalence, a loss of the planetary in its assumption of the Earth as so much matter for 'us', but the planetary – as Anthropocene discourse has made clear – is always given as that which expands or exists beyond the globe, and more often than not it is the globe for 'us' – the global 'we' that recognizes itself through these gestures of political and figural expansion.

Here, it is worth recalling the micropolitical nature of globalism. Our hands, eyes, gestures, ears and bodily habits are formed in a world of devices that produce a private survey of the whole. My smartphone alerts me to the weather, my heart rate, the stock market, what's trending on YouTube and (currently) the progress of a viral pandemic. The globe is embedded in what Bernard Stiegler has referred to as 'epiphylogenesis'; each human body emerges from, and is individuated through, technologies that open the body to the globe. I become who I am by way of the images I view, the music I hear, the screens I touch and the texts I read; my sense of 'the human' is at once composed from the habits of my body, and from the technologies that surround me that orient my attention to others. In the twenty-first century those others are both human and inhuman, both the globe of geopolitics and the planet of the Anthropocene. Globalism is not an ideology – an idea imposed from above – but a comportment or assemblage in which bodies, things, institutions, habits, desires and archives produce relations that demand and institute the constant exchange of forces. If globalism is in part an idea or way of seeing, it is nevertheless engendered through technics: from the writing systems that enabled the traditions of universal science, to the twenty-first-century social media technologies that orient our personal lives to those of a world of virtual others, every 'now' is already transported beyond itself. The systemic technologies that allow our bodies to evolve in tandem with the small screens and devices that orient us to the globe are also planetary. Stock markets, weather systems, viral pandemics, ecosystem crises and trending events are all relayed to each smartphone screen, adjusting for the algorithms of each user. Rather than see an exclusive disjunction between the global and the planetary, or between the human politics of who 'we' are and the environmental politics of life as such, deconstruction allows us to confront the ways in which the smallest of events is always already global *and* planetary, while the planetary, in turn, always opens from an articulated and individuated present.

The End of Globalism

Nowhere is this more clear than in contemporary post-apocalyptic culture, where scenes of the 'end of the world' are really scenes of the end of globalism: the world ends when urban hyper-consumption and mass media collapse, and 'we' become nothing more than bodies nomadically drifting in unmarked stateless spaces. The loss of the world is the loss of global 'man': the being who thought of himself as more than human because of the technologies that allowed him to survey the planet is now threatened with being a mere body in space. Globalism is, therefore, both an expansive force that enables events of difference – allowing any thought in the present to think beyond its locale – *and* at the same time a constant recuperation of events and inflections into a single system. As I have already suggested, one way to think about globalism as a movement is by way of Derrida's deconstruction: any seemingly present or local context always harbours the potential to be opened beyond itself. Yet every articulation of that universality is inscribed from within a locality. The globe would be both an idea or aspiration – a rupturing event – and a violent domestication, or the reduction of potentiality to the already conceived articulation of the whole. The globe and globalism are movements or tendencies that take the analogue difference of the world – each world with its own richness of meaning and sense – and render differences digital. That digitality or grammatization is not merely a possibility of language but can be thought of as marking and making possible life in general:

> No doubt life protects itself by repetition, trace, différance (deferral). But we must be wary of this formulation: there is no life present at first which would then come to protect, postpone, or reserve itself in différance. The latter constitutes the essence of life. Or rather: as différance is not an essence, as it is not anything, it is not life, if Being is determined as ousia, presence, essence/existence, substance or subject. Life must be thought of as trace before Being may be determined as presence. (Derrida 1978: 203)

Life might be thought of as proto-global, not an individual or being (or even matter) that must connect with a milieu or world, but rather a tendency for differing that generates a relative inside and outside, a self–other, world–globe oscillation. This differential operation, or what Stiegler has referred to as the *pharmakon*, takes on a specific modality in globalism in its human sense. Life in general might be thought of pharmacologically. Without exposure and negotiation of an outside there can be no survival, no individuation, but that very relation is also what places any life at risk. For Stiegler, all life individuates by way of articulation and relation to a differentiated milieu, but it is the external memory of human difference – in various archives – that creates the global potentiality of 'the human' (Stiegler 2020). I not only have a sense of who I am by way of the others in my milieu, but I am also able to read, hear, touch and view the present with the sense of humanity in general.

Without what Stiegler refers to as exo-somatization, or the formation of who we are through external technical systems, there would be no sense of the human, no 'we', no future, and certainly neither a sense of a global nor a planetary unity. If the technics that constitute human time and interiority are expansive, they also threaten to return us to a peculiarly human stupidity, where 'we' no longer invest in the various technologies that produce us and instead allow our desires and senses to be 'proletarianized':

> The Entropocene names the disruptive stage of the Anthropocene as it reaches its vital limits, because *reticulated fixed capital*, which is a global technical system, *functionally short-circuits every social system*, and, along with them, all the deliberative processes in which they consist, all the forms of knowledge on which they rest, and all the forms of care they cultivate (justice, law, education, culture, urbanity and so on). (Stiegler 2018: 141)

One might think of the ways in which social media, Wikipedia, crowd-sourcing and viral political memes create expansive global networks at the same time as they can operate with an almost numbing algorithmic repetitiveness. What opens the globe and the future is the possibility of the event – that the inscriptive systems that enable us to think and imagine the whole are never stable but mutate and create unthought-of figures and desires; at the same time, what makes an event possible is also what threatens to contain difference within a single system of inscription and exchange. This is how Stiegler marks the twin tendencies of globalism:

> One might be tempted to believe that the 'market', unfolding at a global level, and exceeding local modes of life as the consumerist 'way of life', therefore constitutes a new process of the individuation of reference. The 'market', however, cannot be a new process for the individuation of reference because, unlike trade, it is founded on generalized proletarianization. For this reason, it can replace those systems of the transindividuation of reference within which it develops only by short-circuiting these systems, rather than by re-individuating them in a new context. This leads to generalized disinvestment and renders impossible the curative adoption of contemporary *pharmaka*. (Stiegler 2015: 184)

Globalism is an ongoing movement of translation, towards one single system of exchange that is both economic and cultural; cultural differences are mediated as an expression of a single humanity, while those differences can then become commodities in global exchange. Nothing sells more than the culturally authentic artefact, while the very possibility of the desire for the singular and unique relies on the reductive and inclusive tendency to globalism. One seeks the singularly authentic in relation to what appears to be an increasingly global indifference. This is as evident in high art and museum culture's rebellion against commodification as it is in the high market value attached to the handcrafted, locally made and supposedly countercultural. The more the globe appears to be disenchanted and digitalized, the greater the sense and value of each unique world promises to be. Yet even though a highly localized and distinct world is different from the mass communication, commodification and translatability of the globe, the experience of a world *as a world* requires some system of articulation, relation and differentiation that enables global expansion.

As I have already suggested, one way to think about the difference between the world and the globe is by way of a distinction between the analogue and the digital. The more global we seek communication to be, the more homogenized must be the means of dissemination. The more reach we seek a message to have, the less it must say. Those who look in horror at the tourists taking selfies in front of the Mona Lisa in Paris's Louvre have to forget that their own reverence for the canvas is made possible by the replication and circulation of the original. In this respect, well before the rise of digital media explicitly, there is already something like the digital, or the tendency for any local mode of inscription to be circulated and repeated outside its context for the consumption of humanity in general. It may appear that increasing globalization and digitization are dehumanizing, but one can only think of one's self *as human*, as being different from the mere existence of non-human and worldless life, through some general concept and system of recognition. The word 'humanity' harbours and enables this double tendency of globalism. On the one hand, 'humanity' signifies the uniqueness of worlds. Humans are never a simple species but differentiate and mark themselves as distinct; humans are culturally rich and differentiated beings. Humans are, to follow Heidegger, beings towards-the-world, and not 'poor in world' like animals (Heidegger 1995: 195). On the other hand, this sense of humanity in general as always culturally distinct presupposes a global sense of who 'we' are in all our worldly distinction. It is this global imperative – that we consider ourselves as distinct beings within a grander and open totality – that also threatens to reduce 'humanity' to nothing more than a quantity in a system of exchange. As I have already argued, Stiegler, writing after Derrida and Heidegger, has argued that humanity and globalism need to be considered in terms of the *pharmakon*, as both enabling and disabling. Without the systems of writing, memory storage and communication that open the present, we would suffer the entropy of falling back into mere existence or stupidity; and yet those same global systems threaten to operate generically and entropically, repeating the same dull round of global indifference. The very movement that allows us to think of ourselves as human – the capacity to regard our own world as a distinct expression of humanity in general – also has a dehumanizing force.

This is why globalism is neither an ideology nor a system but a double tendency that at once enables the rich analogue differences of worlds *and* the empty quantitative differences of late capitalism. One can only experience the distinction of a world if each present is lived as one's own, as different from other possible worlds. Martin Heidegger argued that this sense of ownness and of one's world *as a world* becomes apparent when the flow of everyday existence is interrupted, and we experience the specific way in which our world is composed. Such a composition is inescapably *technical*; it is things (such as hammers, smartphones and books) that enable our sense of the singular (Heidegger 1962). Heidegger had already argued that the very possibility of individuated being-in-the-world was bound up with an inauthentic and technologically intensified worldlessness, where everything we experience is so much matter already determined as 'standing reserve'. For Heidegger the quantifying, homogenizing and 'humanist' reduction of the world to a general matter that is available for logical and mathematical calculation emerges from a more primordial 'technical' capacity, where we regard the beings of the world as if they were simply there and present at hand, and *not* as the outcome of a temporally complex process of appearing that is bound up with our distinct and meaningful world (Heidegger 1977). Meaning and non-meaning, or the sense of one's world versus the abstraction of the globe, are competing tendencies within the very possibility of being human. After Heidegger, Stiegler refers to the present moment as the Neganthropocene: humans become who they are – individuated – by working against the entropy of indifference. But to be human and negentropic one needs to read, write, listen and communicate, all the while risking that one becomes nothing more than a repetition of the already given signs and figures of globalized communication. To make sense of this one need only think of the market in cultural difference. A local and singular artwork that is intended only for the immediate experience of a small community must take on some shareable form, and once it does so it is therefore – in its distinction – available for reproduction and commodification. It might seem to be a travesty that one travels through European cities past small boutiques selling original Indigenous Australian artworks; but those very works can only forge and sustain their local worlds if they take on the material distinction that allows them to be abstracted, exported and exchanged. The world before globalism is always already on its way to becoming global. The McDonald's arches that seem to sully Paris's Champs-Élysées are an *intensification* of globalism, not its sudden eruption; the Champs-Élysées, after all, is itself already rendered iconic and distinct because of its repeatability.

Analogue, Digital and Arche-Digital

Capitalist globalism – along with dehumanization, mechanization, disenchantment and the rendering of the world into so much useable and disposable standing reserve – is enabled by the 'arche-digital'. Derrida had used the term 'arche-writing' to describe the way differential processes enable what appears as fully present life. Both writing and digitalization in their explicit forms offer ways of thinking about the potentiality common to inscriptive systems and life as such, especially life in an era of globalization. Rather than see twenty-first-century life as having fallen into digital quantification, abstraction and the reduction of the differences of worlds

Pharmakon, Difference and the Arche-Digital   171

to a single system of exchange, it is better to see globalism as the becoming explicit of a digitality that makes life possible.

There are several ways in which this proto- or 'arche-' digitality might be theorized. Following Derrida, one might see all life as being possible only because the experience of any lived present – the experience of any body or perception as one's own – relies upon a marking or tracing out of time and space. Before there is a meaningful world, or even the sense of one's own being, there is an inaugural *differentiation* which then makes possible the experience and sense of difference between one quality and another. It would follow, for Derrida, that any appeal to some pure experience or immediacy prior to a radical digitality would be 'metaphysical' – the positing of a ground or presence prior to difference, even if such a ground can be thought and achieved only through difference:

> To think the unique within the system, to inscribe it there, such is the gesture of the arche-writing: arche-violence, loss of the proper, of absolute proximity, of self-presence, in truth the loss of what has never taken place, of a self-presence which has never been given but only dreamed of and always already split, repeated, incapable of appearing to itself except in its own disappearance. (Derrida 1974: 112)

Derrida uses a series of terms – grammatization, writing, difference – all to signal a *technicity* that makes life possible. 'Techne', here, is a repeatability that is not life's own: owness, or the sense of presence, unity and identity, is possible through something like technics. The current era of technology, and especially the global experience of a single technical system of communication and exchange, is an extrapolation and intensification of the technicity that makes life possible. Language is a techne; gesture is a techne. The eye, hand, brain and nervous system are also technologies – systems that are repeated across time and across bodies, maintaining and mutating the differences of the past.

Globalism may be the ultimate technology – a system of exchange, communication, recognition and relation that transcends any living body – but it is the outcome of a history of technologies, where history *is* technology. The lived present, the supposedly pre-linguistic experience of the 'now', is the result of a marking out of time, the tracing of a 'before/after/here/there' that relies on an outside world of sensations that become increasingly differentiated through repetition. Seeing, thinking, having a body, desiring, speaking, feeling: all these are the result not only of evolving organic life's relation to an inorganic outside – the eye evolving in relation to light, the eye–hand–brain evolving in relation to increasingly complex artefacts – each body has its own composed relation to technical objects. This is what has led Stiegler to define human life as a form of epiphylogenesis that requires an organology. 'Epigenesis' is the inheritance of acquired characteristics; epiphylogenesis marks the way in which 'humanity' emerges in relation to its evolving technologies. The eyes and hands that dart quickly across smartphone screens; the attention spans that move effortlessly between social media, writing an essay and online shopping; the auditory capacity to screen out urban noise when one sleeps in a high-rise apartment: these bodily habits and affects have evolved as humans become increasingly attached to twenty-first-century technologies. Globalism would be one such technology, where we learn to read, imagine, see and hear the differences of other worlds through a history of media. We co-evolve with the objects we have created, one of those objects being the media-generated globe. As technical objects evolve, so do our own capacities. One might think, today, of the way in which our desires are made possible by digital technologies – from the songs and images that play through our personal devices, to the dating apps, and the possibilities of texting and social media that structure our inner life. To say that life becomes possible with technicity or digitality is to locate a tendency towards globalization in all organisms; a body can only take on distinction and form through some repetitive relation to an outside or milieu. Derrida (following Husserl) refers to this composition of the interior self-made possible by external traces as 'secondary retention'. The lived present not only retains the immediate past and an anticipated future but harbours and is haunted by the past sensations that compose the self. Consciousness, especially in its human form, is enriched by various external systems (such as language) that allow individuals to remember and imagine beyond their own time. That forging of interiority and the human, by way of a rupture of what one imagines as a living present, is also what threatens the imagined integrity of life:

> The arche-writing is the origin of morality as of immorality. The nonethical opening of ethics. A violent opening. As in the case of the vulgar concept of writing, the ethical instance of violence must be rigorously suspended in order to repeat the genealogy of morals. (Derrida 1974: 140)

For Derrida this dispersed and constantly differing nature of life – where there can be a 'now' only as marked or traced from a series of previously marked or traced differences – has two dimensions. We can only live and experience life through the difference that marks out each now as distinct. In addition, 'life itself' is differential or proto-digital. In the beginning is the mark, trace or event of differentiation, and because those events of differentiation are never gathered into a single perception, *all life* is subject to difference, never its author or master. Stiegler, taking up this conception of a fundamental difference or grammatization from which human life emerges, has argued for a more specific conception of the technics that mark human time. Stiegler insists upon *tertiary retention and memory*:

> Epiphylogenetic memory, essential to the living human being, is technics: inscribed in the non-living body. It is a break with the 'law of life' in that, considering the hermetic separation between somatic and germinal, the epigenetic experience of an animal is lost to the species when the animal dies, while in a life proceeding by means other than life, the being's experience, registered in the tool (in the object), becomes transmissible and cumulative: thus arises the possibility of a heritage. (Stiegler 2009: 4)

Our experience of inner time and who we are is structured by images, figures, sounds, concepts, narratives and rhythms stored outside the human body. Western music, for example, has a technical evolution that shapes the way our ears listen and enjoy tonality; if Westerners hear Chinese or Indonesian music, it may at first not sound like music at all. Of course, globalism and 'world music' have allowed our ears to hear music from systems other than that of Western tonality; synthesizers, MP3 players, streaming services and the algorithms that prompt us to listen to what everyone else is listening to shape the way we hear, and what we want to hear. The various tonal systems that once composed many worlds are increasingly subsumed by a single global system of music made possible by digital media in its specific sense. But music as such is possible only through a broader digitality. To sing, chant, hum, lament or cry is to take up the sounds of one's own body in relation to others and mark out a rhythm. Deleuze and Guattari refer to this as 'the refrain', and in so doing they take up a broader post-structuralist sense that what is experienced today as global digitality – a single system of communication and exchange – is an abstraction of a more complex difference that characterizes all life (Deleuze and Guattari 1983: 310).

What Stiegler, Derrida, and Deleuze and Guattari share – despite significant differences – is a commitment to an original 'technicity' of all life. Any seemingly individuated living being is the effect of dynamic relations that take the form of differential systems. What this means in terms of twenty-first-century globalism is that any appeal to a world or locality before globalism would be a difference of degree, not kind: there can only be the recognizable context of a meaningful niche if there is some marked out series of differences that can be repeated, exchanged and articulated in another context. From our sense of what counts as sensual touch (which follows every movie, television show, love poem and novel we've consumed) to the perception of our own body (shaped by modern medicine's drugs and prostheses), what makes each body unique is its relation to global differential systems.

The hand that touches, caresses, types, writes or gestures is already not simply one's own body part but is organized by way of a system of differences, delays, messages or *digits*. The most obvious case is using the hand to count or add, where the fingers become markers of generic units. But before this explicit digitalization or rendering generic of one's own body, even the body's relation to itself is already one of marked out, repeatable and recognizable differences. To take a phrase from Deleuze and Guattari, the body without organs is what is presupposed by a marked out and differentiated field but is never given as such. One might say that one's sense of 'the human' – of experiencing who I am as a fragment of humanity – in general occurs with this digitalization, rendering global or deterritorialization of one's own body. As Deleuze and Guattari argue, the hand is the deterritorialized paw, a body part that has now been located in a system that is not the body's own – writing, counting and typing (Deleuze and Guattari 1987: 61). If one becomes *more* human by recognizing one's own self as a subject who can recognize truth and the good *in general* (unlike mere life, which would simply react and consume), one also becomes *less* human in this process, becoming generic, no longer bound up with the richness and sense of one's world. If every human were actually operating with the same moral code, all agreeing and behaving in sync, we would have arrived at a clichéd dystopia, a mechanistic nightmare world of coded behaviour. We would have lost the rich diversity of worlds and fallen into homogeneity. This is the risk of global capitalism and neoliberalism, where becoming and relations all occur within the axiom of exchange. If, by contrast, the global remains as an ideal to come, as a deferred principle, it can be set against the actual and highly digitalized forms of global capital, where 'we' are all united and rendered indifferent by a single calculating system. One might therefore mark this difference of ideal globe versus globalism as a division between analogue and digital. As long as the ideal of global harmony remains virtual, it can possess the potentiality for nuance and infinitely rich distinctions; each world can imagine global unity in its own way. If globalism becomes actual, then relations among different worlds and persons become subject to some pre-given and determining system. This yields two conceptions of the global, one that is rich in worlds because the globe is ideal and deferred and one that is impoverished, inhuman and indifferent. There is a name for this problem, and it's the problem of capitalism where persons and things are determined in advance by a general axiom. The problem is also, even before explicit theories of capital, the problem of 'the human' and its relation to the digital.

To make sense of this and come to a conclusion, let's expand what we mean by 'digital' beyond today's digital culture and consider what makes digitality general and necessary. Derrida used terms such as writing or grammatization to refer to the way in which life as such, or experience as such, is already traced out, inscribed, systematized or – I would argue – digitalized. There are three ways one might think of this, perhaps beginning with that beast of the present, 'the human'. In his argument with Levinas, who insists that ethics begins with the singularity of the face, Derrida argues that I can only recognize *this* absolutely singular face here by way of some already given concept that enables recognition; difference begins with the indifference of some generality (Derrida 1978). If one were not to subject the face to some degree of generality, there would be no recognition at all, or what Derrida refers to as the worst violence. In a similar vein, Paul de Man argued that giving a face to something is necessarily defacement, rendering the complex temporality and difference into a stable and fixed figure (de Man 1979). De Man's way of thinking about this violence of inscription was through the language of rhetoric; materiality might be thought of as that which marks out the differences that *then* generate the sense or narrative of signs, and a world those signs represent. In the beginning is difference or differentiation that is not yet the difference between recognizable or given terms. It is the difference that makes sense but precedes sense. If Derrida referred to this as 'arche-writing', it was not only because recognizable systems of writing rely upon differences that have not yet been coded into meaningful units (so that we have 'writing' before we have writing), and not only because so much more than writing in the narrow sense is marked by this inscriptive event of differentiation (so that we can think of speech and gesture as a form of writing), but because writing in its narrow sense is clearly *material*. The illusion of speech and thought is that the self remains fully proximate or in touch with itself, as though one's thoughts were always one's own, as though speech were the simple extension and expression of one's present self. But this seeming proximity is nevertheless a difference; the very experience of one's own self *as a self* requires some distance and objectification that one might think of as digital in general. If one thinks of the digit in the sense that the touching, feeling, gesturing hand is *reduced* to digits that might count anything whatsoever, then one places the meaningful, proximate and owned distinctions of one's body *before* the abstraction of mere difference. Derrida's argument reverses this to argue that the experience of one's own hand, touching and feeling, depends upon what comes to be thought of as digitality. Before the hand can gesture or even touch, there must be a marked out distinction; to touch one's own self requires the unified sense of body part versus body – a marked out difference. If Derrida refers to arche-writing, one might think of this as 'arche-digitality': one's own hand can become a means of counting (digits) *after* the formation of the unity of ownness. One might even say that digitality or a simple 'this not that' is what precedes the sense of richer and more nuanced analogue differences. Further, what we think of as 'the human' is an effect of the digital. This is not only because our sense of who we are requires some concept of identity, or some sense that the world I have before me is the same world that others also perceive; it is also because 'the human' is a technical digital event. The 'human' is the effect of inhuman materiality or digitality. This can either be because one thinks of the inner flow of consciousness as requiring the perceived sensations that mark time (so that who we are relies on the connection of outside events), *or* – somewhat differently – because our perception of who we are is already stored and digitalized elsewhere.

Hyper-Globalism

Negotiating globalism cannot be by way of a difference between originary worlds and the technical abstraction of globalism, and even less can it be an ethics or politics of returning to a pre-systemic moment of rich life and difference. Instead, what is required is a hyper-globalism, and an orientation to the ever finer and more open differences that could be thought *beyond* the actual globe of human capital to the globe of ever-expanding difference. The globe is both a domestication of potentiality, drawing us back to some mythic unity that putatively underpins relations, *and* an idea of an expansive rupture of actual relations for differences not yet marked. Rather than lament a globalism that has disenchanted the world and dehumanized existence, it would be better to push globalism beyond the actual globe of already constituted systems and relations, and to push what counts as viable existence beyond the enchantments of humanism. The problem with globalism is not that it dehumanizes and is world-destructive, but that it maintains the myth of the world. There would be no market in the authentic and local, no fetishization of indigeneity (that goes hand in hand with its dehumanization) if there were not the global myth of a single humanity that begins with difference only to recognize itself in the family of 'man'. An ethical globalism would begin with an abandonment of the world. Imagine a globalism, a relation to others, that does not assume that being human amounts to being rich in world (possessing a sense of one's unique, meaningful potentialities). What if those who are currently without world or poor in world – those deemed to be less than human, merely existing, stateless – were to configure the future of the globe? Such a globalism would be out of this world, the end of the world.

CHAPTER 11

Time–Space Compression
The Long View
Mark Currie

In this chapter I am going to think about what has happened to the notion of time–space compression since its definitive formulation by David Harvey in 1990. The question is a way of developing a conviction that the core ideas of time–space compression have transformed into, or yielded to, something like a conception of uncertainty, by which I mean an account of globalization focussed on the universal opacity and unpredictability of the future. One way of looking at this is that, while the spatial meanings of compression have remained more or less stable, the 'time' of time–space compression seems increasingly to invoke uncertainty about the future as a key concept. It will be my argument here that these questions were always present in Harvey's concept but have acquired additional and perhaps urgent importance in a world that has convinced itself that the future is less knowable than it used to be. The switch from questions about dimensions in time and space to issues of unknowability and instability is not, I recognize, self-explanatory, and I intend first to establish the connection in Harvey's own concept. I also want to show that it holds some promise, in terms of analytical purchase, for those interested in the relation of globalization to writing, language and representation.

The double nucleus of Harvey's idea of time–space compression is spatial shrinkage and temporal simultaneity. The globe shrinks, psychologically, perspectivally, metaphorically, to the point that it feels like a village, and the compression also entails the elimination of delay: things that were perceived as separate in time come to seem co-present or simultaneous. The first time Harvey illustrates the shrinkage in *The Condition of Postmodernity* (1990), he does so in relation to speed, and specifically travel speed. Because in 1857 it took 252 days to reach Australia from England by sea, and in 2020 it takes around twenty-three hours by air, distance has transformed into proximity and presence. Travel speeds seem almost trivial, perhaps irrelevant, in comparison with the infinite speed of modern communications, represented by an infinitely small world by comparison with the contracted globes that Harvey describes, the world in which spatial dimensions have been abolished, and time has vanished. One task for this chapter has to be to think about what the infinite speed of digital technics has done to the concept of time–space compression, and to what extent it has been analysed.

Ideological Murk in the Terminology of Globalization

Harvey attaches some grand theories of capitalist growth and the stages of economic globalization to these core concepts, sometimes as a set of conditions that drive compression and sometimes as its social outcome. A key facet of compression, for example, is the homogenization of space, a commodification and indeed 'pulverization' of space that is an inherent effect of mapping, as well as an outcome of the logic of capital, which fragments space into 'freely alienable parcels of private property, to be bought and traded at will on the market' (Harvey 1990: 254). Homogenization is an obvious consequence, perhaps the central value, of Fordist or industrial capitalism, and this phase of globalization is therefore characterized by standardization. Both within Harvey's argument and in its immediate aftermath, there is often a sense that the current phase, perhaps the postmodern phase of globalization, is characterized by diversification. Understood as diversification, postmodern globalization must either displace Fordist standardization, reversing its homogenizations, or exist alongside it, as a paradox of diversification and standardization. *Diversification* is also difficult to pin down in globalization theory, and two very different political orientations can be heard in the word. On the one hand, there is a business meaning of diversification, whereby corporations turn to new products or services in order to reach new markets, as well as a financial meaning that refers to the spreading of investments to reduce risk. On the other hand, there is diversification as a kind of critique of capitalism: a counter-politics of the local that opposes the standardization of the world, celebrates cultural diversity or seeks to defend difference against the threat of homogeneity. Diversification is thus doubled: it is both the logic of capital in the new phase, and it is the resistance to capitalism's pressures towards global sameness. The doubling of diversification has produced a new crop of political confusions and paradoxes in which corporations can pursue strategies which both produce and disavow the values of global monoculture. Diversification, in this sense, is either a mere appearance of standardization, a new disguise for commercial global ambitions, or, as Michael Featherstone described it in 1993, a paradoxical product of standardization itself (Featherstone 1993: 169–70). A stark contemporary example is the marketing of the HSBC as 'The World's Local Bank', a brand idea launched in 2002, which is credited with an incremental growth of $70 billion in the six years before the crisis of 2008. This paradox of the global and the local was far from new in 2002, but this campaign was more explicit about the glocal marketing strategies that had been pursued by global corporations such as McDonald's and Starbucks since the 1980s. The paradox could be made explicit partly because, like diversification, it contained positive political meanings that derived from environmentalism about acting locally to protect the planet: the concept of the world's local bank seemed to offer the consumer a combination of the security of a global corporation and a sensitivity to local needs or different values. The HSBC brand idea illustrates the entanglement of standardization and diversification, but it also demonstrates the transition to a concept of globalization based in uncertainty. After the banking crisis in 2008 the campaign began to trade on slogans that emphasized the unforeseeability or instability of financial conditions: 'In the future, investors will need to be explorers' and 'Tomorrow will be nothing like today'. Here is the future imaged as the unknown, as the unforeseeable and as a break from the present. Financial corporations, for obvious reasons, are particularly worried about unexpected events and unforeseeable futures and are therefore concerned to address and appropriate these negative conditions for investors. Banks have actually affiliated themselves to the new condition of uncertainty and have sought to blend the unpredictable future of investments with connotations of the creative unpredictability of the corporation itself. We can see this in a campaign such as the one recently launched in the United Kingdom for First Direct Bank, which draws on these more positive meanings of unexpectedness with madcap slogans – 'We are the crab that walks forwards' – to support the campaign's overall self-depiction as 'The Unexpected Bank'. If the negation of sameness took an anti-global stance in the earlier HSBC campaign, we see here a temporalization of sameness as repetition, and the emergence of unpredictability as a positive value in the place of individuality or locality, as if one kind of unpredictability (creativity, novelty, surprise) might help the corporation to respond to the other (uncertainty). Faced with the opacity of the future, the banking corporation becomes a creative guide in adverse, because unknowable, conditions.

The HSBC campaign makes the direction of travel very clear for the global financial corporation which must own and sell the very things that threaten its global services, first in the form of diversity, then in the notion of uncertainty. Marketing has a long track record in this kind of inversion, just as it has a history of appropriating the vocabulary and the concepts of its own critique. The connection between diversification and uncertainty is in fact one of the central strands of the argument that Harvey makes about the stages of globalization that reflect the changing nature of capitalism. For Harvey, the postmodern phase of globalization should be understood as 'flexible accumulation', whereby global corporations challenge the rigidities of Fordist mass production and develop flexible labour processes, labour markets and products. This is, for Harvey, a 'new round of time–space compression', in which the time horizons of decisions and strategies are further reduced, and in which employers have pushed for more flexible work regimes and labour contracts that allow a corporation to respond to changing conditions, patterns of consumption and market volatility. Perhaps most significant, according to Harvey, is a general tendency away from regular employment towards part-time, temporary and sub-contracted work arrangements (Harvey 1990: 150). Flexible working practices appear as a mutually beneficial and positive development, but Harvey also describes a world-system of race and gender discrimination, the erosion of union power, the abolition of permanency, the revival of sweatshop labour systems, and flourishing familial and paternalistic organizations. Uncertainty, therefore, is both the business rationale (market uncertainty; adaptability) and the new condition of labour (precarity of employment); flexibility is thus Janus-faced in much the same way as the concept of diversity, as both the privilege and the despair of the new work arrangements.

Fredric Jameson analysed the positive and negative valences of this terminology as the difference between cultural contents and economic concepts – markedly different and yet co-present within the concept of globalization. If, on the one hand, you insist on the cultural contents of globalization, you will 'emerge slowly into a postmodern celebration of difference and differentiation: suddenly all the cultures around the world are placed in tolerant contact with each other in a kind of immense cultural pluralism that it would be very difficult not to welcome' (Jameson 2009). If, on the other hand, you think in economic terms, the picture turns darker: 'Now what comes to the fore is increasing identity (rather than difference): the rapid assimilation of hitherto autonomous national markets and productive zones into a single sphere, the disappearance of national subsistence (in food for example), the forced integration of countries all over the globe into precisely that new division of labour I mentioned before' (Jameson 2009: 437). Crucially, Jameson goes on to claim that the positive and negative valences can be transferred from the cultural to the economic realm, projecting a sinister vision of standardization onto the cultural domain, threatening cultural difference and diversity, or in reverse, projecting the joyous celebration of difference onto the economic sphere. For Jameson, this dialectic is primarily a description of the ideological murk that results when these two aspects of globalization fuse. Jameson's dialectic is primarily between standardization and diversification, but the murk thickens when it is recognized that the whole axis of resistance is projected onto corporate strategy and vice versa. Harvey, for example, writes from the position of Marxist critique, describing the regime of flexible accumulation as injustice and inequality on a new scale. And yet the core notions of flexibility, of the abolition of time and space, and the elimination of delay are easily overtaken by a kind of atmosphere of celebration, so that human beings begin to grasp capitalism, in Jameson's words, as 'their most fundamental human possibilities and the surest sources of their freedom' (1998: 438). The duality and the confusion of capitalist logic and its critique extends to the concept of postmodernism itself, which rebounds in a comparable way between the cultural logic of capitalism and the resistance to that logic. As a result, in the politics of globalization and in the academic analysis of culture, it can feel as if the left hand completes the work that the right hand has started.

Freedom and the Obfuscation of Inequality

The idea that uncertainty has arisen from the concept of time–space compression, in the form of an ever-worsening flexible accumulation, is plausible but incomplete. Uncertainty and precarity offer a cultural and economic explanation for something that is also emergent in philosophical and scientific contexts. It might be more accurate to say that, in economics, the predictive sciences and philosophy, the concept of uncertainty has an established place, but that it has emerged and developed a new prominence and urgency in the new millennium. In philosophy, the question of uncertainty traditionally resided in 'the problem of future contingents', the problem of attaching truth-values to statements about the future, and in the importance that the mathematics of probability holds for analytical philosophy of the twentieth century. Questions about contingency and chance have irrupted in all areas of philosophy partly as a result of the rise of event philosophy, which seeks to explain change through the analysis of unforeseeable novelty or invisible arrivals in what was assumed to be a stable situation. We see, for example, in the work of Alain Badiou or Quentin Meillassoux, a preoccupation with dice as the ultimate symbol of unknowability, and indeed, in Meillassoux, with a kind of advent not on our list of possibilities for the outcome of a roll of the dice (Badiou 2011; Meillassoux 2008, 2011). We see in Badiou an argument that existing situations can be blown apart by some immanent rupture, driven by chance alone, and understood only later. These are quite different accounts of uncertainty from the economic and cultural logics set out by Harvey and Jameson in the social theory of postmodernity. They are less obviously intentionalist or conspiratorial, and more focussed on the philosophy of contingency and necessity. The same point can be made about the rise of uncertainty in theoretical physics, which has reconciled itself in a number of ways to the unpredictable and the unknowable: that uncertainty is not motivated, strategic or even human, but a category that comes to the fore as a result of accurate scientific prediction: randomness. How do these philosophical and scientific conceptions of the unforeseeable interact with social arguments about the opacity of the future? One answer is that they lend the notion of economically generated uncertainty a metaphysical or scientific credibility and therefore camouflage human interests at work in the new social conditions. It could be argued, conversely, that the abstract or mathematical conceptions of randomness acquire a social importance, as the logical description of an uncertainty that otherwise remains enigmatic within the crises of capitalism. What is clear is that, in this expanded sense, the phenomenon of uncertainty has a temporal logic that departs from the concept of global simultaneity and turns instead towards the relation of the present to the future. Though it was present in Harvey's own argument, the issue of uncertainty in social theory has been reinterpreted and amplified by this new prominence in philosophy. It is also clear that this temporality, the new time structure that turns away from simultaneity towards a question about what is to come, emerges in philosophy for quite literary reasons. For Badiou and Meillassoux, for example, Mallarmé's 'A Roll of the Dice' provides an account of the event, of chance and the unforeseeable arrival that explains and exceeds the more formal descriptions that they develop from set theory and symbolic logic (Badiou 2011; Meillassoux 2012). More generally, the time structures associated with uncertainty, as I shall argue below, find their most complex articulations in literary, and particularly narrative, contexts to such an extent that literature might be thought of as an analytical resource for the concept of uncertainty that cooperates with, and possibly outstrips, the cultural theory of globalization.

Whatever new status the issue of uncertainty has acquired, Harvey's concept of time–space compression, in *The Condition of Postmodernity* and since, takes a longer view. In *The Enigma of Capital and the Crises of Capitalism*, for example, there is a strong sense of an ongoing conjunction between globalization and precarity, which was visible in 1848, when Marx and Engels wrote in *The Communist Manifesto*:

> All old-established national industries have been destroyed or are daily being destroyed. They are dislodged by new industries, whose introduction becomes a life and death question for all civilised nations, by industries that no longer work up indigenous raw material, but raw material drawn up from the remotest zones; industries whose products are consumed not only at home, but in every quarter of the globe. In the place of old wants, satisfied by the productions of the country, we find new wants, requiring for their satisfaction the products of distant lands and climes. In place of the old local and national seclusion and self-sufficiency, we have intercourse in every direction, universal interdependence of nations. (Marx and Engels 2018: 5)

In other words, the basic conjunction between the uncertainties produced when national self-sufficiency and local exclusions are exposed to the forces of globalization were already established before the period of Fordist standardization; the thing that Harvey calls flexible accumulation in 1990 is a worsening and deepening of more basic threats to the long-established national industries, with their stable working patterns and their secure and predictable futures.

The idea that globalization produces uncertainty is therefore nothing new. But the concept of globalization as uncertainty, rather than as spatial and temporal contraction, is a contemporary phenomenon that Harvey himself began to address, from 2005 onwards, under the heading of *neoliberalism*. Despite Harvey's efforts to define and historicize the concept, this is a word that has only deepened the confusion, in academic humanities departments, between cultural contents and economic concepts. Harvey is perhaps the only theorist of neoliberalism to adequately emphasize that the freedom implied in its central morpheme is an equivocation. It aims to present the market freedom of monetarist policy as freedom in general, so that the good freedoms of free speech, civic rights, freedom from poverty and oppression can gather under the banner of the market economy, which is then universalized into what Harvey calls the phase of neoliberal globalization. Quoting Karl Polanyi, he summarizes the argument about freedom as follows:

> The idea of freedom 'thus degenerates into a mere advocacy of free enterprise', which means 'the fullness of freedom for those whose income, leisure

and security need no enhancing, and a mere pittance of freedom for the people, who may in vain attempt to make use of their democratic rights to gain shelter from the power of the owners of property. (Harvey 2005: 37)

Under the concept of neoliberalism, the ideological murk thickens again as a result of the positive and negative valences of freedom and their conflation in the notion of the free market. The liberal content of neoliberalism therefore turns out to be the extent to which freedom can be deployed as a concept that borrows the positive valences of freedom to vote, speak or choose, claims that the free market is their very emblem, and so liberalizes and universalizes the core of neoconservatism. According to this account, the new phase of globalization is a maximal uncertainty and subjection presenting itself in economic policy as a freedom from regulation, and more generally as a synecdoche for freedom itself.

The word neoliberalism is another instance of the left hand completing the work that the right hand has begun, because liberalism is opposed as two completely different entities: as the freedom of market economies and, particularly in the United States, as an unacceptable leftist attitude. It must be discarded because it means nothing and everything, positive and negative, and because it conflates liberal values and conservative economic policies. It is, however, useful to think about the murk that produced it and focus on some of the ways that these issues might actually constitute the legacy of time–space compression. It is clear that the complicities and overlaps that I have been tracing from diversification and standardization, through the concept of postmodernity, and into the terminology of neoliberalism, turn into one of Harvey's own central concerns, but they have also been seen as the most pressing analytical project for others concerned with the terminological valences of diversification, flexibility and freedom. In 'The Global Situation' (2000), Anna Tsing focussed this question on the 'charisma' that globalization holds for social scientists, so that, despite its dark side, it offers images of interconnectedness, travel and transformation. The response to this charisma, she argues, is a kind of endorsement: that anthropologists, and social scientists more generally, engage in a general appreciation of values such as interconnection, circulation and exchange. For Tsing, Harvey's time–space compression is both an aspect of the economics of globalization and the basis for this endorsement in fields such as anthropology and sociology, resulting in a strange kind of complicity between capitalist expansion and social-scientific analysis. In other words, like most of the words associated with globalization, the concept of time–space compression is itself doubled between light and dark meanings. Tsing is particularly interested in the metaphor of *circulation*, and the way that it has taken the place of *penetration* in the rhetoric of globalization. Penetration was part of the Marxist view of world-systems, and if it evokes a kind of rape, circulation 'calls forth images of the healthy flow of blood in the body and the stimulating, evenhanded exchange of the marketplace' (Tsing 2011: 54). The new word is one such endorsement, used just as much by leftist social commentators as capitalist ideologues: 'Circulation is thus tapped for the endorsement of multicultural enrichment, freedom, mobility, communication and creative hybridity. But it is therefore also one of many recent endorsements that participate in the 'process for making the future partake in the obfuscations of inequality for which market models are known' (Tsing 2011: 54).

The emphasis on the future is interesting in Tsing's account of the complicities between money and social-scientific commentary. She sees an inherent futurism in globalization theory that distributes another kind of charisma among social scientists. Globalization is 'a crystal ball that promises to tell us of an almost-but-not-quite-there globality'. The picture we have of experts, such as geographers and anthropologists, is transformed by this future orientation from collectors of ancient survivals into new opportunities to predict, expect and speculate; it casts social scientists as guides in 'an anxious rush into the future' (Tsing 2011: 52). The future orientation of this commentary is founded on an assumption of newness which functions both as a form of analysis of ways in which the present breaks from the past, but also as the basis for prospect, sometimes to the point of discrediting suggestions that interconnectedness might also be old. This analysis, which draws out so many of the complicities and conflations of the commentator with the capitalist, also expresses discomfort with the reception of Harvey's most epochal claims around time–space compression and flexible accumulation. For Tsing, time–space compression has been taken by anthropologists and geographers as too singular a source of evidence of the new epoch – a source which has been reduced and over-factualized as the basis for this new, charismatic and anxious, future-gazing. One such reduction is a tendency to just ignore the central thesis of Harvey's *The Condition of Postmodernity*, which Tsing expresses as follows:

> [W]hen I return to Harvey's book, it seems to me that the central argument is that the 'cultural aesthetic' of postmodernism is related to the economic logic of flexible accumulation. The first section of the book reviews modernism and postmodernism as trends in the arts and letters, including architecture and philosophy. This is 'capital C' culture: a genealogy of great men and their ideas. The second section of the book turns to the economic 'regimes of accumulation' of Fordism and post-Fordist 'flexible

accumulation'. The book's original idea is to juxtapose these two bodies of literature, and to argue that postmodernism mirrors post-Fordism. It takes a certain amount of economic determinism to make this argument work, in which Culture acts as a mirror of economic realities ... But in this gap, space and time come in. For Harvey, the 'experience' of space and time mediates between Culture and the (nonculturally organized) economy. (Tsing 2011: 56)

I am not sure that this is the original idea of the book, and even less sure that the proposition that postmodernism mirrors post-Fordism would count as an original idea. It might be true to say that social commentators have shown less interest in the parts of this argument that relate to cultural representations than those that sketch the logic of capital in the new epoch. I think it is difficult to claim that Harvey's argument rests on an economic determinism, or that its central claim is that cultural representations mirror or reflect economic conditions. But the underlying question is a good one: what is the relation between time–space compression as an epochal concept and the cultural artefacts of that epoch? Tsing suggests that the answer lies in the content of representations which mirror economic conditions, though she does also turn, at the end of the citation above, to a more complicated notion to be found in Harvey, that the experience of time and space mediates between culture and the economy. I want to argue now that the notion of mediation contradicts the idea of reflecting or mirroring, and that the classical account of mimesis needs to yield to something more like this more complex notion of mediation for the relation of culture and economic conditions to make sense.

Epochal Temporalities for the Digital Age

Epochal temporality is a phrase that describes the strand of Harvey's argument that claims to identify a distinct, contemporary experience of time. Many accounts of epochal temporality in the Fordist phase of globalization emphasized speed, acceleration or some kind of increased perception of simultaneity. I have already suggested that this feeling of compression or simultaneity acquires a new importance after the arrival of the internet, and that Harvey's diagram can't represent the infinite contraction that results from digital speed. But what does digital communication in fact do to the concept of time–space compression, and what kind of epochal temporality has to be proposed as a result? Epochal temporality has to be thought of as a doubly temporal concept. It is a temporal concept, in the first place, because it periodizes, and, in the second place, because it proposes that the periodization is based in an experience of time. One of the striking things about Harvey's concept is that it contained within it the economic argument that helps us to understand what it is that arrived along with the internet by way of a new experience of time. This is not only because the internet became the technological medium in which flexible accumulation flourished, but because the uncertainty that Harvey described as an inherent part of the new regime seemed to find its best emblem in the ever-increasing speed at which new technologies arrived from the future. The speed of emergence of world-changing technologies seemed to install emergence itself as the new epochal experience of time, so that the digital present has a more immediate obsolescence than any previous material commodity. We can see this idea of emergence in the vocabularies that have taken hold in cultural commentary, social theory and philosophy, in words that name new and unexpected arrivals: invention, inventiveness, advent, arrivant, event, eruption, irruption, emergence, singularity, unforeseeability, unpredictability, uncertainty, the untimely and the messianic. Some of these were particularly visible in the later stages of deconstruction, while others belonged to the new event philosophy that influenced thinking about change across many disciplines. These words, like the concept of epochal temporality, have a doubleness about them: they are emergent words that name emergence, and they point to the idea that the contemporary moment might be understood as an obsession in the present with a future that cannot be foreseen. Not all, but many of the temporal concepts that travelled alongside Harvey's account of time were linked to this sense of infinite speed in digital communications. Jacques Derrida and Bernard Stiegler, in particular, have linked the notion of a globalized epochal temporality specifically to digital cultures: the phenomenon that Derrida describes as *archive fever* (Derrida 1998), and the question that Stiegler discusses as the delegation of human memory to machines (Stiegler 2010). For Derrida, archive fever is a kind of psychic illness that frantically archives and preserves everything that happens for the future. We might once have been able to think that events and their representations were sequenced, that an event happens first and is represented later, or that a happening and its archivization were strung out in time. For Derrida, the temporality is backwards, in the sense that the archive produces the event that it purports to record. Though Derrida says this in the context of news media, the idea of an event which would not happen but for the fact that it is represented in an archive is immediately recognizable to any user of social media. For both Derrida and Stiegler, this is a basic psychic condition for all memory, but it has an epochal dimension because the technology of the memory device and the internet as a representational medium so significantly encourage and universalize an experience of the present as the object of a future memory. Technology makes the archiving of everything feverish, by turning envisaged memories into the cause of what happens in the present.

In the work of Stiegler, we find perhaps the most interesting attempt to link our Greek inheritance on the subject of memory with contemporary conditions. In *The Fault of Epimetheus* Stiegler develops the notion of *retentional finitude* as the foundational fact about memory – that there are limits to what can be retained in memory, and that we therefore turn to memory machines for help. Human memory is, according to Stiegler, dependent on these hypomnesic devices which externalize and preserve what cannot be retained in interior subjectivity. We increasingly delegate cognitive functions to these devices, and none more significant than the function of remembering the past, increasingly because the externalization of memory is now assisted by memory devices produced and consumed on an industrial scale, in the sense that we have memory in our phones and our laptops, our tablets and our computers, storing on the outside what no longer needs to be stored inside the mind. But this externalization of memory, Stiegler argues, even if it is flourishing with technics, is primordial and originary. Memory has always been externalized, most obviously by writing, or *grammatization*. Memory does not occur first in the interior of the subject before being subsequently farmed out or delegated. Like Derrida's arguments about the presumed externality of writing, Stiegler's account gives the exteriorization a kind of primacy. For Derrida there is a conceptual primordiality, for example, in the exteriority of writing, in the sense that the external form of language as writing constitutes a kind of foundational possibility for what we think of as its inside. This conceptual primordiality might be part of the argument in *Technics and Time*, but for Stiegler there is also a more literal, historical primordiality that underpins this relation between memory and its exteriorization. This tendency to complicate the relationship between what happens and what is recorded, the disruption of sequence in the conceptualization of events and their representations, is one of the reasons that it is difficult to defend Tsing's argument that the core claim of Harvey's book is that postmodernism mirrors post-Fordism: in this kind of thinking about technics, the classical sequence of mimesis, in which an action happens and then it is represented or imitated, is reversed.

Stiegler wants to show that, though we might live in an epoch of memory devices, the externalization of memory was always there in every period of history, and this is partly because it was always the case that we cannot remember everything – that retentional finitude always was our basic condition, and so the requirement for memory to exteriorize itself was always there. This retentional finitude that was always already there is above all a *forgetting*, and Steigler's scheme therefore gives a foundational importance to forgetting in the history of memory. Originary exteriorization is primordial forgetting, and forgetting as exteriorization was there from the beginning of history. Forgetting is the fault of Epimetheus, the forgotten brother of Prometheus, a figure who features in Plato's account of Prometheus in Protagoras, but whose story since then has not been retold. Epimetheus is the forgotten, but he is also the figure of forgetting, because in the story told by Plato, it was his responsibility to distribute attributes to the creatures of the earth, but in carrying this out, Epimetheus forgot to give anything to humans. He gave all the available attributes to the animals and had nothing left. It was this, in Plato's account, that forced Prometheus to steal fire and the arts from Hephaestus and Athena. The figure of Prometheus, for Stiegler, makes no sense by itself. It is only consistent through its doubling with Epimetheus:

> The forgotten of metaphysics. The forgotten of thought. And the forgotten of forgetting when thought thinks itself as forgetting. Whenever Prometheus is spoken of, this figure of forgetting is forgotten, which, like the truth of forgetting, always arrives too late: Epimetheus. (Stiegler 1998: 186)

This, too, is an important foundational characteristic of Epimetheus as the hidden structural double of Prometheus: he is the forgotten, the figure of forgetting, and he stands for delay. These meanings are there in the Greek roots of their names, since *prometheia* means *foresight*, where *epimetheia* is the kind of comprehension that comes afterwards, after a delay. The doubling of Prometheus and Epimetheus is partly a doubling of remembering and forgetting, but it is also a dynamic between retrospection and anticipation, foresight and comprehension, or knowledge in advance and knowledge after a delay.

Stiegler is one of many cultural commentators to focus an account of the present historical epoch on the overcoming or elimination of delay. For Stiegler, delay is eliminated not just as a function of an accelerated cultural tempo, or of the time–space compression that results from speed. It is a function of coverage. If retentional finitude means that we do not remember everything, there must be selection, or the hierarchization of events that is implied by coverage, and significantly, the logic of hierachized coverage is at odds with the temporality of writing and, more specifically, of narrative:

> This new time betokens an exit from the properly historical epoch, insofar as the latter is defined by an essentially deferred time – that is, by a constitutive opposition between the narrative and that which is narrated ... (current events have an already historical feel as immediately out of the past i.e., both present and past) ... In writing, the very medium of history, an event typically precedes its seizure, and the latter precedes its reception or reading. This configures the presentation of the past as the retroactivity of an originary default, of a belatedness of the narrative and of the reception of the event with respect to the time of the event, which nevertheless constitutes itself only in this delayed action. The time of relation, of 'narrative', is always belated with respect to what is narrated, is always cited in being recited. (Stiegler 2010: 80)

In writing, the seizure of an event is separated from its happening by an interval, just as, in Aristotle's account of memory, it was temporal distance that guaranteed the distinction between memory and imagination, where memory traverses the interval between an event and its recollection. In Stiegler's account of hierarchized coverage, meanwhile, the process that he calls the 'daily and industrial fabrication of time' does not merely record what happens: 'rather what happens happens only in not being everything – by being hierarchized coverage' (Stiegler 2010: : 78). With the elimination of delay between an event and its exteriorization or seizure, the event is produced more than it is represented, and therefore invented as much as it is recalled.

In Stiegler's account of technics, a different kind of time compression comes into view, and a different conception of uncertainty emerges from it. For Harvey, we can see the elimination of delay as a condition in which everything arrives sooner than it used to, to the point of instantaneity, but in Stiegler there is an argument that the 'new time' betokens an abolition of any interval at all between an event and its coverage, and an exit from an epoch of belatedness. The language here can feel overblown, but there is an interesting addition in this kind of thinking to the idea of time compression which links technology to the elimination of delay. It also, like Harvey's concept, has an integral link to uncertainty, in Stiegler's case in the form of a primordial forgetting: that forgetting is not something that we do afterwards but in advance, according to hierarchies that determine in advance what will receive 'coverage'. Primordial forgetting is therefore prospective, and by extension globalization is a kind of incomplete representation: just as we cannot remember everything, so too we cannot represent everything, and much of what will happen is therefore forgotten in advance. There is some family resemblance between this idea and some of the influential accounts of globalization that foregrounded ideas such as totalization. Jameson argued in 1990, for example, that 'a significant structural element of the economic system is now located elsewhere, beyond the metropolis, outside of the daily life and existential experience of the home country' (Jameson 1990: 50–1). As a result, the totality of the economic system cannot be grasped and can only be apprehended in fragments: 'To put it in other words, this last – daily life and existential experience in the metropolis – which is necessarily the very content of the national literature itself – can now no longer be grasped immanently; it no longer has its meaning, its deeper reason for being, in itself' (1990: 51). Ideas such as this, about totalization, were spatial orientations that accentuated the ungraspable totality of the globe from any position within the world-system. We might see Stiegler's argument as the complement to this, in the sense that it involves a temporalization of the idea of partiality, and more specifically one that gives the absent, ungraspable content of representation a future orientation.

Jameson's idea of the ungraspable totality is developed in relation to modernist literature of the city. It aims to suggest that the structure of imperialism makes its mark on 'the inner forms and structures of that new mutation in literary and artistic language to which the term modernism is loosely applied' (1990: 44). There is, in other words, something structural that mediates between economic and political conditions on the one hand and cultural productions on the other which goes beyond the idea of mere reflection or mirroring at the level of content. What might we say about the inner forms and structures of contemporary fiction that would eschew in a comparable way the idea that fictional content mirrors post-Fordist conditions? Perhaps that Harvey's concept has been wrongly thought of as a resource for the thematic paraphrase or content description of contemporary narrative fictions. The legacy of time–space compression in literary studies, and other areas of the humanities and social sciences concerned with representations, would lie in inner temporal form, variants in temporal structure, conflations of the past and future which produce as much as they reflect, the elimination of delay. I said above that Stiegler characterizes narrative itself as a form of belatedness. Narrative theory has many established ways of thinking about the interval between the time of an event and the time of its capture, which borrow broadly from the notion of narrative tense, or the relation between the time of an utterance and the time to which it refers. Stiegler's argument is not only that narrative is, in its default settings, a recapitulation of past events, but that there is a further interval between the capture of events and their reception, and that in this chronic belatedness, narrative belongs to a bygone epoch. We can think about the way that contemporary representations often eliminate both of these intervals in, for example, the live representation of news events. But is there something in the inner temporal form of contemporary fiction that might also aspire to the elimination of delay? A hasty answer might be the rise of present-tense narrative verbs, which purport to eliminate the interval between the time of a narrative utterance and the time of events. But any feeling of immediacy, contingency or presence achieved by the present tense is always negated by writing – by the already written character of represented events. The feeling of immediacy in present-tense written narration is no greater or lesser than for the quasi-present of past-tense narration, where completed events are also present to us *as if* they were happening live. There may have been an increased use, in the novel, and in many non-fictional discourses such as television history, of present-tense narration, but this increase is just one sign of a broader kind of anachrony in the inner form of the novel.

The category of tense, and what Genette called anachrony, have been at the centre of time and the interpretation of fiction. Theories of narrative have focussed on a kind of disjunction between narrative tense and temporal reference – the kind of disjunction most easily illustrated by novels written in the present tense. In *Time and Narrative*, for example, Paul Ricoeur finds a version of this argument in Harald Weinrich's book *Tempus – Besprochene und erzählte Welt* (1964), a book about tenses in narrative discourse which argues for a complete break between the tense of narrative verbs and the time to which they refer. Ricoeur is less willing to accept this complete break between tense and time and proposes instead a basic 'semantic kinship' between time and verb tenses which cannot be easily escaped. For Ricoeur there is something inescapably mimetic about this relation of time and tense. Against Weinrich's argument that the use of the preterite tense does not mark any real pastness of the past, but 'signals only the entry into narrative', Ricoeur asks:

> But can we conclude from this that the signal marking entry into narrative has no connection whatsoever with the expression of the past as such? Weinrich does not, in fact, deny that in another communication situation these tenses express the past. Are these two linguistic facts completely unrelated? Can we not recognize, despite the caesura, a certain filiation that would be that of the *as if*? (Ricoeur 1985: 74)

This model of a 'certain filiation' between tense and time is the basis of the temporal *as if*, which posits both a similarity and a difference, a connection and a disjunction, between the real and the narrative past: some metaphorical relation that helps us to explain that narrative tenses are also those of memory, even if, in the case of narrative, this past is a quasi-past. In other words, there is a certain filiation and a disjunction between tense and temporal reference that allows past, present and future to mingle and merge in the hypothetical mode of the *as if*. For Ricoeur, as for Stiegler, the temporal *as if* entails an alteration to the classical sequence of mimesis which would challenge Tsing's account of the core claim of Harvey's *The Condition of Postmodernity*: that postmodernism mirrors post-Fordism. For Ricoeur, mimesis is a circle in which time is not simply reflected in narrative but also reconfigured by it, in such a way that would cast the cultural products of postmodernism as co-producers rather than reflections of the compression of time. We shouldn't therefore expect standardization, diversification, global shrinkage, acceleration, the elimination of delay and uncertainty to be represented as topics in literature, or conclude that the novel's represented contents have changed in response to the precarity that emerged from time–space compression. We might be justified in claiming instead that transformations in the temporal structures of narrative, particularly variations of Genette's categories of order, duration and frequency, which Ricoeur viewed as novelistic resources for the fictional inquiry into internal time consciousness, might also be thought of as participants in the process of time–space compression. Gary Saul Morson views this participation as an affirmation of uncertainty which inhabits the inner form of narrative retrospection:

> To understand one's situation, it is often helpful to imagine the rest of life *as if* it were an epilogue. But it is usually dangerous to forget that such a projection is only one of many possibilities, and that every moment will have options, accidents and sideshadows. The straight line is the rare exception. The laughable results of past predictions and of superseded futurologies should warn us, more often than they do, that contingency reigns. (Morson 1994: 197; his italics)

The dynamic here between the certainty of narrative retrospect and the uncertainty of actual prospect offers a model for Ricoeur's conception of the hermeneutic circle between time and narrative, not as an expertise in internal time consciousness, but as a relation of the internal form of the novel to an ungraspable external reality.

CHAPTER 12

The Matter of Blackness in World Literature

Joseph H. Jackson

In his history of Blackness, *A Critique of Black Reason* (2017), Achille Mbembe entitles his introduction 'The Becoming Black of the World'. This radical and provocative gesture identifies the 'generalization' of Blackness, a 'new fungibility', a 'solubility', 'institutionalized and expanded to the entire planet' (Mbembe 2017: 5–6), the transformation of humanity under globalization into subjects characterized by dispossession of self-determination and of futurity – a global condition for those disinherited from the world. Such a generalization does not deny the specificity and variability of Black experience past and present but recognizes the way that Black history is the persistent shadow of global modernity, now cast over 'all of subaltern humanity' (4). Mbembe's observation echoes an earlier 'worlded' interrogation of Black expressive culture: Paul Gilroy's *The Black Atlantic* (1993). Like *A Critique of Black Reason, The Black Atlantic* argued that, far from being marginal to modernity and its cultural registration, Black history was absolutely central; that it forced a reconceptualization of the emergence of the subjectivities and representational practices attached to modernism and postmodernism. In Gilroy's analysis, 'the supposed novelty of the postmodern evaporates when it is viewed in the unforgiving historical light of the brutal encounters between Europeans and those they conquered, slaughtered, and enslaved' (Gilroy 1993: 44). Both *A Critique of Black Reason* and *The Black Atlantic*, emerging respectively from a francophone and anglophone tradition of Black critique, identify that Blackness needs to be understood in 'worlded' terms, with transnational dimensions and local inscriptions, and an emphasis on the interrelatedness of the world – its 'systematic' character. Moreover, each recognizes that in its engagement with imperialism, racialization and the radical redefinition of subjectivity effected by capitalist modernity, Black writing pre-emptively grasps the spirit of globalization.

Before Franco Moretti's 'Conjectures on World Literature' (2000) provided the impetus for a new formalization of world literature as a critical object, *The Black Atlantic* had already provided a model of systemic critique that eschewed national traditions in favour of a transnational understanding of literary-cultural production enmeshed with that modernity. Gilroy's heuristic of the Black Atlantic world offered a counter-narrative of world history. Its unifying principle was a geographically distributed but shared experience of racialization, rather than a parochial 'cultural nationalism', substantially because '[n]either political nor economic structures of domination are still simply co-extensive with national borders' (7). Key to Gilroy's analysis is an attempt to 're-world' the hegemony of African-American scholarship on Blackness, via thinkers that 'renounce the easy claims of African-American exceptionalism in favour of a global, coalitional politics' (4). References to a global politics rooted in representation, and the cultural registration of transnational 'structures of domination', situates *The Black Atlantic* firmly in the terrain of world literary *systems* – as prototypical of more explicit attempts, such as those of the Warwick Research Collective, to conceive of world literature as a singular system characterized by inequality, and as a discipline dedicated to elaborating the 'literary-cultural implications of combined and uneven development' (WReC 2015: 6). Blackness itself resembles this topography: one, in the respect that it shares a common basis in European colonialism and transatlantic slavery, but unevenly, in that it is context-specific and immensely mutable, prohibiting any 'total' comprehension.

It makes sense for Gilroy to speak of a Black Atlantic *world*, because the Black Atlantic not only gave rise to globally distributed forms of Blackness through diaspora and cultural exportation but was itself the crucible of a 'globalized' world economic system. Mbembe conceives of three historical moments or phases which define the global character of Blackness and its integral part in globalization. The first is proto-globalization. Echoing Marx's observation that 'the turning of Africa into a warren for the commercial hunting of black-skins … signalised the rosy dawn of the era of capitalist production' (Marx 1887: 533), he points to the 'organized despoliation' of chattel slavery, in which the development of plantation economics and racially structured colonies placed the exploitation of Black people at the heart of a new 'planetary consciousness' (2, 79). Recent accounts of capitalist development such as *Slavery's Capitalism* have meticulously established slavery as the basis for a contemporary global economy headed by the United States, not only in terms of labour power but also as a laboratory for innovations usually promoted as resulting from the 'free market'. For Mbembe, the symbolic break from initial conditions of enslavement was precipitated by the technology of writing, which impelled struggles for emancipation bookended by the Haitian Revolution at the beginning of the nineteenth century and the fall of apartheid at the end of the twentieth. Both examples are local struggles with deep global roots. C. L. R. James's *The Black Jacobins* (1938) – itself a work embedded in an internationalist tradition of Black radicalism – chronicled the revolution in then Saint-Domingue, led by Toussaint Louverture, who mobilized the language and philosophy of the French First Republic in opposition to imperialism and slavery, and in the formation of the first independent, Black-led republic. Apartheid was the culmination of centuries of imperial-raciological thought, a national policy that relied on tacit international tolerance and endorsement of its racial logic for stability; conversely, its disintegration relied on local activism coupled with a marked transnational Black consciousness that galvanized anti-apartheid movements around the world. The era of acute and organized resistance gives way to a final phase characterized by a simultaneously fragmenting and totalizing neoliberal ideology: the 'privatization of the world', the totalizing of financial markets, digitalization and 'the postimperial military complex' (Mbembe 2017: 2–3). While in Mbembe's account the neoliberal moment constitutes the generalization of Blackness across the world's subaltern people, Kamari Maxine Clarke and Deborah Thomas reinforce that Blackness retains its own specificity, that 'contemporary transformations in the production of blackness are as relevant to the globalization of late capitalism as deployments of "race-thinking" … were to earlier periods of imperialism, state formation, and nationalism' (Clarke and Thomas 2006: 9).

Insofar as four centuries of global Black history can be captured in epochal terms, these phases provide a historical schema for approaching the literary registration of the mutual development of Blackness and globalization. Evidently, the uncodified experience of Black proto-globalization – a literary era but an oral one – offers little if any extant basis for literary analysis. But slavery and the early formation of the 'New World' has recurred as a vital representational challenge for writers interrogating Black history and global capitalism alike. The global dimensions of Black political resistance have had their own significant literary character, from early narratives opposing slavery, through the poetics of anti-imperialism, decolonization and civil rights, to anti-apartheid writing. The twenty-first century, meanwhile, has supplied ample evidence that raciologies, and structural inscriptions of Blackness, remain present in both familiar and evolving forms in an increasingly integrated world that nevertheless perpetuates old forms, and perpetrates new forms, of racial inequality. These are recorded and shaped by the literary imagination, in narratives dominated by the racialized unevenness of the world-system and its prevailing neoliberal governmentality.

Harlem and Black Internationalism

In its critique of nation-bound thought, *The Black Atlantic* takes aim at the insularity of the English New Left (14–15) and at a preoccupation with 'Caribbean authenticity' (31), but it is clear from the sweep of Gilroy's project that the United States represents the powerful gravitational field that any worlded understanding of Blackness must negotiate. Despite the hegemonic power accorded to the United States in terms of contemporary discourses of Blackness, the national was never the single horizon for Black thought even in the United States itself. In keeping with the geographical coordinates of *The Black Atlantic*, the main extra-territorial object of Black political consciousness in America was Africa, understood as a resource for cultural autonomy but also as a site of diasporic return and as a territory of racial solidarity and empowerment. The politics that mobilized around Blackness often took the form of an explicit Black nationalism. While some forms of Black nationalism focussed more intently on the struggle against racism within the United States, many – such as Garveyism – had Pan-African aspirations with a global character, loosely understood as the principle that 'all peoples of the Afroworld – those separated from their roots by the slave trade's involuntary diaspora as well as those still resident within the ancestral homeland – should work together for their mutual benefit' (Van Deburg 1996: 8–9). Overlapping with the political ambitions of Black nationalism and Pan-Africanism, the cause of international socialism also attracted many Black activists, thinkers and writers in the United States. Surviving, or evolving past, the catastrophic failures of Stalinism, Black Marxism sought an explanation of the 'global regularities of war, expanding poverty and exploitation, the concentration of wealth, and the extension of repression' inherent to capitalism, informed directly by a Blackness that demanded the expansion of a radical frame beyond Eurocentric forms (Robinson 2004: 288–9). These political orientations, fundamentally global-diasporic in their logic and orientation and developing from a longer trajectory of internationalism in Black politics in the nineteenth century, were well represented in literary terms, and many of the primary exponents of such politics were the foremost poets and prose writers of Black arts.

The New Negro movement and the Harlem Renaissance were significant waypoints in the development of cultural expressions of a Black international consciousness. Much of their reformative political ambition was national in scope, but the work of the Renaissance was entangled with world-historical events – the 'pulses of decolonization' experienced in the Caribbean itself, in Ireland, in Mexico, in Russia and in China (Chaney 2007: 41). Crucially, the Black diaspora as a world phenomenon with Africa at its heart informed some of the most iconic works of the Renaissance, such as Langston Hughes's 'The Negro Speaks of Rivers', of 'rivers ancient as the world', a hydro-arterial world-system that maps that diaspora through the Euphrates, the Nile, the Congo and the Mississippi (Hughes 2001: 36). Caribbean writers such as Claude McKay and Eric Walrond were prominent in the Harlem scene, providing not only a non-American perspective but a distinctively global scope. McKay was himself a dissident international socialist, a writer of '[i]tinerant impulses' (Chaney 2007: 50) who travelled to Russia in the early 1920s under the auspices of the African Blood Brotherhood. He championed a global 'socialist cosmopolitanism' which found expression in his works such as *Banjo* (1929) (Nickels 2014: 3), a novel of ad hoc social organization set against a backdrop both sharply local and world-systematic. The titular story of Walrond's collection *Tropic Death* (1926), meanwhile, detailed the construction of the Panama Canal using Black labour from the Caribbean. The canal is a major symbol of the world-system, a jigsaw piece of infrastructure connecting the Atlantic and the Pacific; 'Tropic Death' dramatizes the lives of an international Black working class, drawn from the Caribbean, whose deprivation and precariousness are set against the macroeconomic interests instrumental in bringing about the construction of the canal. The Caribbean, a developing-world context of Blackness, also provided an extra-territorial geography for writers such as Zora Neale Hurston, who travelled to Jamaica and Haiti (Chaney 2007: 51) to expand the world horizons of the movement.

The movement from national to world scope in political and literary terms is a recurring one for many of the major Black writers after the Harlem Renaissance too, impelled by opportunities for self-expression and political solidarity that lay outside pre-civil rights America. Richard Wright's ground-breaking and highly influential *Native Son* (1940) represented the sharp inequality of racialized America via the sudden and violent autonomy, and epiphany, of the protagonist Bigger Thomas. *Native Son* had its own international dimensions in its registration of communist organization, but after its publication Wright emigrated to Paris and commenced a new intellectual phase. The sequel to *Native Son*, *The Outsider* (1953), reflects this evolution towards what Gilroy calls an 'intercultural hermeneutics' underlined by his extensive writing while travelling in Africa, Asia,

Spain and Central and South America (Gilroy 1993: 150–1). The overt political dialogue of *The Outsider* makes clear Wright's understanding of a singular and unequal global modernity, defined by 'industrialization' and racially stratified, 'all modern history tied together by one overall meaning', an uneven progression towards 'modern industrialization' perpetrated on 'black, red, brown, and yellow men' whose resources are expropriated by the white 'hands of the West' (Wright 1991: 474–5). Wright was not the only significant Black American novelist at work in Paris in the 1950s either – James Baldwin, who disagreed with Wright over the way Black experience in America could translate in literary aesthetics, lived on and off in France for most of his adult life. Baldwin's fiction foregrounded the violent exclusion of individuals – particularly gay men – but he was a socialist who knew that racism effected the division of a working class for the benefit of an owner class. Both were unified by a transnational socialist politics, but also by an internationalist outlook and experience, recognizing the ways Black life in America could be rendered anew by 'outsiders'. It is only from the vantage point of Europe, for example, where he encounters white people to whom he is a complete novelty, that Baldwin can observe that 'the interracial drama acted out on the American continent has not only created a new black man, it has created a new white man, too' (Baldwin 1955: 175).

Négritude and the Fact of Blackness

Wright and Baldwin were part of a large international network in Paris that included prominent francophone Black writers, many of whom were part of an intellectual and aesthetic vanguard in the representation and analysis of global Black modernity. *Négritude*, the foremost movement of Black consciousness in francophone terms, derived much of its impetus from the rhetoric of empowerment of the American New Negro movement and the Harlem Renaissance (Gilroy 1993: 211). Pioneered by the poets Aimé Césaire, Léopold Senghor and Léon Damas, *Négritude* espoused a poetics of worlded and anti-colonial Black consciousness. It was literary in expression, transnational in its political implication and attentive to the racialization and inequality inherent in the world-system – an example of what Mbembe calls a 'luminous sign of the possibility that the world might be redeemed and transfigured' in the Black imagination (6). Eschewing a 'territorial response', one bounded by national or even imperial parameters, the works of the *Négritude* poets constituted no less than 'epochal projections and projects', which reflected a 'world-making ambition to reconceptualise and reorganize the global order' (Wilder 2015: 8). These global ambitions are expressed clearly in Césaire's modernist epic *Notebook of a Return to My Native Land* (*Cahier d'un Retour au Pays Natal*, 1995), which emplaced Black life in the narrative of world development. Proceeding through scattered national, territorial and metropolitan references, the poetic persona claims that

> not a piece of this world that does not bear my fingerprint
> and my calcaneus on the backs of skyscrapers and my filth
> in the glitter of gems!
>
> (Césaire 1995: 91)

The imprint of the Black body – the hand, the heel ('calcaneus') – is a claim made upon the whole world, the 'skyscrapers' that index a hyper-development inseparable from the economics of slavery, and the besmirched 'glittering gems' redolent of both class signification and colonial resource extraction. *Notebook* offers a panoply of world visions, many of which suggest an opposition between the extant 'white' world and the possibility of a different global order, one established by those who are 'indifferent to subduing but playing the game of the world':

> truly the eldest sons of the world
> porous to all the breaths of the world
> brotherly zone of all the breaths of the world
> undrained bed of all the water of the world
> spark of the sacred fire of the world
> flesh of the flesh of the world palpitating with the very movement
> of the world
> [...]
> Listen to the white world
> horribly weary from its immense efforts
> its refractory joints crack under the hard stars
> its stiffnesses of blue steel piercing mystic flesh
> listen to its proditorious victories trumpeting its defeats
> listen to its pathetic stumbling in its grandiose alibis
>
> Pity for our omniscient and I conquerors!
>
> (Césaire 1995: 115)

Defiance of the white world is personified in *Notebook* by the figure of Toussaint Louverture, figurehead of the Haitian Revolution, 'a man alone who defies the white screams of a white death' (91). Louverture's centrality endorses Gilroy's Black Atlantic world; with the publication of *The Black Jacobins* in 1938, a year before *Notebook*, the anti-imperial and republican spirit of the Haitian Revolution over a century before was a shared preoccupation in francophone and anglophone writing, even if Césaire had not actually read C. L. R. James in English. Juxtaposed against a filial, ecological and embodied planetarity, the world-system fashioned from the 'immense efforts' of white conquerors is pathological: sterile, fragile, exhausted, self-deceiving. Césaire's reiterative, 'palpitating' language of 'world' is likewise a contrast to the singular 'white world', suggestive of a plurality of worldly vision that stands against reification, against the impermeable and impregnable edifice of an imperially and racially ordered world. This is an ambiguous vision, however, as the 'worlds' accorded to Blackness remain bound up in a racial mythology: a profound spiritual connection to ecology and planetary consciousness that substitutes for claims to a *material* world and legitimates the expropriation of the wealth of that material world through colonialism.

In *Black Skin, White Masks* (*Peau noire, masques blancs*, 2008), Frantz Fanon confirms with biting satire this relationship between the colonial invention of Blackness and the world understood as a cosmological inheritance deprived of human agency:

> I am black: I am the incarnation of a complete fusion with the world, an intuitive understanding of the earth, an abandonment of my ego in the heart of the cosmos. (Fanon 2008: 31)

Distant to and critically reflective on *Négritude*, *Black Skins, White Masks* is likely the most influential work on Blackness ever written and proceeds in part by an extensive interrogation of Césaire's writing and his situation in French society and French letters. Although Fanon discusses his treatment as a Black artist in France specifically, the epigraphic use of Césaire's *Discourse on Colonialism* and *Et les chiens se taisaient* emphasizes the worlded scope of Fanon's theorization of Black psychology:

> In the whole world no poor devil is lynched, no wretch is tortured, in whom I am not degraded and murdered. (Fanon 2008: 61)

Fanon does not work through 'globalization' as a named process, but the global dimensions of colonialism and the marks of world-consciousness recur throughout *Black Skin, White Masks*. The resonant opening of Chapter 5, 'The Fact of Blackness', makes clear that to be racialized is to be dispossessed of the world through a process of objectification:

> I came into the world imbued with the will to find a meaning in things, my spirit filled with the desire to attain to the sources of the world, and then I found I was an object in the midst of other objects. (Fanon 2008: 82)

This denied world is the 'white world', which persists throughout Fanon's work – that raciology and imperial development are inseparable and global – and underscores the wished-for equality and actually lived inequality of the 'real' world: 'we asserted the equality of all men in the world. ... And then the occasion arose when I had to meet the white man's eyes. An unfamiliar weight burdened me. The real world challenged my claims' (83). Indeed, for Fanon, the disruption to the 'bodily schema' of the Black subject is a disruption of a world relation, an ontology that exceeds the 'slow composition of my *self* in the 'real dialectic between the body and the world' via the weaving of Blackness through 'a thousand details, anecdotes, stories' by the white man (83–4). These observations indicate the way in which, for Fanon, the discursive or 'fictional' dimension of Blackness was its dominant feature, to be undone, contrasted directly against Césaire's political reclamation of *Nègre* as part of a 'stubborn struggle for liberty and indomitable hope' (Mbembe 2017: 159). These divergent critiques of race nevertheless shared a common object of interrogation, namely the larger, transnational scope of imperial-racial hierarchy.

The tremors from Fanon's work were felt instantly across linguistic divides, and the poetics of *Black Skin, White Masks* – 'Out of the blackest part of my soul, across the zebra striping of my mind, surges this desire to be suddenly *white*' (Fanon 2008: 45) – helped to carry its theoretical and psychoanalytical premise through the world literary system. Even before Charles Lam Markmann's translation in 1967, Fanon's theatrical staging of ideas and experiences was being translated into literary expression outside of French by writers attentive to the global conditions of Blackness. In Sam Selvon's *The Lonely Londoners* (2006), for example, the Trinidadian migrant Henry 'Sir Galahad' Oliver is 'objectified' in the street and experiences a racial-ontological epiphany that is nearly identical to that which Fanon describes in *Black Skin, White Masks*:

> 'Mummy, look at that black man!' A little child, holding on to the mother hand, look up at Sir Galahad.
> 'You mustn't say that, dear!' The mother chide the child.
> [...]
> Galahad watch the colour of his hand, and talk to it, saying, 'Colour, is you that causing all this, you know'.   (Selvon 2006: 76–7)

The reference to the ontological moment is more than coincidental. Galahad is a proxy Fanon and becomes 'so interested in this theory about Black' he goes to inform the novel's main focalizer, Moses Aloetta, only to be dismissed summarily: 'Take it easy, that is a sharp theory, why don't you write about it' (77–8). Moses's acerbic reaction is more about Selvon's longstanding scepticism of organized Black politics in Britain than a real reckoning with Fanon, whose work was quickly established as a reference point in Black thought, especially with shared antecedents in the Caribbean.

In its representation of 'the boys', a set of Black migrants largely from the West Indies but also from Africa trying to make their way in a hostile post-war London, *The Lonely Londoners* offers a vision of a diasporic return to the colonial centre. In the case of writers such as Selvon, or his fellow traveller to Britain, the Barbadian novelist George Lamming, this is a return to the centre of imperial culture – the well-trodden path that writers from the global periphery must tread to gain access to the literary marketplace in the 'core', as Pascale Casanova describes in *The World Republic of Letters* (1999). Moses, enraptured by the cultural cachet of London as the imperial capital, and channelling the reputations of writers such as Césaire and Fanon, ponders that in France 'all kinds of fellars writing books what turning out to be best-sellers' and wonders 'if he could ever write a book like that, what everybody would buy' (139). For 'the boys' of the novel, immigration to England is a different mechanism of globalization, to 'reconstruct' war-damaged Europe as part of an internationally mobile Black working class, following similar but distinct lines of travel established under colonialism. The interrogation of Black experience in *The Lonely Londoners* is also suggestive of the mutability of race discourses, their historically contingent character: the way in which, at a certain point in British history, an Indo-Caribbean writer from Trinidad such as Selvon would be identified with, and consequently be understood to write 'authentically' about, Blackness, a racial demarcation that would be inconceivable in the United States, Kenya, South Africa or, for that matter, contemporary Britain.

Neo-Imperialism and Neoliberal Globalization

Césaire, Fanon, Selvon and Lamming wrote from experiences of Black majority countries still formally part of European empires – indeed, Martinique remains a component of the French Republic. Black writing in a *postcolonial* sense demanded new forms and new orientations that were nevertheless acutely sensitive to the continuation of global relations of dependency constructed under colonialism and maintained in new forms in a neo-imperial era. Ngũgĩ wa Thiong'o's *Decolonising the Mind* (1986) places the United States firmly at the centre of that 'new' imperial project, wherein military power preserves the 'freedom for western finance capital and for the vast transnational monopolies ... to continue stealing' from the colonized world; neo-imperialism 'presents the struggling people of the earth and all those calling for peace, democracy and socialism with the ultimatum: accept theft or death' (Ngũgĩ 1986: 2–3). The threat of military action is only latent, however, and the main site of ongoing domination is the cultural sphere, and particularly language:

> But the biggest weapon wielded and actually daily unleashed by imperialism ... is the cultural bomb. The effects of a cultural bomb is to annihilate a people's belief in their names, in their languages, in their environment, in their heritage of struggle, in their unity, in their capacities and ultimately in themselves. (Ngũgĩ 1986: 3)

Not configured as an explicitly Black politics, Ngũgĩ's idea of decolonization nevertheless implies breaking free from the constraints of racial hierarchy and demanding redress for the material impacts of colonialism, which themselves establish racial difference preserved globally in perpetuity. Moreover, in its resemblance to American militarism more generally, the 'cultural bomb' successfully conveys the remoteness of the operation of this new imperialism – globally distributed, but at a remove. For Ngũgĩ, globalization is the mechanism through which the racially stratified extractive processes of colonialism can be continued even after the administrative and military occupation of the world has largely ceased, under a neoliberal rhetoric of free-market enterprise imposed by neo-imperial states.

One explicit observation of the effects of the new imperialism and its economic logic is Jamaica Kincaid's *A Small Place* (1997), a satirical evisceration of the national condition of Antigua in the period after formal independence in 1981. *A Small Place* is a sharply 'global' articulation channelled through tourism both as a mode of ethnographic observation ('the guidebook') and as an evidence base for combined and uneven development: tourism, along with finance, are primary economic motors in Antigua. The text shows the way racial hierarchies of class and wealth, entrenched during plantation economics and colonialism, continue into a new phase in which postcolonial countries are embedded anew into global economic and cultural flows, and where the mark of governmental corruption is their ready access to globally marked commodities such as new-model Japanese cars (Kincaid 1997: 7). Observing the importation of foodstuffs from Miami to Antigua to cater to the tastes of American tourists, the narrator reflects that the food likely originates from some other subordinate economy in the world economic system to begin with: 'There is a world of something in this, but I can't go into it right now' (14). The globalized world of financialization, in which Caribbean nations such as Antigua are now enmeshed, is construed as the 'inheritor' system of slavery in a narrative manoeuvre that anticipates Mbembe's 'becoming Black of the world': the Barclay brothers 'may have been visionaries and agitated for an end to slavery, for look at how rich they became with their banks borrowing from (through their savings) the descendants of slaves and then lending back to them' (26).

Reaction to *A Small Place* in the Caribbean observed that Kincaid was an adopted American writer pouring scorn on a society she had abandoned, which highlights the way that America has supplanted European colonial powers as Casanova's centre of cultural sanctification and promotion for authors of the colonized world, at least in anglophone terms, in the world literary system. That certainly holds for celebrated contemporary African writers such as Chimamanda Ngozi Adichie or NoViolet Bulawayo, both African-born novelists whose literary 'training' was delivered via MFA programmes at high-profile American universities and whose work reflects on race as produced in transnational space. Bulawayo's prize-winning *We Need New Names* (2013) consciously channels anterior works, in particular a genealogy of world-conscious African fiction. 'Hitting Budapest', the first chapter and prize-winning piece of short fiction in the novel, establishes the profound hunger of the children at its heart: 'We didn't eat this morning and my stomach feels like somebody just took a shovel and dug everything out' (Bulawayo 2014: 1), invoking the defining narrative of Zimbabwean emigration to the colonial centre, Dambudzo Marechera's *The House of Hunger* (1978). A similar invocation follows in the mass emigration from the persecution and instability of the Zimbabwean state, referencing Chinua Achebe's *Things Fall Apart* (1958): 'When things fall apart, the children of the land scurry and scatter like birds escaping a burning sky' (145). Zimbabwe, emblematic of postcolonial states in various stages of disintegration, is thus captured in the language of the African novel: 'who wants to be in a terrible place of hunger and things falling apart?' (49).

The effects of the 'cultural bomb' on postcolonial Zimbabwe are made visible in *We Need New Names*, where the language of an America-dominated global hierarchy infiltrates the everyday play dynamics of Zimbabwean children; each sees their destiny as escape to a land of plenty. The children at the heart of the narrative bear witness to the neo-colonial ministrations of white American non-governmental organizations, aspire to be part of the cast of *ER*, wear hand-me-down and/or counterfeit branded American clothes, and play the 'Country Game' wherein all participants want to 'be' the United States rather than 'rags of countries' such as Zimbabwe itself (49). While America surmounts the global food chain in Bulawayo's novel, the text signals the larger geopolitical conflicts in which Zimbabwe is caught. This is marked in a visit to 'Shanghai', a construction site where a Chinese corporation is building a new mall:

It's just terrible madness inside Shanghai; machines hoist things in their terrible jaws, machines maul the earth, machines grind rocks, machines belch clouds of smoke, machines iron the ground. Everywhere machines. The Chinese men are all over the place in orange uniforms and yellow helmets; there's not that many of them but from the way they are running around, you'd think they are a field of corn. And then there are the black men, who are working in regular clothes – torn T-shirts, vests, shorts, trousers cut at the knees, overalls, flip-flops, tennis shoes. (Bulawayo 2014: 42)

This globalization is not one of frictionless networks or cosmopolitan exchange but industrial ecocide and commodity abstractions, part of China's geopolitical ambitions in Africa. What remains undisturbed in this new geopolitics is the position of Blackness in the global order of race. The protective uniforms of the Chinese workers mark them out as professionalized, if not managerial; the 'black men', meanwhile, are recognizable as the same international proletariat as in *Tropic Death* or *A Small Place*, lending their labour power to global infrastructure projects, facilitating the concretization of commodity highways in flip-flops and tennis shoes.

Representing Slavery

The labourers of Shanghai in *We Need New Names* indicate the way that globalization has returned the Black labouring subject to Africa without changing its relationship to a global economic or social order. The ill-equipped and vulnerable labourers of Shanghai, working to build in service to global capitalism and the geopolitical advantage of others, are suggestive of what Saidiya Hartman calls the 'incomplete project of freedom' for Black people, wherein Blackness is understood as the 'precarious life of the ex-slave' (Hartman 2008: 4). Slavery is understood here as a continuity; while chattel slavery as a formal system that dominated the Atlantic world recedes in the historical record, slavery remains a world formation 'inseparable from writing the history of the present' (4). Representing slavery consequently has contemporary urgency: it is not past, and every narrative act that engages with slavery is attuned to a present-day politics. In 'Venus in Two Acts', Hartman constructs a 'critical fabulation' marked by an intentionally 'failed' attempt to reconstruct the eponymous Venus who stands in for all the Black women glimpsed partially through the mutilated and mutilating archive of slavery. The silence of the archive has some proximity to Gilroy's description in *The Black Atlantic* of the 'topos of unsayability', a condition of linguistic mutilation under slavery produced by practices such as enforced illiteracy and the separation of slaves sharing common languages (Gilroy 1993: 74). Hartman's radical methodology of enquiry commits to 'do more than recount the violence' of the life of Venus – to reproduce the violence through a violence of narration – and instead tell a story that feels the contours of the impossible task of constructing the 'biography' of the enslaved from an archive of violence and objectification (2–3). In the same 'dispossession of the world' recognizable from Fanon and Mbembe, Venus is 'driven out of the world', a 'worldless' figure (7, 8); Hartman's critical reflection effects a journey 'out of the world and back' for Venus, one that aspires to both a 'way of living in the world in the aftermath of catastrophe' and a 'home in the world for the mutilated and violated self' (3).

'Venus in Two Acts' is a radical exploration of the representational limits of the literary imagination in reconstituting the violence of slavery, but it also recognizes the importance of *attempting* that project, which comprises no less than an exploration of the incarceration, brutality and subjection of a Black present. The pursuit of a 'critical fabulation' is not unprecedented – narratives which examine the partiality, and reflect on the impossibility of reconstituting, the history of slavery are a crucial part of contemporary Black writing. An archetypal example is Toni Morrison's *Beloved*, which provides a reconceptualization of the 'hauntological' dimension of slavery in the United States, in which the eponymous Beloved is the absent presence of Black suffering that stretches back through postbellum lynching to the depravities of slavery itself. It is in *A Mercy* (2009), however, where Morrison addresses the *world* most directly, the spatiality of a world 'taking shape', the networks of mobility and exchange, and the widespread exploitation of unfree labour that define early globalization. *A Mercy* depicts colonial America in the late seventeenth century, 'a world so new, almost alarming in rawness and temptation' (10), in a moment of global formation, in which narrative threads of the lives of unfree workers are woven together. The proto-globalization of *A Mercy* is bound by the sea, as the 'contracted wife' Rebekkah reflects on her voyage from Europe to America: 'you own the globe and land is afterthought to entertain you; that the world beneath you is both graveyard and heaven' (71). The women brought to America to work are symbolically united in their ship-bound experiences, although profoundly differentiated by racial disenfranchisement emblematized by the moment when Rebekkah proposes to sell Florens, the enslaved Black girl around whom the narrative coheres. This new vision of 'world' is an acknowledgement both of the global dimension of the Black Atlantic, which transcends the land-bias of nation through the 'modern machinery' of the ship (Gilroy 1993: 12), and of the non-national idea of 'archipelagics', another Black-authored theory of globality, from Glissant's *Treatise on the Whole World* (*Traité du tout-monde*, 1997), in which '[t]he entire world is becoming an archipelago' poised between isolated island and massified continent (Glissant 1992: 194).

Extending the concept of world as a dynamic process, the allegorical night of colonial America in *A Mercy* is a form of 'dark matter', 'thick, unknowable, aching to be made into a world' (Morrison 2009: 154). On the one hand, this darkness is a Manichaean foreshadowing of what transpires in the historical record – the centuries-long slave economies of the Americas. On the other hand, it seems to strike a note of *contemporary* global agitation, consonant with Hartman's identification that slavery narratives are really histories of the present: the world that aches to be made is the world of the present. The transnational reach of a contemporary formation such as Black Lives Matter, propelled especially by the death of George Floyd in 2020, shows that Black politics, like many contemporary and globally distributed forms of Black expressive culture, has firm roots in the United States. But it persistently overgrows and penetrates far beyond that territory. Black Lives Matter speaks with a different voice in Britain, in France, in South Africa, in Brazil, in Haiti and in many other contexts, each with a distinct inflection based on histories of racism and imperialism. As Mbembe articulates, 'to build a world that we share, we must restore the humanity stolen from those who have historically been subjected to processes of abstraction and objectification' (Mbembe 2017: 182). The 'unknowable dark matter' of *A Mercy* may be the protean character of Blackness itself, a global formation, dispossessed but aching – activating – for the task of restoration, and the reshaping of the world.

CHAPTER 13

World-Systems, Literature and Geoculture
Matthew Eatough

The term 'geoculture' was first coined by the sociologist Immanuel Wallerstein in his ground-breaking four-volume study *The Modern World-System*. In a move that would come to be famous, Wallerstein proposed that capitalism had created the first-ever 'world-system', a new 'kind of social system' that aspired to 'encompass the whole world', and which 'was larger than any juridically-defined political unit' (Wallerstein 2011: 15). The nations, city-states and empires that made up this modern world-system were bound together by trade networks, systems of taxation, modes of resource extraction and the international division of labour. But they were also bound together by a shared 'geoculture' that instilled certain social and political norms essential for the smooth functioning of international trade. Such norms included a belief in the sanctity of state sovereignty and the interstate system, as well as a widespread institutionalization of the state's role in guaranteeing and protecting property. Over time, these basic principles would eventually develop into what Wallerstein calls the 'triumph' of 'centrist liberalism': the creation of a group of 'liberal states' in Europe and North America, each of which provided a number of welfare programmes and 'guarantees against arbitrary authority' in return for acceptance of the capitalist system and its unequal distribution of wealth (Wallerstein 2007: 65).

Unfortunately for literary scholars, Wallerstein leaves the term geoculture somewhat under-theorized (Shapiro 2008a: 35–40). Novels, poems, plays, music and other expressions of popular culture receive scant mention in *The Modern World-System*. Wallerstein tends to focus instead on pervasive political beliefs that have become institutionalized in either the state apparatus or mass social movements – phenomena closer to what literary studies would call 'ideology' than culture properly speaking. For example, Wallerstein identifies the liberal dictum that 'the inclusion of all' is 'the definition of the good society' as the foundational premise upon which the entire geoculture of the modern world-system has been built (Wallerstein 2007: 60). But while it is certainly true that the history of political action from the French Revolution through the rise of anti-colonial nationalisms and beyond has been driven by debates over who and what constitutes the inside and the outside of the state – the 'us' versus the 'them', to adapt Carl Schmitt's well-known definition for politics – this does not tell us much about how structural transformations in the capitalist world-system have influenced the development of specific culture industries over the last 500 years.[1]

This means that when we opt to use world-systems theory as a lens for examining literature's function within a global world-system, we must first attend to a number of methodological and epistemological considerations. How can we trace the effect of a large, abstract capitalist system within particularized works of literature – and without generalizing to the point that we are mimicking Wallerstein's social-scientific approach? To what extent has the emergence of specific literary genres been shaped by forces originating within the world-system, and how can examining such forces lead to a better understanding of the history of literary production? And finally, how can we best attend to literature's unique status both as a *commodity* (subject to the same global economic forces as any other product that is bought and sold) and as a *representation* that projects its own world – one that can simultaneously reflect, contest and interrogate socio-economic realities?

In this chapter, I outline two possible approaches to geocultural analysis. In the chapter's first section, I discuss what I call a *phenomenological* approach to literary texts. Scholars who adopt this mode of interpretation argue that literature provides a unique glimpse into the experiential worlds produced by capitalist systems. For such scholars, capitalism is not simply an economic system characterized by autonomous agents in a public marketplace (as envisioned by rational-choice theory and free-market ideology) but is instead a complex web of discrete processes, industries and modes of production, each of which organizes workers' experiences, affects and environments in unique ways. What makes literature valuable for world-systems analysis is thus its attention to phenomenological experience – its unique ability to describe how subjective experiences are sutured together with material realities and institutional norms to form a lifeworld.[2] By attending to these representations of lived experience, world-systems analysts are able to construct genealogies and comparative anatomies of what the French philosopher Jacques Rancière calls capitalism's 'distribution of the sensible' – that is, the way in which particular socio-economic dispensations shape how people see and feel the world (Rancière 2004: 3).

In the chapter's second section, I turn from the world projected by individual works of literature to the marketplace they inhabit. As I explain, the fact that the capitalist world-system is constituted by a mixture of residual and emergent modes of production – what Leon Trotsky famously termed 'uneven and combined development' – means that it is populated by any number of overlapping ideological and experiential 'worlds' (Trotsky 1967: 432). Some of these lifeworlds are structures of feeling inhabited by different classes, nations, regions, genders and so on. But many are inhabited by the same persons, who experience living in them as a state of prolonged contradiction. I propose the term *genre-system* as a conceptual tool for examining how literary fields make sense of such contradictions by dispersing their representations of economic processes and ideologies across a range of literary genres. As I show, literary genres tend to render capitalism's contradictions logically coherent by allegorizing particular stages of the production process within self-contained narrative forms. When we examine such genres together, as the constituent parts of a totalizing genre-*system*, we are able to see how narrative forms work together to create a series of partial, dissonant, yet nevertheless legible representations of the capitalist world-system.

In practice, there is a good deal of overlap between these two methods, and much of the best scholarship on literary world-systems moves seamlessly between analysing the representational strategies of individual texts and placing them within their wider institutional context. For the sake of clarity, though, I treat these two techniques separately so as to better explain the methodological principles embedded within each.

The Phenomenology of the World-System

In 2008, Farrar, Straus and Giroux published the first English-language translation of Roberto Bolaño's 900-page epic *2666*. Set in the fictional town of Santa Teresa (a thinly disguised version of Ciudad Juárez), Bolaño's novel is ostensibly about a gruesome series of femicides that have plagued the city in recent years.[3] But as the novel proceeds, readers are treated to an eclectic narrative that ranges widely across time, space and genre. Bolaño regularly shunts the locus of his story away from Santa Teresa, with lengthy episodes set in the post-industrial wastelands of 1990s Detroit, Nazi-era Germany and early Soviet Russia. As he does so, he freely mixes generic frames in a manner that gives a jarring, jagged feel to the book's narrative structure. The novel's first section, for instance, consists of a sort of literary detective story in which four academic colleagues search for their idol, the reclusive German writer Benno von Archimboldi. After this hunt eventually leads the scholars to Santa Teresa (where their quest flounders), Bolaño abruptly jumps to a patchwork of metaphysical reflections and anxious worryings from the 'mad' professor of philosophy, Óscar Amalfitano, followed by a hybrid road trip/coming-to-political-consciousness narrative, a parody of the objective language of journalism and police reports, and finally a panorama of twentieth-century European history that borrows its stylistic cues from everything from Alfred Döblin's *Berlin Alexanderplatz* (1929) to early Soviet science fiction (particularly the work of Yevgeny Zamyatin).

As this brief overview may suggest, *2666* is a big, baggy and self-consciously *global* novel. Its foundational thesis appears to be that Mexico's femicides can only be fully understood if one contextualizes them within a heterogeneous (and radically uneven) capitalist world-system. This is a belief that the novel shares with a number of other notable post-2000 novels, including Marlon James's *A Brief History of Seven Killings* (2014), Amitav Ghosh's Ibis trilogy (2008–2015), Neal Stephenson's Baroque Cycle (2003–2004), and David Mitchell's *Cloud Atlas* (2004). Like *2666*, each of these novels adopts an expansive spatial and temporal scope: a Cold War-era U.S.-Caribbean domain bound together by the international drug trade, and populated by a disparate cast of gangsters, assassins-for-hire and CIA operatives; the transnational Sino-Indian supply chains that sustained the opium trade prior to the First Opium War (1839–1842); an early modern Europe in the midst of the series of social, political and scientific revolutions that would eventually culminate in the creation of a modernized financial system; and a discontinuous sequence of Anglo, Asian and American 'civilizations' ranging in time from the nineteenth-century Pacific to a dystopian Hawaii on the verge of human extinction.

Unsurprisingly, these epic, globe-trotting novels have been a key object of interest for scholars working on literary world-systems, serving not only as representations of particular moments in capitalist history, but as models for how to understand the workings of the capitalist world-system. Nowhere is this truer than in the case of *2666*, which has often served as a foundational ur-text for theorizing the relationship between literary representation and capitalist form. The Warwick Research Collective (WReC), for example, identifies *2666* as a 'world-systems novel', a '"novel-in-parts" whose narrative structure self-consciously encapsulates the structural relations of the world-system, mapping the periphery in relation to other centres and peripheries' (2015: 98). Sharae Deckard, herself a member of the WReC, presents the novel as an 'insurgent attempt to reformulate the realist "world novel" in order to overcome the changed historical situation of Latin America in the era of millennial capital, when as Natasha Wimmer eloquently puts it, "capitalism, the World Bank, and the international drug trade replaced caudillos, death squads, and political persecution as the new forces of evil'" (Deckard 2012: 353). And José Enrique Navarro notes that even Bolaño's penchant for inserting highly academic disputations on literature alongside gritty depictions of North American hyper-capitalism reflects his interest in the 'neoliberal policies' that have led to 'the creation of publishing conglomerates', 'book overproduction' and 'a reduction of ... sales channels' (Navarro 2017: 144).

Part of the reason for this collective fascination with Bolaño's *2666* may have to do with how the novel speaks to one of the core methodological challenges involved in geocultural analysis – namely, the problem of how the fictional representations found in novels relate to the economic transactions that constitute the capitalist world-system (labour contracts, trade agreements, tax levies, resource extraction and so on). These material processes would seem to operate on a different level than that of literature, which, as Pheng Cheah, Eric Hayot and many others have shown, is defined first and foremost by its capacity to project its own self-contained 'world' (Hayot 2012; Cheah 2016). Fictional worlds may reflect, refract or allegorize the material world that produced them, but there will always remain some degree of dissonance between representation and reality. Even when an author strives to be as faithful to reality as possible (as in, say, the documentary realism of a Mahasaweta Devi), there remain any number of complicating factors that open up a gap between reality and its fictional representation: the impossibility of reducing complex economic processes into a tidy narrative form; genre conventions that endow texts with their own independent meanings; the distorting effects of ideology; and the irreducible difference between language (as a system of arbitrary signs) and material reality.

What has made Bolaño's *2666* such a compelling object for world-systems analysis is the way in which its vast spatio-temporal scope and multi-generic structure have provided a model for how to finesse the representation–reality divide. If, on the one hand, the novel's epic size seems to gesture towards the sheer scale needed to tackle an object as large as the world-system, Bolaño's penchant for suturing together a diverse array of generic frames helps to capture both the complex, multi-layered nature of the capitalist world-system and the impossibility of fully documenting such an object in fiction. We can see this clearly if we turn to the third and fourth parts of Bolaño's novel, 'The Part About Fate' and 'The Part About the Crimes'. After two initial parts in which the femicides feature more as background material than as primary subject matter, 'The Part About Fate' and 'The Part About the Crimes' finally turn the narrative's attention directly to the killings of women in Santa Teresa. Bolaño begins this section of the novel by focalizing the narrative through the perspective of Oscar Fate, an African-American journalist who is sent to Santa Teresa to cover a heavyweight boxing match, only to be gradually introduced to the femicides. As Fate tries to understand the killings by contextualizing them within a series of uneven global systems, the narrative breaks from its typical third-person limited style and lapses into other generic modes: densely allegorical renderings of the somatic effects of the factory labour system; detached descriptions of the urban decay that has beset U.S. cities under NAFTA and deindustrialization; autobiographical accounts of the death of 1960s radicalism (as emblematized by the Black Panthers); self-help lectures that performatively enact the self-regulating entrepreneurialism of the neoliberal subject; sociological treatises on the slave trade (which are used to comment upon the similar dehumanization of women in the *maquiladora* factory system); and dream sequences that register a felt experience of unreality accompanying modern capitalist life. The ultimate failure of these interpretative frames to fully represent the totality of a North American import–export economy leads the narrative to discard them in the following section, 'The Part About the Crimes', in favour of the more objective language of journalistic reportage and police reports. And yet even this form proves limited. As Bolaño proceeds to describe murdered woman after murdered woman in a series of concise, emotionally flat vignettes, the victims eventually lose their individual identities and merge into an indistinguishable mass. As we near the end of the section, we learn that these interchangeable accounts of raped and mutilated women merely replicate the perspective of the Mexican state and its representatives in the police, who regard women as abject, disposable objects – 'vagina[s] surrounded by a more or less organized bunch of cells', as one officer crudely jokes (Bolaño 2008: 552).

While this fragmentary collage of narrative forms might seem like a testament to literature's inability to provide a holistic picture of the global capitalist system, it is a perfect demonstration of the world-system's indirect effect on narrative *style*. For many world-systems analysts, the fundamental un-representability of global capitalism means that what literature depicts is not capitalism-in-itself, but rather the phenomenological *experience* of capitalist life.[4] When, for example, Bolaño provides a detailed description of a mural in Detroit 'representing the twelve stages in the [factory] production chain', the bizarre, haunting imagery is intended to replicate the disjunctions that govern life in the post-industrial United States:

> It was circular, like a clock, and where the numbers should have been there were scenes of people working in the factories of Detroit ... In each scene, there was one recurring character: a black teenager, or a long-limbed, scrawny man-child, or a man clinging to childhood, dressed in clothes that changed from scene to scene but that were invariably too small for him. He had been assigned the role of clown, intended to make people laugh, although a closer look made it clear that he wasn't there only to make people laugh. The mural looked like the work of a lunatic. The last painting of a lunatic. In the middle of the clock, where all the scenes converged, there was a word painted in letters that looked like they were made of gelatin: *fear*. (Bolaño 2008: 241)

Bolaño's mural identifies many of the sensations produced by the Fordist factory system: the strict adherence to tightly managed time (the clock); the atomization of the production process into discrete stages; promises of upward mobility and the good life (as implied by the juxtaposition of person and clock, which seems to affirm an evolutionary development to wealth and maturity); the failure of the factory system to deliver on these promises (as emblematized by the stunted growth of the 'man child'); and the repetitive nature of factory work (as represented by the circular imagery of the clock). These images are tied together by the final injunction to '*fear*', a word whose ambiguous placement enables it to refer simultaneously to conscription under the factory-labour system *and* the dangers of being left outside that system (the results of which we see in the urban decay that has overtaken post-industrial Detroit).

Note in particular how these overlapping meanings are conveyed through the scene's stylistic register. The description of the mural shows clear debts to surrealism's opaque mode of symbolism, as well as to the types of detached affect common to Euro-American modernism (e.g., James Joyce's *Portrait of the Artist as a Young Man* and Ernest Hemmingway's *A Moveable Feast*).[5] In Bolaño's hands, these narrative devices provide us with a concrete insight into the lived realities of Fordist capitalism – the long hours, the repetitive work, the intimate connection between affective disposition and ideological interpolation. I call Bolaño's approach here a 'phenomenological' one because it draws a direct line between what Stephen Shapiro and Philip Barnard term the 'experience-system' of capitalism and the tactile-affective-ideological world projected by the fundamental components of narrative style (genre, point of view, tone, etc.).

(Shapiro and Barnard 2017: 27). Indeed, to the extent that Bolaño is able to describe how abstract economic processes (i.e., the Fordist factory system) are embedded in subjective dispositions, habitual behaviours and distributions of material goods, he does so through the narrative vocabulary provided to him by the conventions of specific literary genres. The images present in the clock mural, for instance, adopt the surrealist technique of defamiliarizing objects in order to gain access to the unconscious (in this case, the political unconscious of (post-)Fordist capitalism). The power of these images – their potential for critical reflection and understanding – thus proceeds from their refusal to represent the North American import–export economy as a set of objectively describable functions, and their recourse to a narrative style that instead treats the extraction of human labour-power from physical bodies as a process shaping workers' thoughts and feelings on the most intimate of levels.

In this sense, *2666*'s multi-generic structure serves as a testament to the multiple, overlapping experiential worlds produced by the capitalist world-system. As Deckard puts it, the 'welding of multiple genres [in *2666*] … can be understood … as corresponding to the radical mixture of residual and modern temporalities, cultural formations, and social relations in the uneven space–time sensorium of millennial capitalism' (Deckard 2012: 356). According to this logic, when the novel splices together a hybrid campus novel/detective story ('The Part About the Critics') with a road trip/coming-to-political-consciousness narrative ('The Part About Fate'), the discrepancy between these narrative frames is a tacit admission on Bolaño's part that the worlds of the university and of literary publishing are structured by a different experiential reality than the world of Santa Teresa's *maquiladors* – as they are also structured by a different experiential reality than that of the Santa Teresa police, the Black working class in post-industrial Detroit or any of the myriad other groups we see in the novel. These lifeworlds are bound together in a complex web of transactions, but each individual one is by definition a partial perspective determined by a person's place in the capitalist supply chain. Bolaño's abrupt stylistic shifts try to approximate the provisional, overlapping quality of these realities, while admitting that no single one can provide a definitive description of the world-system – just as the novel will ultimately abdicate any unified theory of the femicides plaguing Santa Teresa.

By using works such as *2666* to investigate the relationship between narrative forms and the phenomenology of capitalism, world-systems analysis has slowly begun to move away from some of the staples of Marxist literary criticism (such as ideology critique and Lukácsian reflection theory), and towards a mode of analysis that synthesizes insights drawn from the work of Fredric Jameson, Franco Moretti and Raymond Williams. Like Jameson, world-systems scholarship tends to treat genre as the site at which capitalist modes of production most directly shape literature, with traces of older generic forms (the folktale, epic, romance, etc.) indicating the persistence of 'residual' socio-economic structures (subsistence economies, pre-capitalist communalism, feudal modes of production, etc.), even as newer generic forms (e.g., the novel) announce the temporal co-existence of emergent socio-economic functions (the nation-state, the marketplace, finance capitalism, etc.) (Jameson 1981, 1986). But where Jameson relies on terms borrowed from ideology critique to describe how genres internalize capitalist processes (e.g., 'ideologeme' and 'cognitive map'), world-systems analysts argue that narrative forms are not ideological mystifications so much as key diagnostic tools that enable readers to see how capitalism structures the experiential and affective lives of its workers. Indeed, to the extent that literature provides a privileged view into the affective experiences of modern life, it is a perfect vehicle for exploring how subjective impressions are sutured together with social, political and economic institutions, in the constellation of practices that Raymond Williams terms 'structures of feeling' (Williams 1977: 128–35).

The result, as we can see from our reading of Bolaño's *2666*, is a mode of analysis that treats literary texts as having a certain level of descriptive agency. Not only do works of literature reveal the 'experience-system' of particular modes of production, as well as how these phenomenological worlds overlap with one another; but as perhaps *the* dominant medium for representing the subjective matrices of modern life, literature helps to actively construct the terms through which people understand their place within the capitalist world-system. *2666*'s stylistic pyrotechnics make it an ideal text for theorizing a mode of interpretation fit for analysing such experience systems. But as a methodology that seeks to delineate between narrative form and the workings of the capitalist world-system, the same general mode of analysis can (and has) been used to assess the narrative structures of any number of capitalist formations, from the those of petro-capitalism and the sugar plantation economy to those of water extraction and public utilities (Rubenstein 2010; Barrett and Worden 2014; Cheah 2016; Deckard 2019).

World-System as Genre-System

Of course, no novel exists in a vacuum. While works such as Bolaño's *2666* may describe what living and working under particular capitalist dispensations *feels* like, these representations are by their very nature internal to the world projected by the novel. Things begin to look quite different when we step outside the world of the novel and ask how fictional texts operate as commodities within a transnational literary marketplace. How, for example, should one make sense of the spectacular critical and commercial success that *2666* has enjoyed in the English-speaking world? To what extent should we credit the novel's publication by Farrar, Straus and Giroux, an imprint of the multinational publishing conglomerate Macmillan specializing in quality fiction, for the novel's positive reception? Would the public response have been any different if the novel had been published by New Directions, the independent press that has released most of the English-language translations of Bolaño's novels? And how does Bolaño's fiction relate to other writings about Mexico – or writings about Bolaño's native Chile, or ones about Latin America more generally? How might we map Bolaño's fiction onto a Latin American literary field that includes everything from *narco* fiction and political thrillers to magic realism and neorealist reportage?

Such questions pose a very different set of methodological challenges for world-systems analysis. To examine literature as a commodity in this manner requires stepping back from the world projected by the novel in order to investigate the networks of production, distribution and reception governing the literary marketplace. We need to consider not only how literature functions as one commercial industry among many but also how literary culture is dispersed across a wide range of reading communities, each with its own preferences, reading practices, ideological vision and shared mores. Some audiences will read, say, pulpy science fiction alongside quality literary fiction, but more often than not the choice to consume one or the other speaks volumes about a person's occupation, race, gender, financial status, political values, mainstream and/or subcultural affiliations and perceptions about insider/outside status. Taking these considerations into account is essential if we are to understand how texts' representations of the world-system are never produced in isolation but are instead informed by their structural placement within historically situated literary fields.

One way to approach this issue is to examine what I call *genre-systems*. If we begin from the Jamesonian premise that genre conventions reflect the ideological beliefs and affective experience of living within a particular mode of production, then the co-existence of multiple genres in any given literary field should alert us to the fact that the capitalist world-system's overlapping matrix of residual and emergent modes of production produces an inherently plural set of experiential realities. By studying these representations of experiential lifeworlds in their totality, as a dynamic *system* of capitalist processes and their attendant narrative forms, we can begin to see how literary fields render contradictory socio-economic structures into coherent form by distributing their effects across a multiplicity of literary genres. More specifically, we can see how each particular genre within a given literary field encodes the perspective of one link in a much larger capitalist supply chain – the habitus of, say, a particular industry, mode of production, class identity or ideology. Due to the complex nature of economic activity, these genres often present incompatible visions of the capitalist world-system. But by identifying each one's place within a larger genre-system, we are able to discern how these disparate images work together to construct a legible picture of the global economy.

In order to better understand how genre-systems work in practice, let's take a look at a relatively straightforward example. The late nineteenth century was a moment of intensive globalization, as new breakthroughs in shipping and telecommunications technologies created the first truly 'global' market for goods (primarily in the form of the international grain market, but also in markets for meat, silver and commodity futures) (Pomeranz and Topik 2006; Belich 2009). Such markets were heavily centralized in London, whose long-standing dominance over financial capital and newly minted imperial telegraph system supplied key infrastructure for trade and speculation (especially in the case of futures markets) (Potter 2003; Pike and Winseck 2007; Cain and Hopkins 2016). They were also buoyed by a new wave of imperial expansion driven by the Long Depression of 1873–1896, when a fall in the price of goods (partly caused by the aforementioned consolidation of global commodity markets) forced venture capitalists to search for new outlets for investment (Hobson 1933). By the end of the century, European nations had made their way into Africa and Asia, the last remaining major markets on the outside of the capitalist world-system, and carved them into a patchwork of colonies, protectorates and spheres of influence. With these last outposts incorporated into the capitalist world-system, one could speak for perhaps the first time in human history of a world economy that spanned the entire globe.

At the same time as this global economy was being consolidated, equally transformative developments were revolutionizing *fin-de-siècle* British literary culture. The rise of mass literacy, a product of several Education Acts passed between 1870 and 1893, had expanded the demand for reading materials of all sorts. Newspapers were the prime beneficiaries of this increased demand, with the number of titles in circulation more than quadrupling between 1875 and 1903 (Keating qtd. in Daly 1999: 20). But fictional literature, too, experienced a parallel (albeit smaller-scale) boom. The average number of new novels published per year jumped from just over 400 in 1885 to more than 1,300 in 1894 (Daly 1999). And as the number of novels increased, so, too, did the diversity of publishers' lists. In place of the *Bildungsromanae*, condition-of-England novels, and sensation novels that had dominated the mid-century literary field, the *fin de siècle* witnessed an explosion of new literary genres: imperial romances, Gothic adventure tales, detective stories, science fiction, naturalism, and the stylized writings of the Decadent, Symbolist and Aesthetic movements. Genres common to the mid-nineteenth century certainly did not completely disappear, but those that remained, such as the estate novel and the *Bildungsroman*, were often transformed in ways that would have been unrecognizable to nineteenth-century readers.

For contemporary readers, this changed literary landscape was indispensable for apprehending structural transformations within the capitalist world-system. While no single genre provided its readers with a complete picture of the world-system, each element of Britain's *fin-de-siècle* literary culture supplied its readers with a way of imagining their place within a global economy defined by imperial expansion, market integration and the rise of finance capitalism. At times, this aim was quite explicit. The imperial romances popularized by H. Rider Haggard and John Buchan, for instance, presented an unsubtle justification for Britain's resource extraction in southern Africa by inventing implausible tales of lost civilizations and their abundant riches. Haggard's novels in particular describe fantastical locations that are stumbled upon by English adventurers, each one awash in unclaimed gold and diamonds simply there for the taking. Of course, what Haggard fails to mention is that the British were currently extending their control over southern Africa and its abundant gold and diamond mines, which were being funded by a newly expanded financial sector and manned by conscripted African workers. By writing these historical realities out of novels such as *King Solomon's Mines* and *She*, Haggard was able to cast the British as the rightful owners of Africa's mineral wealth, which they had 'earned' through manly feats of valour and professional expertise. In doing so, his novels both displaced some of the more troubling aspects of the so-called Scramble for Africa (such as its annexation of independent African territories and its coercive labour policies) and provided an ideological justification for those same activities (through the strategic deployment of discourses of manly virtue and unowned riches).

In other cases, writers sought less to defend an aggressively expansionary imperialism than to affirm an enduring set of English values – or to worry about the potential erasure of such values in a rapidly modernizing world. This objective was especially pronounced in the country-house and pastoral fictions that returned to popularity during the 1880s and 1890s. In the hands of an Anthony Trollope or a Harriet Ella Ernle Money, country estates and family farms in such varied colonial outposts as Ireland and South Africa functioned as metonyms for what the English politician Charles Dilke coined 'Greater Britain' – that is, the belief that imperial expansion had created, as the historian J. R. Seeley put it, 'a great homogenous people, one in blood, language, religion, and laws, but dispersed over a boundless space' (Seeley 1931: 184). Trollope in particular contrasts the 'orderly' governance of colonial estates (itself an effect of the 'English ... character') with the violent chaos that was forever threatening to engulf these outposts of civilization (tenant unrest, rural conspiracies and habitual idleness) (Trollope 1848: 50).[6] Here we see little of the adventurism that characterized Haggard's imperial romances. Instead, country-house novels tend to naturalize and legitimate British ownership of colonial lands by pointing to an idealized set of social mores that circumscribe any need for violence. The spread of English-style country estates across the empire was thus presented by Trollope and his contemporaries both as a metonym for the expansion of 'English' society to the colonies, and as the central vehicle through which such values were engendered in new lands – a social and architectural form that could transform foreign lands into mirror images of English society.

These country-estate novels and imperial romances were joined by a number of genres that sought to make sense of such diverse phenomena as increasing competition to Britain's commercial empire (especially from Germany and the United States), the entrance of women into the workplace and the rise of what Harold Perkin has memorably dubbed 'professional society' (Perkin 1989). There were invasion novels that transformed anxieties over the German and American consumer goods flooding British markets into fantastical stories about alien invaders (from the literal aliens of H. G. Wells's *War of the Worlds* (1898) to the orientalized vampires of Bram Stoker's *Dracula* (1897)) (Arata 1990; Shapiro 2008b). There were detective stories that sought to enshrine the expertise of the professional at the apex of a technocratic capitalist society (as in, e.g., Arthur Conan Doyle's Sherlock Holmes series). There were naturalist novels that incorporated the empiricist sociology of Charles Booth and Seebohm Rowntree into their analyses of how living conditions affected the quality of life of the working classes (e.g., the work of George Gissing) (Keating 1989: 318–20). There were New Woman novels that dramatized women's entrance into new professions while arguing for increased access to education and employment opportunities (Ledger 1997). And there were the varied compositions of the Decadent, Symbolist and Aesthetic movements, whose self-conscious orientation towards a niche audience of refined readers anticipated the professionalized type of literary writing that in future years would develop into modernism (Teukolsky 2009).

What is important to recognize about this heterogeneous collection of texts is that it only provides something close to a picture of the late nineteenth-century world-system when it is considered in its totality – as a genre-*system*. While each of the aforementioned novels renders abstract social and economic processes into particularized genre conventions, the representational codes employed by each narrative form often jar with those of other genres. For example, we can see such a disjunction in the contrasting imaginaries of the imperial romance and the alien invasion narrative – the former mimicking both the wars of imperial expansion and the flow of finance capital outwards from London to the colonies in the journeys of its male adventurers, and the latter expressing anxiety over Britain's potential eclipse by emerging imperial powers. Note how each of these narratives tells a very different story about Britain's status in the late nineteenth-century world-system: one a story of optimistic expansion, the other a tale of decadence and ruin. Yet neither account is strictly speaking 'wrong'. As J. A. Hobson's classic analysis of *fin-de-siècle* finance capitalism, *Imperialism* (1902), observed, Britain's imperial expansion into Africa and Asia in the late nineteenth century was largely driven by diminishing rates of return in agriculture and manufacturing, both direct consequences of the fall in prices that attended the consolidation of global markets and increased competition from Germany and the United States. Imperial romances and invasion novels simply look at this process from different positions within the capitalist supply chain. On the one hand, the imperial romance regards the British world-system from the vantage point of finance capital and military expansionism, for which the *fin de siècle* was a period of unmitigated success. Invasion novels, on the other hand, focus more on allegorizing concerns about the domestic market for consumer goods, where an influx of German and American products seemed to portend an economic 'invasion'.

The disparity between these two representations of Britain's late nineteenth-century world-system speaks to how genre-systems makes sense of capitalism's uneven processes. Insofar as the world-system combines any number of different industries, functions, modes of production, class systems and ideologies, the distribution of these across multiple genres helps to render legible what might otherwise be perceived as a chaotic network of contradictory phenomena. This is the case for the allegorical representations of finance capitalism and consumer marketplaces that we find in imperial romances and invasion novels, but the same is true of the other genres present in the *fin-de-siècle* British genre-system. The valorization of professionalism present in detective stories is in marked contrast to the neo-feudal class politics that characterize country-estate novels. Women are afforded avenues to education and professional employment in New Woman novels but are also completely excised from the imperial enterprises depicted in imperial romances. Aesthetic poetry and other proto-modernist writings champion an elite art for refined connoisseurs, while popular fiction identifies craftsmanship with commercial success.

All of these are examples of how genre-systems project contradictory processes into different representational frames. What is important to keep in mind is that these meanings are fundamentally effects of two types of *structure* – the structure of the genre-system, and the structure of the world-system itself. As such, they are effects we can only see when we shift our focus away from the study of individual genres and onto the workings of the genre-system as a whole. Without this more expansive view, it is impossible to see how what might otherwise appear as idiosyncratic stylistic choices are in fact important components of a wider representational vocabulary for describing the dynamics of the world-system.

In addition to enabling the structural analysis of literary fields, the concept of a genre-system also raises a number of interesting possibilities for transhistorical comparison. If genres operate in tandem as a structural unit, then what could be learned, one might ask, by comparing a genre-system such as the one we see at work in *fin-de-siècle* Britain with one from a very different time and place? Do imperial romances, country-house novels, invasion narratives and other contemporary genres retain an unchanging kernel of meaning no matter when and where they are written – a strong 'socio-symbolical message' that 'persists' even when those genres are imported into 'quite different social and cultural contexts' (Jameson 1981: 141)? Or is there a certain elasticity to genre – so that, say, a science fiction tale written in *fin-de-siècle* Britain may use motifs drawn from colonial tales of exploration to describe a proto-professional gentleman-scientist's encounter with unfamiliar species (an in Wells's *Time Machine*),[7] but one set in twenty-first-century Nigeria will refashion the colonial encounter narrative to imagine alien technology as a metaphor for the revolutionary potential of an emerging Afropolitan professional elite?[8] Similarly, what might we learn from such a comparison about genres' enduring *structural* roles within literary fields? Might we, for instance, trace a connection between the pigeonholing of Haggard's fantasy-laden imperial romances as mere 'popular' fiction, and later uses of fantasy to shore up minoritarian positions within literary fields (e.g., the anti-modernism of J. R. R. Tolkien and C. S. Lewis, or the subcultural fan groups that dominate today's science fiction and fantasy industry)?[9] And finally, how might we map the rise and fall of particular genres and genre-systems against the economic cycles that constitute the dominant mode of capitalist time?[10] Only time will tell if these avenues of investigation prove fruitful. For now, they serve as intriguing possibilities for what is still an evolving methodology.

Notes

1 Schmitt's term for this distinction is 'friend'/'enemy'; see Schmitt (2007).
2 I take the term 'lifeworld' from Edmund Husserl; see Husserl (1970).
3 For a detailed account of the rising number of femicides in Mexico and other parts of Central America, see Rodríguez (2012).
4 The classic account of capitalism's un-representability is to be found in Jameson (1991: 1–54).
5 On the modernist use of affective detachment, as well as the persistent use of this narrative device in the present, see Moody (2018).
6 Trollope would later update this portrait of Irish society in his unfinished novel *The Land-Leaguers* (1883).
7 On how the identity of the 'professional' grew out of the earlier concept of the English 'gentleman', see Perkin (1989: 116–23). On how the connection between gentlemanly ideals and professional identity plays out in English literature, see Gopinath (2013).
8 I allude here to Nnedi Okorafor's novel *Lagoon* (2014). On the connection between *Lagoon* and Afropolitanism, see Eatough (2017).
9 For an analysis of how Tolkien and Lewis exploited fantasy's minor position to consolidate their anti-modernism, and the persistence of this anti-modernism in young adult literature, see Maria Sanchico Cecire (2019).
10 For attempts to read literature against long-wave economic cycles, see Shapiro (2008a); WReC (2015); Shapiro and Barnard (2017).

CHAPTER 14

World Author
On Exploding Canons and Writing towards More Equitable Literary Futures

Rebecca Braun

In Frankfurt International Airport, Terminal 1, an over-sized Johann Wolfgang von Goethe sits in an elevated position at the centre of the Goethe Bar (Figure 1). Dressed in late eighteenth-century travelling clothes, the sculpture has been lifted from Johann Heinrich Wilhelm Tischbein's 'Goethe in der Campagna' (1787, Goethe in the Roman Campagna). The original painting has been on display in the Frankfurt Städel Museum ever since it was donated to this museum in the town of Goethe's birth in 1887, and it is considered of artistic value not least for the way it articulates Goethe's importance as a cultural and intellectual figurehead for European letters of the time. Accordingly, in the painting, too, Goethe is larger than life, and he reclines against a scenery of assembled Roman ruins with a gaze that implies a great mind occupied by matters of intellectual enlightenment that transcend a specific time and place. The painting encapsulates a whole cult of Goethe that took hold in the nineteenth century and has gone on to cement not just his German, but his

Figure 1   Statue of Goethe on display in Frankfurt Airport's Goethe Bar. Photograph by R. Braun, 2016.

global reputation. The modern sculptural mock-up, by contrast, places Frankfurt's best-known author at the heart of a contemporary commercial space, ostensibly offering 'full service' to harried international travellers and, in so doing, perhaps appealing to a slower pace of life for the length of time it takes to drink a coffee. His physical elevation above the coffee tables continues the intellectual veneration expressed in Tischbein's painting, as Frankfurt Airport celebrates its city's most famous son, but it also has a distinctly practical purpose: for the bar to catch the eye of passers-by as they look for somewhere to kill twenty minutes and eat a snack.

When Goethe caught my eye, it was about five in the morning and I was on my way back from a Comparative Literature conference in the United States. Although the bar was closed, it opened up a way of articulating much of what I had been trying to express. In the presentation I had just given I had borrowed the term 'network intellectual' from Fred Turner and Christine Larson's 2015 work in Celebrity Studies and inflected it through the work of sociologist Bruno Latour to argue that 'world literature', as a more or less canonical product that can be mapped at any one time, is necessarily underpinned by a thoroughly networked practice of 'world authorship'. This latter is subject to considerable flux and expansion as it draws ever more people, places, processes and things into its orbit, and it is therefore here that the questions of what literature 'is' and 'does' are most live (Latour 2005; Braun 2016). Now, as Goethe gazed serenely past me and into the shuttered window of the airport shop opposite, he embodied back at me my multidirectional musings on authors' relationship to the world around them. Goethe's 'world author' persona demonstratively on display in the transit lounge is the product of his own writing and repeated self-projection during his lifetime, of course, but also of Tischbein's late eighteenth-century cultural framing, Frankfurt city's late nineteenth-century desire to stake its claim in the nascent German Empire, and Frankfurt Airport's early twenty-first century attempts to infuse its generic airport architecture with local tourist connections that reinforce a certain cultural cachet whilst also driving commerce. As Goethe literally grows in stature, his agency in mediating his own world authorship diminishes and the multiple agendas of others take over.

Here, quite literally personified, was in fact my guiding research observation on how authorship relates to the world: the diverse ways in which an author is mediated necessarily place his or her writings into other contexts that significantly affect what this writing can be, as well as who exactly exerts agency over this process of ongoing reception. Thus, the baristas serving coffee in cups bearing Goethe's signature all make an infinitesimal contribution to Goethe's work as it is experienced by the international travellers who drink in his shadow. This kind of agency goes well beyond the human. Indeed, to my eye that had just recently finished reading Latour, the plaster mould of the statue itself, the wood-veneer countertops around it, the shatter-proof glass balcony above and the hazard tape stuck to the floor below are all part of what Goethe's authorship has become in a world that needs safe, individual figureheads that can provide intellectual orientation as well as help with cash flow in the complex, ever-shifting world swirling around them. This leads to a paradox in how both he and his work are valued. Where Goethe rails against the strictures of artistic convention in his early writing precisely in order to celebrate instead man's inherent dynamic, creative connection with nature, his very body has become canonical for a whole host of interrelated economic and cultural spheres by the early twenty-first century, such that now an entire airport transit lounge has been constructed around him. By association, his literary material, which draws its life blood from offering new ways of seeing and celebrating the world's harmony, has been allied with diverse physical materials, each of which leaves its own small trace on who and what that author can be and all of which collectively tend towards solidification, if not to say ossification, of that intellectual spirit. It becomes literally immured in the physical environment as well as intangibly appropriated by multiple other discourses with their own, often contradictory, take on cultural value that – the point hardly needs to be stressed – are unequally accessed by different demographic groups (notably all those people who will never walk through Frankfurt airport).

Yet this mediation is not one-way. If the airport, one of the ultimate nodes in the flow of twenty-first-century global capitalism, subtly affects the way we see and value Goethe's authorship, Goethe's authorship also makes us think in unexpected ways about the wider world in which literature exists. Polymath that he was, Goethe not only greatly valued the chance intermingling of people from all different walks of life passing through the Central European hub of the Weimar court – an airport of sorts for his times. He also particularly appreciated how architecture could tangibly express the ideal of an underpinning universal harmony that he otherwise explored in the abstract in literary narrative or made the subject of extended scientific hypothesis. Thus, in an essay from 1772, he wrote passionately about the way Strasbourg Cathedral, for all its gothic detail, displayed the same kind of overarching unity as a natural organism. Indeed, this concern with the interconnectedness of often seemingly divergent things – whether individual styles or spheres of life – not only would go on to shape much of his later work but is particularly prevalent in the image of Goethe himself acting as a major figure at the helm of a sizeable, markedly interdisciplinary intellectual network, as detailed by Johann Peter Eckermann in his influential three-volume chronicle *Conversations with Goethe* (Goethe 1998). It is here, in fact, that Goethe's oft quoted pronouncement on the advent of world literature in 1827 is recorded, and thus here that the points are set for the subsequent reception of Goethe's putative authorship of the very term 'world literature'. In scholarship from the early twenty-first century onwards, which coincides with a renaissance of interest in the whole subject area, this has generally been relayed as a form of cultural circulation that has the power to change the way we see the world around us, and thus, as John K. Noyes has argued, might not only shape but also partly counter dominant political and economic models of globalization (Noyes 2015).

As Goethe discourses to Eckermann on the circulation of books from different cultures in early 1827 and subsequently further actively facilitates this circulation through his role as a journal editor, he is therefore metaphorically setting out an alternative space for the flow of cultural goods. This flow of cultural goods will lead to a genuine interpersonal exchange that has the potential to affect the very fabric of society as different people and traditions are brought into contact with one another, albeit of a certain elite subsection of what we might now call our globalized world. Goethe, as captured in Eckermann's diaries, repeatedly conceives this as part of a universal experience of reflecting on being human in the world and seeing this human experience as part of a larger contextualized whole that includes architecture, natural landscapes and the laws of physics as much as belletrist and philosophical endeavours. Crucially, however, both in his own activities and in the scant direct comments he made about the emerging canon of 'world literature' that might sustain such exchanges, Goethe repeatedly stressed the importance of person-to-person interaction. This human element, together with the obvious inequality of opportunity that must accompany it, is the overlooked aspect of his own thinking on the notion of 'world literature', and it has remained a blind spot in almost all subsequent research on the topic. In what follows, I therefore outline both theoretical and practical approaches that allow us to do 'full service' to literary studies and globalization by bringing the world author and its significance as a cultural and economic construct for contemporary globalized society back into view.

Theoretical Approaches to World Authorship

The idea that literary texts represent worlds of their own underpins both scholarly analysis of literature and popular engagement with authors.

Traditionally, literary scholars seek to describe and evaluate the success with which a particular literary world is created, whether this is done in a realist, modernist, surrealist or any other manner, and regardless of whether they are attributing the success with which this is done to an individual author or to a much wider set of discursive factors. Similarly, the ability of what one might call the 'literary imagination' manifest in these textual worlds to foreshadow possible real-world scenarios, as well as to provide entertaining or otherwise instructive counterfoils to our collective lived experience, is what is generally being honoured when authors receive prizes or other forms of social accolade during or after their lifetime. The stipulation in Alfred Nobel's will, generally considered rather cryptic, that the Nobel Prize in Literature be awarded to the work of literature 'in the most ideal direction' is in fact a case in point for this. Philosophy too has made much of these literary worlds. For Martin Heidegger, for example, the potential achievements of literary texts go well beyond those of the individual author. For him, literature as a whole provides a particular view on the world that both is the defining feature of literature in the first place and provides a broader philosophical insight into the human condition. He considers the work of art fundamentally to undermine simple notions of chronology and causality by being 'ever non-objective' (because of the fact that it unfolds within the human consciousness) (Heidegger 1971: 42). From this vantage point of radical subjectivity, the work of art reflects on the phenomenon of the world's 'worlding', of which it too is a part. It does this through its inherent ability to evoke messy ontological truths in an experiential way for those who engage with its particular space and time and is therefore defined precisely by the way it is only ever unfolding in the present, as a broader network of people, places and things engage with it.

Where for Heidegger and a number of other influential twentieth-century philosophers, including Michel Foucault and Jacques Derrida, literary texts are thus able to make the complex interconnections between language, cognition and the material world around us tangible in ways that ordinary speech and other forms of human interaction do not, the literary scholar Leslie Adelson specifically links the potential inherent in this literary imagination to the need for finding new ways of navigating the challenges posed by twenty-first-century globalization. Her key argument is that globalization in the contemporary sense has mutated from being merely a case of ever greater connectivity in actual space and time to also entailing a shift in how space and time are perceived in the contemporary individual's mind. Her associated premise is that while some contemporary literary texts echo experiences of globalization in a 'symptomatic' way (by engaging with obvious themes, such as migration, or exhibiting an aesthetics of connectivity, for example), there are others that have the potential to be 'future-making' by capturing 'more than meets the eye' (Adelson 2015: 680, 679) within our contemporary world. By this, she means the way in which they engage with intangible experiences of being connected in multiple contradictory ways with the world around us that conventional understandings of time and space would not allow. Such texts give us the tools for articulating our existence differently in the world, working from the literary imagination outwards with performative power for shaping a potentially different future.

In the context of this chapter, we can link this back to the ineffable 'more than meets the eye' that Goethe perceived in Strasbourg Cathedral. To communicate the profundity of his experience there and link it up to his own broader enactment of the power of the creative individual who acts in harmony with the world around him, Goethe avails himself of all the licence of fiction: the thirteenth-century master builder Erwin von Steinbach appears in a vision to the incredulous young Goethe as he tries to make sense of a Gothic aesthetic that the dominant art theory of the time had previously decried to him as ugly and overburdened. The result is a radically new appreciation not just of the cathedral, but of the whole world:

> How fresh was its radiance in the misty shimmer of morning light, how happily I stretched out my arms towards it and looked at the vast, harmonious masses animated by countless components! As in the works of eternal nature, down to the smallest fiber, all its form, all serves the whole. How lightly the immense, firmly-grounded edifice soars into the air, how like filigree everything is, yet made for eternity! I owe it to your instruction, noble genius, that I no longer reel when confronting your profundities, that my soul is touched by the blissful calm of a spirit who can look down on such a creation and say, as did God, 'It is good!' (Goethe 2016: 870)

Linking Goethe, Heidegger and Adelson is the focus on the world-revealing power of creative perception on the one hand and, on the other, the belief that worlds beyond literature (real worlds and possible future worlds) are formed by the creative act even as they also condition it. This imbrication of an apparently individual act with an endlessly recursive set of mediations between literature and the world is also at the heart of world authorship. For, as all the examples above have made clear, authorship is a process that is not exhausted by the writers who first set pen to paper and compose a literary work; rather, it is repeatedly modulated by the many different ways in which responsibility for the literary world of the text and the various iterations of the real world that surround it are perceived and acted upon by different people and things at different times.

A writer's 'world authorship' as I am defining it here, then, is the sum of all these actions and interactions, of which those of the writer herself are but a part (albeit an important one). World authorship referred to in the abstract invokes the extended process of making a text that includes all these diverse practitioners. It is not bound to the initial drafting, publishing and reception of a work but extends right up to the present moment, as different sets of people and circumstances condition what a work can mean and where it sits in society. The more a piece of work gets caught up in global processes, not just of publishing but of the global flow of goods and services in a much broader sense too, the more its world authorship is going to expand. It might be useful to call the writer we conventionally think of as the individual author an 'originator' in line with the conventional modern understanding of the author as the creative origin of the text, but only in order to differentiate this person's input in this iterative process from that of the many others involved. This originator author remains a significant agent within the process, but one whose overall agency is significantly relativized by that of all the other agents, both people and things, influencing the real-world circumstances in which the work exists at any one point in time, from editors, through rights managers and translators, to festival organizers, and indeed architects and baristas. To speak of an individual as a 'world author' is therefore both to acknowledge an individual's success in having his or her work taken up and iteratively inserted in different ways into the world around it, but also to evoke the originator's diminished actual agency in controlling what the world(s) of his or her text may be. This is in fact almost the inverse of traditional understandings of the author as a Romantic genius whose creative inspiration precedes the text and determines all subsequent engagement with it. The term therefore means something quite different to lay understandings of being either a global bestselling writer (such as Paulo Coelho) or a major point of reference in the Western canon (such as Homer, or indeed Goethe). These latter understandings evoke absolute numbers (in terms of global sales) or an 'achieved' status that becomes largely self-enforcing in line with observations about fame, and both phenomena are best interrogated through the lens of literary celebrity (Boone and Vickers 2011; Braun and Spiers 2016). Remaining within debates about world literature and drawing out our terminology expressly from them, the world author is not an honorific badge in either neoliberal or elite cultural terms, but a simple fact of writing that reaches an audience and is continually modified by the recursive acts of mediation that ensue. These acts are particularly diverse in the contemporary context of global capitalism, such that studying world authorship entails studying a wide range of social and economic actors as inherent parts of the literary process.

By this definition, the question of who can be a world author is answered in the most expansive way possible: nominally, everyone. This stretches from everyone who writes to everyone who engages with what is written, which could technically be everyone, full stop. There are, however, some limiting factors that can usefully be applied at this point. Foucault's observations on the author function from 1969 remain relevant, as he points out the entrenched social desire to limit a work's potential for meaning and hold an individual accountable for what is produced (Foucault 2000). The promotional structures that sustain world authorship today – both the commercial considerations within publishing as well as other cultural and intellectual conditions determining the mediation of literary work around the world – still require the illusion of individual determinacy, even if only for the expediency of having a shorthand. In my example above, Goethe needs to look like he is the wellspring of European letters if people are going to carry on wanting to engage with both them and him. Thus, the processes underlying world authorship, in themselves potentially endlessly inclusive, will all point towards a seemingly exclusive world author figure who both emerges out of this massive collaborative effort and justifies its existence in the first place. The world author is both the start and end point of the world authorship process. This sense of monumentality, however, is quite different from defining world authors as canonical authors. The potentially endlessly inclusive process of collaborative mediation applies in principle to any author whose work finds an echo, no matter how small, in the real world. In fact, world authorship as a fundamental process linking the world created in the literary text and the highly networked real world around it is easiest to see when we move away from canonical figures and the well-known circumstances of their mediation and reception. We can look instead at the ethical questions of access thrown up by wider mediating infrastructures underpinning the whole neoliberal system of publishing on the one hand, and individuals expressly setting out to challenge them on the other.

Practical Manifestations of World Authorship

In order to effect this shift, the rest of this chapter will consider the growth of the publishing infrastructure in West Germany in the latter half of the twentieth century, which was followed by a discernible turn towards acknowledging more diverse authorial practices into the first two decades of the twenty-first. The literary history to be traced briefly in these pages is one that gives particular consideration to the 'modes of authorship' that emerged in response to the way both politics and economics were perceived in the post-war period, but whose roots go right back to the emergence of Goethe's world literature. Although my examples are specific to the German-language context, the underlying ontology of world authorship that I am setting out can be adapted to other areas of the globe, certainly in the West and with some modification elsewhere too. The idea of classifying authorship by mode, which I have developed in depth elsewhere (Braun 2022) and present necessarily summarily here, follows directly on from the considerations above about how best to articulate the relationship between an individual writer and the potentially limitless world in a way that acknowledges mutually imbricated agency on both parts.

A mode of authorship, then, describes a certain attitude towards being an author in the world, whether on the part of that author or of the wider world that yields and validates her authorship. It can be inferred from close analysis of literary practices, whether these practices reside in the tangible structure of a literary text, are reconstructed through archival traces of relations across the literature network, or are intangibly subject to philosophical concepts or social conventions. It is not necessarily directly perceived by either an author or any other actor as significant in its own right. With respect to German literary history of the latter half of the twentieth century, four modes suggest themselves: the celebratory, commemorative, satirical and utopian. I have alighted on these modes by distilling attitudes towards authorship displayed in and around German literature and culture to a basic set of elemental blocks. I took as broad a brush as I possibly could in order to do so, starting out with just two modes and only adding to them when I found compelling evidence that there was a significant body of work that didn't fit to at least some degree into either category. The original modes – the celebratory and the commemorative – acknowledged the foundational force of the Romantic genius at the turn of the nineteenth century (broadly speaking, Goethe's oeuvre both presumes and enacts this mode) and the cultural imperative of memory and memorialization that sets in over the course of the twentieth century. The satirical and utopian modes were added when I realized the extent to which extended critique of the dominant paradigms that earnestly foregrounded individual achievement needed to be factored into the schema. Immersing myself in the German literary world from the 1950s through to the late 2010s, I found there were ultimately four modes of authorship that

I couldn't do without. When used either alone or in combination with one another as a way of explaining both the fine detail and the wider significance of a writer's work, they opened up a whole new way of, literally, seeing authorship. The product of significant two-way interaction between an individual and the wider world, authorship became both a textual and an inherently social phenomenon with significant constitutive power for the way we grasp the worlds, real and imagined, around us. With this, we are able to see how forces of late twentieth-century globalization both shape and are themselves shaped by key parameters of the literary worlds invoked by Heidegger and Adelson above.

These points can be illustrated through reference to another picture, this time the so-called *Verlagscollage* (publisher's collage) inserted by one-time publisher and freelance literary journalist Fritz J. Raddatz into his memoir of working for the Rowohlt publishing house in the 1960s (Raddatz 2015). Originally established by Ernst Rowohlt in Leipzig in 1908 and with headquarters in Berlin during the Weimar period, the publishing house was re-established first in Stuttgart directly after the war and then in Hamburg in 1950. The post-war business was so successful that in 1960 the famous architect Fritz Trautwein built a brand-new headquarters in the nearby Reinbek which remained the central seat of the business until 2019 and now enjoys listed status. The publisher could be compared to Penguin in its wide range of literary fiction and early introduction of diverse paperback series in the 1950s. Raddatz played a particularly important role in developing the paperback, particularly in support of left-wing political causes, as well as spotting talented upcoming writers in both German and other major languages, such as French and English. Having previously worked for the East German Volk und Welt (People and World) publishing house, where he sought to increase the number of modernist texts available for East German readers throughout the 1950s, he brought extensive experience of trying to navigate between different literary systems with him to the West German Rowohlt. He was thus particularly well placed to conceive of the potential literary space that hung between communism and capitalism in a manner not so dissimilar to Goethe's concept of world literature as something that should transcend nationalist political structures, and he certainly understood the value of human contacts in building transnational literary connections.

By his own account, his entry into West German publishing was facilitated by the grand patriarch Ernst Rowohlt taking him on in his literary salon of sorts. Here he would quickly learn the markedly male mores that would set him up for a lifetime in twentieth-century letters that was characterized by elite gatherings and colourful soirees and would repeatedly see him rubbing shoulders with all the major names of late twentieth-century German letters. Although the commercial infrastructure underpinning the network of independent publishers that characterized mid-twentieth-century German publishing is dwarfed by the twenty-first-century context – where six global companies with multimedia holdings account for 80 per cent of the US market (McIlroy 2016) and control well over half of other Western countries' sales (Brown 2006) – West German publishing was not short of cash, prestige, nor wider powerful networks by the standards of the day. In fact, as the 1960s progressed, contemporary authors and their publishers wielded considerable soft power as they were increasingly seen to be leading on debates about what German values should be, based on both the recent past and hopes and dreams for the future. Accordingly, while the individuals working in these broader publishing structures were not themselves literary authors in the conventional sense (although Raddatz did make various attempts at writing fiction), they are all key figures in the iterative process of world authorship through the way they edited, promoted, networked and funded many writers who went on to become household names both in German-speaking Europe and beyond.

The 'publisher's collage' pictured in Figure 2 captures some of this pioneering spirit of 1960s West German publishing and offers a limited critique of it. Pasted onto a background representing the front entrance to the newly built headquarters in Reinbek, the collage shows five men posing in swimming trunks to create a human pyramid. The CEO Heinrich Maria Ledig-Rowohlt (Ernst Rowohlt's eldest son) stands on the shoulders/thighs of the crouching Fritz J. Raddatz, with three further senior managers balancing on Ledig's shoulders and left and right thighs respectively. The collage has been judiciously doctored to give all five men something approaching body-builder physiques, although the famously large Ledig retains a paunch. Raddatz in particular has acquired a particularly sporty physique and is otherwise depicted as the strong foundation on which the charismatic Ledig balances while the other three work together on top to provide the finishing visual touches. Raddatz does not explicitly comment on this image in his memoir, but it clearly supports the general picture he paints as being Ledig's trusted second-in-command, who was in many respects shouldering many of the publisher's business decisions. The collage also supports the image of an almost exclusively male environment in publishing that emerges, equally uncommented, from Raddatz's various accounts of both the years at Rowohlt and his subsequent decades spent first as literary editor-in-chief for the weekly broadsheet *Die Zeit* and then as a freelance journalist and literary commentator.

Figure 2 The 'Verlagscollage'. Fritz J. Raddatz at the base of the pyramid; Hans Maria Ledig-Rowohlt above him; on his shoulders Kurt Busch, Chief Financial Officer; to his right, Distribution Manager, Karl Hans Hintermeier; to his left, Edgar Friedrichsen, Print Production Manager. Reproduced in Raddatz 2015.

In terms of the modes of authorship that I outlined above, this picture unquestionably evokes a celebratory mode on the part of the whole industry designed to mediate literary work. Not only are the men themselves posing as a glamorous and powerful ensemble, which is of course itself a tongue-in-cheek engagement with the tradition of honouring strong men on the one hand and, perhaps, on the other a humorous gesture to the capable support team on which Rowohlt authors and readers can draw. More importantly, the built environment around them also underscores the self-evident nature of the position publishing occupies in society. The low-rise building with the large swathe of landscaped ground in its forecourt gestures to investment in real estate, while the notion that senior business leaders might have time to frolic on the lawn to create a sort of inverse pin-up calendar points to a certain *esprit de corps* (pardon my pun) that can either literally afford not to take itself too seriously or that sees further commercial benefit in the undertaking. All of this reinforces the secure position of their underlying business, namely mediating the work of the authors they have taken on in such a way as to enhance both the cultural and economic status of all involved – and to provide entertainment in tune with the mores of the economically booming post-war society as they do so.

Alongside the celebratory mode and for reasons already partially outlined above, the satirical mode is therefore clearly also in play. While the material infrastructure of publishing and the core ideology of the strong male provide the basic frame of reference for understanding this picture and are uncritically invoked, satire is evident in the way the individuals are depicted and insinuations made about the relations between them: who carries whom and how stable the whole construction really is. Although the (demeaning) tradition of the female pin-up calendar is also referenced, it is hard to suppose that any of the satire is directed at critiquing the gender imbalance in publishing. Rather, the satirical mode crowds out the space for even acknowledging women's potential role in the industry. Just as in Shakespeare's day male actors were deemed perfectly able to play female parts, here too an all-male cast perceives no need for women. Themselves occupying the subservient or otherwise objectified position within their own self-satire, the five men as displayed here manage to foreclose any actual critique from a position of alterity by merging the satirical mode with the celebratory mode in a way that ultimately serves to strengthen the message of male power emanating from the collage.

A certain complicity, then, can be seen in the way the celebratory and satirical modes of authorship are brought into play within this collage, which is very much a picture of its times – times when, for example, nobody appears to have raised an eyebrow that lucrative publishing deals were often concluded in Hamburg's red-light district. These modes of authorship describe both the confidently un-self-critical spirit in which the collage itself was put together, but also the underlying assumptions about the value of authorship that can be read from the publishing personnel involved in the frame, as well as the material infrastructure around them. Although none of the individuals – and certainly none of the buildings or landscape features – are likely directly to perceive themselves as operating within these modes, the underlying attitudes of celebrating and/or satirizing within a thoroughly normative frame of skewed gender relations and elitist cultural practices can be intuited from the collective world that their multiple interactions create.

What is therefore necessarily missing from the publisher's collage is any sort of commemorative gesture that might point to the recent traumas and attendant absences in German letters, as well as any indication that society might aspire to organize itself otherwise, around different values and/or different lines of communication that veer away from honorific models of individual achievement and seek instead dialogical development – the commemorative and utopian modes respectively. This is not to berate an image that probably only ever set out to be something of a passing joke for a particular, in-crowd audience. It is merely to acknowledge its limits: the collage is part of a thoroughly normative approach to the wider business of authorship, and neither the person(s) who put it together nor the individuals and broader sector represented within it have any interest in fundamentally changing this status quo. This is not least because the whole network of social contacts, meeting places and cultural habits that drive the literary ecosystem themselves act broadly within and thus in turn replicate these modes, and they do so in such a way that keeps both money and books circulating in the broader economy. Maintaining the mystique of the desirable (male) author is the bigger game that the most influential actors in German letters across the latter half of the twentieth-century play, even – or in some cases particularly – when they appear to be trying to poke fun at it.

Nevertheless, the premise that authors, through the works they initiate, might be able to look beyond their own willing commodification and help us capture 'more than meets the eye' with a view to alternative ways of being in a globalized world remains central to this chapter. Nor, for all its endemic blind spots, does German literary history of the late twentieth and early twenty-first centuries disprove this thesis. Indeed, if my reading of the modes of authorship evident in the publisher's collage above is correct, then perceiving the normative use to which the celebratory and satirical modes are put already helps us see blind spots that were in fact always hidden in full view. This in turn encourages us to think differently about current normative forms of world authorship: on what current practices and relations might we wish to build, whether as writers, readers or any one of a range of cultural mediators in a world that now consciously labels itself globalized?

One answer has been given by the long-running institution of the Ingeborg Bachmann Prize, which is awarded annually in the eponymous author's hometown of Klagenfurt, Austria, and run as a highly publicized live competition between aspiring writers. In recent times, its list of winners has shown marked linguistic and ethnic diversity, including a significant number of laureates whose first language is not German and many of whom have operated in multiple different cultural contexts. The 2014 winner, Katja Petrowskaja, is one of these, and her winning entry, an extract from her autobiographical text *Vielleicht Esther* (*Maybe Esther*), can be taken here as broadly representative for a whole swathe of writing whose starting point is well outside the normative German canon but which is considered to be articulating a new set of world experiences that significantly expand and enrich this canon as much as they challenge its very existence. These questions of access are economic as much as they are cultural, for often the mother tongues in question are from the former Eastern bloc, which has both a smaller home readership and (even) less chance of being picked up for translation into English than the more major language of German. Yet the way in which such authors are breaking into the German-language market is also profoundly changing what this market looks like, precisely by pushing against the post-war normative frame in which the dominant modes of authorship unfold.

'History begins when there are no more people to ask, only sources', writes Petrowskaja's autobiographical narrator (Petrowskaja 2018: 22–3), as she works outwards from scraps of recipes and half-remembered labels on jars to try to piece together a picture of who her ancestors were and how they lived over the twentieth century.[1] The resulting text tells the story of how what started out as simple research into her Jewish family history quickly revealed multiple lives that had been lost, as well as unexpected connections across an extended network that stretched from Vienna and Warsaw through to Kiev and further into small provincial towns in Ukraine, Poland and Russia, as well as France and North America. Strikingly, one of the recurring connections is her maternal family's work in establishing schools for deaf and mute people: literally giving a voice to those who would otherwise routinely not be heard in society. In this respect, her task becomes one of hearing those who have been doubly not heard, even as these lives and stories have been multiply erased from her background: she is not a practising Jew herself, the stories she wishes to uncover are mostly of those who did not survive the Soviet and National Socialist regimes, and many of these characters were even in their own day intricately allied with people whose voices and experiences were pushed to the margins of society.

Bearing all this in mind, Petrowskaja's narrative takes direct aim at official memory narratives, many of which informed a wide swathe of both German and European cultural initiatives across the late 1990s and early 2000s. The main ethical thrust of her text is to write against the fact not that commemoration of her community has not happened, but that it has happened in such a way as actively to silence it. Writing about the official commemoration of the siege of Leningrad that would take one million lives, she observes, 'We were called on to forget no one and nothing in order that we forget who or what was forgotten' (Petrowskaja 2018: 31). This sense of how the commemorative mode can itself cast a shadow is particularly clearly set out when she attempts to look at the house in Warsaw where her grandmother was born in 1905. The only information she can access compels her to look at the area through the lens of the Jewish ghetto:

> In an attempt to fend off such references, I repeated that of course the ghetto was the most important thing, but I was looking for my history here, which started much earlier. My grandmother was born in Warsaw in 1905, my great-grandfather had a school for the deaf-mute here up to 1915, and that was that. Yet the people I was talking to, those in the fields of Warsaw historiography and its well-equipped outposts in the Internet and in scholarship, were in the majority, and they all said ghetto. Ghetto here! Ghetto there! Ghetto up! Ghetto down! (Petrowskaja 2018: 88–9)

The rhetorically cacophonous repetition of the word 'ghetto' conveys the sense of being drowned out, with the narrator forced to allow her own perspective, which does not fully mesh with the well-known narrative of trauma and loss, to be submerged. She will counter this by doggedly piecing back together what she can and, in so doing, challenging what exactly is remembered. In fact, the whole thrust of her text becomes one of filling in the very considerable blank space on the metaphorical map of memory narratives that draw on the lives and experiences of millions of people right across Central and Eastern Europe, but which all too frequently treat them as a homogeneous mass. Precisely because it has become so difficult to trace individual family members with any certainty, she finds herself taking on the fates of all the people she finds listed who share the more common names in her family tree. However, in recognizing 'that I had to consider each person on the lists one of my own' (Petrowskaja 2018: 20), Petrowskaja's narrator is also determining that she must provide a qualitatively different kind of commemorative mode to that which has hitherto guided the kind of monolithic memory narratives that she encounters online and in various social and scholarly exchanges across the German-, English-, French-, Polish- and Russian-speaking worlds. She wants to know not how these people were deported and died, but how they lived, and how those lives that were lived still shape the world today.

With this in mind, the entirety of Petrowskaja's text is underpinned by her deliberate performance of her particular kind of commemorative mode against the backdrop of the German- and European-inflected norm that she finds so lacking. Yet in critiquing the shadow cast by dominant memory narratives, Petrowskaja is not interested in some kind of nationalist or ethnically led tally of relative suffering or ethical oversight. In fact, central to her endeavour is the ability to step outside any one linguistic or political frame. Having learned German as an adult, she is particularly positive about how researching and writing through this language makes it easier to see and hear the untold stories that run through her extended family in Russian, Polish and Yiddish. Drawing on Russian etymology, she explains how 'German' in Russian, *'nemetskiy'*, literally means the language of the mute, *'nemoy nemets'* (Petrowskaja 2018: 68). Unexpectedly, then, the German language itself places her in a similar situation to those deaf-mute children to whom her ancestors would give a voice, and, as also the 'language of the enemy' (Petrowskaja 2018: 69), it provides her with both an escape route from and a way back into her family history. This sets the whole creative process of research and writing in motion for Petrowskaja: 'I thought in Russian, looked for my Jewish relatives, and wrote in German. I was lucky to be able to move in that space between languages, swapping words and switching roles and viewpoints' (Petrowskaja 2018: 100).

The idea that a multiplication of languages, roles and perspectives might be helpful when trying to establish how one should live in the world takes us directly into the utopian mode of authorship. This mode requires the ability to co-locate oneself in different, partially mutually exclusive systems, just as Thomas More's *Utopia* gains its full impact from shuttling back and forth between the newly discovered world of Utopia and sixteenth-century England, and the various writer figures invoked within it are both everywhere and nowhere at once. Petrowskaja will repeatedly be overwhelmed by the unexpected signifiers she encounters in her family's past and which cannot be incorporated into her present – the newspaper reports from 1932 that disintegrate in her hands as she tries to find out the truth about her great uncle, shot by the Soviet state for apparently attempting to assassinate the German ambassador, for example, or the perfect horror of the paradise apple trees that link her long-lost grandfather and suspected beneficiary of early Stalinist purges with Nazi atrocities. When the narrator learns about these, she finds she has to rewrite some of the happiest memories of her childhood. Even her own German-language authorial persona later seems eerily pre-figured in the place of her birth, as she reflects on how she is the product of two streets in Kiev, the Ulitsa Engelsa (Engels Street) and Ulitsa Liebknechta (Karl Liebknecht Street), birthplaces of her father and mother respectively (Petrowskaja 2018: 249). However, this sense that material objects, places and language itself also have agency that can seriously undermine the individual's attempt to orient herself in the world is also distinctly liberating. If the author stops trying to control and order the narrative around what she can immediately perceive and thinks she knows, and instead lets the deaf and mute connections between people, places and things come to the fore, then she is also able to create a text that has many more points of access for many different people.

Against a background of too much – history, language, global connectivity – Petrowskaja's autobiographical narrator is representative of many writers in German in the twenty-first century who are deliberately trying to give a voice to the lives and things that have tended to get drowned out or have gone unnoticed, and they do so by marshalling the innate ability of the literary text to hold multiple intangible things in view. As such, the utopian mode of authorship is harnessed to a critical reconsideration of how dominant celebratory and commemorative modes have unfolded up to now and how they should be oriented for the future. This is a different kind of world authorship, one that is not necessarily on view in airport terminals, but which is quietly servicing a growing need to connect differently, with both global pasts and global futures. While Petrowskaja remains the shorthand 'world author' who has won the Bachmann Prize and profited from the subsequent international attention and book sales, everything about her book points away from the individual and towards the multiple. This is consciously presented within the narrative itself as a move away from the grand narratives that dominate world history towards the unvoiced attitudes of people, places and things that collectively make up actual shared pasts, presents and futures and the way these might carry meaning for a wide variety of stakeholders. In this utopian mode of authorship, the reduction of agency on the part of the originator author is therefore not a structural irony brought about by the global flow of capital as ever more people become involved in mediating the work, but rather the beginnings of more equitable literary futures where other non-monetized connections across countries and cultures, time and space, come to the fore. The multilingual, pluralistic spaces opened up in and by texts such as Petrowskaja's allow us to author a more modest but perhaps also a more meaningful place for our human activities and geopolitical interconnections as we collectively reflect on what it means to move together through the world.

Note

1 All subsequent references are to this English-language edition.

PART III
Application

CHAPTER 15

The Globalization of the Enclave

Matthew Hart

In his book of essays *Hold Everything Dear*, the English writer John Berger offers two apparently antithetical descriptions of our globalized age. The first concerns the migrants who, whether in Lesbos or Arizona, Calais or Cueta, find themselves trapped outside the fortified barriers meant to deter the unwanted and deflect the desperate:

> The poor are collectively unseizable. They are not only the majority on the planet, they are everywhere and the smallest event speaks of them. This is why the essential activity of the rich today is the building of walls—walls of concrete, of electronic surveillance, of missile barrages, frontier controls, and opaque media screens. (Berger 2008: 98)

The second passage is from the micro-essay 'Wanting Now' (2006), which concludes by defining freedom not as getting what we want but as the ability to acknowledge desire's unfulfillable supremacy. It begins with this capsule summary of the twenty-first-century world:

> The world has changed. Information is being communicated differently. Misinformation is developing its technique. On a world scale emigration has become the principal means of survival. (Berger 2008: 7)

In the last quotation, we encounter that familiar trope of our changing millennial world: information, misinformation, people on the move. In the first, the building of walls: blockage, surveillance, opacity, control. These are not, however, contradictory statements. For Berger, the 'offshore demented dream of the new ongoing power' is the fantasy of an entire planet transformed into 'a single fluid market' (Berger 2008: 122). This process involves the cultural deracination, as well as the depopulation, of provincial zones such as the alpine Haute-Savoie region of France to which Berger himself emigrated in 1962. But just as capital puts poor people on the move, so must it keep those movements under control – must, in Berger's terms, attempt to seize the unseizable by building walls and throwing up all kinds of obstacle, material and immaterial, to the goings and gatherings of poor humans. In the words of China Miéville, another visionary writer of the British left, under the 'internationalization of capital', the oligarch's dream isn't of 'open borders but of mobile ones, as ferociously exclusive as those of any other state, and more than most' (Miéville 2007: 261). This explains why, in response to fears about the movement of people into the United States, a traveller from Ontario to New York goes through US customs and immigration while still in Toronto Pearson Airport, or why US Border Patrol now routinely stops vehicles and sets up checkpoints many hundreds of miles inside US territory.[1] The border is not a line but a volume within which people move and live.[2]

Such a position is hardly controversial. Writing in 2007, Manfred B. Steger distinguished between globalization as an ongoing and uneven complex of social developments and the ideological formation he called 'globalism': a 'hegemonic system of ideas that makes normative claims about a set of social processes called "globalization"', and which thereby presents a certain model of neoliberal economic development as an inevitable fact of contemporary history (Steger 2007: 369). For Steger, 'globalism' was the overt ideological project of neoliberal elites in the 1990s and early 2000s. That ideological project was already under strain during the 2000s, with the new security and immigration restrictions that followed the so-called Global War on Terror pushing against the liberalization of trade and travel. In the political realm, the early 2000s had witnessed right-wing populist demands that states '[tighten] national borders and [maintain] sharp cultural divisions' (Steger 2007: 379). At the same time, critics in the Global South were revolting against 'economic, political and cultural structures of global apartheid that [divided] the world into a privileged North and a disadvantaged South' (Steger 2007: 380). It's in this context that Miéville felt able to declare, in 2007, that the 'era of the crassest globaldegook is over – the supposed imminent demise of the state, the perforation, dissolution, and evaporation of its sovereignty and borders under the onslaught of commerce and capital are asserted with considerably less vigor than during the boosterish early 1990s' (2007: 261). Similar accounts of globalization's inextricability from bordering and border regimes were developed in this period by scholars such as Étienne Balibar, Brett Neilson, Sandro Mezzadra and Saskia Sassen (Balibar 2004; Sassen 2007; Mezzadra and Nielson 2013). And events the other side of the 2008 financial crash only affirm the inextricability of wall-building and border-crossing. To take just the most pressing current example: as I write, a global pandemic has demonstrated the fundamentally interconnected state of our global communications systems, with the novel coronavirus spreading through transnational human movement systems more quickly than governments can react. At the same time, in the absence of a vaccine, the most effective response to the pandemic has been to throw up barriers to human movement and association, whether in the form of national border closures, local and regional travel bans, immigration-based quarantine regimes or national 'lockdowns'. World scale, meet local wall.

I return to the historical and theoretical implications of this situation in the concluding section of this chapter. First, it's time to consider the chapter's major subject, which is how the interdependence of globalization and bordering regimes leads to the practical and symbolic parcellization of contemporary social and political space, as epitomized by the proliferation of enclosed zones and enclaves as diverse as luxury business parks and desolate refugee camps. These enclave zones, as we shall see by analysing contemporary literature and its recent historical context, are crucial areas in which twenty-first-century nationalisms and nationalities are born and fostered.

Enclaves, Utopian and Otherwise

An enclave, strictly speaking, is an area of territory surrounded by a different kind of territory – another political nation, perhaps, or just a region that's socially or culturally distinct in a way that is marked upon a landscape or streetscape. Formal examples include the Kingdom of Lesotho, landlocked within South Africa, or the English unitary authority of Nottingham, which is entirely surrounded by the administratively distinct County of Nottinghamshire. More relevant here, however, are informal zones such as gated communities or university campuses with their own police or security force. Or, to cite one of the cases we'll come to later, an enclave might be a settlement such as the Calais refugee camp known as 'the Jungle', which was under French jurisdiction but populated by a multi-racial and multi-national group of foreign migrants and asylees, many of whom sought to leave France for residence in England. 'The Jungle' was not administratively or legally distinct from the area around it, but it was socially, culturally and spatially distinct; at times, it was jointly policed by French and British law enforcement officers, making it a zone apart in another respect. In this chapter, we shall be more concerned with such complicated and often informal enclaves rather than with national or municipal islands.[3]

The study of such geographic and architectural developments has been pioneered by Keller Easterling, whose books *Enduring Innocence* (2005) and *Extrastatecraft* (2014) analyse how governments and corporations, encouraged and assisted by transnational institutions such as the World Bank and International Monetary Fund, cooperate so as to subdivide national space in order to produce the infrastructure necessary for the creation and operation of the global economy. Paramount among such kinds of 'infrastructure space' are what she calls 'zones'. These include areas such as the many Special Economic Zones in the People's Republic of China, within which liberalized tax and trade regulations enabled the development of export-oriented economic development in the 1980s and 1990s, as well as more recent developments such as the Dubai International Finance Centre (DIFC), an autonomous 'Financial Free Zone' within the United Arab Emirates, with its own civil and commercial legal system based upon English law, and one of twenty such zones in that city-state of only 1,500 square miles. Such infrastructural zones, Easterling argues, are essential for the operation of global trade and finance; they do not, however, embody the evacuation of national sovereignty so much as a process in which states willingly subdivide and punctuate their own territory. The zone, she writes, is a 'site of multiple, overlapping, or nested forms of sovereignty, where domestic and transnational jurisdictions collide' (2014: 15).

Joseph O'Neill captures this sense of the zone's ambivalent freedom in his novel *The Dog*, published the same year as Easterling's study of infrastructural space. O'Neill's narrator-protagonist is an American lawyer, X., who, in the wake of an ugly breakup and a foundering career, takes a job as legal factotum to an incredibly wealthy Lebanese foundation located in the DIFC. About halfway through his narrative, X. slips into one of his regular moments of cod-anthropological observation:

> The semi-autonomous Dubai International Financial Centre, with its regulatory structures that remove it from the emirate's archaic justice system, is not just a financial free zone. It is also an architecturally free-floating environment. In contrast to almost any other place in Dubai, substantial amenities are offered to the person who wishes to be a pedestrian. Here are broad gray plazas and pools with charcoal or dove gray water. There are green lawns, and blue-gray-brown footbridges, and cafés with silver chairs, and cool gray-brown breezeways and charcoal gray sculptures. The beautiful office buildings are gray and gray-blue and silver-gray. Gray-brown doves go about near the dove gray pools and beautiful women go coolly across the plazas in dark jackets over white or blue shirts, and the men on the plazas have charcoal or silver hair and blue shirts and dark suits or beautiful white robes. These harmonies and consistencies of tone and demeanor are nothing other than indicia of an agreement in feeling between all of us who partake in and of this polity, namely that, in essence and in potential,

The Globalization of the Enclave

ours is a zone of win-win-win flows of money and ideas and humans, and that somewhere in our processes and practices, as we sense in our bones and sometimes almost sniff in the air, are the traces of that future community of cooperative productivity, that financial nationhood, of which all of us here more or less unconsciously dream. (O'Neill 2014: 106–7)

X. doesn't believe everything he says here – after all, this passage follows yet another of his bruising encounters with his capricious boss. Still, it's worth noting how O'Neill modulates the tone and syntax of X.'s hymn to the zone's extra-statecraft. He is at first factual, reserved. He connects the DIFC's position within the emirate's pluralistic legal geography to its aesthetic and infrastructural difference: in contrast to the rest of the desert city-state, a person can stroll here – and, at times, X. even does, visiting the coolly depopulated museums that dot the vestibules and atria of the DFIC. But then X. lapses into a reverie that is no less ideological for being part of his ongoing self-delusion. His self-consciously poetic repetitions, his gormless polysyndeton, prepare us for the vapidity of phrases such as 'a zone of win-win-win flows' and his dream of a 'financial nationhood' untrammelled by social commitments. X. even commits the offence of twice writing 'dove gray', the very expression that Ezra Pound singled out as a perfectly useless lexical ornament (Pound 1913: 202). For a keen reader of modernism such as O'Neill, such defects of expression are keenly linked to defects of thought and morality. It's no surprise, then, when X.'s brief vision of a life in a 'free zone' ends badly, abandoned by his patrons and arbitrarily subject to investigation by the Dubai police. The DFIC's usefulness to the free movement of capital may let his crooked employers off the hook, but the Dubai authorities still retain their teeth as the agents of a sovereign power for whom the DFIC is a means to an end, not a 'polity' in which X. is a world citizen among world citizens.

Zones are not, as all this suggests, just infrastructural spaces. They have a strange symbolic and affective identity that partakes of their position at once within and without the areas by which they are surrounded. Enclave spaces are, Fredric Jameson argues, the kinds of space most associated with utopian thinking. As a zone differentiated from the social and spatial world that surrounds it, the enclave can serve as a 'pocket of stasis within the ferment and rushing forces of social change' (Jameson 2005: 15). As such, enclaves foster and give shape to fantasies about how the world might be different, or better; enclaves, that is, are powerful repositories for social dreams and projections. The irony, of course, is that enclaves are at once the product of social and spatial differentiation (the compounded racial, religious, economic, and legal inequalities, for instance, that produce ghettoes) and places we go in order to imagine how, and to what end, the direction of social change might be arrested, altered or reversed. The enclave's utopian function is inextricable from the very social pressures that make us want to imagine the world differently in the first place (Jameson 2005: 15–16).

Examples of utopian enclaves abound, in both literature and history. In the former, we might include the precincts devoted to the Guardians in the *kallipolis,* or ideal city-state, imagined in Plato's *Republic*; in the latter, experiments in living and governing such as Freetown Christiana, a communal settlement of around 1,000 people on a disused military base in Copenhagen, or the Capitol Hill Autonomous Zone, established in June 2020 by anti-racist and anti-capitalist protesters in the several city blocks surrounding the abandoned East Precinct police station in Seattle. But not all enclave societies are experiments in how to live freely or well. Enclaves are also zones into which societies project their worst fantasies. The best example of this phenomenon – best because of its extremity but also, for this chapter's purposes, because it's an ideological reaction against global migration flows – is the right-wing discourse about so-called No-Go Zones: supposed immigrant ghettoes or neighbourhoods in which 'sovereign nations allegedly cede authority to Muslim immigrants' (Jaffe 2015). Thus does a popular Islamophobic internet meme, 'The Path of Islam is Always the Same', begin its itemized run-down of a supposed Islamist agenda as follows: '1. Establish Mosque 2. Create an Enclave 3. Grow the Population'.[4]

The existence of this last sort of enclave, however, has been impossible to prove. Even the British nationalist Raheed Kassam has to begin his book *No Go Zones: How Sharia Law is Coming to a Neighborhood Near You* (2017) by admitting that the very existence of such areas has come under sustained attack (Kassam 2017: 1–10).[5] When the former Louisiana governor (and then-US presidential candidate) Bobby Jindal said in a speech in London that, 'In the West, non-assimilationist Muslims establish enclaves and carry out as much of Sharia law as they can without regard for the laws of the democratic countries which provided them a new home', his remarks were swiftly debunked as relying on false accounts of actual conditions in European cities (McMurry 2016). And journalistic and academic research has indeed demonstrated that claims made about the existence of Islamic No-Go Zones are inflated and inaccurate.[6] Yes, there exist areas identified as 'Sensitive Urban Zones' (*Zones Urbaines Sensibles*) in some French cities, some of them poor suburban neighbourhoods (*banlieus*) with significant Muslim populations. And, yes, the United Kingdom's Arbitration

Act 1996 allows for the operation of Muslim Arbitration Tribunals, under which people of Islamic faith can consent to have civil and commercial disputes arbitrated by religious courts. But the *Zones Urbaines Sensibles*, far from puncturing the sovereignty or administrative competence of the Fifth Republic, actually form part of a geographically differentiated strategy through which central government intervenes within the social fabric of the nation's suburbs and cities.[7] And the Muslim Arbitration Tribunals, rather than embodying the state's judicial surrender to an alien legal code, operate only on the basic of parties' mutual consent, must act in accordance with English law and make rulings subject to review by regular appellate courts.[8]

Evidence for the existence of actual No-Go Zones is, such examples suggest, very thin on the ground. Indeed, to the extent that the social-scientific literature supports the existence of the phenomenon, the label appears to suit not immigrant neighbourhoods that have somewhere seceded from the national state but ethnic-majority populated urban areas that immigrant youth find to be violently inhospitable.[9] There's an obvious parallel between the No-Go Zone myth and other populist narratives about globalization. Just as immigrants from the global south are blamed for the unemployment and deskilling suffered by industrial workers in metropolitan states, so are the real bad effects of globalization's parcelization of national space deflected onto already-marginalized Muslim populations.

'The Urbanization of the Enclave'

Islamophobic projections aside, contemporary culture has responded in lively fashion to the reality of actually existing enclave zones. In the literary realm, nobody's body of work better illustrates the ubiquity of enclave geographies than that of the late speculative novelist, J. G. Ballard. And nowhere has Ballard depicted enclave settings more fully than in his final four novels: a loose sequence joined by their exploration of the detective genre and by the thesis that, as a psychologist puts it in *Super-Cannes* (2000), only 'a voluntary and sensible psychopathy' can provide the route to 'a shared moral order' (2000: 264). In Ballard's enclave world, the utopian and dystopian aspects of enclave spaces collide and entwine.

In *Cocaine Nights* (1996), the relation between madness and morality is explored within two expatriate enclaves on Spain's Mediterranean coast, each of which is compared to Kowloon Walled City, the fortified Chinese settlement that lay within the Hong Kong New Territories when they were leased to Britain in 1898 (Ballard 1998: 247). The second novel, *Super-Cannes*, features a remarkably similar plotline and setting: for Spanish resorts, see instead the high-tech French Riviera business park, Eden-Olympia, the very name of which aptly signifies its utopian apartness: 'the only place in the world where you can get insurance against acts of God' (Ballard 2000: 16). In *Millennium People* (2003), we switch from the Mediterranean to London, but much else remains the same. The action mostly takes place in Chelsea Marina, a gated community inhabited by an economically stressed class of media professionals and academics, variously described as an 'anomalous enclave' and a 'republic' (Ballard 2004a: 256, 294). Finally, in *Kingdom Come* (2006), we encounter the Metro-Centre, a massive suburban leisure and shopping complex once again described as a 'Republic' as well as 'a self-contained universe of treasure and promise' that becomes the site of struggle between the state and a rag-tag army of nativist suburban guerillas (Ballard 2006: 213, 218).

Besides the fact of being set apart from the world, these enclaves have other things in common. They count among their populations an outsize proportion of Ballard's stock characters: doctors, media types, retired pilots, technocrats, crypto-fascists and people with a taste for rough sex. Enclave settings also share an obvious novelistic utility, in that, as with the country house detective yarns that these novels parody and resemble, they enable Ballard to gather his characters in one place. Meanwhile, as exceptional spaces they are also doubly useful in that they can be made to epitomize common qualities of everyday life (consumerism and nationalism, for instance, in *Kingdom Come*'s Metro-Centre) while also standing apart as zones of utopian intensity or speculative perversion – the kind of place you might construct, to refer again to the Metro-Centre, in order forge a 'new religion' or 'a Fourth Reich' (Ballard 2006: 235). Most importantly, Ballard's enclave settings symbolize what he considers an essential quality of contemporary urban society: how, 'for reasons of security' and economic self-interest, 'middle-class professionals [....] [are] subtracting themselves from the whole [arena of] civic interactions that depend on them, virtually conducting an internal immigration' into gated communities (Sellars 2005).

The architectural theorists Rafi Segal and Eyal Weizman call the social development fictionalized by Ballard the 'urbanization of the enclave', in which the 'end condition of urban and architectural formations' is discovered in 'enclaved suburban neighborhoods and gated communities' that epitomize 'capitalist globalization and its spatial fallout' (Segal and Weizman 2003: 25). In an essay co-authored with Anselm Franke and Ines

Geisler, Weizman has further described contemporary social and political space as a 'territorial patchwork of introvert enclaves located side by side, each within the other, simultaneously and in unprecedented proximity' (Franke et al. 2003). Pier Vittorio Aureli speculates about the economic logic behind this spatial order when he argues that enclaves are peculiarly suited to capitalism's dual injunctions to specialize in production and consumption (so as to maximize profit) while, at the same time, segregating and protecting the already-privileged when it is time for accumulated wealth to be enjoyed (Aureli 2011: 26). Again, it bears emphasizing that such fracturing is far from antithetical to globalization. Talking about the post-1960s popularization of airline travel, for instance, Ballard remarks that, when one travelled overseas 'back in the '30s and '40s', cultural shifts registered 'very dramatically [....] national boundaries were real and one had to make huge mental adjustments to cope. Today, of course, the changes are imperceptible' (Ballard 2004b: 192–3). This does not mean, however, that the 'global' traveller of today has become a deracinated planetary citizen. She is, rather, a member of the 'unitary global culture of the departure lounge', the beneficiary of a political economy in which international airports and hotels are built cheek-by-jowl with 'festering slums' that the international traveller barely sees, let alone sojourns within (Ballard 2004b: 192–3). The middle-class protagonists of Ballard's final tetralogy live in a unitary world not because its smooth surface no longer admits of divisions of wealth, security, liberty or culture; their world is 'global' because they can stalk, like animals crossing a river by stepping-stones, from enclave to enclave over the gaps in-between. That the poor are arrested, if only for a while, by the walls around such enclaves only brings us back to Berger's original point about what happens when people and borders are mobilized at the same time.

Ubiquitous and National

Enclave spaces are, to begin to summarize, the insular results of global social processes. Because they are the results of social and spatial differentiation, they can stand apart as areas of utopian hopefulness or dystopian fear. They are, by definition, exceptional – and yet their apparent ubiquity means they can also stand in for general social problems or trends. All these traits come together in the work of two more British authors, both of whom have taken on the challenge of writing literary fiction that responds directly to the pressures of twenty-first-century history, and both of them especially concerned with nationalist xenophobia and racism. This chapter will conclude by considering two novels that draw together its several themes and arguments: one by the queer Scottish novelist Ali Smith, the other by the Black British author and journalist Caryl Phillips.

Smith is, among many other distinctions, the author of the celebrated seasonal tetralogy of novels, written rapidly in the wake of the 2016 Brexit referendum, which address the travails of post-Thatcher Britain through a series of linked stories, each set in a different natural and political season. Beginning with *Autumn* (2016), the series continued with *Winter* (2017) and *Spring* (2019) and concludes with *Summer* (2020). The key scene for us comes in *Autumn*, when the protagonist's mother, Wendy, takes out an old Ordnance Survey map of the rural area of England in which she lives. Wendy has marked where the nearby coastline has been diminished by tidal erosion – here picking up a theme established by one of the novel's several epigraphs: a 2016 news story declaring that, at current rates of erosion, 'Britain has just 100 harvests left' (Smith 2017: n.p.). She points to where, ten days ago, a 'World War II pillbox fell into the sea' (Smith 2017: 55). And then she points away from the coast, to the other edge of the map:

> That's where the new fence has gone up, she says. Look.
> She is pointing to the word *common* in the phrase *common land*.
> Apparently a fence three metres high with a roll of razor wire along the top of it has been erected across a stretch of land not far from the village.
> It has security cameras on posts all along it. It encloses a piece of land that's got nothing in it but furze, tufts of long grass, scrappy trees, little clumps of wildflower.
> (Smith 2017: 55)

The passage develops a theme that is important throughout *Autumn*: the privatization of that which was once held in common, whether common land for pasturage and recreation or, more metaphorically, the sense of common purpose and cosmopolitan solidarity that, for Smith, underwrites threatened institutions such as the British welfare state and the European Union. That double sense of the commons helps explain why, just a few pages later, a long passage of lyrical prose, marked by the anaphoric repetition of the phrase 'All across the country', concludes with figures of geographical division that epitomize the general social, cultural and economic fractiousness of the United Kingdom in the post-Brexit season of 2016:

> All across the country, the country split in pieces. All across the country, the countries cut adrift.
> All across the country, the country was divided, a fence here, a wall there, a line drawn here, a line crossed there,
> a line you don't cross here,
> a line you better not cross there.
> (Smith 2017: 61)

In this passage, the nationalism and xenophobia that the novel associates with Brexit are given geographical form by the division of common land into an enclave demarcated by fortified wire walls. This enclave is a metaphor for an island culture becoming ever-more insular – but it is also, crucially, more than a metaphor. Wendy's anger about the enclosure of common land reaches its pitch when she hears on the radio news that the government has scrapped the position of Minister for Refugees and announced cut-backs in funding for asylum seekers. Her temper breaks and she rushes to the wire fence, short-circuits its electrical defences by throwing an antique barometer at it, and later pledges to return every day in order to assault it 'with people's histories and with the artifacts of less cruel and more philanthropic kinds' (Smith 2017: 255). The fence, the scene implies, is not just a figure for abstract cruelty or some general betrayal of the commons: it is the fortified outer ring around an immigration detention and removal centre, in which asylum-seekers would be imprisoned without the possibility of judicial review pending deportation or admission. It thus represents, in the eyes of Wendy and the ethos of *Autumn* (the co-protagonist of which is an elderly Jewish refugee from Nazi-occupied France) one of the worst possible betrayals of the idea of common purpose and collective destiny: the victory of nationalist self-interest over empathic identification with ethnic, national, generational, religious and sexual others.

Yet the curious thing about *Autumn* is that Smith leaves much about her fortified enclave unclear. While we know that it's the project of the same conglomerate, SA4A, that, in *Winter*, also polices online intellectual property violations, we never go inside the wire and never learn for certain why it has been built (Smith 2018: 25).[10] The enclave's very anonymity therefore testifies to its ordinariness: the way, for Smith and her characters, the privatization and disaggregation of common space has come to epitomize basic aspects of British society in the new century – a theme also taken up in *Winter*, with its scenes commemorating the Women's Peace Camp that, from 1981 to 2000, protested against the presence of American nuclear weapons at the fortified Royal Air Force base at Greenham Common (Smith 2018).

This same sense of the enclave's generality also characterizes Phillips's *A Distant Shore* (2003), which has proven remarkably prescient about the direction of social change in the United Kingdom since the turn of the century. The novel focusses on two protagonists: Dorothy Jones, a teacher who has been forced into early retirement and now lives in the small, planned community of Stoneleigh in northern England, and a man we are introduced to as Solomon, the development's 'handyman-cum-nightwatchman', whom we learn was once called Gabriel and who emigrated to Britain from Africa, having run away from the violence of his country's inter-ethnic civil war (Phillips 2005: 13). As this description suggests, the question of immigration is at the heart of *A Distant Shore*. Mike, the English lorry driver who helps Solomon as he attempts to settle in the north, sees no contradiction between his fraternal bond with a black African and his assertion that 'I'm an old traditionalist [...] I want fish and chips, not curry and chips. I'm not prejudiced, but we'll soon be living in a foreign country unless someone puts an end to all this immigration' (Phillips 2005: 258). Describing her father's increasingly conservative opinions, Dorothy admits: 'Well, you know, to some people everything's to do with immigration' (Phillips 2005: 196). And in Phillips's novel, 'everything's to do with immigration' in more ways than one. For it's not just that people like Mike and Mr Jones learn to blame all social ills on immigrant scapegoats; rather, *A Distant Shore* shows us a modern Britain in which almost everyone is, to some degree or other, an immigrant. It does this not by leaning on sentimental clichés about Britain as a land populated by immigrants and invaders, from the Romans to the Normans and so on. Instead, its novelistic world emerges as a fractured social geography in which lonely people shuttle between isolated enclaves.

Solomon emigrates to Britain from an unnamed African country. His story is written so as to be at once hugely dramatic and highly generalizable, with Phillips developing a kind of characterological technique we might call abstraction without stereotyping. Although we don't know the name of his home country or the ethnolinguistic group to which he belongs, Solomon's story draws on various national and regional histories, so all we can really say is that he appears to come from a sub-Saharan location in which at least some of the people speak English and some of them have biblical names. Parts of his dramatic personal history are clear. We know that he is at once the victim and perpetrator of war crimes in a vicious inter-ethnic conflict; we know that, after reaching a refugee camp in northern France, he travels to the southern coast of the UK by hanging off the side of a passenger ferry; and we know that he is detained almost immediately after reaching land, having been falsely accused of assaulting an English girl. We know a bit more, here and there, but most of all we know Solomon as a man whose story is defined by sudden, often desperate, dashes and leaps between discrete locations. Setting therefore becomes discontinuous, fractured. Just as Solomon's story jumps back and forth between past and present, so does his geographic journey stutter rather than flow. When we first see him in the development where he works as a caretaker, he is recently arrived at just the latest in a series of enclave-like spaces that include army camps and prisons as well as Stoneleigh itself, which we are introduced to early in the novel as a place that, much to the chagrin of locals and the postman, has differentiated itself by rejecting the name of the nearby former mining town of Weston. Overlooking the main road and separated from Weston by a steep hill, Stoneleigh's 'dozen bungalows arranged in two culs-de-sac' epitomize a drab kind of gentrification, designed to appeal, so Dorothy reports, to what 'a vulgar woman in the post office calls "newcomers, or posh so-and-sos"' (Phillips 2005: 5). Before we even meet Solomon, then, the world of *A Distant Shore* has already been introduced to us as one in which its protagonists are both migrants of a sort, their current life and former histories defined by their movements into and out of enclaves. Stoneleigh is not, like Ballard's Eden-Olympia, a properly gated community. And it is not, like the French ferry port Solomon breaks into, or the English jail in which he is held, a walled and fenced area patrolled by guards. But it is, like the tent city in France from which Solomon embarks for Britain, a discontinuous settlement marked by social and spatial difference. The novel's settings therefore create an important kind of connection between Solomon and Dorothy that persists despite their widely different racial identities and personal histories. That connection is felt by the reader when, at the end of the novel, Dorothy's mental breakdown leads to her confinement in a psychiatric hospital – yet another zone at once within but outside the broader society. But by the time Dorothy's story ends in her locked-down isolation, her spatial connection to Solomon has already been fixed by her status as the one resident of Stoneleigh who grieves for him after he is murdered in a racist attack by young white men from Weston. Dorothy's own experiences of isolation and fear are not the same as Solomon's: her whiteness and Britishness affords her a level of safety and privilege he cannot enjoy. But she joins Solomon in being a perpetually lonely migrant to a series of isolate enclaves, assailed by the judgement and suspicion of outsiders, and unable to escape a tide of nativist feeling that alternately grows within, and overwhelms from without, a world that is global because it is cut into fortified pieces.

Conclusion

The empirical hypothesis underlying this chapter is that the globalization of social, economic and political structures is not defined by the removal of borders and barriers to movement, any more than it is characterized by the erasure of cultural or ideological difference. Our 'global' world remains a multiverse, not a singular universe, even if the interconnected nature of twenty-first-century societies means that events in one place are now more likely to have observable effects in other parts of the world-system. Neoliberal capitalism has not torn down borders; it has caused them to multiply and go on the move, such that we now encounter social or political boundaries in the middle of territories, rather than only at the edge. States willingly participate in these processes, subdividing and parcelling out their geographies so as to build the formal and informal infrastructure of a 'global' space that is one because it is divided and unequal.

The proliferation of enclave spaces is just one symptom of this broader reality – an aspect of social space richly attested to in the settings and themes of twenty-first-century fiction. In some novels, for example Ballard's late series, those enclaves become the overt subject of the narrative, the friction between the enclave and its outside driving much of the plot and symbolizing many of its themes. This is especially the case, as we see in both factual and fantastic examples, because enclave spaces so easily become repositories for utopian dreams and dystopian nightmares. In other novels, such as Smith's *Autumn* and Phillips's *A Distant Shore*, readers might at first miss how enclave settings give form to the text's moral and political implications. An analysis of how enclaves operate in such novels shows how they enable authors' principled and creative engagement with a social reality in which the global movement of peoples is increasingly accompanied by rising tides of nativist reaction.

Notes

1. For details of US Customs and Border Protection operations at the Toronto airport, see 'US Customs at Pearson'. For checkpoints operated north of the US–Mexico border, see US General Accountability Office (2009). For accounts of US Border Patrol checks south of the Canadian border, see Woodard (2011).
2. For this argument, see Hart (2015).
3. Both sets of enclaves can, however, be distinguished from *exclaves*, which are fragments of one territory geographically separated from a mainland by one or more other territories – though it should go without saying that one nation's exclave is often another's enclave.

4 See the much-circulated version of the meme found on Google Images (The Path).
5 Kassam's solution to the probative issue is to dilute his definition of a No-Go Zone such that any question of sovereignty or judicial writ has been suspended and the only criteria are: (a) a higher-than-average likelihood that one might be attacked or abused 'on the basis of your appearance of the bigotry of locals' *and* (b) that the policy *may* 'require authorization or acceptance from a religious or community leader before entering' *or* (c) 'where the rule of law has either broken down or been supplanted by a foreign set of rules' (13). These are, it should be obvious, a very flexible set of criteria, which could accommodate all kinds of urban zone, many of them with no discernible religious, ethnic or legal difference from surrounding areas.
6 For a round-up of research, including citations of several uses of the term by national and international politicians, see Graham (2015).
7 This is no less the case simply because that intervention sometimes takes the form of the relaxation of (e.g.) laws around sales and property taxes. That kind of fiscal exemption is wholly consistent with Easterling's description of the globally oriented infrastructural zone. Even the American neo-conservative commentator Daniel Pipes, a known critic of Islamism, decided after visiting several *Zones Urbaines Sensibles* to retract his description of them as 'No-Go Zones'. See Pipes (2013).
8 For information on this see Muslim Arbitration Tribunal. For the legislative framework for binding arbitration, the vast majority of which takes place in secular contexts, see UK Govt (1996).
9 For this use of the term 'No-Go Zone', see the analysis of British Muslim youths' experience of urban space in the Lancashire town of Haslingden, as described in Quraishi 2008. Another alternate use of 'No-Go Zone' is developed by Ruben Andersson, who uses it to describe transnational regions considered inhospitable to Western states, NGOs and private citizens. These areas (*e.g.*, the Pakistan–Afghanistan borderlands, or the sub-Saharan Sahel) are at once objects of concern – even places of active military activity) for Western governments and areas, even as they are places many others are averse to enter. See Andersson (2016).
10 Pun on 'safer' aside, the name 'SA4A' possibly riffs on G4S, the British-based multi-national security corporation, which has run immigration detention centres and prisons in the United Kingdom.

CHAPTER 16

Geopolitics and the Novel
The Case of the Mediterranean Noir

Caren Irr

If global histories describe the organization of the world's regions and their relations with each other, then from this point of view, globalization can be understood as a process of reorganization. By de-territorializing and re-territorializing the spaces of the globe, globalization draws attention to an existing order under threat, outlines emerging trends, and exposes old patterns.[1] Global historians thus often see globalization not as a new phenomenon but rather as a recurring period of transition, a period that arises when world-systems open themselves to reflection as they undergo transformation.

For Michael Denning, for instance, the discourse of globalism that arose in the 1990s displaced the 'three worlds' model associated with the height of the Cold War while drawing on the internationalism of the 1930s (Denning 2004). Where mid-twentieth-century popular narrative had consistently described a 'free world' competing with the 'Soviet bloc' to rule the 'third world', '90s-era globalization talk introduced a new paradigm in which a dominant multinational consumer capitalism centred in the United States stitched together a network of 'world-class cities' around the globe by means of cheap air travel, communications technologies and high-end lifestyle products. Teetering over 'developing' and 'least developed' economies alike, as well as their own increasingly depopulated hinterlands, this emerging network of urban hubs remapped the sites and conflicts that had previously ordered the globe (Sassen 2001). It simultaneously released a delirious celebration of consumerist opportunities for the wealthy (vacations in Bangkok! Iceland! Rio!), together with the peril of literally riding in the undercarriage of the global system for a rapidly expanding population in what came to be known in some circles as the Global South.[2] Following a wave of development schemes, this phase of globalization also prompted reflections on so-called clashes of civilization and neo-nationalist reaction. That is, the wave of globalization that was launched in the 1990s and seems to be subsiding in the 2020s opened up a period of reflection on the global arrangements that preceded and undergirded the Cold War. A significant feature of this phase of globalization was the attention it devoted to the work of culture in sustaining patterns that arguably generate political resistance to consumerist globalization. The rise of culture as a source of political coherence supplanting ideology was one symptomatic response to conditions of globalization during this period.

This treatment of culture as a totality (a position strongly associated in the academic humanities with cultural studies and New Historicism) owes a tremendous debt to the global histories of the Annales school, especially the work of Fernand Braudel. Braudel's masterwork, *The Mediterranean and the Mediterranean World in the Age of Philip II* (1949), is centrally concerned with globalization and geopolitics. Exploring the shift from the Mediterranean to the Atlantic as the seat of global power in the sixteenth century, Braudel traces the quotidian business of political events back to the geographic, demographic, cultural and sociological processes underwriting the totality of the Mediterranean world. From Braudel's perspective, a coherent trans-Mediterranean culture bound together by climate, trade and social life ruptured during the competition between the Hapsburg and Ottoman empires, making it vulnerable to northern invaders (England, Germany, the Netherlands). After the rise of the North Atlantic powers, the Mediterranean survived as a distinctive yet somewhat lagging semi-periphery. Nonetheless, its culture did not disappear, because culture has many material determinants. For Braudel, this persistence of culture reflects its geographical conditions and the temporal contradiction between geo-historical processes and political economy (Braudel 1987: 5–12).

Since the 1950s, this contradiction between immediate geopolitical necessities and the longer flows of global history has resulted in the culturally resilient and formerly politically dominant Mediterranean becoming a tourist region. Its residents have, in other words, shifted towards marketing a Mediterranean history and way of life to the beneficiaries of a global economy centred elsewhere. This project has been successful; the twenty-one nations comprising the Mediterranean collectively make up 40 per cent of the destinations of world travel and account for 30 per cent of the world's tourist revenue (Apostolopoulos and Sünmez 2000). At the same time, with another twist of the dialectical knife, these high rates of tourism not only preserve a place for the Mediterranean in a global economy, they also exhaust natural resources and trigger waves of cultural transformation that erode the conditions tourists travel to experience – the pristine beaches, vivid blue water, traditional modes of agriculture, and so on.

With accelerated information flows and ease of air travel, the twenty-first-century Mediterranean also competes with other sun-and-sand locations, especially the Caribbean and the South Pacific. For this reason, in hopes of staving off further decline in a four- to five-century long process that has peripheralized the Mediterranean, leaders in the area's tourist industry have advocated for political initiatives (e.g., Euromodernization) designed to reposition the region within the global economy. Seeking to improve an integrated infrastructure and upgrade the protections of natural resources, these efforts seek to reposition the Mediterranean in a geopolitical struggle by creating a regional superstate entity of sorts. Accordingly, they also inevitably revive the concerns of earlier phases of global reorganization – prompting reflection on the rise and fall of empires, the ebbs and flows of human migration and the enduring role of climate and nature in cultural life. In other words, these immediate geopolitical efforts to combat 'decline' are situated with the *longue durée* of globalization.

One interesting form in which we can plumb the deep currents supporting the geopolitical phenomena that bob atop them is the popular Mediterranean noir novel. In Cold War thrillers set in the North Atlantic (think John Le Carré) complex conspiracies at the level of ideology proliferate: spies and double agents wrestle with the uncertainty of motive and belief, and national allegiances are assumed and tested. But starting as early as the 1970s, in the Mediterranean noir, a postnational and explicitly global form of capital begins to provide the menace. In the Scandinavian crime novels of Stieg Larsson and Henning Menkel, for example, multinational operations menace the social democratic states built on the ruins of failed empires, and detectives explore their collective disillusionment with state-level reform. Similarly, the cynical detectives of Mediterranean noir fiction explore the corruption that permeates political systems, and they move swiftly through the circuitry of multinational and usually illicit capital that undergirds politics, exposing its workings without having the power to directly oppose it. In this respect, they satisfy the expectations for noir thrillers that have been set in place since the heyday of Raymond Chandler and his compatriots in the 1940s.

These elements of noir cynicism about the distorting force global capital exerts on geopolitical distributions of power have been attractive to writers from around the Mediterranean basin. Unsurprisingly, a number of French authors have continued the mid-twentieth-century obsession with noir fiction; the genre-defining author of police fictions Jean-Claude Izzo and the Nobel Laureate Patrick Modiano are two of the names associated with two very different versions of francophone noir writing. Noir writers have also thrived in Franco-era Spain, Italy after the World Trade Organization protests in Genoa, and in debt-ridden Greece. The nations of the former Yugoslavia, Turkey, Israel and Lebanon have all proved welcoming to interesting noir fiction, as has Egypt, Sudan, Morocco and Algeria. In a profusion of languages and cultures, the noir investigator familiar from Los Angeles in the 1940s finds his place.

A distinctive feature of the Mediterranean noir, however, is the sharp contrast this familiar tale of corruption provides with the brilliant sun, sea and sand of the region's climate. Veering between the intense sensory pleasures of the natural environment and the chaos, murder, torture and exploitation that invoke the economic and political powers that be, writers from across the region develop a shared repertoire of figures for interpreting their condition. Referring regularly to Albert Camus's *The Stranger*, they collectively emphasize their existential solitude. And yet, randy, ravenous, bruised and tired, the hero of the Mediterranean noir is a resolutely physical creature, tempted by pleasure even as he muses metaphysically on his own nothingness. His friends are cooks and whores, petty criminals and police on the take. His enemies the big men, the high rollers, and politicians. His world is gritty and urban, but he has his domestic side and usually finds himself a cosy hide-away where he can indulge his nostalgia, lick his wounds and enjoy a generous pour of the local wine.

The recurrence of these genre features does not, however, prohibit differences among noir fictions set in the Mediterranean. These are, after all, novels keenly attentive to material conditions and preoccupied with injustices, the left-behind and the shadows of consumerist/touristic illusion. More particularly, as Gretchen Head has persuasively demonstrated, the currents of migration still flow northward and westward, and the Mediterranean noir reflects that unevenness (Head 2015). North Africans envision an arrival in Marseilles or Barcelona, while Greeks, Spaniards and others head towards the North Atlantic. The movement of peoples creates multicultural and non-national energy that is usually celebrated in the Mediterranean noir, but nonetheless to be southern is still to be associated with various degrees of underdevelopment. Capital, by contrast, is not static or national; it rushes into the Mediterranean basin from America, Russia or farther abroad, radically transforming the economic landscape, creating nodes and hubs, bumps and barriers, peaks and ravines. In the Mediterranean noir, the northward flow of regional migrants takes place on the treacherous terrain of a globally mobile capital that overpowers residual national distinctions.

Even more than genre features, what unites these noirs from the northern, southern and eastern perimeter of the Mediterranean is the figure of the sea itself. Scenes of rapturous, transformative and even redemptive liquidity occur in all the major Mediterranean noir novels. The sensuality and temporality of the sea offers a crucial source of succour to the depressive noir detectives, and it suggests another sort of utopian globalization. The geopolitical particulars of this oceanic globalization vary. Sometimes this alternative is spiritual, other times historical, cultural, epicurean or archly atheistic, but the encounter with the sea always energizes not only the individual hero but also ultimately the port cities he or she lovingly inhabits. The sea always provides an important option for escaping the exploitative reach of conspiratorial capital. From the maritime depths, a source of intense light emanates in the noir novel. It will be the project of this chapter to map that light, as it were, and enquire into the prospects for a proto-ecological alternative to capitalist globalization arising from the Mediterranean noir novel. In these writings, among other anchoring figures, we can discover a utopian geopolitics of the sea.

Faded Empires

Essential to the Mediterranean noir as a genre is a certain bemused reflection on previous stages of globalization. Complicated memories of imperialism, in particular, permeate these novels. The writer credited with founding the genre, Jean-Claude Izzo, explicitly builds this motif into *Total Chaos*, the first of his trilogy devoted to the French port city of Marseilles. As Izzo's narrator describes it, Marseilles is the 'gateway to the East. To foreign lands, adventure, dreams' (Izzo 2005: 197). The city absorbs immigrants from around the Mediterranean – from Italy, Spain, Corsica – as well as from former French colonies in North Africa, Comoros, the West Indies and South-east Asia. Izzo's hero regularly notes but does not romanticize this multicultural mélange. To the contrary, the plots are often built around virulent race politics. 'Our former colonies were here', this Italian immigrant's son sardonically reflects on racist reactions to migration in the

> capital: Marseilles. Here, as there, life didn't matter. The only thing that mattered was death. And violent sex. It was a way to express your hatred of being nothing but a ghost waiting to fight. The unknown soldier of the future. One day or another. In Africa, Asia, the Middle East. Or even two hours from home. Wherever the West was threatened. Wherever there were foreigners hungry to fuck our women, our pure white women, and soil our race. (Izzo 2005: 229)

The detective Montale's vision of Marseilles as a tense mélange braids the migrant and nationalist remainders of empire together with an account of the phenomenon that the narrator considers the failed experiment of social democracy. Probing the decaying housing projects that ring Marseilles's historic centre, Montale identifies corrupt schemes that prey on the migrants who inhabit them. The novel melancholically meditates on the mutually reinforcing intersection of colonialism, racist reaction and a diminished state.

Similar reflections occupy noir fiction set in the capitals of even older empires – Barcelona, Istanbul, Cairo. Manuel Vázquez Montalbán's *Southern Seas*, for instance, compares the 'patina of history' of the 'ugly poverty' in one neighbourhood to the 'completely different. ugly, prefabricated poverty of a neighborhood prefabricated by prefabricated speculators' (Montalbán 1986: 132). A fascist visitor to the detective's office interprets this newer planned poverty of post-Franco Spain as a sign of the lack of virility in countries north of the equator 'where democracy and communism are ruining everything' (Montalbán 1986: 180), but as the novel proceeds we learn that the corpse at the heart of the novel's mystery belongs to a wealthy bourgeois traveller who had explored these 'cement islands' as if they were 'Polynesia'; 'the natives he had found there were a hardened race – the same hardness that Gauguin had discovered in the Marquesas, where the natives had come to know that the world was a huge market in which they too were up for sale' (Montalbán 1986: 202). As a symbolic crossroads of north and south, the slums of Barcelona depicted in the novel partake of the colonial vision exhibited in '*the South Seas*—the first poem published by Pavese, an Italian poet much influenced by American literature' (Montalbán 1986: 95). Inspired by Melville, Pavese described the contrast between adolescent fantasies of a South Sea paradise and a sailor's disillusioned view of the region as just another landscape of work. In other words, Franco-American explorations, filtered through Italian fantasy, anchor the Spaniards' relations to each other and their location. In Montalbán's elaborate vision, the cityscape of Barcelona is interpreted by way of its location in an imperial global imaginary. Like Izzo's Marseilles, it absorbs literal and symbolic migrants and wrestles with the political and economic consequences of its ambivalent position. While some of Montalbán's additional twenty-one novels featuring the same detective (especially *Tattoo*) tackle migration to and through Spain more literally, *Southern Seas* is particularly notable for its layered account of a port city whose former glory has been overwritten by several waves of imperial and political failure.

Imperial history also provides the explicit structure of Ahmet Ümit's *A Memento for Istanbul* (2011). Organized around the investigation into a sequence of murders occurring at major sites around the city, Ümit's novel tutors its readers in the long history of the city as the detective discovers corpses at the feet of its Greek, Roman, Christian, Ottoman and Turkish monuments. Under threat by both Islamic fundamentalists and a business conspiracy, these sites prompt the investigators to re-envision their surroundings, calling up the quiet of a time when 'the city was basically a small harbor and a fortress encircled by the sea and the forest' or the Ottoman glory of a time when 'the waters of the Golden Horn flowed like liquid gold into the mouth of the twisting and winding Bosphorus. Standing back a little, Fatih Mosque was no longer visible but those two unparalleled shrines, the Hagia Sophia and the Süleymaniye Mosque, could be seen standing serenely atop two of the city's renowned hills' (Ümit 2011: 50, 147). Menaced by tourist infrastructure and CIA operations, the architecture of the city encodes clues to a high-stakes battle between good and evil, as well as a complex regional history.

The sense of occupying the heart of a fallen empire overwritten by subsequent waves of occupation and turmoil also pervades Parker Bilal's *The Golden Scales* (2012). Set in a corrupt, politically conflicted Cairo, Bilal's novel entwines the fortunes of a British expatriate, a soccer star and a gangster-turned-real estate magnate, asking how their paths converged. Asides on Cairo's long history punctuate the narrative, as the detective (a scientifically minded Sudanese exile) sorts his way through the facades thrown up by the various players. At the beginning of Chapter 26, for instance, while cooling his heels in an impressive foyer, Makana muses on 'the giant finger of the Cairo Tower':

> modeled on the lotus flower, symbol of life in Ancient Egypt, it was built in the 1950s to broadcast the *Sawt-al-Arab* radio signal. The legendary broadcasts united the Arabs around the bold leadership of Gamal Abdel Nasser and his defiance of the West. ... He was said to have built the tower with a $3 million bribe the Americans threw his way after refusing to finance his construction of the High Dam. It had never struck Makana as a particularly attractive object. There was a restaurant up there which revolved as you ate. Spinning around in the air as you ate struck him as a strange idea. Was that what had become of Egyptian independence? (Bilal 2012: 233)

A single monument here compresses moments of ancient glory, national independence, client-state dependence and nauseating consumerist inequality. Looking back on the state projects that drew on memories of imperial glory to animate anti-Western and anti-colonial defiance, Makana does not indulge in nostalgia so much as he ironically observes its dispersal. From the point of view of one taking refuge in Cairo, he remains a distinctly alienated witness to Egyptian mythology.

This shared emphasis on a faded imperial grandeur characterizes all of the urban centres we find in Mediterranean noir fiction. These cities are grounded in the infrastructure of former conquests, populated by a multilingual and international migrant population, and wrestling with their own mythologies, as the world-system moves beyond them. Their world-weary and politically savvy detectives appreciate the complexity of urban history and consistently mark the uneasy juxtaposition between modernist state projects, like the Cairo Tower, and monuments to former glories, such as the Fatih Mosque. The moments when these building projects signalled optimistic renewal has faded into the past in the noir novel, because the site of energy lies elsewhere.

The Horrors of Contemporary Economic Globalization

The second trope anchoring the Mediterranean noir is a grim, horrified view of the global system operating in the novel's present. While the wreckage of former empires can be (and often is) associated with a melancholic appreciation for lost glories, contemporary globalization most commonly appears in these novels as something abrasively new, corrupt and violent. Typically, American and Russian figures signal the forces of global capital in these novels. These figures engage in violent predatory acts, but often these are described as having aesthetically or affectively disturbing effects rather than national ones. That is, the noir novel tends to be less interested in nationalist revival than in assessing economic globalization from the point of view of the weakened observer.

Parker Bilal's novel provides an especially clear treatment of the ravages of contemporary economic globalization. His detective Makana makes several visits to the Big Blue, a tourist resort being carved out of traditional fishing villages; there he encounters the force behind this development:

> Vronsky sat up to reveal a torso covered in tattoos. Both shoulders were decked with feathers that descended down his back and along his arms as far as his elbows, giving the appearance of wings. On his forearms were words in Chinese and what might have been Sanskrit. Makana would have put his age close to fifty, though a man ten years younger would have been happy with that body. There was no excess fat. It was all muscle. (Bilal 2012: 212)

The menacing multilingual body of the Russian mobster emphasizes his angelic, ageless presence. Arriving from elsewhere, as an agent of a form of globalization that caters to international travellers and international capital, Vronsky lands in Egypt and undertakes a forceful transformation of land and social relations. In particular, he ransacks traditional fishing villages in order to develop a glittering tourist resort and a shady real estate shell game.

The transformative effects of foreign capital are also a major theme in Petros Markaris's *The Late-Night News* (2004). Set in Athens, Markaris's police procedural takes note of the peripheral role allowed to Greeks in the global system. When his investigator withdraws money from an ATM, the message '"Touch here for Greek", ... [appears] on the screen, to show that it was cosmopolitan and [he] was a peasant' (Markaris 2004: 6). The infrastructure of international banking reinforces domestic class differences, such as those exhibited by the big-wigs at a local television station who 'gave [him] a meaningful look – apparently he regarded all police officers as backward and coming from the Third World, so speaking to them rudely wasn't enough, you also had to browbeat them with looks and hints to be sure the message had sunk in' (Markaris 2004: 65). The officer resents his positioning as an apparently 'Third World' figure in the domestic class structure, while also recognizing the distance between his situation and labourers in the global system of labour. When canvassing witnesses, for instance, he reflects on labour trends: 'The times were well past when well-to-do families brought girls from the villages to do all the jobs and, in addition, to give their darling son his first lessons in screwing. Today, you ring the bell, some Filipino girl opens the door, her English is broken, yours is irreparable, and you're supposed to communicate' (Markaris 2004: 139). Markaris's grouchy, ethnocentric investigator regularly discovers gaps in communication that arise in a global system of exploitation. International capital flows, as depicted in the novel, create hierarchies, barriers, and gaps as often as they integrate nations. Confronted with the 'Filipino girl', he notes the new forms of exploitation faced by a globally mobile labouring population.

The potential for criminal abuse latent within the infrastructure of global economies is, after all, the main theme of Markaris's novel. As the novel unfolds, a complicated trafficking scheme emerges, one that brings children and organ donors from impoverished countries of the former Soviet bloc (especially Albania, Bulgaria and Romania) to the West by way of trucking routes controlled by blackmailers with geopolitical motives inherited from the Cold War. The extreme vulnerability of those being displaced and rendered newly mobile in a global economy that treats their bodies as mere commodities is exposed in Markaris's plot, and the resulting horrors are observed from the vantagepoint of the Greek semi-periphery, that is from the point of view of a nation that experiences some of the benefits of serving as a transit point for global capital without being dominant within that system.

The sheer physical vulnerability of dazed Albanian trafficking victims in Markaris's novel is magnified in Massimo Carlotto's *Master of Knots* (2004). This Italian novel investigates a ring of brutal sadomasochistic kidnappers, and it begins with a by now familiar litany of global violence reshaping the local. The detective

> switched on the TV to watch the regional news. In Padova, a gay rights center had been set on fire. Rival criminal gangs, all of North African origin, had clashed near the train station. A couple of gang members had ended up in A&R with stab wounds. In the Vicenza area, a police quick-response team had uncovered yet more sweatshops employing Chinese labour in conditions of semi-slavery. Near Treviso, on the other hand, a gang of Albanians had attacked an isolated villa. (Carlotto 2004: 36–7)

The passage finally comes to an end when, exhausted by this swarm of brutality, the detective 'switched off the TV, picked up another remote and selected a Bob Dylan CD. "Tombstone Blues" poured out of the speakers' (Carlotto 2004: 36–7).

His world feels the shockwaves of brutality coming from all directions. The global media circuitry that brings Carlotto's hero the music of Bob Dylan also exposes him and others to international gangsterism and exploitation. As the detective is drawn deeper into the case, he learns that blackmail schemes have entangled S&M practitioners in horrific snuff films, and he identifies the leader of the blackmail ring as an American Mafiosi who is covered in Japanese tattoos that simultaneously indicate his adherence to the arts of bondage and a multinational circuit of exploiters. Explicitly set in the context of the street battles surrounding WTO meetings in Genoa, then, the novel examines the complex knotting together of the infrastructure of capital and the gangsterism of state and non-state actors.

In all these novels, the tattooed, tied and carved-up human body is an object of fascination. While national and linguistic markers are noted, they do not inspire investigation so much as they serve as a shorthand for multinational mobility. It is the brutality of a global system that treats Chinese sweatshop workers, Filipino maids and Albanian children as interchangeable, largely silent bodies that these novels explore. The melancholic detectives of the Mediterranean noir novels are often themselves alienated from nationalist efforts to reinforce borders. Carlotto's detective Alligator was a former political prisoner; Bilal's hero is in exile; and Markaris's Haritos finally depends more on family networks than the corrupt Greek legal system depicted in the novel. Theirs is a world in which contemporary networks of global power override the regulatory force of weak states at the expense of rootless populations of working people.

The Moods of the Sea

At the heart of the grim, exploitative world of noir narratives, we consistently find passages devoted to description of the Mediterranean Sea. In the action-driven detective plot, these passages often serve as moments of meditation and transformation that anticipate a turning point in the action. They launch a form of Aristotelian *anagnorisis* or recognition. Because noir fiction is usually not deeply invested in character, the recognition in question normally relates to the social and political scene of these novels. The noir detective's encounter with the moods and qualities of the sea reveal a relation to globalization that exceeds physical horror and post-imperial nostalgia. This potentially redemptive sea washes the shores of all of the port cities on the northern, southern and eastern perimeter of the Mediterranean. It provides a common imagery that suggests at the level of mood and affect an alternative to the perilous prospects of globalization.

That said, the sea does pose dangers in noir fiction, but they are dangers that open up new modes of perception and new possibilities for action. Rather than presenting an external threat, immersion in the sea puts the hero at risk in order to allow her to flourish in a new way. Bilal's hero Makana certainly experiences such a moment. After being thrown overboard by his antagonist, Makana 'suddenly had the sense that he was no longer alone. Within the darkness around him a deeper, darker shadow was moving in the water'; bolstered somewhat, he strikes out, hits a reef and reaches the shallows. At this point, 'the world looked different. The palm trees towering over him were still. He got to his feet and looked about him' (Bilal 2012: 345). The invisible shadows and lifeforms populating the sea renew Makana's own efforts to survive and ultimately provide him with the necessary momentum to solve the case.

A similar confrontation with the perils of the sea revives the hero of Rawi Hage's poetic novel about a refugee fleeing from the Lebanese civil war. At the climax of *DeNiro's Game*, Basaam is overcome by terror and despair at the death of his closest friend, and he bathes in the sea, attempting to cleanse himself of his sins. In this passage, 'the sea turned purple, like the onyx that had once filled the shore. And the blood screamed louder than the seagulls, louder than the ancient invaders'; 'the pebbles behind [him] rocked back and forth; the clams shut their shells'; Basaam vomits, 'spitting out the yellow substance that joined the sea foam and rushed past me to shatter on the massive rocks' (Hage 2006: 272–3). Hage's hero's immersion into political and personal crisis is thus reflected back to him by the sea and the sensations it provokes. This nauseating purple, yellow, screaming sea provides the ultimate confirmation that he must leave Beirut.

On board the ship that transports him to the relative safety of Marseilles, Basaam has another more restorative experience of the sea. He talks with a career sailor who has found in a life at sea access to a magical world of new sensations, and he enters into a meditative state:

> for days the ship slid over the waves, and waves passed by and never came back, and the sailors pulled their sails, and the wind puffed and huffed and pushed us north and stole the smoke from our breath, and when the winds were high up, the sea slowed down and the water slowed, and the sail slowed, and the fish slowed, and the partridge glided above our heads under the sheet of the Hellenic skies, and one-eyed nymphs saw us and gathered to listen to our fantastic tales, charmed by the smell of our burning plants, mistaking it for the incense of their dying gods. (Hage 2006: 189)

In this passage, travelling by sea pulls Basaam into a hypnotic Odyssean world of myth and fantasy. Metamorphosed by this reverie, Basaam provisionally escapes the terrors of social crisis, recovering his capacity for storytelling and his appreciation for a slowness that opens up the senses.

As in the scene of Odysseus's entrapment by the sirens, maritime fantasy can produce a more embarrassing or negative revelation, though. Patrick Modiano explores this theme in his elegant unravelling of the motifs of the detective novel. In *Sundays in August*, this Nobel laureate opens the narrative with two small-time criminals seeking refuge in the faded glories of the seaside promenade at Nice. They hope to blend in with the 'refugees in the Free Zone, exiles, Englishman, Russians, gigolos, Corsican croupiers from the Palais de la Méditerranée' who have clustered there, but soon find themselves instead the targets of another pair of crooks (Modiano 2017: 37). After a seductive encounter at poolside in a borrowed mansion, the second couple offers to take them to dinner at Coco Beach: 'Where is this Coco Beach?' Sylvia asked. 'Near Antibes? Cap Ferrat? Or even farther? Coco Beach…. The name had the sound and the scent of Polynesia, associated in my mind more with the beaches of Saint-Tropez: Tahiti, Morea…' (Modiano 2017: 91–2). Entranced by fantasies of the south seas, the narrator and his beloved Sylvia are scammed into giving over their own stolen diamonds. As in Montálban's *Southern Seas* (discussed above), the allure of the sea risks an erosion of caution and an overwhelming absorption into ahistorical tropical fantasy, even as it allows a release from the outright horrors of geopolitical turmoil. The narrator comes face to face with his own fatal delusions.

At its best, in Mediterranean noir, the sea offers the exhausted, jaded heroes a period of reprieve and a form of historical, rather than mythic, memory. In *Zagreb Cowboy* (2012), Alen Mattich's hero finds such sustenance in memories of time spent with his father during his boyhood on the Istrian peninsula in the Adriatic. He recalls days when

> they'd drive down to the coast and spend the day swimming, careful to avoid the spiny urchins that made a hazard of the stony sea floor. They'd picnic ... while sitting on cushions of stacked Mediterranean pine needles. [And] ... sit in cafes in the old parts of town, the broad, smoothed blocks of white Istrian stone underfoot, in among high, narrow, Venetian-styled Renaissance houses with their ogee windows. (Mattich 2012: 132)

These natural, gustatory and familial pleasures survive shifting political fortunes and anchor the beleaguered hero in a stable set of sensations.

Perhaps the most direct and most influential vision of the sea as an alternative to the corrupt past and dangerous present of globalization appears in the final passages of Izzo's genre-defining *Total Chaos*. Exhausted by the case he has been pursuing and plagued by visions of 'formless, decomposing masses of gristle and blood', the hero writes a letter of resignation from the police force and goes for a long swim (Izzo 2005: 248). Concentrating on physical exertion, he releases the impurities he has accumulated into the sea and finally finds himself capable of returning to 'the land of the living' (Izzo 2005: 249). This purgative or negative experience does not complete the significance of the sea for Izzo's hero, Montale, however; instead, this purifying bath fits him for a reunion with his beloved. The two then set out in a boat together, rowing past the sea wall, until in the final sequence of the novel:

> at last Marseilles was revealed. From the sea. The way the Phocian must have seen it for the first time, one morning many centuries ago. With the same sense of wonder. The port of Massilia. I know its happy lovers, a Marseilles Homer might have written about Gyptis and Protis. The traveler and the princess. In a soft voice, Lole recited:
>
> > O procession of Gypsies
> > May the sheen of our hair guide you ...

One of Leila's favorite poems.
> Everyone was invited. Our friends, our lovers. Lole placed her hand on mine. It was time for the city to burst into flame. White at first, then ocher and pink. A city after our own hearts. (Izzo 2005: 252. Ellipses in original)

Interweaving historical legend about the founding of Marseilles with Homeric verse and lines from the contemporary translingual Lebanese poet Sarah Stétié, Izzo's hero and his Roma lover view the beloved city from the sea. Looking back at the city from the sea, they adopt a perspective characterized by cultural engagement and radical pluralism; they inhabit an aesthetic alternative to the poisonous life versus death imagery adopted on land. Marseilles can then appear to them in the flames of sunrise shaded with ochre and pink. The view from the sea reveals a vivid and glorious alternative to the darkened image available on land.

The Environmental Shadow

Since the heyday of the Mediterranean noir in the 1980s and 1990s, other visions of passage across this sea have become particularly pressing. Political turmoil, escalating economic inequality, and climatological changes have led to a rapid escalation of migration across the sea. Not only the horrifying deaths of migrants crowded into unseaworthy vessels but also their extremely mixed reception on northern coasts have rightly become the object of a great deal of media attention. At the same time, journalistic and scientific inquiries explain the dramatic consequences of overfishing and pollution in the Mediterranean, as well as the potential for desertification, erosion, and salinification of the aquifer related to climate change (Wainwright and Thornes 2004). With tourism, population growth and demand for water-intensive agriculture, groundwater resources are vastly diminished, and the aquifers become vulnerable to seawater intrusions.

By attending to the global flows that disturb historic boundaries, these twenty-first-century narratives of the environmental issues in the Mediterranean region complement the noir novel's critique of economic globalization. They also suggest new directions in which that story might grow. Reckoning with environmental crises in the Mediterranean and elsewhere seems an especially urgent geopolitical question and a live one for the social, political and economic concerns of noir-influenced writing. From the vantagepoint of the twenty-first century, in other words, we can return to the dark scepticism directed towards globalization in the Mediterranean noir novel and find there some points of reference for an emerging green critique of the effects of global capitalism.

Flowing through such a new green noir – or, perhaps, a dark green – sensibility, one surely will find some of the utopian drive towards the sea surviving from the earlier form. As we learn to think of the sea not only as a nationless maritime commons and deep blue wonder but also as a historically and culturally marked phenomenon, new prospects for geopolitical narration become visible. From the perspective of globalization, the sea can figure the complex thermodynamics of fluid systems. Its ebbs and flows, its waves and tides, currents and calms can model for us some narrative forms for depicting geopolitical tensions while also exhibiting the boundless energy that flows through such global situations, restlessly pushing them beyond their current structures.

Notes

1 See Middle and Naumann who also use this language.
2 See, for example, Topham (2015).

CHAPTER 17

Spy Fiction in the Age of the Global
Maria Christou

In an article published in *Foreign Policy* in 2009, David C. Earnest and James N. Rosenau set out to tell us about 'the spy who loved globalization'. This, as it turns out, is none other than James Bond. Here, Ernest and Rosenau note that Bond is described in *Goldeneye* (1995) as 'a relic of the Cold War', but, they argue, he is in fact 'more modern' than that (Earnest and Rosenau 2009: 88, 89). If, their argument goes, the Cold War is about tensions between sovereign states (or between coalitions of states) then what Bond stories typically dramatize is something different: they are about tensions between the sovereign state (or states) and what Earnest and Rosenau call the 'sovereignty-free' actor (or actors). And this, they admiringly highlight, is something that the Bond story came to explore before globalization theorists and scholars even 'pondered such ideas' (Earnest and Rosenau 2009: 88). It is in this sense that they dub Bond the 'spy who loved globalization'.

If this description is eye-catching, it is not only because Earnest and Rosenau are in this specific instance wrong. It is also because, more broadly, globalization and the figure of the spy seem to be incompatible concepts. The scholarship on spy fiction suggests as much insofar as, in one way or another, it flags up the key role of the sovereign state in the genre. Michael Kackman's *Citizen Spy* (2005), for example, opens with an introduction entitled 'The Agent and the Nation', in this way explicitly foregrounding this link. Allan Hepburn goes further in that he associates the very origin of the spy story 'proper' with the state (specifically the British state) and its protection. Hepburn acknowledges that narratives involving spies have always existed – citing, for instance, Homer's *The Iliad* – but argues that 'spy narratives come into their own in the first decade of the twentieth century', when they come to address a certain 'unease' about 'the end of empire and the encroachment of foreigners into the United Kingdom' (Hepburn 2005: 10–11). Similarly, Sam Goodman's *British Spy Fiction and the End of Empire* (2015) – which, as the author is at pains to stress, is not about making 'crude' associations between British spy fiction and 'a homogenised form of British identity' – also affirms the link between the work of the spy and the state (Goodman 2015: 6). In an 'era of rapid decolonisation', Goodman shows, spy fiction betrays anxieties about the loss of national identity and of 'territorial control', in this way appearing to acknowledge their fluctuating nature, but those anxieties are channelled towards 'the preservation of British sovereignty': 'individual spies' – who, as Goodman writes, constitute 'manifestations of the British state' – are seen to be striving to 'render spaces safe and assert the power and presence of their government within them' (Goodman 2015: 6–7).

If we were to leave the fictional context aside for a moment to turn to Peter Szendy's *All Ears: The Aesthetics of Espionage* (2017), we would see that even as far back as the fifth century BC the concept of the spy was understood primarily in relation to a country and its enemies. Sun Tzu's *The Art of War*, for instance, identifies different types, or 'sorts', of spies: there are, for example, 'native agents', defined as 'those of the enemy's country people' who are employed by 'us'; 'doubled agents', described as spies who ostensibly serve the enemy country but in reality serve ours; 'inside agents', designated as officials of the enemy country 'whom we employ' – and so on, with the description of each type further highlighting that the profession of the spy is definable in relation to a sovereign country and its enemies (qtd. in Szendy 2017: 4). The same associations emerge in religious contexts, too. Having found 'more than a hundred references to spies and intelligence-gathering' in the Bible, Szendy points out as an example the incident in which Joshua sends spies to the Promised Land (Josh. 2) – an incident in which the practice of spying is, again, bound up with the notion of one's country and what are seen as threats against it (Szendy 2017: 4). In short, whether fictional or non-fictional, ancient or modern, the significance of a spy's actions emerges in relation to the impact they have on the state.

Even Ernest and Rosenau's analysis does little to counter this link, despite this being exactly what one might expect, given the title of their piece. Highlighting the role of the sovereignty-free actor in the Bond novels, Earnest and Rosenau refer to the example of SPECTRE (Special Executive for Counter-Intelligence, Terrorism, Revenge and Extortion), a global criminal and terrorist organization. They describe SPECTRE as an organization made up of 'sovereingty-free' actors in that they do not work for, or have any allegiances to, a particular state; SPECTRE, they write, 'seeks to squeeze money from states and to humiliate governments' (Earnest and Rosenau 2009: 89). Far from undermining the relevance of the state in a globalized world in which its power is dwindling, then, the actions of these so-called sovereignty-free characters are prompted, and, as such, are ultimately made possible, by the state, and so it is clearly in relation to the state that these actions – and, by extension, the actions of the spy who seeks to foil them – acquire their significance.

The importance of the state is manifested not only at the level of the typical spy novel plot but also at what we might think of as the genre's ontological ground. In *Mysteries and Conspiracies* (2014), Luc Boltanski puts forward the thesis that spy novels and detective stories present us with two realities. Both genres depend on the notion of the mystery or on that of the conspiracy, notions which in turn imply the existence of, on the one hand, the official reality that the mystery or the conspiracy disrupts, and, on the other, the unofficial reality that the mystery or the conspiracy points toward. The former reality, Boltanski observes, is formed by the state and its institutions: these institutions 'underwrite' order and normality – what might be referred to as 'ordinary reality'– and so spy and detective fiction, he maintains, are ultimately conservative genres since it is this state-sanctioned, stable, and rather exclusionary, reality that they typically consolidate once the spy or the detective solves the mystery or tackles the conspiracy (Boltanski 2014: 19, 3, 19–20). It is in this sense that we can see spy fiction as being ontologically bound up with the state, insofar as, in Boltanski's account, the perception of reality (formed by the state) constitutes the very foundation of what the spy story *is*. And so, although, as Earnest and Rosenau's reading of the Bond story suggests, authors of spy fiction do engage with concepts and scenarios that can in some ways appear to be relevant to the globalized world, a true diminution of the significance of the state in the genre would appear to be equivalent to a reconfiguration of the genre's very ontology.

It is just such a reconfiguration, I want to suggest, that we witness in William Gibson's Blue Ant trilogy. Globetrotting and, more generally, life and work in a globalized world is certainly one of Gibson's key concerns here, so much so that Olga Tarapata describes *Pattern Recognition* (2003), the trilogy's first instalment, as 'Gibson's acclaimed novel *about* globalization' (Tarapata 2019: 67, emphasis added). And yet, as the title of the second instalment, *Spook Country* (2007), makes clear from the outset, this also constitutes Gibson's engagement with the genre of spy fiction. Criticism on the Blue Ant trilogy typically approaches one of these concerns (primarily the former), with Fredric Jameson's 'Fear and Loathing in Globalization' (2003) being a notable example. What is notable about it is that, despite his focus on globalization in *Pattern Recognition*, Jameson here also gestures towards Gibson's preoccupation with the genre of spy fiction even though this does not emerge as clearly until *Spook Country*, which Jameson's piece predates. In regard to this preoccupation, Jameson refers to what he calls 'Gibson's Russian episode' in *Pattern Recognition* (Jameson 2003: 109). As it is ultimately revealed, the secret 'maker' of the mysterious footage that Hubertus Bigend employs Cayce Pollard to find is located in Russia, and, as it turns out, some powerful Russians end up being involved too, attempting to thwart Cayce's mission because they become (unnecessarily) suspicious of her motives, having discovered that she is the daughter of an American spy who operated in Soviet Russia. For Jameson, this 'brings a residual Cold War mentality' into play, which he finds 'less interesting' than Gibson's take on globalization in this novel (ibid.). In other words, even in the rare occasion when both of these concerns of Gibson's have been picked up on in the same piece, the implication seems to be that they cannot be treated in conjunction with one another but, instead, ought to be juxtaposed, the Cold War – and, by extension, the bipolar world of spies with which it is typically associated – being precisely what the globalized world officially replaces. In this chapter, I attempt to think about these two apparently incompatible concerns – globalization and the figure of the spy – in conjunction with one another, and in so doing I aim to identify how Gibson reconfigures the genre of spy fiction in the age of the global.

Gibson, as we will see, does not reconfigure the spy novel in the way that, say, Luis Borges does in 'The Garden of Forking Paths' (1941), or John Barth appears to do in *Sabbatical* (1982). Following from critics such as William V. Spanos, who, in engaging with postmodernist rewritings of the detective story, prefer to use the term '*anti-detective* detective story', we can similarly label Borges's and Barth's above-mentioned texts as *anti-spy* spy fictions (Spanos 1972: 147–60). This is so in the sense that, in typically postmodernist fashion, Borges and Barth do not so much rewrite the spy genre as undo it by rejecting its key distinguishing elements. They confront us, for instance, with narratives in which initial uncertainty does not give way to certainty, and different perspectives or interpretations do not get superseded by a final revelation of the truth. Indeed, if, according to Jean François Lyotard's now canonical formulation, postmodernism can be defined as 'incredulity toward metanarratives' (Lyotard 1984: xxiv), and, by extension, as a rejection of the very notion of the totality, then, unlike Borges's 'The Garden of Forking Paths' and Barth's *Sabbatical*, the Blue Ant trilogy cannot be described as postmodernist. On the contrary, this trilogy presents us with something similar to what Joel Evans identifies in

Conceptualising the Global in the Wake of the Postmodern (2019) – namely, a return to the totality. Here, Evans argues that the pronounced preoccupation with the global that characterizes much of contemporary literary and cultural production constitutes a renewed engagement with the idea of the totality. In what follows, I demonstrate how Gibson's trilogy engages with the global, arguing that this signals a return to the totality. As such, this suggests both a return to classic spy fiction – to the very (totality-related) principles that are rejected in postmodernist iterations of the genre – but also, and inevitably, a movement away from, or a radical reconfiguration of, the genre and its attachment to the state. More specifically, I will argue that Gibson's engagement with the totality effectively reverses the structure of the spy story – a reversal, however, which does not, as we will see, amount to a transformation of what, as Boltanski demonstrates, is a fundamentally conservative genre into a progressive one.

Mirror-Worlds

Hubertus Bigend occupies a central position in all three novels, and unsurprisingly so since he is the character who joins together the three instalments of the Blue Ant trilogy. This is a central position which is akin to that identified by Michel Foucault in the opening chapter of *The Order of Things* (1966), in his discussion of a Diego Velázquez painting. In the background of the painting in question, *Las Meninas* (1656), but at a 'more or less completely central' position, Foucault observes, is a mirror which reveals what the figures who are in the foreground of the painting are looking at: namely, the king and queen (Foucault 2002: 8). Though the mirror is small and so the figures it reflects barely take up any space on the canvas, they in fact constitute, Foucault shows, the centre around which everything is organized and without which nothing that the painting depicts could have been depicted; they are the subject of Velázquez's painting within the painting and, as such, they are the reason why the scene we witness in the foreground is occurring in the first place. As with *Las Meninas* so too with Gibson's trilogy it is not the character or set of characters we encounter in the foreground that constitute the driving force behind what happens across the three novels, but, rather, Bigend and Blue Ant, his advertising agency. Though Foucault does not channel his reflections on *Las Meninas* into an explicit discussion about power and sovereignty, it is obvious that these questions are very much at stake. After all, the king and the queen clearly bespeak power; in particular, they signal a model of power that is associated with feudalism – with land and its ownership.

Bigend and his advertising agency, on the other hand, bespeak an order of things that is apparently fundamentally different. We will return to this observation later in order to unpack and complicate it further, but, for now, it will suffice to point out what seems to be a key difference – one to which we are alerted when, in the first chapter of *Pattern Recognition*, we are told that Blue Ant's operations are not wedded to land. Blue Ant is here described as 'globally distributed, more post-geographic than multinational' (Gibson 2011a: 6) – a description that immediately sets the scene as a world in which national borders and sovereign countries have, in effect, become irrelevant.

This order of things also emerges through the character of Cayce Pollard, who, like the Infanta in *Las Meninas*, finds herself in the foreground of *Pattern Recognition*; but, unlike the Infanta – whose presence bespeaks a continuation of the model of sovereignty embodied by her parents – Cayce inhabits a different world: a world in which sovereign power and its limits are not determined by land borders. This, in fact, is a world in which the notion of sovereignty, at least as this is understood in the genre of spy fiction – that is, as being attached to the state – is virtually absent. Significant in this respect is the relation between Cayce's role in the novel and that of her father, Win Pollard, who, as we learn, worked for 'twenty-five years [as] an evaluator and improver of physical security for American embassies worldwide', and whose 'idea of a bedtime story had been the quiet, systematic, and intricately detailed recitation of how he'd finally secured the sewer connections at the Moscow embassy' (Gibson 2011a: 44). Win was, in other words, a spy, and it is particularly telling that he never appears in the novel, having apparently gone missing. By contrast, Cayce and the spy-like mission that Bigend assigns to her – namely, to track down the secret maker of the footage that is being mysteriously uploaded on the internet – are very much at the forefront. With Win's disappearance on the one hand and the foregrounding of Cayce's new job on the other, we seem to be confronted with a mutation of the role of the spy: from the traditional variety embodied by her father – the spy, that is, whose work was bound up with sovereign countries and hostilities between them – to the role that Cayce comes to embody: what we might think of as a version of the spy in the age of the global.

Cayce, like most spies worth their salt, features as an expert in pattern detection. But, while the traditional spy's pattern detecting skills are typically used to help a country avert dangers, maintain its power, and advance its interests, in this new iteration of the role of the spy pattern detection serves corporations or individual entrepreneurs, as though they have come to occupy the place of the sovereign state. In this role, and as required by her current mission, Cayce is seen to be travelling ceaselessly from one part of the world to another, and to be doing so with such ease and speed that her travels suggest a growing irrelevance of national borders. It is important in this respect that the narrative tends to describe her as travelling from city to city – from New York, to London, to Paris, to Tokyo, to Moscow – rather than from country to country: from the United States, to Britain, to France, to Japan, to Russia. When references to these countries do appear, they are at times especially telling. When, for instance, Boone Chu spots the ventilator in Damian's flat in London, he observes that 'we' (Americans) 'don't have' these 'things', but '[t]hey're everywhere here' (in Britain). The following exchange ensues:

> 'They're part of the mirror-world', Cayce says.
> 'Mirror-world?'
> 'The difference. [...] They invented that [the ventilator] here, probably, and made it here.
> This was an industrial nation. [...] They made all their own stuff. Kept imports expensive. Same thing in Japan. All their bits and pieces were different, from the ground up'.
> '[...] I don't think it's going to be that way much longer. Not if the world's Bigends keep at it: no borders, pretty soon there's no mirror to be on the other side of'. (Gibson 2011a: 105–6)

Though the emphasis here is clearly on sovereign nations rather than on individual cities, the discussion serves not to affirm their relevance but to call it into question. And, while Boone in this exchange projects the waning importance of the state – and, by extension, the emergence of the world-as-a-totality – into the near future, Cayce's experience suggests that this is already underway. Despite, for example, referring to London as 'mirror-world', she does not – ventilators notwithstanding – experience it as such, but, rather, thinks that 'London and New York feel more like each other', as though 'the membrane between mirror-worlds' is 'dissolving' (Gibson 2011a: 94). Even when she later finds herself in Russia, where she is admittedly 'presented with serious cultural novelty' and 'her mind [begins] doing the but-really-it's-like thing' – 'but really it's like Vienna, except it isn't' – this impression is finally overturned (Gibson 2011a: 276). During a dinner in Moscow, she notes the absence 'of toasts', toasting being something she regards as characteristically Russian. '[P]erhaps', she concludes, echoing Boone's observation, it should not be described as 'a Russian meal' at all but, more accurately, as 'a meal in that country without borders that Bigend strives to hail from', that 'country' being, of course, the globalized world in which individual sovereign countries are all but redundant (Gibson 2011a: 264).

Such a disappearance of 'mirror-worlds' seems to be consistent with the information we are given about Cayce's defining characteristic: her 'sensitivity' to brands and logos, which curiously causes her to suffer allergic reactions. Tellingly, we are at one point made aware of what appears to be an exception to this sensitivity: namely, the flags and symbols of sovereign nations. For instance, we read that the 'national symbols of her homeland don't trigger her', as if to suggest that the concept of the sovereign country is becoming irrelevant, the significance of national symbols by extension becoming less potent, and as a result failing to affect her as the much more potent commercial logos do (Gibson 2011a: 106). Indeed, despite it being made clear that Cayce is American, and despite the fact that, as we have just seen, even the term 'homeland' is used to designate this, Cayce's idea of 'home' does not really appear to be firmly tied to a specific geographical location, let alone a country. There is, in fact, a certain sense in which Cayce may be described as 'homeless'. Though she rents a flat in New York and, therefore, does not technically lack a permanent residence, at no point in the narrative does she appear to live in it on account of the travelling she is obliged to do as part of her job – a predicament that Sean Scanlon associates more generally with the condition of workers in the globalized market and its demand for constant mobility (Scanlon 2016: 145). When Cayce is not on a plane, she stays in hotel rooms, or at her friend Damian's flat, which, though clearly not a hotel room, seems to resemble one in its 'semiotic neutrality' (Gibson 2011a: 89). The same is true of Cayce's own flat, which is described as a 'whitewashed cave, scarcely [...] demonstrative of self' (Gibson 2011a: 89). And if the anonymity of Cayce's flat signals less a 'home' and more a hotel-like environment that could, theoretically, be found anywhere in the world, then this is even more obviously the case with the place that, as we are told, most closely 'approximate[s] [...] home' for Cayce now, in the present of the narrative: namely, F:F:F, an online forum where subscribers from all over the globe anonymously share their opinions about the enigmatic footage (Gibson 2011b: 4).

In short, both in the foreground and in the background of *Pattern Recognition* we are confronted with characters who in one way or another operate in the age of the global, that is, in the world-as-a-totality, where the relevance of sovereign states and their borders is on the wane. While Cayce's work can in this sense be contrasted to that of the traditional spy, the fact that the global points to the notion of the totality complicates matters. Indeed, Gibson's engagement with the totality extends to the more general idea of the 'bigger picture' or the 'whole', which serves to bring these complications to the surface in that it more explicitly signals conformity to key conventions of spy fiction (at least at first glance). This is particularly pronounced in *Zero History* (2010), the third instalment of the trilogy, where the lives of the characters encountered in the previous instalments are weaved together into one 'whole' story, but also in *Spook Country*, where the rotation between three different plotlines immediately gives us to understand that the individual lives of the characters on which each of these plotlines focusses will by the end form parts of a 'bigger picture', and all the seemingly disconnected pieces will eventually fall into place.

Spook Country gestures toward the existence of not simply a bigger picture but also a 'whole' in the sense of the 'totality'. Bobby Chombo's 'locative' art is key here. This is a form of art which is linked to a specific geographical location determined with military precision, using GPS technology, but which also simultaneously constitutes an opening up to a wider world. Chombo's dead River Phoenix hologram, for instance, brings into the present a past event – that is, River Phoenix's death – at the exact location where the event in question took place, and so locative art suggests that what we see around us is not all there is to see in a very literal sense; as Gary Westfahl puts it, what may seem like 'a deserted city street' is, with the right 'headgear', in fact revealed to be nothing of the sort (Westfahl 2013: 148). This, in turn, points to a further, striking possibility: the possibility of theoretically creating enough holograms to capture, in a palimpsest-like manner, all events that took place at each spot of the planet at any point in time. What is being gestured toward here, in other words, is the possibility of constructing a world that can be genuinely designated as a totality – the most totalizing totality imaginable – in this additional sense.

It is the affirmation of the totality that Jameson sees as a key attribute of spy fiction, something which he associates with the global. In Jameson's now familiar formulation, the world-system – like postmodernist architecture – is centre-less, complex, fragmented, disorientating, and, in short, un-navigable by the human brain. The conspiracy tale, which, he says, typically finds expression in the genre of spy fiction, strives to offer an antidote to this: it is, as he puts it, 'a degraded attempt [...] to think the impossible totality of the contemporary world system' because it implies that beneath the fragmented and un-navigable reality there lie connections that point to a deeper, truer, more total or complete reality that can become comprehensible when hidden connections are revealed (Jameson

1991: 38). With this in mind, then, what we appear to have arrived at by this point is a paradox: while globalization and the figure of the spy, as we saw at the beginning of this chapter, appear to be incompatible with one another, Gibson seems to present us with a return to classic spy fiction *through* – not in spite of – his engagement with the global. This is so to the extent that the global is here associated with the notion of the totality – a notion which, as we have seen, finds multiple expressions in the Blue Ant trilogy and which is key in the genre of spy fiction.

Gear-Queer

And yet, while Gibson does in this sense confront us with a return to key principles underlying the classic spy story, these principles have been emptied of their meaning. It is, we might say, as though the 'shape' of the story has been preserved but its implications changed. Once again, the global and the idea of the totality are instructive in this respect. It is, for example, particularly important that they feature in pointedly anti-climactic ways in the trilogy. In *Pattern Recognition*, for instance, the fact that Cayce has to traverse the globe in order to complete her mission of discovering the 'maker' of the enigmatic footage, coupled with the fact that this maker is proved to be located in Russia, and with the fact that powerful Russians (some associated with the oil industry) turn out to be involved, suggests that this is a mission that will be revealed to carry political significance, perhaps even on a global scale. By the end, though, it becomes clear that this is rather far from the truth: the secrecy which surrounds the whole enterprise, giving the impression that something truly 'big' is going on, is finally shown to be rather unnecessary. Indeed, Jameson, as we have seen, complains that this 'Russian episode' is ultimately uninteresting, but this seems to be exactly the point. It is, I would suggest, the anti-climactic that lies at the core of Gibson's reconfiguration of the spy novel. While classic spy fiction typically ends by pointing up the spy's work in a climactic ending which may reveal that the significance of what has been achieved is even bigger than was expected, what we have here instead is a movement from a build-up toward an expected climax to what turns out to be rather anti-climactic, and, more specifically, a movement from a gesture toward the global and the totality to what turns out to be extremely localized in the sense of being individual and idiosyncratic instead. The fervour with which 'Footageheads' from around the world discuss the uploads, for example, in conjunction with the amount of resources that Bigend throws into the discovery of their 'maker' help to create the expectation that the footage is the bearer of some profound meaning that will turn out to be of global or universal significance. The truth, by contrast, is that the 'maker', Nora Volkova, started putting this together without a grand artistic plan and not even in a fully conscious state, while being treated at the hospital, an explosion having seriously injured her, and a fragment from it still remaining inside her brain. Not only did the project begin without a plan in mind, but once Cayce meets Nora it becomes clear that there is also no vision of a revelatory end with a final upload, or indeed a message that the footage at-large seeks to communicate.

Jameson, on the other hand, convincingly argues that the footage does have a 'deeper meaning' for Cayce, in that 'its utter lack of style' constitutes a 'relief', 'like black-and-white film after the conventional orgies of bad technicolour'; it is, he continues, 'an epoch of rest, an escape from the noisy commodities themselves, which turn out, as Marx always thought they would, to be living entities preying on the humans who have to coexist with them' (Jameson 2003: 114). Jameson is right to suggest that there does exist a message here regardless of the artist's intentions, but what is more important is that this message is finally cancelled out, and spectacularly so: what throughout *Pattern Recognition* signals 'an escape from [...] commodities' ironically ends up, as we find out in *Spook Country*, being channelled, of all things, to the sale of commodities. As Bigend reveals, the anonymous pieces of footage allowed him to develop a 'viral pitchman platform' that has enabled him 'to sel[l] shoes' by doctoring old films (Gibson 2011b: 108). Once again, in other words, we are following a trajectory from climax to anti-climax, from that which promises to resonate meaningfully on a global or universal scale to that which turns out to be nothing if not mundane – the sale of shoes – and which is extremely localized in that it serves one individual.

This trajectory – from the global to the very particular or idiosyncratic, and, more broadly, from an expected climax to an anti-climax – defines not just the fate of the footage but it is at the heart of *Spook Country* more broadly. Here, Hollis Henry (on whom the novel's first plotline focusses) is employed by Bigend to investigate the emerging 'locative art', the main proponent of which is, as we have seen, Bobby Chombo, who, as it gradually emerges, works in a different capacity for someone enigmatically referred to as 'the old man'. Also working for the old man is Tito (second plotline), a teenager from a Chinese-Cuban family of spies that worked for Castro before moving to the United States, where they take on various non-governmental assignments. Tito is being monitored by Brown and his captive Migrim (third plotline) with the aim of discovering the old man and what he is planning. As it turns out, the old man 'used to be in national security, American government' – a spy, that is, of the traditional variety (Gibson 2011b: 319). Having resigned from his duties of serving the state, we learn that he is currently pursuing a mission related to a ship container carrying American aid money which was supposed to be used in war-torn Iraq, but has been diverted and is now transported around the world until it is deemed safe to unload it. The mission includes a distinctly complex method of marking the money to render it unusable, and involves, in the run-up to this, Chombo's task of 'compiling elaborate logs of fictional searches for the container's signal', in this way creating data recounting his 'ongoing search for and utter failure to find the key he already has' – data which will then be purposefully lost in order to mislead those who are seeking to monitor the old man's activities (Gibson 2011b: 196). The great complexity of, and commitment required by, the old man's mission builds up the expectation that this mission carries some sort of global resonance. In reality, though, the global or the totality give way to the individual or idiosyncratic. While at stake in this instance are practices like money laundering and profiting from the war in Iraq – practices, that is, the opposition to which would appear to promote a universally worthwhile anti-corruption message – what features as the driving force behind the project is not the old man's moral compass but what Gareth describes as the personal obsessions of an eccentric individual, who 'uses his various connections' to find out things people have done in relation to the topics he happens to be 'queer about' so that 'he can fuck with them, frankly. Fuck them up. Over. Sideways if he can manage it' (Gibson 2011b: 319).

With the above in mind, we can describe Gibson's reconfiguration of spy fiction in the age of the global through an analogy with the phenomenon of 'gear-queer'. In the context of *Zero History*'s plot, where the term appears, the phenomenon of gear-queer serves to explain the hype around military trousers and the power of exclusivity in the market, which is also at the core of the popularity of the secretive 'Gabriel Hounds' – the paradoxically 'brand-less' brand whose designer Bigend employs Hollis Henry to discover. The term is defined as 'equipment fetishism' – an attempt, more specifically, to own the 'costume and semiotics of [...] police and military units', and 'in turn to be associated with that world, with its competence, its cocksure exclusivity' (Gibson 2010: 213). Gear-queer, we learn, applies neither to individuals who want *to be* soldiers, nor to those who want to *pretend* to be soldiers; the former, after all, would require more than owning the equipment while the latter could be achieved with less, for example with imitation gear.

In Bigend's words, the phenomenon denotes not an attempt *'to be'* but to be 'mistaken for', or 'at least associated with' that which the equipment points toward (Gibson 2010: 213–14). Beyond the specifics of its importance in *Zero History*'s plot, the notion of 'gear-queer' resonates in reference to the trilogy at-large and its formal elements in that it effectively encapsulates a trajectory such as that we have been tracing above: from an expected climax – a climax in this instance promised by the associations the gear serves to draw – to an anti-climax, in that at stake is ultimately an *association* with (as opposed to *being*) the 'real thing'. As a metonymical figuration of the trilogy's relation to the genre of spy fiction, the notion of gear-queer would suggest that what we are confronted with is not a case of the trilogy merely *pretending* to be a spy story – a case, that is, of simply appearing to be something other than what it really *is* – but rather as a case of possessing the genuine 'equipment', 'costume', and 'semiotics' of the spy story but without *being* a spy story in the traditional sense.

In effectively raising the question of what a spy story really *is*, the phenomenon of gear-queer leads us back to the beginning of the chapter and the claim that Gibson's Blue Ant trilogy effects a reconfiguration of spy fiction that we can describe as ontological. As we have seen, Boltanski argues that the spy story typically presents us with two realities, whereby, in the course of the story, the state-sanctioned or 'official' reality comes under threat but is by the end restored with the completion of the spy's mission. In the Blue Ant trilogy, on the other hand, there is no state, and so it seems to follow that there is no discrepancy between two realities either, and, by extension, no restoration task is needed. Indeed, the analogy with gear-queer already steers us away from the two realities model – a model that would point to a case of pretence, whereby something on the outside is different to the inside. Although it does not involve such a clash between an external and an internal reality, which would by definition suggest a degree of superficiality, gear-queer is nevertheless a phenomenon that – despite the commitment it clearly demands – is inextricable from a sense of an emptying or hollowing out, and, once again, this proves instructive for the trilogy at-large and its formal characteristics. I want to linger a little longer on this sense of a hollowing out – which is precisely what underpins the movement from an expected climax to an anti-climax that we have been tracing here – and to conclude by suggesting, firstly, that this is very much connected to the absence of the state from Gibson's trilogy and, secondly, that this, in turn, is at the heart of the emerging, and rather bleak, world that Gibson's trilogy points toward.

Conclusion: The Kingdom to Come

The absence of the state does, of course, theoretically open up the possibility of channelling the spy story towards a more progressive direction, freeing it from some of the suspect values with which it has been associated. An example of such values is brought up in *Spook Country*, during a discussion about the US government's practice of spying on its own citizens. In response to the claim that this otherwise unacceptable practice is justified because of exceptional circumstances – in this instance, the threat of terrorism post-9/11 – Milgrim says:

> A nation [...] consists of its laws. A nation does not consist of its situation at a given time. If an individual's morals are situational, that individual is without morals. If a nation's laws are situational, that nation has no laws, and soon isn't a nation. (Gibson 2011b: 139–40)

It is, indeed, with just such objectionable suspensions of the law that the spy is traditionally associated with. Spies, Goodman writes, are the 'figures that seek to protect and preserve' the 'nation-state, its laws, and its values' but they are also simultaneously the figures that repeatedly suspend those same laws and values (Goodman 2015: 8); or, as a 1966 article in *Esquire* magazine puts it, in more vivid language, spies can 'kill, steal, maim, rape, lie, cheat', and can do so 'without penalty' (qtd. in Kackman 2005: xvii). Though Gibson's spy figures do not have such a status of being 'outside' or 'above' the law, this does not, as I have suggested, translate as a progressive reconfiguration of the spy story. The role of the state here is not exactly removed entirely but is, rather, in a certain sense reconstructed in that it effectively becomes a role that is played by Bigend. This is a role replacement, I would suggest, that alerts us to a transition from what Boltanski deems to be the conservative worldview associated with the genre to a different worldview that could in fact be worse.

Hints of this substitution – the substitution of the state by Bigend – are present from the first instalment of the trilogy, and become more obvious by the third, where the implications become clearer. One initial hint is given in *Pattern Recognition*, when we realize that Cayce here features as a spy figure but, unlike typical spies, she works not for a country but for Bigend, who in this way appears to have taken the role traditionally played by national governments. By *Zero History*, the assumption of the role of a sovereign nation's government by businesspeople becomes more insidious. Early on in this novel, we witness Milgrim thinking about 'radio-frequency identification tags' and the fact that they are now embedded 'in every recent U.S. passport', which means that one 'could sit in a hotel lobby and collect information from the passports of American businessmen' (Gibson 2010: 25). The passport, then, which would have otherwise stood as proof of a sovereign nation's relevance and power is not rendered redundant here in what might have turned out to be a progressive development in a globalized, borderless world, but is, rather, transformed into something whose function is to serve one businessperson at the expense of another. What we have here, in other words, signals a transition to a situation whereby a corporation or an entrepreneur replaces, or at least assumes a status that seems equivalent to, a sovereign state. The same kind of transition emerges through Milgrim's journey in the trilogy – a character whose name, in evoking the Milgram experiment, raises the question of being subject to authority, and in so doing inevitably highlights Milgrim's own experience of such subjection. In *Spook Country*, where he first appears, Milgrim is held captive by Brown, whom he assumes to be an undercover police officer or a spy. In *Zero History*, Milgrim still is, for all intents and purposes, a captive, although here responsible for his captivity is not someone who has represented, or was associated with, the authority of the state but, rather, Bigend. Such a shift from the authority of the state to the authority of a businessperson or entrepreneur is also what underpins one of the central thematic threads of this novel: gear-queer. After all, the 'gear' here refers specifically to police and military equipment – equipment, that is, which is explicitly associated with officers serving the state, but which in *Zero History* is co-opted to advance the interests of the businessperson that manages to secure the original designs.

The dynamic between climax and anti-climax in *Zero History* cements this notion of a new structure of power within the contemporary world-system. At the end of this novel, it appears that Bigend has in fact made an important discovery: he has obtained the 'order flow' of the market, which allows him to anticipate future events and gain control over the totality of production and consumption, albeit momentarily. In this instance, then, the deflatory quality of mundane or very particular events that defines the endings of the previous instalments of the trilogy seems to have been avoided: here we end with something of genuine, universal significance. But there remains a sense of anti-climax nevertheless; regardless of its various objectionable qualities, the classic spy story ends with a sort of gravity, in that the spy's mission is defined by the idea that it is carried out for a collective body – that of the nation-state. In *Zero History*, on the other hand, we are confronted with an emptying or hollowing out in that any sense of collectivity is removed; the representative model of politics which has gone hand in hand with the idea of the nation-state since its inception is replaced by a model of politics centred on an individual who upstages any residual form of collectivism (however illusory) we might locate in an earlier concept of the corporation. Indeed, capture and control of the market, as Milgrim points out, suggests that 'the market would cease to be real' because 'the market *is* the inability to aggregate the order flow at any given moment' (Gibson 2010: 177). What Bigend has achieved, in other words, in a sense spells the end of the market as a free trading ground (cultivated by the state) where different individuals can compete. Bigend thus exceeds any bourgeois or even neoliberal concept of the entrepreneur, and in turn transcends what he perceives as the limitations of representative or liberal politics; his dominion of the market, we might say, signals the coming of a figurative kingdom of sorts in which he would be the one performing the role of the king.

In this sense, Bigend is perhaps the first properly *neo-feudal* character in a reconfigured spy genre. As suggested by my earlier comparison between Bigend's operations in the Blue Ant trilogy and the function of the king and queen in Foucault's reading of *Las Meninas,* Bigend's power is post-geographic rather than being tied to land, but he nevertheless does conjure up such figures of (absolute) sovereignty. Indeed, Bigend's power and influence, like that of feudal lords, is exerted remotely, and the territory over which he has oversight is worked out along the lines of dominion rather than nationhood. He also exceeds any of the prudence associated with entrepreneurial or bourgeois models of investment; his investments, as he brags, are often based on whim rather than on a clearly defined or pre-calculated expected return, and in this sense he appears to tap into the model of unproductive expenditure that figures like Georges Bataille associate, in works such as *The Accursed Share* (1949–1976), with the concept of sovereignty more generally.

The project Bigend hires Cayce to work on constitutes just such a whimsical undertaking, but even the fact of her employment in the first place, regardless of the specifics of the project in question, points toward a neo-feudal state of affairs. Lauren Berlant aptly summarizes the service that Bigend hires Cayce for when she refers to the latter's 'professionalisation of intuition': what Cayce is 'selling', after all, are her affective reactions to logos (Berlant 2008: 846). For Berlant, this epitomizes one of 'the sovereign figures of neoliberalism' – namely, 'the freelancer': 'the person on contract who makes short-term deals for limited obligation' (Berlant 2008: 855). What is key here, though, is the fact that Cayce's situation in *Pattern Recognition* makes it impossible to maintain any belief (however erroneous) in the sovereignty of the freelancer. Far from presenting her as a sovereign figure, the terms of Cayce's employment point instead to what Jodi Dean describes as the 'neo-feudalizing tendencies' of the capitalist system – tendencies which Dean sees emerging, among other things, in certain iterations of the freelancer or the so-called self-employed worker such as the Uber driver (Dean 2020: 1). Just as the Uber driver's car 'is not for personal transport' but 'for making money' for 'the lords of the platform' (Dean 2020: 5), so too Cayce's affective reactions to logos are not personal but are instead used to make money for 'the Bigends of this world' (Gibson 2011a: 106). Cayce, in this sense, is not entirely unlike the Uber driver who, according to Dean, constitutes an example of a 'tendency toward becoming-peasant, that is, becoming the one who owns the means of production but whose labour increases the capital of the platform owner' – a tendency which she describes as 'neo-feudal' (Dean 2020: 5). From this vantage point, then, the spy in Gibson's trilogy seems to have entered into the service of something which is rather more regressive than the nation-state – something that is emergent and yet all too imbued with the qualities of the existing global system.

CHAPTER 18

The Twenty-First-Century Global Slave Narrative Trade

Laura T. Murphy

'O what crimes are perpetrated under a mask of democratic liberty!'
-Frederick Douglass, 1847

Paul Gilroy suggested in *Black Atlantic* that global modernity was inauspiciously conceived in the cargo holds of slave ships travelling between the slave forts and plantations that mark the distant – though increasingly connected – shores of the Atlantic (Gilroy 1993: 16–17). And indeed the global capitalism that was born of that exchange of currency, culture and commodified bodies continues to survive on the blood of enslaved people who even today toil in Congo's mines, Cambodia's fishing boats and China's factories. The nearly global legislative abolition of the slave trade between 1807 and 1888 may have largely eradicated the institutions that legitimized and profited from slavery, but it did not dismantle the global systems of trade that support the use of forced labour. Slavery proliferated globally after the end of the slave trade, transforming and even expanding under ever more opaque disguises.

Even as globalization purports to be the disseminator of rights, it nonetheless thrives on a foundation of slavery. Estimates from the International Labour Organization and Walk Free Foundation suggest that forced labour is not as anomalous in the twenty-first century as we might imagine. Indeed, the global economy benefits from the forced labour of at least 40 million people (Walk Free 2018). Affecting practically every consumer good in the market including our mobile phones and laptops, clothes, jewellery and home goods, slavery very much undergirds the global economy and is practically invisibly integrated into international supply chains. Siddharth Kara has called contemporary slavery 'the shadowy underbelly of the global economy' (Kara 2017: 270), but forced labour is not so much shrouded in darkness as it is a widely accepted though studiously ignored feature of the system of global capitalism (LeBaron 2015: 1–3). The twenty-first-century global slave trade employs all late capitalism's most powerful tools – elaborate systems of credit, diversified supply chains, shadowy transoceanic shipping, lightly – or even entirely un-regulated labour standards and unprecedented human mobility – to ensure that consumer goods are produced rapidly and at the very lowest price. At the same time, slavery most typically is enacted through the most local and intimate of interactions – small villages are conscripted to labour in factories, children are stripped from their parents to fight in wars, impoverished women are coerced into trading sex – ensuring that forced labour remains nearly invisible to the vast majority of the globe's consumers. Practically all governments, ostensibly formed to protect their citizens from such violations, benefit, whether through more overt forms of forced labour such as the state-sponsored forced labour regimes emerging in China's western regions (Zenz 2019) or the hyper-availability of sexual transactions for deployed US military (Hoots 2019: 739, 748–52), or through less visible but nonetheless economically and politically lucrative collaborations with corporations that mask corporate reliance on slavery through opaque and largely unregulated international networks of commerce (Peksen et al. 2017: 675–9). Slavery is neither inherent to any one community or caste or region of the world, nor is it unavoidable – it is *created* through generations of neoliberal policies and investments that require the enslavement of the most marginalized in order to produce and sustain the wealth of the elite and of the nations (democratic or otherwise) whose economies depend on cheap production costs.

Generic Contexts

A contemporary anti-slavery movement has emerged in response to the diverse array of forms of forced labour that proliferate in the twenty-first-century global economy. The movement has encouraged survivors to speak out about their experiences of enslavement and to work as activists in a new abolitionist cause. As a result, the genre of the slave narrative, so popular among nineteenth-century abolitionists, has re-emerged as a form of protest literature. Not to be confused with the neo-slave narrative (a genre of historical *fiction* in which the central protagonist or narrator is an enslaved person, typically in bondage in nineteenth-century America), the new slave narrative that emerges in the early twenty-first century is a *non-fictional* account written from the first-person perspective of the person who has suffered contemporary forms of forced labour and is driven by an activist's ambition to redress wrongs committed against him or her and others who are enslaved today (see Bell 1987; Rushdy 1999; Cox 2000; Keizer 2004). These new slave narratives are penned by authors who were child soldiers in Sierra Leone, child domestic labourers in Haiti and child brides in Yemen. They are written by domestic servants in Lebanon and France or forced sex workers in London and the United States. While the new slave narratives available on shelves now represent a wide spectrum of slavery today, we still have only a small sampling of narratives to analyse relative to that available to the scholar of nineteenth-century slave narratives. Published book-length new slave narratives are often co-authored by an amanuensis, and typically employ tropes familiar to the nineteenth-century narratives, perhaps as a result of the author's or ghost writer's familiarity with the historical genre as well as the conventions of memoir and autobiography (Murphy 2019: 49–58). Resonance with the nineteenth-century narratives and reliance on particular tropes of slavery make it more likely that a slave narrative will be published. The slave narrative is a didactic project, one that seeks to perform for the reader the conditions of life among the poorest and most oppressed people in our societies. The depiction of life under the yoke of slavery is, thus, determined largely by the kinds of experience that will indicate the extraordinary suffering and brutality that is characteristic of the system. Ghost writers and the non-profits who support the slave narrators often fixate on these details, encouraging survivors to include the most intimate details of their subordination, in an effort to make contemporary forms of slavery legible.

The slave narrative tradition catapulted to prominence in the late eighteenth and early nineteenth centuries as a global anti-slavery movement took shape, but the genre largely lay dormant between the era of the Works Progress Administration of the 1930s and the early 1990s. At least two forced labourers identified their experiences as 'slavery' in the 1990s and adapted the genre of the slave narrative as a platform from which to describe their experiences, but it was not until the civil war in Sudan became a concern in the West that the slave narrative really gained traction as a revivified genre (Muhsen and Crofts 1991; Cadet 1998). Francis Bok's 2003 life narrative of Sudanese forced child labour was explicitly framed as a slave narrative. Together with Mende Nazer's similar story of capture by the mujahedeen published in the same year, which she titled *Slave: My True Story* (Nazer 2003), these stories of enslavement in Sudan seemed to inaugurate a re-emergence of the genre of the slave narrative in the twenty-first century. In the years since Bok and Nazer published their slave narratives, at least forty new book-length narratives have emerged alongside hundreds of shorter testimonies collected for non-profits, court testimony, congressional hearings and journalistic accounts, all of which recount the first-person non-fictional lived experience of contemporary enslavement (see Bales and Trodd 2013; Murphy 2014).

Despite an overwhelming shift in the anti-slavery movement towards concern for domestic sex trafficking victims, international slave narratives maintain traction in the US publishing industry, especially when they take up issues considered to be of geopolitical significance.[1] In the early years of the genre's re-emergence, Francis Bok's *Escape From Slavery* and Mende Nazer's *Slave: My True Story* lent a face to the oppression of the Dinka of southern Sudan. Indeed, since those early Sudanese narratives, the new slave narrative seems to be growing in its popularity, and it has been mobilized for political ends by influential public figures. More recently, the new slave narrative has been mobilized to make a sentimental case against the Islamic State with Nadia Murad's slave narrative *The Last Girl: My Story of Captivity and My Fight Against the Islamic State* (Murad 2017). New slave narratives have garnered their authors' invitations to the White House (Bok's *Escape from Slavery*), have been promoted by Starbuck's (Ishmael Beah's *Long Way Gone*, 2007), have been featured on Oprah and Tyra (Somaly Mam's *The Road of Lost Innocence*, 2009), and have even led to the awarding of the Nobel prize (Murad's *The Last Girl*). In many ways, the unassailable gravity and ethical unacceptability of slavery that is made flesh in the slave narrative is used to emphasize the radical injustice of armed conflicts, gender-based violence, child abuse and domestic servitude around the world.

Narrative Contours

Francis Bok's new slave narrative is exemplary of the form and conventions of the genre as it has emerged since 2000, including clear echoes of the tropes of the nineteenth-century iteration of the genre. Bok opens his narrative with a story of growing up as a young Dinka boy, proud of his heritage and destined for greatness. His family was poor by Western standards, but they were influential within their community and provided a home of love and support for Francis when he was young. While he was shopping in the market one day, however, an eerie tension descended upon this otherwise peaceful setting, as armed men on horses galloped into the bustling town centre and furiously whipped the shoppers, herded the men into one section of the market, kidnapped the children and rode with them into the desert. For the next decade, the young narrator was forced to work for a family of people who did not share his language, religion or culture, never to see many of his family members again. The family who enslaved him call him 'abeed' (slave) and beat him like an animal for even the smallest transgression. The father of the family is a figure of utter horror and brutality, much like the Simon Legree character from Stowe's *Uncle Tom's Cabin*.

As was the case for so many slave narrators before him, Bok's young mind obsessed over freedom, and his plot to escape is the focus of the bulk of the middle of the narrative (Lovejoy 2011: 91). When he did finally manage to run away, he was met with various impediments (including the police) that episodically reiterate his subjection to slavery. When he was eventually able to escape Sudan, he found sanctuary in neighbouring Kenya in a pestilential displaced persons camp, but quickly followed his dream to move to the United States, where he took up residence in Lynn, Massachusetts, the onetime home of Frederick Douglass, the famed slave narrator. Given a new Christian name in his new community, Francis was by then in his twenties, over six and a half feet tall, gifted with a brilliant smile and an affecting charm. He recounts that when he met Charles Jacobs, a self-styled 'modern-day abolitionist' from Boston's American Anti-Slavery Group, they both immediately recognized their value as a team. Bok's narrative recounts how the two men collaborated to present a case to American audiences that slavery still exists and to campaign against oppression in Sudan under Omar al Bashir. Jacobs coached Bok in his speeches and encouraged him to highlight some of the events that he thought the Christian and Jewish audiences to whom they spoke would respond: being called 'abeed' or slave, being forced to embrace Islam, his later conversion to Christianity, his redemption in freedom in the West. Jacobs located an amanuensis for Francis, and they composed *Escape From Slavery: The True Story of My Ten Years in Captivity and My Journey to Freedom in America*, giving it a title that most certainly echoes those of his nineteenth-century predecessors and advertising it as 'a touching modern day slave narrative' on the back cover (Bok 2003). In many ways Bok's narrative can be usefully read as an unconscious blueprint for the new slave narrative that emerged in the ten years after its publication, as the arc and tropes of his narrative are quite similar to those adopted in other new slave narratives published by survivors from the Global South.

Globalization's Failures

It might seem on the surface that because Bok's labour was localized and served only a single, small, geographically isolated, family farm, we could assume that his enslavement would not suggest a critical engagement with the global circuits of capital or our own complicity in slavery. For this reason, he was a 'perfect victim' for the early anti-slavery movement, as he was both a child whose innocence could not be impugned when he was enslaved, and also because his oppressive life circumstances pointed to a world outside the West that did not value freedom or rights (Murphy 2019: 186–9). Embracing capitalism, Bok celebrates his freedom through that consecrated American pastime of shopping, eagerly consuming jeans and glasses and shoes and other markers of his entry into a Western liberal economy that liberates through consumerism, as Yogita Goyal has noted (Goyal 2019). Bok says that 'one American habit came to me very naturally: shopping' (2003: 255). He explains: 'Sometimes I would buy things because it made me happy. I had known sadness and misery and real pain. I preferred being happy, and sometimes I just out and bought some happiness' (2003: 176). Instead of concerns about consumer responsibility for slavery around the globe, Bok's narrative often celebrates his entry into consumer culture.

However, the very fact of having been enslaved in the first place undermines the neoliberal concept that the prosperity ushered in through globalization trickles down to the most impoverished to lift up the entire global economy in consumeristic bliss. The poverty of Bok's childhood before enslavement that made him and his family vulnerable to the mujahideen and invisible to most human rights agendas for decades is taken for granted in his narrative. His subsequent enslavement is figured in his narrative as culturally embedded; that it is an invention of the people of Arab descent who attacked his community, made them captive, and 'brainwashed' them into 'Muslim life' (2003: 244). However, Bok's enslavement, though menial and localized, is part of a global struggle to control the lucrative oil wealth of his nation. Omar al-Bashir's violent drive to maintain the integrity of his nation was at least in part motivated by his need to keep the south's oil supply under his control. Oil was first exported from Sudan in 1999, and it is no coincidence that the brutality of the government's oppression and displacement and even enslavement of the Dinka and Nuer increased at this time, nor is it surprising that a significant rights response to Sudan's oppression of their citizens of African descent only emerged in the years that followed. The Sudanese civil war, which had left 2 million people dead and 4 million people displaced over twenty years before oil was exported from southern Sudan, had largely escaped global humanitarian notice. Bok and his community's displacement was part of a deliberate government campaign that made way for Western and Asian oil companies to build the infrastructure for oil extraction (Human Rights Watch 2003). Though Bok and his amanuensis stress the terror of Omar al-Bashir's rule, they do not complicate their historical narrative, which emphasizes instead the 'centuries of [Arab] racism…and almost twenty years of religious arrogance and cruelty' perpetrated by the 'fanatical Islamist government' on a par with bin Laden and the Taliban (2003: 231–2). They never suggest the significance of the global flows of oil and wealth that undergirded his power and violence. To do so would implicate the globalized fossil-fuel-based economy (and thus everyone in the West who was poised to consume Sudan's oil riches) that underwrote Bok's oppression.

By historically contextualizing Bok's narrative and other slave narratives, it becomes clear that in documenting the very fact of enslavement in the twenty-first century the narrators collectively reveal the widespread failure of the promises of globalization, even if they celebrate their own atypical ascent to freedom and prosperity. Now in America, the narrators, too, turn away from their own new-found complicity in the oppression endemic to globalization. They repeat their own erasure through consumption as well as through their emphasis on Western freedom and rights in their narratives. However, by contextualizing these narratives in which we learn that there are millions of people enslaved, we are able to discern the true contours of globalization, the radical inequalities that remain and are fed by the transnational flow of commodities, including but not exclusively labour, and the slavery that is endemic and even encouraged in these global transactions.

The cooptation of Bok's narrative by the human rights establishment reveals another betrayal of globalization's promise. Bok's patron Charles Jacobs had recently taken up the cause of slavery in Sudan when he met Bok, but it wasn't the only cause he was invested in. Jacobs was the most well known for being an instigator of take-down campaigns against universities, professors, mosques, community centres and individual clergy that he deemed anti-Semitic (Blumenthal 2010; Nevel 2013). Jacob's other politicized non-profit endeavour, the David Project, ran training and leadership camps for Jewish youth to take up the Zionist cause (Davidproject.org; Dillon 2004; Sasson 2013: 44–5). When Jacobs met Bok, he was in the midst of fighting several defamation lawsuits lodged against him by Boston-area mosques and Islamic community groups that he regularly libellously attacked in newspapers as being radical jihadists, acts which has garnered his most recent non-profit, Americans for Peace and Tolerance, the label of a hate group and repudiations by the Anti-Defamation League (Council on American-Islamic Relations-MA 2015). Jacobs explicitly promoted himself as a white saviour who would transcend the left's cowardice exhibited by their 'human rights complex' – their supposed refusal to 'protest evil' done by those who come from non-Western communities (Bok 2003: 273). In his radical misinterpretation of American race relations, Jacobs believed that he alone was willing to be a white activist fighting oppression perpetrated by people of African and Arab descent. What Bok could not have predicted was that as part of his campaign to destabilize Islamic power globally, Jacobs had become a central figure in a large-scale fraud that purported to be purchasing the emancipation of enslaved Sudanese people with US donor funding, but which was in fact arming a rebellion in southern Sudan. Bok disagreed with Jacobs's stated position that slave 'redemption' (or the purchasing of enslaved people's freedom) was an appropriate response to slavery (2003: 250), but he did not seem aware that the talks he gave were raising funds that Jacobs sent to Sudan to equip the Sudanese People's Liberation Army (SPLA) to fight against Omar al-Bashir because Jacobs and his colleagues were hiding this information from their donors and the public until it was exposed by journalists and scholars (Lewis 1999: A7; Miniter 1999; Skinner 2008: 87–92). Jacobs's mission was not related to Sudan's potential oil dividends so much as a perceived Huntingtonian ideological 'clash of civilizations' that suggested that in this more globalized world, a war would be fought for ideological domination. As Bok puts it, mimicking his 'American father' Jacobs, 'Sudan's conflict was the result of an irrational fanaticism, and nothing seems to be able to fuel that kind of radical commitment better than religion' (2003: 232); it was up to Bok and Jacobs to ensure that Islamic fanaticism was defeated, not just in Sudan but in Mauritania and elsewhere (2003: 276). The universal façade of rights provided a mask for their sense of Western superiority and the concomitant anxiety about the expansion of Islamic ideas, norms and cultures.

It is in this post-9/11, ideologically driven, Islamophobic milieu that the new slave narrative sees its rebirth. Slavery is nearly universally reviled; the slave narrative thus acts as a vehicle for condemning those who would most explicitly benefit from it. In the context of this global ideological battle, however, it can be fashioned as a powerful weapon that invokes slavery's gravity and unassailability for political goals that can at times be at odds with the explicit liberatory politics of the narratives. Jacobs and his team at the American Anti-Slavery Group knew precisely how powerful the façade of slavery could be for their Islamophobic cause that they not only helped Bok publish his narrative and headline speaking events, but they published a collection of slave narratives themselves, half of which were about people who had been enslaved by Muslims (Sage and Kasten 2006).[2] But the American Anti-Slavery Group was not alone in using anti-slavery as a proxy for Islamophobic sentiments. Mende Nazer's narrative (co-authored with Damien Lewis who has written numerous biographies of ordinary citizens who fight against Islamic extremism) tells the story of a woman who grew up Muslim but in the process of narrating her enslavement authorizes the consistent theme in US and UK rhetoric post-9/11 that Islam had been hijacked by men with 'wild staring eyes and long scraggy beards' who kidnap and enslave other innocents (Nazer 2003: 3). Grace Akallo's narrative of being a child soldier in Uganda (co-authored with Faith McDonnell, who works for a conservative evangelical think tank concerned with Christian persecution), blames Omar al-Bashir and the pernicious spread of Islam for the oppression and enslavement of Acholi children of Christian faith, even though the enslavers themselves are Christian and animist (Akallo and McDonnell 2007: 25). In 2015, Shyima Hall published a narrative of her kidnapping from Syria, in which she rails against the strictures of Islam (Hall 2014: 101) and is so scarred by her experience that she concludes that 'adult Muslim men had done nothing worthy of my respect' (152). More recently, shorter narratives condemning Boko Haram for engaging in sexual enslavement have gained popularity, and even more popular are the narratives condemning the sexual enslavement of Yazidi women by the Islamic State, including Jinan's German-language slave narrative titled *Esclave de Daech* (2015) and Farida Khalaf's *The Girl Who Escaped ISIS: This Is My Story* (2016). Nadia Murad's *The Last Girl: My Story of Captivity, and My Fight Against the Islamic State* (2017) won her the Nobel prize for a book that is providing US government officials further ammunition against IS.

The narrators are not necessarily themselves Islamophobic, but, read together, they could suggest that slavery is over-represented in Islam and make a case for humanitarian and military intervention. However, read contextually, their narratives collectively reveal the powerful influence the post-9/11 Islamophobic anxiety has on the publishing industry to determine the shape of what we know and believe about slavery in the twenty-first century. This is not to suggest that we should refuse to condemn the use of rape as a weapon of war or the deployment of child soldiers in civil conflict or forced religious conversion or enslavement by people of the Muslim faith in general, as Charles Jacobs accuses the progressive left of doing. But it must give us pause that more than one in five of the full-length new slave narratives published in the West over the course of about fifteen years publicized human rights violations committed by Muslim people. These narratives appeal to Western audiences because they affirm a widely held misconception that Islam stands against the human rights regime that globalization ostensibly offers and because of a seemingly contrary fear that globalization has empowered Islamic networks of communication and piety that are understood as antithetical to the Enlightenment values that are considered intrinsic to capitalism.

Neoliberal Exclusions

Ironically the one aspect of slavery's radical injustice that seems to be excluded from the increasingly crowded shelf of new slave narratives is the forms of unfreedom that emerge from the globalization of the labour force within the capitalist economy today. The twenty-first-century slave narrative, like its nineteenth-century predecessor, typically tells the uplifting, Enlightenment, *bildungsroman*-esque story of a rise to freedom, rights and prosperity as the markers of escaping slavery. Those life narratives that make it to the publishing market are typically packaged to celebrate freedom as a gift of Western democracies and as inherent right enshrined in international human rights protocols. As we can see through a critical reading of Bok's new slave narrative and its depictions of slavery, freedom and anti-slavery activism, however, an historicized reading of the slave narrative as a genre calls into questions the very triumphant liberal narrative of globalization that is celebrated in its pages.

Strikingly, there has not been even one full-length slave narrative published in the United States, United Kingdom, France or Germany that depicts a factory worker, producing the products that would expose the complexity and opacity of global supply chains that constitute the majority of cases of enslaved labour around the world today. Where is the narrative of uplift for the factory worker in Bangladesh who rises up from her sewing machine where she has been making our cheap t-shirts to resist the system and rise to prominence on speakers' circuits in the United States? Where is the Oprah book club memoir of a Congolese child miner who crawled out of a pit of gems to wear his own designer jewels? It's both extraordinarily rare for people to escape these supply chain tragedies, but even less likely that a mass market press would promote such a book. It is perhaps the case that Western complicity in global enslavement is what makes these stories so unpublishable. The publishing industry, and significant sectors of the anti-slavery movement, have virtually ignored the relationship between, say, Francis Bok's enslavement and global oil production or the ways Western geopolitical manoeuvring made Uganda's civil war or crisis in the Middle East fertile ground for the exploitation of people reduced to vulnerability machines by the radical inequality of the global economy. Even worse is the lack of recognition of the enslavement of people who work at the far ends of our supply chains, whose voices are virtually excluded from the genre and from anti-slavery activism.

The slave narrative of the twenty-first century embraces the ambivalent Enlightenment philosophies of the nineteenth-century abolitionist movement to lionize individualism and promote a freedom that is almost unattainable for those from the Global South, even after emancipation from freedom's ostensible antagonist slavery. The new slave narrative reveals that the freedoms supposedly delivered through globalized capital exchanges are elusive even for those privileged few who migrate to the West and attract the attention of global audiences through the publication of their life stories. Despite (or perhaps because of) their failure to address the failures of globalization, their narratives become the fodder of politicians, think tanks, celebrities, corporations and prize committees, who use narratives of oppression to pursue ideologies of hate, exclusion, inequality and warfare. Within these high-stakes contexts, the figure of the enslaved person is rendered the embodiment of globalization's gravest of contradictions, and the slave narrative its articulation.

Notes

1 Initially focussed on international forced labour and child soldiering, the first years of the re-emergence of the slave narrative reflected the initial notion that slavery and trafficking could only truly exist in other parts of the world. The anti-slavery movement seemed to retrain its focus in the 2010s, however, when there emerged a perceived crisis of domestic child sexual exploitation in the United States and United Kingdom. Most new slave narratives published in the United States and United Kingdom today thus focus on young women who have been coerced into the sex trade. The narratives are typically undergirded by a 'carceral feminist' approach best documented by Elizabeth Bernstein, which has as its ambition the abolition of sex work, rather than only sexual enslavement (2010: 313).
2 Full disclosure: I was employed by American Anti-Slavery group for a few hours a week over four months to assist with the development of this collection. I cut ties with the organization when I discovered that they were committed to embellishing the narratives and coaching survivors to emphasize aspects of their enslavement related to Islam, and when I discovered they were embroiled in law suits charging them with Islamophobic fear-mongering, which I found to be accurate in my time working there.

CHAPTER 19

Planetary Poetics

Christian Moraru*

I have repeatedly insisted, and it bears re-emphasizing in a book published in a 'critical concepts' series, that terms such as 'world', 'globe', and 'planet' can no longer be bandied about interchangeably at this point in intellectual history.[1] Ever since Gayatri Chakravorty Spivak's and Masao Miyoshi's 1999–2003 influential 'turn to the planet' – to recall the main title of Miyoshi's (2001) oft-quoted landmark article – planetary theory and criticism have not only made inroads into enquiry domains whose canvassing had previously been sponsored, oftentimes reductively, by global studies' quasi-uniformly anti-globalist and 'altermondialist' epistemology and rhetoric, but they have also drawn key philosophical, political and methodological demarcations among the members of the aforementioned notional triad, in English and other languages.[2] Such dissociations have meanwhile become foundational to the fast-expanding field of planetary scholarship. A main objective of the 'planetary turn' – to invoke another characteristically titled intervention of the previous decade – has been in fact the dismantling of the deceptive synonymies entangling together 'world', 'globe', 'planet', as well as 'earth' (or 'Earth') and other cognate vocabularies and muddling up, accordingly, conversations around these notions and germane thematics all over the humanities.[3] This has been an uphill battle, and terminological haziness has yet to clear up in lay and specialist venues alike.

I will not rehearse the debates around such a woolly issue here. But, to set the stage for a presentation of what I have called 'planetary poetics' and thus reach the goal of this chapter, a few distinctions are worth reiterating.[4] So, to begin with, let me underscore one more time that to critics like myself, not only are 'globe' and 'planet' hardly equivalent, but they are not givens either, unless what one designates by them is Terra's spherical shape, astronomical classification, natural environment and other features suggesting that what one is talking about is in all actuality the earth or, again, Earth. Rather, 'globe' and 'planet' are *products*, something

305

done *to* the world, made *in* and *out of* it; they are *world-making and remaking forms*. To be more precise and thus lean, albeit half-heartedly, on Heideggerian lingo, they are *outcomes of worlding*, that is, of highly complex, interrelated changes leading to intensified and vastly transformative interactions of the world's various parts economically, culturally and otherwise, much though – and this too needs to be said – the same world's animate and inanimate systems, at whose expense socio-economic growth and integration have been de facto unfolding, are concomitantly coming under unprecedented threat or even disintegrating. Both 'globe' and 'planet' are, then, objects or, as Timothy Morton might dub them, 'hyperobjects' resulting from the cultural and physical modification of the world as shaped and experienced by human and non-human actors at a certain moment, a world makeover yielding another kind or form of world to be known, lived in, and felt as such by humans and non-humans past a particular point in time.[5]

Historically, the quintessential world-making dynamic or, as I call it, world poetics underwriting this evolution has been one of incremental de-distancing, coming together, and co-presence. Increasingly frequent, extensive, and intensive in the modern age, these are *worlding* or, better yet, *re-worlding* processes that have occurred both peacefully and violently, beneficially or less so, at close quarters (more and more of the world's previously separate entities now in the same place) and at distance (more and more of the world's still geographically discrete elements and locales interfacing and 'touching' over the wide expanses between them). These transforming 'touches', these world 'haptics', as Jean-Luc Nancy and Jacques Derrida might name them, have been triggered by epochal events such as the first documented intercontinental and transoceanic travels, 'discoveries' of 'New Worlds', technological breakthroughs in all manner of communication, data exchange, and commerce, and geopolitical realignments, whose main vectors and applications have invariably been de- and re-localizing, proximity-inducing, connective, multiply relational and world-systemically so – in brief, 'worlding'.[6] Thus, the medieval world re-worlded into the early global Renaissance world. Or, closer to us, the more fragmented, Cold War world further worlded, and thus re-worlded, into the post-1990s, late global world, one of revved-up global rearrangements, shifts and morphings.[7] Among those, most critics have unrelentingly latched onto accelerated socio-cultural and linguistic homogenization, neo-imperialism, runaway rationality of lucrative management and speculation, environmental damage, depletion of natural resources, species extinction, neoliberal monetization of life, growth of transnational corporations at the expense of national sovereignty, indiscriminate imposition of deregulatory and austerity measures, and the like.

Derived from this scrutiny is a kind of police sketch of the contemporary world-as-globe. Monochrome as this ritually rehashed doom-and-gloom account has struck some, it has alerted us to the centripetal/centrifugal, organizing/disorganizing, constructive/destructive double bind of worlding qua globalization and of 'progress', 'development', 'modernization' and 'Westernization' more broadly, even though, I might add in passing, these are by no means synonymous either. More importantly still, the *factuality* of what the pre-1989, pre-Internet world has changed into post-1989 does not coincide with that world's worlding *potential*, viz., with what the world in general could and, planetarily minded critics contend, should become. The present world-system, the 'globe' thus understood and by and large actually existing despite ongoing disputes about its nature, equity and sustainability in the wake of the disastrously mismanaged Anthropocene, is not and arguably has not been all the world could and at times did turn into, for globalization is and historically has been just one worlding type. There are, some of us believe, alternatives to it and, implicitly, to 'world' as 'globe'.

Planetarization

One of these alternatives is planetarization, the world's planet-becoming. Because globalizing phenomena are so widespread and advanced, planetarization re-worlds the world in an iterative and differentiating mode at once, working so as to both refashion the world into a worlded, integrated aggregate *and* rescind the worlding logic underwriting the current, dominant global setup. In a similar vein, it is worth pointing out the two-pronged, *descriptive* and *prescriptive* driver of this work and, by the same token, of *planetarism*, to wit, of the planetary critical-theoretical project dedicated to fleshing out and furthering the concrete impact and import of planetarization. That is to say, while the planetary critic may be taking stock of one-world developments defining, for better or worse, what our shared world demonstrably *is* nowadays mostly, but not solely, as a consequence of worldings of the global sort, he or she is also committed to a normative tack. Going beyond analysis of what is, this approach reaches into the ethical territory of that which might and should be, sometimes drawing from enclaves of and responses to the globalist world's makeup that, already in the post-Berlin Wall present, bode well for a different, more markedly planetary future. Where 'global' implies, at least in its mainstream constructions, a 'globalist' worldview that, given the globalist 'values' enumerated earlier, scarcely affords us a future, planetarity opens up descriptively and conjures up, sets in train theoretically a futurality.

For both 'globe' and 'planet' are not only world realities, and disjunct, asymmetric, disproportionately extant realities at that, but also theoretical constructs. Moreover, they are competing paradigms. As discursive formations, they have been pressed by politicians, commentators, and scholars across disciplines in the service of either legitimizing the global world, the world as for the most part is, or, alternatively, the planetary world, the world as planet, as it should be. The work I and others have been engaged in for some time now has negotiated the fine line between, on one side, planet as geocultural actuality consisting of a range of intertwined 'natural' and humanmade, animate and inanimate material ecologies, and, on the other side, planet as object of the inquisitive mind, more specifically, as modality of comprehending and articulating, as *reading algorithm*. This interpretive model has been keyed to a 'reading for the planet' in the mundane fine print of the contemporary world's material-symbolic realities but also to an aspirational reading for – and, in that, a summoning of – a time in which the planetary ideal itself might become a reality. Such a planetary cognitive mapping of our world has then a 'critique' component as well as a 'post-critique' flipside to it. Dissatisfied with the foregone conclusions and political despondency of run-of-the-mill global-studies analysis, planetary reading is poised not only to 'unmask' the sometimes less conspicuous and yet by now predictable, *The Matrix*-like dissimulating workings of globalization. Where a certain poverty of the critical imagination limits standard takes on the late global era to self-congratulatory '*un*covering' of the worlding realities effectively or putatively conveyed by the said police sketch, the planetary approach is keen on enriching the obtaining critical vista by *re*covering a ampler, less morose, hope-giving, present-grounded yet future-oriented picture in which such workings can be reframed and reset to the benefit of more propitious, planetary worldings: less exploitative socially and environmentally, less profit-oriented, more equitable and more protective of the planet's wealth of biomaterial constellations of being and expression inside and outside the sphere of the human. On this account, and unlike the catastrophism prevailing in mainstream representations of the globe as sensible and intellectual object, planetarity is, to stress it one more time, both of the 'now' and of the 'not yet', irreversibly compromised as the latter may seem at present. The planetary critic looks or reads, consequently, for what is but also looks ahead to and reads, sows the intellectual seeds of, and advocates, for what ought to be, straddling the ontological divide between existence and projection, surrounding and projected worlds.

This critic must dwell, then, first, on the world-making or world-poiesis that has brought us where we are. As a literary and cultural critic, he or she attends, in other words, to world poetics, to the worldings that have led to the world geocultural aggregate as we know it. His or her basic procedure is something like a *reverse engineering* of this world in its concrete, large-scale as well as local, site-specific, often highly idiomatic, and ethnographically bounded instantiations. Simply speaking, this modus operandi analytically unmakes world-making, retracing the genealogical pathways and breaking down the linguistic-cultural amalgamations that have taken those world formations to what and where they are. Otherwise put, for a planetary critic, a certain artifact or, more generally, a certain place in the world displays or, more often than not, encodes – flaunts and disguises concomitantly – a world-poiesis process. But he or she is reading, as noted before, for this worlding phenomenology also with an eye to decoding its downside as well as its more propitious and uplifting potential. In his or her unpacking of planetary poetics, the *suspicious* hermeneutic of the portentous, ominous, and apocalyptic makes room, accordingly, for a more *auspicious* hermeneutic of the possible, which, incidentally, goes to show, the Jamesonian doxa notwithstanding, not so much that the present is incapable of imagining itself outside its economic and political configurations, but that such imaginings need not be utopian, nor that should they play back – quite *un*imaginatively – twentieth-century dystopias in order to come true. These two hermeneutics work like the arms of a scissors, cutting out from the same ontological cloth of the world different images, meanings, lessons, and prognoses, all of them 'out there', all of them necessary. Where the former interpretive vector ordinarily piggybacks on a narrative of unchecked capitalization of the modern world and subsequently on a critique of the technology instrumental to capital expansion, the latter hews disproportionately neither to ascriptions of globality hamstrung by economic determinism nor to germane and equally hampering, Martin Heidegger-inspired anti-globalist technology critique.

In assenting as it does to the Heideggerian stance and, by the same movement, to the ethical and epistemological disqualifications of technology's and science's overall planetary and circumplanetary appurtenances, even an important intervention such as Philip Leonard's *Orbital Poetics: Literature, Theory, World* (2019) remains only partly devoted to the poetics platform billed in the title of the book.[8] The conflation of the members of the conceptual triangle referred to at the outset of this chapter comes into play in Leonard's reluctance to fully value and even practice this sort of poetics at all. For, whatever discoveries the geo-orbiting and, by extension, planetary positioning and planet-scale examinations of world-making might eventuate, such revelations are predicated on 'world', 'planet', and technology concepts that are, descriptively speaking, globalist, that is, of the 'globe' kind, one that follows in the line of Heideggerian apprehensions and presumptions of 'greatness', 'giganti[sm]', and 'Americanism', all of these in turn interchangeable as scalar tropes and measuring ('planning and calculating') procedures (Heidegger 2013: 135). Therefore, *Orbital Poetics* carries on the classically anti-globalist critique of the author's previous book on the subject (2013) rather than earnestly venturing into the planetary and the worldly *poiein* of the planetary sort, in spite of his reiterations of Heidegger's lyrical incantations of *techne* as *poiesis*, as 'making' in an 'artistic' sense (Heidegger 2013: 34).

Once the orbital and, more broadly, the planetary perspective on things mundane are chalked up to the same globalist rubric, the 'Apollonian gaze' of the satellite, space station, or astronaut cannot but resubject the world down below to the same totalizing epistemologies, political calculations, and profit-driven rationalizations that have globalized it in the first place. No wonder, then, that this kind of elevated technoscrutiny – this radical literalization of the 'globalization from above' mantra – ads, for Leonard and others, geostationary injury to global insult, and so, understandably, such critics have met with suspicion what they perceive as satellite-technology-induced, euphorically all-encompassing macro-narratives of common humanity, harmonious 'interconnectivity', and fairly shared earth, often treating the altruistic, grandiose and verve of such lofty intimations as cover for self-centred and parochial designs. To them, the notion 'that it is necessary to leave the earth in order to see and know it adequately' – a 'hypothesis' (Leonard 2019: 53) undergirding 'Apollonian' discourse from orbital accounts to *The Divine Comedy* and beyond, deep into modernity – is dehistoricizing at best (although, if you cared about climate change, you would probably appreciate satellite photography's unrivalled ability to capture the *historically* unmatched pace of the Polar ice caps' melting and of Amazonian deforestation). At worst, said notion is *de*-worlding, accounting for the world's 'loss' (Cheah 2016: 95–130) or, as Morton contents, even for the world's end', one that has already 'occurred', and so '[w]e have no world' anymore (Morton 2013: 7, 104).

This is one instance in which *Hyperobjects* does not spare its critical hyperboles, rather uncritically for my money – if the world has ended, where in the world do you begin? Is there a beginning anymore? A starting over? A possible world 'reset'? Is there a point in even asking? At any rate, elsewhere in the book, however, or in the more recent *Humankind: Solidarity with Nonhuman People*, Morton is far more nuanced, and this is important because nuance, the measured ability to master one's object interpretively and terminologically, to handle level-headedly its woolly semantics as well as the language one speaks while making sense of it, is crucial to planetary criticism. No less notable is, along the same lines, Morton's revisiting of some of the more provocative vocabulary of object-oriented ontology (OOO). 'It's not', he writes

> that there is no such thing as world, but that *world* is always and necessarily incomplete. Worlds are always very cheap. And this is because of the special non-explosive holist interconnectedness that is the symbiotic real; and because of what OOO calls 'object withdrawal', the way in which no access mode whatsoever can totally swallow an entity. 'Withdrawn' does not mean empirically shrunken back or moving behind; it means—and this is why I now sometimes say 'open' instead of 'withdrawn'—*so in your face that you can't see it*. (Morton 2013: 37)

Worlds are anything but cheap (regardless of what you make of Morton's *faux pensée*). Quite the contrary. A world – the world, ours – is all we have got to go on even though it is not enough, as the 007 movie would tell you. And we have got it at present *so much*, in point of fact, that this present is defined by the world's presence – by one that *is* with such an intensity that we risk becoming desensitized to its being-here, 'so in your face that you can't see it'. In our face: this is where, I would argue, the world as planet lies right now, ontologically and critically speaking. This is, more exactly, what an entire host of worlding histories, both globalizing and planetarizing, have turned the world into, and where they have brought it – to a sort of Heideggerian 'clearing' in which clarity itself or, more likely, pseudo-clarity gets in the way and blocks out the planetarity of the mundane, oftentimes by showcasing only globalization at the expense of worldings of a more 'nuanced' category.

Furthermore, the face – or the gaze – in question is not 'above', in an 'Apollonian' sense, nor does it 'look down' (in all senses). But then again, one need not be at an orbital distance or at any distance at all for that matter to come to grips with the world-poetic operations of geocultural de-distancing and, on this very basis, accrue the cognitive profits of planetary critical investments. Far more than other objects that nowadays challenge us emphatically to grasp them, the world as planet is neither 'withdrawn' nor 'lost', let alone utterly 'dead' or 'absent'. Instead, it is *present*, and often *hyper*present, planetarily, as planet. More than anything, and more than anything else today, the world *presents itself* – presents itself qua planet, *refers* to itself in this geo-existential modality. 'The world', observes a character of Don DeLillo's strangely prescient 1982 novel *The Names*, 'has become self-referring', 'This thing', the hero goes on,

> has seeped into the texture of the world. The world for thousands of years was our escape, was our refuge. Men hid from themselves in the world. We hid from God or death. The world was where we lived, the self was where we went mad and died. But now the world has made a self of its own ... This is my vision, a self-referring world, a world in which there is no escape. (DeLillo 1989: 297)

'Now that the world has made a self of its own', and now that this self is planetary in its quasi-ubiquitous pull, the world as planet points to itself with every new app, anime and pandemic, with every back-and-forth between face-to-face and Facebook, and pretty much with any genuinely significant post-Cold War event of language, discourse, fashion, identity and culture.

Criticism as Reverse Engineering

This means, again, that one does not have to be in the International Space Station to get a serious purchase on the planetary nature, scope, aspect, or predicament of worldedness. In effect, one can be a literary critic and access this dimension so as to locate and reinscribe argumentatively bits and pieces of the world as well as the world as a whole in genetic chains of actions and actors spanning long spaces and deep times of planetary breadth. But this geolocative knack is, or can be yours also, if you happen to be a planetary critic, because it was literature's first. Not unlike most previous ways of reading, planetary criticism follows the lead of a certain way of 'geolocational' writing, and it is worth remembering that planetary poetics is a way of making, of meaning-making or meaning-engineering, before it becomes reverse engineering at the hands of the critic. Leonard himself shows that Christoph Benda's 2012 'geo-novel' *Senghor on the Rocks*, which incorporates Google Maps pictures, manages to spin a story as 'sited' as plugged into the wider world the story's nonfictional settings are. The critic highlights the role of tele-technologies of location such as GPS in the rethinking of contemporary aesthetics (2019: 96), but literature and the arts too can be seen, particularly in the wake of such advancements, as *sui generis* geopositioning systems, not to mention that, when compared with some of the orbital fiascos reviewed by Leonard, *literary* GPSs seem – with an apparent paradox – more reliable.[9]

But if writers and artists themselves do not have to get up into Yuri Gagarin's privileged observation post to gain planetary insights into the world, planetary critics must do so even less. Instead, what they must do, now as in previous ages of literature and criticism, is, as suggested earlier, walk the trail blazed by literature itself. For, if one cannot see from or like a satellite, technically speaking, one can imagine and one can write, however, like David Mitchell, Mohsin Hamid, Dave Eggers, Colson Whitehead, China Miéville, Ben Lerner, Emily St John Mandel, Gary Shteyngart, Joseph O'Neill, Jonathan Lethem, Nicole Krauss, Jonathan Safran Foer, T. C. Boyle, Richard Powers, Daniel Kehlmann, Michel Houellebecq, Ian McEwan, Mircea Cărtărescu, Nuruddin Farah and Orhan Pamuk, to name, somewhat at random, but a few. One can gravitate around Earth and take pictures of the steadily expanding deserts and shrinking glaciers; or, more down-to-earth, as it were, one can work out new *ecologies of writing* susceptible to undertake the biographies of world ecologies. The former would narrate, as they magnificently do in Powers or Mitchell, not only how the latter have been coming together into today's planetary ensemble but also how the Anthropocene has been deepening their distress, a two-pronged fictional recordkeeping that would forefront historically and diachronically *the presence of the world*, of a world that actually becomes hyper-present when its systems start failing one after another.

This is, in fact, a core feature of the new aesthetic that has been making headway in literature and other arts after the Cold War, whether their subject matter is environmental or not. Where the world-systemic frenzy of the 1990s brought the world into being in one panoramic story of smooth and lucrative interconnectedness after another, a good many contemporary writers seem now drawn preponderantly to the dysfunctionalities of the world-system. Theirs is a world that presents itself with supreme acuity as its systems stutter, shut down, or overload. In their works, the world's body parts acquire unprecedented 'being-hereness' as the world body, and thus the world as an integrated body of myriad organs, goes into shock or malfunctions. These parts – a rock, a tree, a newspaper, a laptop – spring into presence and call out to humans, to fictional characters or readers, not just when these non-human entities' actual presence is threatened. Phantom limbs of the withering tree-planet, they do so even in their sheer absence, when their very existence has been compromised already or is a thing of the past, as *most* things are in Emily St John Mandel's 2015 world-pandemic classic *Station Eleven*, where yesteryear's banal utensils retain no more than a museal value.

The *phantom limb* figure is at play in more ways than one in Powers's 2018 novel *The Overstory*, whose heroes and heroines are trees, actually: pines, chestnuts, oaks, redwood and many other species. They all are, as a character pointedly designates them, 'presences' (Powers 2018: 160, 165, 172, 178, 211, 213). They sprout, channel and shape life *across* species, habitats and spaces inside and beyond North America, underpinning and effectively making up a planetary system that becomes visible and acutely 'real' to the human observer once they start disappearing. Their endangering or, worse, their *not being there* anymore, Powers hints, brings them counterintuitively into being, into the very *Lichtung* from which Northwestern logging companies, sprawling developments, or disease pulled them. The Heideggerian term is somewhat apt here, for it points to a phenomenology of hyper-appearance, of a presence that, unlike in Heidegger, becomes painfully present, like a missing limb, both to people and plants when the majestic trees are cut down abusively and more broadly when they are treated not as life sources but as resources for alleged human life-improvement, as one item stocked in the warehouse of usable *Zuhandenheit* ('readiness-to-hand', to employment and manipulation). As we know, all sorts of natural, artificial and hybrid systems cry foul as such – they appeal to us as systems in the language of various and invariably world-systemic crises, shortages and calamities – when system components suffer, in this case when existents are instrumentalized, consumed, used, used up, and otherwise objectified. *The Overstory* too reiterates this symptomatic global scenario and typical script of the global itself as trees die off, are turned into lumber, or even replanted with an eye to exploitation domestically or overseas. But, all of a sudden, they assert a reality heretofore unequalled. They proclaim a significance of their own, for themselves as well as for the planetary systems, living and nonliving – or all of them living, rather, in ways whose ontological range humans are only beginning to make note of – affording *anthropologists* such as Eduardo Kohn to talk about 'how forests think' (Kohn 2013: 7). Whether they resist objectification, industrialization and commodification or they lose the fight against such developmentalist excesses, Powers's trees affirm a thoughtful and nurturing presence, a biopolitical resilience, and a planetary world-systemic modality of being, action, and cogitation that ironically tops the human environmentalists' themselves and gives the lie to the anthropocentric arrogance of Heideggerian pronouncements about the 'world-poor' non-human kingdom. A world-rich world of plants – not just of Pascalian thinking reeds – blossoms in a planetary novel that, it turns out, writes like a tree itself so as to possibly 'overwrite' the global (Spivak's dream) or at least a certain version of it (Spivak 2003: 72–3).

The Overstory would not be, and entire continents-spanning Latourian networks of life and culture would not exist either, without a rhizomatic understory sprouting occurrences, growing plotlines, tying them all into knots, and buttressing narrative branches that cross and cross-pollinate centuries, countries and ethnicities. Thus, as major characters interact, formerly discrete family trees enjoy an unforeseen yet fruitful proximity, and each fictional location, tiny and humble as it may strike you prima facie, becomes a planetary crossroads. Prior to global disasters and picking up its own pieces in their wake, wounded and vibrant, the planetary presents itself, persists in its presence.

The small and the modest looking, the anodyne and unremarkable, the miniature even, telescope – make visible and concentrate, compact and fold up – planetary multitudes and expanses, which is what planetary fiction challenges, and guides, the planetary critic to make out, unpack, and account for in his or her reading. It is in this descriptive 'decompression' that the basic mechanics of reverse engineering inheres. Both the challenge and the guidance posed and required, respectively, by this intellectual venture are conspicuous in Orhan Pamuk's 2002 novel *Snow* in the 'telescoping' episode where Ka, the protagonist, talks about 'All Humanity and the Stars', the 'constellating' poem he composes in reaction to his companion's comment that 'the history of the small city [of Kars] has become as one with the history of the world' (Pamuk 2005: 306). 'In the notes he made afterward', Ka 'described [the poem's] subject'

> as the sadness of a city forgotten by the outside world and banished from history; the first lines followed a sequence recalling the opening scenes of the Hollywood films he had so loved as a child. As the title rolld past, there was a faraway image of the earth turning slowly; as the camera came in closer and closer, the sphere grew and grew, until suddenly all you could see was one country, and of course – just as in the imaginary films Ka had been watching in his head since childhood – this country was Turkey; now the blue waters of the Sea of Marmara and the Bosphorous and the Black Sea and the Nişantaş of Ka's childhood, with the traffic policeman on Teşvikiye Avenue, the street of Niğar the Poetess, and trees and rooftops (how lovely they looked from above!); then came a slow pan across the laundry hanging on the line, the billboard advertising Tamek canned goods, the rusty Gutters and the pitch-covered sidewalks, before the pause at Ka's bedroom window. Then a long tracking shot through a window of rooms packed with books, dusty furniture, and carperts, to Ka at a desk facing the other window' p[anniong over his shoulder, the camera revealed a piece of paper on the desk, and following the foundtian pen, came finally to rest on the last letters of the message he was writing, thus inviting us to read:

ADDRESS ON THE DAY OF MY ENTRANCE
INTO THE HISTORY OF POETRY: POET KA,
16/8 NIGÂR THE POETESS STREET,
NISANTAS ISTANBUL, TURKEY. (Pamuk 2005: 306–7)

Sometimes, however, *teléscopy* flips over into its opposite, or apparently opposite, *microscopy*. Thus, the forests of North America await, as in Powers, in a Norway spruce seed. Or, the whole earth telescopes into the poet's room, as in Pamuk. Either way, the planetary world opens itself up to us in its most intimate, 'local', or culturally specific embodiments. And so, the more one peers into the micro and its geocultural gamut – the different, the truly or seemingly chaotic, asystemic and standalone, the fragmentary, the discontinuous, the cloistral and the isolated – the more one gets a sense of worldly, macro units, of the planetary 'longer spaces' and 'deeper times' in which 'micro' topologies and histories participate. A multi- and hetero-scalar dialectic of the micro and macro thus takes hold, setting itself forth as ontological fulcrum of both the wide planetary world-as-world and the smaller worlds without the worlding of which the bigger one would just not be. It would then be prudent, and perhaps necessary in today's theoretical context, to insist explicitly on a planetary concept seized not so much – and certainly not exclusively – as capaciousness, supreme expanse, and world-systemic extension, which would only reawaken all manner of imperialist angsts, but as co-presence and mutual, inevitable yet still to be ethically managed interlocking of the small, limited, marginal, odd, endemic, grainy and vernacular, on one hand, and the wider, centripetal, integrated, disseminated and ecumenical, on the other. It would behove the planetary critic to do so, over and over again, on a tone unfriendly to the 'Apollonian' grandiose and rhetorically apposite, instead, to the one-of-a-kind, singular and culturally granular.

Notes

* This project has received funding from the European Research Council (ERC) under the European Union's Horizon 2020 research and innovation program (grant agreement no. 101001710).
1 I have made this argument in a series of recent books and articles. See, in particular Moraru (2015, 2017).
2 See Spivak's 1999 article 'Imperative to Re-imagine the Planet', reprinted as chapter 16 in Spivak (2011); also Spivak (2003); and Miyoshi (2001). On 'globe' and *monde/mondialisation* in French philosophy, see, among others, Moraru (2011: 51–52 and 2015: 19–76); Apter (2013: 175–190), and Cheah (2008, 2016).

3 On the 'turn' theorized as such, see Elias and Moraru (2015) and Moraru (2015).
4 I have briefly talked about 'planetary poetics' in Moraru (2015: 63, 70–73, 75).
5 'Planet' is a strong candidate to 'hyperobject' status, as Timothy Morton defines the term in Morton 2010 and then exemplifies it abundantly in *Hyperobjects* (2013).
6 On touching, haptics and Jean-Luc Nancy, see Derrida (2005).
7 On 'thick' or 'late globalization', see Moraru (2011: 33–37; 2015: 35–36), among other places in my work. David Held has also described this world reality in his books and articles.
8 I have reviewed Philip Leonard's *Orbital Poetics* extensively in the forthcoming 2020 issue of *The Comparatist*.
9 I talk about contemporary fiction as an apparatus of narrative geopositioning in Moraru (2015).

CHAPTER 20

Addressing Globalization in the Anthropocene

Sam Solnick

When addressing the transnational flows of globalization or the geological dimensions of the Anthropocene, it matters not only what texts speak about, or even who (or what) is speaking, but to whom (or to what) they speak. This chapter argues that 'address', one of poetry's most fundamental – if sometimes overlooked – dimensions, offers important ways of thinking about the concepts, affects, and scales of our planet's interpenetrating economic and ecological systems.

In several poems in her 2017 collection *Fast*, Jorie Graham experiments with dashes and arrows to rapidly jump between different concerns and discourses. These paratactic shifts render the simultaneous operation of different economic, cultural and technological forces, and their effects on and in the Anthropocene – the term for a geological epoch where, thanks to activities such as anthropogenic global warming, plastic pollution and nuclear testing, humanity has woven itself into the fabric of the planet. Below is the opening of the collection's fourth poem, 'Self Portrait at Three Degrees', the title of which alludes to one of the most iconic poems of the twentieth century, John Ashbury's 'Self Portrait in a Convex Mirror'. Graham replaces the convex mirror with a picture of the planet at 'three degrees', a phrase charged with the sense of future global heating, two degrees being one of the headline targets for Intergovernmental Panels on Climate-Change.[1]

> Teasing out the possible linkages I – no you – who noticed – if the world – no – the world if – take plankton – I feel I cannot love any more – take plankton – that love is reserved for an other kind of existence – take plankton – that such an existence is a form of porn now – no – what am I saying – take plankton – it is the most important plant on earth – think love – composes at least half the biosphere's entire primary production – love this – love what – I am saying you have no choice – [...] within fifty years if we are lucky – I am writing this in 2015 – like spraying weed killer over all the world's vegetation – that's our raw material, our inventory, right now, we are going through the forms of worship, we call it news, we will make ourselves customers, we won't wait, how fast can we be

delivered – will get that information to you – requires further study – look that's where the river used to be .... (Graham 2017: 8)

This is a fragmented portrait of person and planet. By teasing out Graham's possible linkages one can find several of the common tropes found in contemporary environmentally orientated fiction, poetry and drama: a sense of the planetary ('on earth') alongside local ecosystem change ('that's where the river used to be'); environmental despoliation via pollution ('like spraying weed killer'); uncertainty about the future ('if the world', 'the world if'); and importance of particular species or ecosystems – in this case plankton, which composes 'half/the biospheres' production of oxygen and is crucial to CO_2 absorption. Other registers mingle with the ecological, in particular when the language of capital infects other discourses. A sense of consumerism slides into both the religious (impatient customers waiting for a delivery mutates into a sense of 'being delivered' from evil) and the scientific (where the withheld 'information' might be customer service or climate-change denialists demanding 'further study').

The poem sucks the reader into the maelstrom of global crises happening even as they read. This sort of effect is common in poetry and some forms of performance, but less so in narrative fiction. As Jonathan Culler argues, lyric poetry 'is not the description and interpretation of a past event but the iterative and iterable performance of an event in the lyric present, in the special "now", of lyric articulation' (Culler 2015: 43). Poetry does not rely on narrative time, where past events are reported. The poetic event can repeatedly occur in the present of readerly articulation. Or to put it another way 'Fiction is about what happened next; lyric is about what happens now' (Culler 2015).[2] So, even though Graham acknowledges she is 'writing this in 2015', the poem – for the reader – is articulated in a lyric present. The effect is ramified by the poem's suggestion of a catastrophic future ('within fifty years if we are lucky') caused by activities already under way in the lyric present which is itself, chronologically, the reader's past.

These nuanced and conflicting experiences of different temporalities are bound up with how and to whom the poem is addressed. Initially the 'you' seems to implicate a fellow *hypocrite lecteur*, complicit in the actions that have collectively brought the planet to catastrophe. But the stability of the 'you' begins to slip. It is potentially neither singular nor simply identifiable with the reader. In fact, the I/you division might also be read as the speaker in dialogue with herself – which would make sense for a 'self-portrait'. At points though the speaker and addressee's positions are even further fragmented ('I – no you – who'). Indeed, the poem seems to acknowledge this fluctuation of possibilities for how what passes as the 'lyric I' might be read ('I change shape→it is allowed'). At its end, the poem adopts the second-person plural, but it is unclear whether this 'we' encompasses speaker and addressee (I and you) or instead is operating almost at a collective species-level: 'define Anthropos. Define human [....] Are we ahead of/time or too late' (Graham 2017: 8–9). Moreover, by dating the poem in 2015 Graham acknowledges that, at least in part, the poem is addressing anticipated readers who are absent (or, rather, not yet present). Such indeterminacies of address highlight the event of address itself as an act, 'whose purpose and effects' – Culler argues – 'demand critical attention' (Culler 2015: 187).[3] It is my contention that the interrelated systems and scales associated with globalization and the Anthropocene have given rise to new modes of address and recalibrated old ones.

This chapter analyses poems directly concerned with some of the central features of the Anthropocene, particularly the ways this is bound up in the socio-economic-technical processes of globalization. Negotiating these issues involves displacements in space (acknowledging the impact on subjects and ecosystems in other parts of the globe) and time (including those who will live in a future of radical environmental change, aspects of which might already be unavoidable). Furthermore, this engenders questions of agency and influence – not least the power (or lack thereof) to influence those separated from us by space or time as well as the operation of what is sometimes called 'non-human' agency, the knowledge that just because humanity may have shifted the planet's ecological systems absolutely does not mean that it can control them.

With this question of influence/agency in mind, as well as the question of address, it is significant that, as Isobel Galleymore has noted, the 'three degrees' of Graham's title probably also refer to the 'three degrees of influence': Nicholas A. Christakis and James H. Fowler's description of how we influence others in our social network, especially given the emergence of another key technology of globalization, social media (Galleymore 2017).[4] While in an increasingly globalized world, individuals might famously be 'connected to everyone else by six degrees of separation', this does not mean that 'we hold sway over all of these people at any social distance away from us'. Instead, Christakis and Fowler posit the 'Three Degrees of Influence Rule':

> Everything we do or say tends to ripple through our network, having an impact on our friends (one degree), our friends' friends (two degrees), and even our friends' friends' friends (three degrees). (Christakis and Fowler 2009: 27–8)

In what follows below I use this idea as a loose framework to think through poetic address in relation to globalization and the Anthropocene. I begin with poetry addressed to those with whom we are intimate (our friends and relations – one degree of separation) before moving to those we might influence (friends-of-friends, and friends-of-friends – two and three degrees). Then, because thinking the planetary and the global requires an engagement with thinking various forms of collectivity, the chapter turns to the challenges of addressing the totality of humanity (the Anthropos) or the totality of life (the planetary biosphere) and, finally, being addressed by inorganic manmade matter.

One Degree of Influence: Here's Looking at You (Future) Kids

One of the most widely disseminated poems on climate-change, with many millions of online views, is Marshallese writer Kathy Jetñil-Kijiner's 2014 'Dear Matafele Peinam', addressed to her infant daughter. The poem describes their ocean lagoon home and the fear that the waters will rise to inundate their island. At an average of two metres above sea level, the Marshall Islands are considered to be at severe risk of inundation from even two degrees of warming. Jetñil-Kijiner assures Matafele Peinam that this will not happen, that no one will become a climate refugee 'rootless/ with only/a passport/to call home'. The poem suggests that it is the global impact of corporate capitalism ('greedy whale of a company') alongside ineffectual or corrupt governance ('blindfolded bureaucracies') that risks tipping 'mother ocean over/the edge'. In the face of these threats, the second half of the poem offers an ameliorative vision of global societies in protest ('fists raised', 'petitions blooming') alongside technological adaptation ('radiance of solar villages'), behavioural change ('recycling, reusing') and cultural engagement ('painting, dancing, writing') in a sustainable future (Jetñil-Kijiner 2017: 70–2).

What I want to highlight here is not the poem's important but relatively unremarkable identification of environmental threat and hopeful vision for change, but how this is intertwined with its specific mode of address – in particular, how the effects of addressing a poem to a beloved are further complicated by the fact that this is an occasional poem whose genesis is in a spoken-word tradition where the specific positionality of the speaker/performer takes on increased importance.

Jetñil-Kijiner's work – and the Marshal Islands more generally – offer a compelling example of thinking through globalization and the Anthropocene from what world-systems thinking calls 'the periphery'.

As Sharae Deckard explains, environments peripheral to the cores of capitalist production often endure 'intensified resource extraction, waste outsourcing, and environmental degradation' (Deckard 2012: 8). Climate-change is not the first Anthropocene-linked environmental crisis to befall the Marshall Islands. American nuclear testing in the 1940s and 1950s led the Atomic Energy Commission to declare them 'by far the most contaminated place in the world' (quoted in Nixon 2011: 7). This nuclear colonialism not only permeates into the landscape for generations, but it constitutes one of Rob Nixon's examples of somatized 'slow violence', a mutagenic force written into the cells of the islands inhabitants, not least the mothers who, decades later, were still delivering headless and limbless 'jellyfish' babies (the subject of Jetñil-Kijiner's poem 'Monster').[5] Nuclear testing led to environmental refugees migrating both within and away from the islands. Jetñil-Kijiner herself, despite being born on the islands and living there now, was raised in Hawaii as part of the Marshallese diaspora.

Michelle Keown explains that, because of their strategic importance, many Pacific islands 'were drawn into processes of economic globalization long before the United States' rise to world military dominance' and 'this contributed to the erosion of indigenous Pacific lifeways' (Keown 2017: 933). Jetñil-Kijiner's poetic project, in both its primary concerns and in its online modes of dissemination, is partly an attempt to engage with and connect to her Marshallese heritage threatened by ecological as well as socio-economic forces. Within this context it is interesting to think about 'Dear Matafele Peinem's' vision of deracinated climate refugees with 'only passport to call home'. Globalization challenges the nation-state. As Joel Evans explains, 'one of the most prominent themes in all writings on globalization is the world without borders' (Evans 2019: 14). But such visions of globalization run up against ecological limitations. The increase of resource stress and uninhabitable landscapes has led to a renewed awareness of the physical integrity of the nation-state – both in terms of a retrograde nationalism that would reinforce national borders against environmental migration and in relation to cultures inhabiting the peripheral territories most under threat from climate-change. Were the Marshall Islands to be inundated, an older Matifele Penem would in some way literally become a citizen of nowhere – a citizen of a place that was formerly somewhere but now exists only on paper passports and under water. Jetñil-Kijiner's poetry renders a Pacific heritage now at risk of being subsumed not (or not only) by globalization, but by the water rise linked to globalization's hydrocarbon-based modes of production.

'Dear Matifele Penem' is an occasional poem, first performed at the opening ceremony of the 2014 United Nations Climate Summit, where Jetñil-Kijiner was invited to speak as the representative for civil society. The video of that performance has since been watched millions of times on various online platforms. As such, the poem not only has a claim to be one of the most famous literary texts about climate-change, but in being initially performed to an audience of international delegates, this is a rare moment where, *pace* Auden, poetry could actually have made something happen. Despite the diplomatic standing ovation, it is hard to say whether the poem modified any of the delegates' behaviour, but it is worth noting that Jetñil-Kijiner was part of the successful '1.5 to stay alive' campaign a year later during the Paris talks, which successfully reduced temperature rise targets to offer island nations a better chance of survival (see Jetñil-Kijiner 2016). It is striking how this occasional poem performed, firstly, to international diplomats and, secondly, with an awareness of a much wider online audience, complicates a fairly traditional mode of address (poems written to children), that has taken on new significance against the backdrop of environmental crisis.

The child has become one of the most ubiquitous symbols in environmentally concerned writing, found in texts ranging from scientific nonfiction (e.g. Hansen 2011) to eco-disaster theatre (e.g. Kirkwood 2017). As Adeline Johns-Putra points out, the 'idea that our relationship with the biosphere is automatically a matter of posterity is a powerful one'. If calls for stewardship can 'trail off into the reaches of time' or be attenuated by distributions in space, 'the modelling of our attitude to future generations on our responsibilities to our offspring' anchors stewardship to the 'sentimentality of parental caring, sharing and nurturing' (Johns-Putra 2019: 4). (Though of course, the affective charge of parenthood might also stymie our ability to think of those places, communities, and species that do not easily coincide with the child as metonym for the future.)

Evoking the child addressee situates the poem in a long tradition of poems written to and for children; but writing in the context of the Anthropocene's environmental crises marks a transformation of this tradition of address. Dorothy Wordsworth, in 1832s 'Loving and Liking: Irregular Verses Addressed to A Child', could direct the child's affections to a fecund and generative sense of the natural world, asking children to love each creature in their habitat. A reader of that poem today has to acknowledge that such Romantic sensibilities are now terminally modified with habitat loss and species extinction. Or take the sense of possibility found in Sylvia Plath's 'You're', a poem echoed by anaphoric 'You are' with which the first three lines of 'Dear Matafele Peinem' begin. Plath's can see in her son's future the limitless possibility of a 'clean slate' (encompassing both personality and opportunity) (Plath 2006: 51). Matafele Peinem, like all children born into the contemporary Anthropocene, will grow up on a planet inscribed by environmental crisis that limits options for development, travel and even secure inhabitation. It is no longer tenable to feign innocence at the environmental limitations future generations will inherit.

In formal terms, by addressing a child who, if not absent is not (yet) capable of understanding, 'Dear Matifele Peinam' employs a type of apostrophe. Apostrophe is an address to someone or something that is not the actual audience – abstractions (e.g. nature, melancholy), inanimate objects (e.g. a Grecian urn) and persons absent or dead (or, in this instance, uncomprehending). 'Dear Matifele Peinam' is an instance of what Culler calls 'triangulated address', 'addressing the audience of readers by addressing or pretending to address someone or something else' (Culler 2015: 8). Matafele Peinam is the nominal addressee, but the audience is (i) initially the assembled delegates of the UN meeting who themselves represent collective national and international interest and (ii) later on, readers and viewers of the poem, many of whom will come to it via the video performance of the UN performance rather than as a printed work.

This complicates the relationship between audience(s) and addressee, particularly in terms of sections which invoke urgency and collective action such as 'we are drawing a line here'. The 'we' encompasses Matafele Peinam's parents and the Marshallese ('your mommy / daddy [...] your country') but also gestures towards the assembled audience in an exhortation to the delegates to use their influence 'here' and now. There is a biting irony in the experience of viewing the original performance and reading these lines five years later. This 'line' (by inference, drawn in the Marshall Islands' sand) has been ignored, or perhaps submerged, by rising waters and broken commitments: at the time of writing in mid-2020, key nations have recently sought to attenuate or exit international climate agreements. This use of the second-person plural both includes and does not include the implied audience. On the one hand 'we' suggests a generalized humanity who can, and should, act. On the other hand it is specific and coalesces around those most at risk (grammatically within the poem 'we' refers, at different scales, to Jetñil-Kijiner's family unit, to the Marshallese and to other populations who face environmental disasters). Hence some of the effects of the poem pivot on the degree to which any reader/viewer finds their actions and interests align with, or act at cross-purposes to, those threatened communities who fall under the poem's 'we'; engendering a sense of both solidarity and guilty complicity that are in tension with each other.

This tension behind the use of the second-person plural distinguishes 'Dear Matafele Peinem' from some other significant – at least in terms of their reach – climate texts emerging from a performance-poetry tradition. 'We', in the context of climate-change poetry, often signifies an accusatory sense of generalized complicity, the effect of which is both magnified and simplified when articulated in performance. Take Prince Ea's 'Dear Future Generations' (23 million YouTube views) which uses, in a comparable way to 'Dear Matafele Peinem', a generalised apostrophe to children of the future to offer a strident (if predictable) apocalyptic warning demanding action from audiences in the present. Prince Ea's 'we' falls foul of a problem of collective address that correlates to one of the key critiques of the Anthropocene – treating humanity as an undifferentiated geo-ecological force, when in fact neither the responsibility nor the risks are evenly distributed. The last line of 'Dear Future Generations'– 'if we don't all work together to save the environment/We will be equally extinct' – is not just glib, it is untrue (Ea 2015: n.p.). Different populations will face different challenges. For those hailing from the peripheral territories such as the Marshall Islands, these will probably be more extreme and more urgent. As Nixon puts it 'We may all be in the Anthropocene but we're not all in it in the same way' (Nixon 2014: n.p.).

'Dear Matefele Peinem' uses intimate address (one 'degree of influence' – mother to daughter, the 'we' of the family unit). But the second-person plural also slides to more generalised levels. Firstly, those in the 'peripheral' territories adversely affected by globalization and climate-change ('we' who are most under threat and now take action). Secondly, by forming an ambivalent relationship with an implied species-level 'we', where some are more complicit in perpetuating these conditions and others are more at risk. This reminds readers of an important question: for whom, as well as to whom, does the second-person plural speak? Who are 'we' and what can we do? In the Anthropocene, neither address, nor the planet, is stable.

Two & Three Degrees of Separation: #AnthropoceneAddress

Juliana Spahr and Josuha Clover's acerbic *Misanthropocene:24 Theses* is a pamphlet-length prose poem that mashes together the aesthetics of the philosophical treatise (especially Walter Benjamin's 'On the Concept of History') with those of Twitter. Its twenty-four expletive-filled sections range across the disintegrations of social and ecological life under late capitalism. This is from the tenth thesis:

> Tenth of all. Fuck the propelling of sand from the bottom of the ocean floor in a high arc so as to construct new islands [...] fuck Palm Jumeirah and Palm Jebel Ali and atrazine. Fuck everyone who has bought a big bag of ant poison because ants have a social stomach and you are one selfish motherfucker if you can't let them have the very small amounts of food they want to share equally among themselves. And fuck this list with its mixture of environmental destruction and popular culture smugness and fuck every one of you that laughed at that rock banjo joke and fuck us all for writing it. And fuck not just the Googlebus but the Googledoc this poem rode in on and fuck us for sitting here reading you a rock banjo joke while the New Mexico meadow jumping mouse went extinct. Fuck that this happened two days and twenty hours ago. And fuck that next up is the Sierra Nevada yellow legged frog because we've always liked frogs their vulnerable skin our vulnerable skin. (Clover and Spahr 2014: 5)

Spahr and Clover take aim at the Anthropocene activity of creating new landmasses, whether that is China's territorial expansion in the South China Sea or grotesque resort islands such as 'Palm Jumeriah', funded by Dubai's petro-dollars. The lament about insecticide goes beyond a Rachel Carson-esque sense that these poisons might leach into the food-chain, into an implied analogy where some human social collectives (us poor worker ants) are forced to exist with various types of corporate-caused toxicity. Spahr and Clover, who were both involved in the anti-globalization Occupy protests, attack Google – icons of globalized tech with their own massive ecological footprint – for their Googlebus, a shuttle service for Google workers that in 2013 became a symbol of the gentrification in Silicon Valley. But even in their attack, the poets acknowledge their own reliance on these digital tools in the creation and dissemination of polemical poetry even while the sixth mass extinction continues to unfold as we read.

The poem mimics the tough-talking 'fuck this and fuck that' of the Twittersphere, with the numbered theses recalling the numbered linked posts that construct Twitter threads. But to whom are such threads addressed? Who are the 'you all' of the poem's opening thesis 'first of all, fuck y'all'? The most obvious answer is that 'you' encompasses anyone likely to read them. This is not quite the same as everyone who might read them. Twitter's algorithms mean that the influence of most individuals' (and certainly most poets') tweets normally dissipates fairly quickly (notwithstanding the occasional viral hit). This is the realm of two and three degrees of influence: friends-of-friends and friends-of-friends-of-friends who might see our posts, and indeed re-circulate them across other feeds by using retweets and 'likes'. Hence 'Y'all' speaks to coterie and online community. One way of increasing online reach is to add a hashtag (e.g. #Misanthropocene).

Hashtags function as a form of indexing or taxonomy, searchable to anyone, not just those in our immediate networks. Hashtags can also constitute a form of self-conscious display, even virtue-signalling. In which case #*Misanthropocene*'s title can be read as a critique of the speed and ease of which we share things online, including of course ecocritics' ability to incessantly tweet news of present and future climate-change into their online echo-chambers accompanied by the appropriate environmentally conscious hashtag: #slowviolence, #aliveat1.5. Sometimes effective, but often merely symbolic resistance.

If the Anthropocene names a geological epoch where human impact leaves a detectable and pervasive mark on the strata of deep geological time, then by implication a misanthropocene names a concomitant cultural epoch, one typified by a detectable and pervasive misanthropism in response to the impact of humans on the planet. Turning the word Misanthropocene into a hashtag gestures towards a scorn for online-only outrage that can only muster an anaemic clicktivism rather than collective action against it; loling at memes and 'rock banjo' jokes while animals go extinct.

What is striking is how the poem's online mode of address brings different forms of temporality into play: not just unfolding crisis or even apocalypse but also the time for action. One of the most interesting critical approaches to the relationship between online lives and ecological crisis is philosopher Bernard Stiegler's notion that the 'Anthropocene is an Entropocene'. What Stiegler means by entropy is the destruction of knowledge – knowledge here not meaning information, as much 'know how'; how to live, how to make, how to think. For Stiegler 'so-called "big data"' – in which we should include user-behaviour analytics associated with Twitter and Google – is a 'key example of this immense transformation that is leading globalized consumerism to liquidate all forms of knowledge (*savoir vivre, savoir faire* and *savoir conceptualiser* [...])' (2018: 51). Stiegler, explains the poet Jonty Tiplady (2016), laments a kind of winding down and short-circuiting of all cognitive capacities, a digitally induced global attention deficit disorder that makes it impossible to focus on what needs to be focussed on: mental 'entropy'. Against the entropocene, Stiegler posits a kind of 'negentropy', a reactivation of care and particularity. Poetry can act as a crucible for such reactivations of care and particularity, but it is also a site for critique. Spahr and Clover's poem renders the enervating distractions of social media. It yearns not only for attentiveness to what is already being lost in the Anthropocene, but for action in the face of the Misanthropocene; not just reflection but revolution.

The poem's gestures towards revolutionary potential draw on its primary intertext, Benjamin's 'Theses on the Philosophy of History' where Benjamin posits a notion of 'messianic time' against what he calls homogenous or empty time of historical progression (Benjamin 2019: 208). The messianic would constitute a moment of rupture in the flow of progress, allowing for revolution or redemption. Messianic time offers an opportunity for change rather than being passive observers blown into the future by the disaster of the Misanthropocene in the manner of a Benjaminian Angel of History.

While much of the first half of *#Misanthropocene* is typified by almost paralysed (and paralysing) rage against mass extinction, consumer culture, and the mental entropy of social media, the final few theses shift away from the apocalyptic into the messianic and revolutionary.

> Twentieth of all. This is how the misanthropocene ends. We go to war against it. My friends go to war against it. They run howling with joy and terror against it. I go with them. (Clover and Spahr 2014: 8)

Spahr and Clover play off T. S. Eliot's famous ending of 'The Hollow Men', 'This is the way the world ends/Not with a bang but with a whimper', inverting it to posit rebellion against extinction, against quiescent despair. There is no going gentle into an Anthropocene night, but rather collective joy and terror. There is a shift from the excoriating direct address (Fuck y'all) and rage at the Anthropocene and globalization (the 'fuck this and fuck that' of most of the poem) into a kind of surreal instruction manual:

> Twentythree. Here is how to capsize container ships. Swim along behind it in a train then grip with the teeth and continue to swim as you insert your claspers into the cloaca and pump. (Clover and Spahr 2014: 8–9)

Both the activists (with teeth and insect-like claspers) and the containership targets are figured as animal. The sexualised 'pumping' of the ship's 'cloaca' (the urinary, digestive, and reproductive tract of some animals) becomes a monstrous vision of blocking emissions.

The question remains as to whether this presentation of a kind of fantastical (and impossible) activism serves to open up imaginative possibility or whether taking on the misathropocene would mean transformations that are so vast they can only be rendered in terms of the irreal. Do the scales of the Anthropocene or globalization lead to a kind of despair where individual and collective agency seems so etiolated that it prevents even trying? As Elizabeth Callaway puts it in her essay on Benjaminian messianic time and climate-change, a 'moment seized could be a moment grasped and taken up, or it could be a moment paralyzed and "seized up"'

(Callaway 2014: 31). Calls to action must also negotiate the doubt, paralysed despair, or even cynicism that circulate on and offline.

Clover and Spahr's experimental Twitter-style address foregrounds both the way we speak to those at two and three 'degrees of influence' online and the key digital-communication technologies of globalization (social-media platforms, collaborative software, big data, search engines). The poem calls attention to how these digital phenomena function alongside other intertwined technological and ecological concerns (e.g. hydrocarbon extraction, pollution, extinction) and shape our engagements with the Anthropocene: our attentiveness, our capacity for concern and critique, and the ways that digital technology both enables and attenuates agency and activism. If 'we' are to wage war on a minsanthropocene then who do we act with and for? One way of exploring that is to test the limits of collective address by asking: how to speak to a global population, and also the living planet on which they dwell?

Beyond Three Degrees of Influence: Addressing Planetary Collectives

> People of earth
> there are no islands now
> the planet is peninsular
> jutting in space
> one blue-green growing
> brown orb attached to
> disease we've made.   (Collis 2013)

The above lines are from 'Almost Islands', Stephen Collis's long poem about global crises emerging from unchecked industrialization on a 'drowning earth' where 'no economy is an island' (Collis 2013: 127–36). The address to 'People of earth' speaks the collective Anthropos of the Anthropocene, positioning all humanity as complicit in the 'disease we've made'. Such species-level address always runs the aforementioned risk of collapsing difference into a totalising category. But Collis's poetry counterbalances gestures towards the species and the planetary with an awareness of the particularity of the challenges faced by specific places and populations. Moreover, his address to collective humanity is itself about ecological community with other species.

Instead of us asking 'to know for which/species science tolls', the poem intertwines the fates of different species. In the Sixth Extinction 'no species//is an island'. The poem's continual nods to John Donne's

'Devotions Upon Emergent Occasions' take perhaps the most famous lines about interrelated responsibility and reworks them for a shared ecological emergency: no human is entire of themselves, one species death diminishes the rest of the ecosystem, the bell that tolls for others always tolls for us too.

'Almost Islands' employs the idea of peninsulas not only as a metaphor for interconnection (between humans, between species, between places) but it is also about the particular peninsular where Collis lives: Tsawwassen, in British Columbia, itself now under risk from the expansion of coal and container ports. In a striking apostrophe, Collis addresses the peninsular directly:

> River built place
> grassy sea
> island rivered to land
> what have we done?. (Collis 2013: 134)

In 'Almost Islands' to speak of place (or indeed of species) is also to speak of a planetary organic collective in which all life is imbricated.

> No species
> is an island
> entire of itself
> piece of the continents planets. (Collis 2013: 128)

Collis pointedly eschews grammar here: no possible comma after 'itself', no possessive apostrophe at the end of 'continents'. This engenders a lack of hierarchy. The poem slides from species to planet without separation; organisms and environments interpenetrate at different scales, species are a piece of planet. In this vision of what we might call 'peninsularity', the poet's address to his own 'River built place' also gestures to a broader sense of Earth's organic life.

This sort of apostrophe is a familiar aspect of the Romantic lyric. As Culler, building on Harold Bloom, puts it, 'to invoke the Spirit that is in the West Wind is not to invoke the wind or the autumn only' but to address a kind of unseen power behind it (Culler 2015: 239). However, the Anthropocene complicates such Romantic notions. In Collis's poem, the unseen power of the interlinked operations of organic life on a planetary scale are always bound up with industrial and technological forces. 'Almost Islands' is the first appearance in Collis's work of the term 'biotariat', a concept he uses to explore organic life under late globalized capital.

In a later poetic manifesto for the biotariat, Collis provisionally defines it as:

workers and commoners; most animals and plants, including trees and forest and grassland ecosystems; water; land, as it provisions and enables biological life; minerals that lie beneath the surface of the land; common 'wastes' and 'sinks' too, into which the waste products of resource production and use are spilled—the atmosphere and the oceans. It's that large. The enclosed and exploited life of this planet. (Collis 2014).

It is worth differentiating Collis's notion from the biotariat from another planet-sized conceptualization of organic life, to which poems are sometimes addressed, Gaia. James Lovelock followed his friend William Golding's suggestion to use the Greek name of the Earth goddess to personify Lovelock's theory of the Earth as a self-regulating system. One side effect of this naming has been that Gaia can too easily become a kind of avenging goddess or a kind of planetary body from which humans might be expunged (Solnick 2016: 210). Collis self-consciously turns away from Gaia, moving from the singularity of goddess or mother into a messy multitude:

> This would be to project not a divine earth goddess (Gaia), but earth as a repressed commons, lowly, levelled, and exploited. Not as singularity, but as the multitude of life, coming, under the impetus provided by globalization and climate change, into a new and necessary solidarity. (Collis 2014)

Awareness of the 'new and necessary solidarity' of the biotariat supplements the poem's repeated address to 'people of earth'. The poem's peninsular vision, which always connects species and places to a broader totality, means that the 'people of earth' refers not just to everyone who lives on a living planet, but acts as a reminder of our own materiality, our being 'of earth': the substances and systems that create the conditions for biological life. As Bruno Latour argues it in his own exploration of the Gaia concept, the Anthropocene necessitates making humans into an 'Earthbound' species who can recognize their complex material dependencies on the planet (Latour 2017: 248–53).

The poem closes with an image of being anchored on:

> an imaginary spit [ie a kind of peninsula] that holds
> a slim midden in the mind
> weaving us into spider looms
> and the dream passing there
> over shoals of the common good. (Collis 2013: 135)

The imagined peninsula that weaves us into spiderwebs refers, at least in part, to the peninsulas of poem itself. The new images and concepts fostered by poetry and criticism (whether peninsularity, the biotariat, or Gaia) can act with an ecological force by reminding readers they are people of earth, woven into the webs of a living planet and must act accordingly for an expanded sense of the common good. Collis's goes beyond identifiable individuals and groups to a species-level address ('people of earth') that is part of his broader consideration of how we conceptualise the collectives needed to interrogate globalization and the Anthropocene. This means invoking both the implied Anthropos (humanity unevenly bound together by the networks and flows of globalization) and the planet that our species inhabits and shapes along with other organic life. His ideas of peninsular relationships and the biotariat enforce the idea of the multitude over the singularity: of fostering interdependence without forgoing particularly and difference.

Conclusion: 'Hello' from the Inorganic

Plastic is not part of planetary commons of the biotariat but rather 'one of several noxious systems that signify the Anthropocene' (De Loughry 2019: 2). It is a key marker of globalization's processes, an output of hydrocarbon industry that flows across bodies and ecosystems. Perhaps the most iconic image suggesting that the Anthropocene is also a 'plasticene' (Macfarlane 2016) is 'Midway' (2009), Chris Jordan's photograph of an albatross choked by the plastic of the Great Pacific Garbage Patch. The photo is the inspiration for Adam Dickinson's ekphrastic poem 'Hail'. It begins:

> Hello from inside
> the albatross
> with a windproof lighter
> and Japanese police tape. (Dickinson 2013: 7)

Plastics from around the world gather in the organism's stomach and address the plastic-using reader directly, interpellating them in a system of toxic materiality. In having this noxious plastic as non-human addresser rather than addressee, Dickinson is employing prosopopoeia, a figure of speech that, like apostrophe, focusses on the inanimate thing, abstract concept or absent/dead person. The difference is that, rather than addressing the non-human, prosopopoeia gives it voice. In doing so, prosopopoeia turns the non-human into 'a potentially animate subject', and by giving it a voice offers 'a radically different perspective on the world, imagining and animating 'an otherness to which we can lend credence'. Such moves, continues Culler, fulfil 'a longstanding lyric task of making a planet into a world' (Culler 2015: 242).

Poetry represents one of the oldest cultural traditions for the 'worlding' of the inanimate planet: transforming the material into something lived and living, imbued with meaning and even a non-human agency. Poetry about globalization and the Anthropocene has to adapt to new conditions, to locate the human reader within a nexus of geological, ecological, and technological systems that have given rise to new materials and processes that will shape future environments and societies.

Throughout this chapter I have argued that thinking about the twinned concepts of globalization and the Anthropocene means a mutation in (rather than a departure from) poetry's modes of address. The examples of these emergent modes of address I have detailed here (to oneself, to an uncomprehending child, to an online community, to the Anthropos, to the biotariat, to the polluting reader from the non-human) each offer different ways of helping readers to negotiate the spatial and temporal scales of their socio-ecological position and the material and technological forces that shape it: expanding and evolving poetry's addressers and addressees to change the ways readers might address global crises in their own thoughts and actions. In doing so such poems participate in the challenges of (re-)making the planetary future determined by Anthropocene-epoch globalization into a liveable world yet to come.

Notes

1 The Paris agreement of 2016 sought to limit the increase in temperatures to a more ambitious 1.5 degrees above pre-industrial levels.
2 This is not to say that there are not counter-examples within prose fiction, but that sequential relation of events is the dominant mode.
3 Culler here is talking specifically about apostrophe, but it holds true for other modes of address.
4 Graham's poetry has an interest in social media and online lives. The second poem in *Fast* (2017) is about Prism, the NSA surveillance project which, according to the Panama Papers, used the principle of 'three hops' (degrees of separation on social networks) to establish targets for surveillance. It is also worth noting that Christakis works at Harvard with Graham.
5 'Monster' can be found on Jetñil-Kijiner's website: www.kathyjetnilkijiner.com/new-year-new-monsters-and-new-poems/. For an extended reading of 'Monster' see Keown (2018) which, along with her other article on Jetñil-Kijiner (2017), provides a detailed account of Jetñil-Kijiner's career, including its relationship to this nuclear context.

References

Abu-Lughod, Janet L. 1989. *Before European Hegemony: The World System A.D. 1250–1350*. New York: Oxford University Press.
Achebe, Chinua. 1990. 'An Image of Africa: Racism in Conrad's "Heart of Darkness"'. In *Hopes and Impediments: Selected Essays 1965–1987*, edited by Chinua Achebe, pp. 1–20. New York: Doubleday.
Adelson, Leslie A. 2015. 'Literary Imagination and the Future of Literary Studies'. *Deutsche Vierteljahresschrift* 89 (4): 675–83.
Adorno, Theodor. 1974. *Minima Moralia: Reflections from Damaged Life*. London: NLB.
Aejmelaeus, Anneli. 2007. *On the Trail of the Septuagint Translators: Collected Essays*. Vol. 50. Paris and Dudley, MA: Peeters.
Ahmad, Aijaz. 1992. *In Theory: Nations, Classes, Literatures*. London: Verso.
Akallo, Grace and Faith McDonnell. 2007. *Girl Soldier: A Story of Hope for Northern Uganda's Children*. Grand Rapids, MI: Chosen Books.
Allam, Lorena and Nick Evershed. 2019. 'The Killing Times: The Massacres of Aboriginal People Australia Must Confront'. *The Guardian*, 3 March. Accessed 25 September 2021. www.theguardian.com/australia-news/2019/mar/04/the-killing-times-the-massacres-of-aboriginal-people-australia-must-confront
Allen, Joseph. 2019. 'The Babel Fallacy: When Translation Does Not Matter'. *Cultural Critique* 102: 117–50.
Almond, Philip. 1987. 'The Buddha of Christendom: A Review of the Legend of Barlaam and Josaphat'. *Religious Studies* 23 (3): 391–406.
Amis, Martin. 1984. *Money: A Suicide Note*. London: Cape.
Anderson, Benedict. 2006. *Imagined Communities: Reflections on the Origin and Spread of Nationalism*. London and New York: Verso.
Anderson, Clare. 2000. *Convicts in the Indian Ocean*. Basingstoke: Palgrave.
Anderson, Perry. 1991. 'Marshall Berman: Modernity and Revolution'. In *A Zone of Engagement*, edited by Perry Anderson, pp. 25–55. New York: Verso.
Andersson, Ruben. 2016. 'Here Be Dragons: Mapping an Ethnography of Global Danger'. *Current Anthropology* 57 (6): 707–31.
Andrews, Walter G. 1996. 'Speaking of Power: The "Ottoman Kaside"'. In *Qasida Poetry in Islamic Asia and Africa: Classical Traditions and Modern Meanings*, edited by Stefan Sperl and Christopher Shackle, pp. 280–300. Leiden and New York: Brill.

Annesley, James. 2006. *Fictions of Globalization: Consumption, the Market and the Contemporary Novel*. London and New York: Continuum.
Apostolopoulos, Yorghos and Sevil Sünmez. 2000. 'New Directions in Mediterranean Tourism'. *Thunderbird International Business Review* 42 (4): 381–92.
Apter, Emily. 2013. *Against World Literature: On the Politics of Untranslatability*. New York: Verso.
Arata, Stephen. 1990. 'The Occidental Tourist: *Dracula* and the Anxiety of Reverse Colonization'. *Victorian Studies* 33 (4): 621–45.
Aravamudan, Srinivas. 2009. 'Fiction/Translation/Transnation: The Secret History of the Eighteenth-Century Novel'. In *A Companion to the Eighteenth-Century Novel*, edited by Paula Backscheider and Catherine Ingrassia, pp. 48–74. Malden, MA: Blackwell.
Armstrong, Guyda. 2015. 'Coding Continental: Information Design in Sixteenth-Century English Vernacular Language Manuals and Translations'. *Renaissance Studies* 29 (1): 78–102.
Auerbach, Erich. 1965. *Literary Language and Its Public in Late Antiquity and in the Middle Ages*. Translated by Ralph Manheim. London: Routledge and Kegan Paul.
    1969. 'Philology and Weltliteratur'. *The Centennial Review* 13 (1): 1–17.
    1984. 'Vico and Aesthetic Historism'. *Scenes from the Drama of European Literature*. Translated by Ralph Manheim, 183–200.
    ed. 1984. 'Figura'. In *Scenes from the Drama of European Literature*. Translated by Ralph Manheim, pp. 11–76. Manchester: Manchester University Press.
    2003. *Mimesis: The Representation of Reality in Western Literature*. Translated by William R. Trusk. Princeton, NJ: Princeton University Press.
Aureli, Pier Vittorio. 2011. *The Possibility of an Absolute Architecture*. Cambridge, MA: MIT Press.
Badiou, Alain. 2011. *Being and Event*. Translated by Oliver Feltham. London and New York: Continuum.
Baldwin, James. 1955. *Notes of a Native Son*. Boston, MA: Beacon Press.
Bales, Kevin and Zoe Trodd, eds. 2013. *To Plead Our Own Cause*. Ithaca, NY: Cornell University Press.
Balibar, Étienne. 2004. 'World Borders, Political Borders'. In *We, the People of Europe?: Reflections on Transnational Citizenship*, edited by Étienne Balibar, pp. 101–14. Translated by James Swenson. Princeton, NJ: Princeton University Press.
Ballard, James Graham. 1998. *Cocaine Nights*. Berkeley, CA: Counterpoint.
    2000. *Super-Cannes*. New York: Picador.
    2004a. *Millennium People*. London: Harper Perennial.
    2004b. *Quotes*, edited by V. Vale and Mike Ryan. San Francisco, CA: RE/Search Publications.
    2006. *Kingdom Come*. London: Fourth Estate.
Ballaster, Ros. 2005. *Fabulous Orients: Fictions of the East in England 1662–1785*. Oxford: Oxford University Press.
Banks, Iain. 1999. *The Business*. London: Little, Brown and Company.

Barad, Karen. 2011. 'Nature's Queer Performativity'. *Qui Parle* 19 (2): 121–58.
Barber, Benjamin R. 1995. *Jihad vs. McWorld*. New York: Random House.
Barker, Sara K. and Brenda M. Hosington, eds. 2013. 'Introduction'. In *Renaissance Cultural Crossroads: Translation, Print and Culture in Britain, 1473–1640*, pp. xv–xxix. Boston, MA: Brill.
Barrett, Ross and Daniel Worden, eds. 2014. *Oil Culture*. Minneapolis, MN: University of Minnesota Press.
Barth, John. 1996. *Sabbatical: A Romance*. Funks Grove, IL: Dalkey Archive Press.
Bataille, Georges. 1991–1993. *The Accursed Share*. 3 vols. Translated by Robert Hurley. New York: Zone Books.
Bate, Jonathan. 1996. 'Living with the Weather'. *Studies in Romanticism* 35 (3): 431–47.
Baudrillard, Jean. 1998. *The Consumer Society: Myths and Structures*. London: SAGE.
  1983. *Simulations*. Translated by Paul Foss et al. New York: Semiotext(e).
Bauman, Zygmunt. 1998. *Globalization: The Human Consequences*. Cambridge: Polity Press.
Bayart, Jean-François. 2007. *Global Subjects: A Political Critique of Globalization*. Translated by Andrew Brown. Cambridge, UK and Malden, MA: Polity Press.
Bayly, Christopher A. 1989. *Imperial Meridian: The British Empire and the World, 1780–1830*. London: Routledge.
Beah, Ishmael. 2007. *A Long Way Gone: Memoirs of a Boy Soldier*. New York: Farrar, Strauss and Giroux.
Beaujard, P. 2019. *The Worlds of the Indian Ocean: A Global History*. Cambridge: Cambridge University Press.
Bec, Pierre. 1994. *Pour un Autre soleil: Le Sonnet Occitan des Origines à Nos Jours: Une Anthologie*. Orléans: Paradigme.
Beck, Ulrich. 2000. *What Is Globalization?* Translated by Patrick Camiller. Cambridge: Polity Press.
Beckert, Sven and Seth Rockman. 2016. *Slavery's Capitalism: A New History of American Economic Development*. Philadelphia, PA: University of Pennsylvania Press.
Beecroft, Alexander. 2008. 'World Literature Without a Hyphen: Toward a Typology of Literary Systems'. *New Left Review* 54: 87–100.
  2015. *Ecology of World Literature: From Antiquity to the Present Day*. London and New York: Verso.
  2018. 'Rises of the Novel, Ancient and Modern'. In *The Cambridge Companion to the Novel*, edited by Eric Bulson, pp. 43–56. Cambridge: Cambridge University Press.
Begam, Richard and Michael Valdez Moses, eds. 2007. *Modernism and Colonialism: British and Irish Literature, 1899–1939*. Durham, NC: Duke University Press.
Belich, James. 2009. *Replenishing the Earth: The Settler Revolution and the Rise of the Anglo-World*. New York: Oxford University Press.
Bell, Bernard W. 1987. *The Afro-American Novel and Its Tradition*. Amherst, MA: University of Massachusetts Press.

Bellos, David. 2011. *Is That a Fish in Your Ear? Translation and the Meaning of Everything*. New York: Penguin Books.
Benjamin, Walter. 2019. *Illuminations: Essays and Reflections*. Translated by Harry Zohn. Boston, MA, and New York: Houghton Mifflin Harcourt USA.
Berger, John. 2008. *Hold Everything Dear: Dispatches on Survival and Resistance*. New York: Vintage.
Berlant, Lauren. 2008. 'Intuitionists: History and the Affective Event'. *American Literary History* 20 (4): 845–60.
Bernstein, Elizabeth. 2010. 'Militarized Humanitarianism Meets Carceral Feminism: The Politics of Sex. Rights, and Freedom in Contemporary Antitrafficking Campaigns'. *Signs: Journal of Women in Culture and Society* 36 (1): 45–71.
Bilal, Parker. 2012. *The Golden Scales*. London: Bloomsbury.
Black, Iain. 1999. 'Imperial Visions: Rebuilding the Bank of England, 1919–39'. In *Imperial Cities: Landscape, Display and Identity*, edited by Felix Driver and David Gilbert, pp. 96–116. Manchester: Manchester University Press.
Blois, François de. 1990. *Burzōy's Voyage to India and the Origin of the Book of Kalīlah Wa Dimnah*. Hove: Psychology Press.
Bloom, Allan. 1987. *The Closing of the American Mind: How Higher Education Has Failed Democracy and Impoverished the Souls of Today's Students*. New York: Simon & Schuster.
Blumenthal, Max. 2010. 'The Great Islamophobic Crusade'. *CBS News*, 10 December. Accessed 1 October 2021. www.cbsnews.com/news/the-great-islamophobic-crusade/
Boehmer, Elleke. 1998. *Empire Writing: An Anthology of Colonial Literature 1870–1918*. Oxford and New York: Oxford University Press.
  2005. *Colonial and Postcolonial Literature: Migrant Metaphors*. Oxford: Oxford University Press.
  2016. 'The View from Empire: The Turn of the Century Globalizing World'. In *Late Victorian into Modern*, edited by Laura Marcus, Michèle Mendelssohn and Kirsten E. Shepherd-Barr, pp. 305–18. Oxford and New York: Oxford University Press.
Boehmer, Elleke and Dominic Davies. 2018. 'Planned Violence: Post/Colonial Urban Infrastructure, Literature, and Culture'. In *Planned Violence: Post/Colonial Urban Infrastructure, Literature, and Culture*, edited by Elleke Boehmer and Dominic Davies, pp. 1–25. London and New York: Palgrave Macmillan.
Bok, Francis and Edward Tivnan. 2003. *Escape from Slavery: The True Story of My Ten Years in Captivity and My Journey to Freedom in America*. New York: St Martin's Press.
Bolaño, Roberto. 2008. *2666: A Novel*. Translated by Natasha Wimmer. New York: Farrar, Straus and Giroux.
Boltanski, Luc. 2014. *Mysteries and Conspiracies: Detective Stories, Spy Novels and the Making of Modern Societies*. Translated by Catherine Porter. Cambridge: Polity Press.
Boone, Joseph and Nancy Vickers, eds. 2011. 'Celebrity Rites'. *PMLA* 126: 4.

Booth, Howard J. and Nigel Rigby, eds. 2000. *Modernism and Empire*. Manchester: Manchester University Press.

Borges, Jorges Luis. 2000. 'The Garden of Forking Paths'. Translated by Donald A. Yates, pp. 44–54. *Labyrinths: Selected Stories and Other Writings*. London: Penguin.

Braudel, Fernand. 1987. *The Mediterranean and the Mediterranean World in the Age of Philip II*. London: HarperCollins.

Braun, Rebecca 2016. 'The World Author in Us All: Conceptualising Fame and Agency in the Global Literary Market Place'. *Celebrity Studies* 7 (4): 457–75.
  2022. *Authors and the World: Literary Authorship in Modern Germany*. London: Bloomsbury.

Braun, Rebecca and Emily Spiers, eds. 2016. 'Introduction: Re-viewing Literary Celebrity'. *Celebrity Studies* 7 (4): 449–56.

Brooke, John L. 2014. *Climate Change and the Course of Global History: A Rough Journey*. Cambridge: Cambridge University Press.

Bregman, Dvora and Ann Brener. 1991. 'The Emergence of the Hebrew Sonnet'. *Prooftexts* 11 (3): 231–9.

Brennan, Timothy. 2004. 'Edward Said and Comparative Literature'. *Journal of Palestine Studies* 33 (3): 23–37.

Brown, Neville. 2001. *History and Climate Change: A Eurocentric Perspective*. London: Routledge.

Brown, Stephen, ed. 2006. *Consuming Books: The Marketing and Consumption of Literature*. Abingdon: Routledge.

Brynildsrud, Ola B. et al. 2018. 'Global Expansion of Mycobacterium tuberculosis Lineage 4 Shaped by Colonia Migration and Local Adaptation'. *Science Advances* 4 (10): eaat5869.

Bulawayo, NoViolet. 2014. *We Need New Names*. London: Vintage.

Büntgen, Ulf et al. 2011. '2500 Years of European Climatic Variability and Human Susceptibility'. *Science* 331 (6017): 578–82.

Burgess, Seth et al. 2019. 'Deciphering Mass Extinction Triggers'. *Science* 363 (6429): 815–16. http://science.sciencemag.org/content/sci/363/6429/815.full.pdf

Burton, Antoinette and Isabel Hofmeyr, eds. 2014. *Ten Books That Shaped the British Empire: Creating an Imperial Commons*. Durham, NC: Duke University Press.

Bush, George H. W. 1990. 'Address Before a Joint Session of the Congress on the Persian Gulf Crisis and the Federal Budget Deficit, 11 September 1990'. Accessed 1 October 2021. https://en.wikisource.org/wiki/Address_Before_a_Joint_Session_of_the_Congress_on_the_Persian_Gulf_Crisis_and_the_Federal_Budget_Deficit

Butzer, Karl W. 2012. 'Collapse, Environment, and Society'. *Proceedings of the National Academy of Sciences of the United States of America* 109 (10): 3632–9. www.pnas.org/content/109/10/3632.full.pdf

Buzard, James. 2018. 'Race, Imperialism, Colonialism, Postcolonialism, and Cosmopolitanism'. In *The Oxford Handbook of Charles Dickens*, edited by John Jordan et al., pp. 517–31. Oxford: Oxford University Press.

Cadet, Jean-Robert. 1998. *Restavec: From Haitian Slave Child to Middle-Class American*. Austin, TX: University of Texas.

Cain, Peter J. and Anthony Gerald Hopkins. 2016. *British Imperialism, 1688–2015*. New York: Routledge.
Callaway, Elizabeth. 2014. 'A Space for Justice: Messianic Time in the Graphs of Climate Change'. *Environmental Humanities* 5 (1): 13–33. https://doi.org/10.1215/22011919-3615397
Callinicos, Alex. 1989. *Against Postmodernism: A Marxist Critique*. Cambridge: Polity Press.
Carlotto, Massimo. 2004. *The Master of Knots*. Translated by Christopher Woodall. London: Orion.
Carroll, John. 2001. *The Western Dreaming*. New York: HarperCollins.
Casanova, Pascale. 1999. *The World Republic of Letters*. Translated by M. B. Debevoise. Cambridge, MA: Harvard University Press.
Cawdrey, Robert. 1617. *A Table Alphabetical, Containing and Teaching the Understanding of Hard Usual English Words*. 4th ed. London. Available online at: http://leme.library.utoronto.ca
Cecire, Maria Sanchico. 2019. *Re-Enchanted: The Rise of Children's Fantasy Literature in the Twentieth Century*. Minneapolis, MN: University of Minnesota Press.
Césaire, Aimé. 1995. *Notebook of a Return to My Native Land*. Translated by Mireille Rosello and Annie Pritchard. Newcastle upon Tyne: Bloodaxe Books.
Chaney, Michael A. 2007. 'International Contexts of the Negro Renaissance'. In *The Cambridge Companion to the Harlem Renaissance*, edited by George Hutchinson, pp. 41–54. Cambridge: Cambridge University Press.
Chang, Kang-i-Sun and Stephen Owen. 2010. 'Introduction'. In *The Cambridge History of Chinese Literature*, edited by Kang-i-Sun Chang and Stephen Owen, pp. xx–xxxii. 2 vols. Cambridge: Cambridge University Press.
Chatterjee, Partha. 1993. *Nationalist Thought and the Colonial World: A Derivative Discourse*. Minneapolis, MN: University of Minnesota Press.
Cheah, Pheng. 2016. *What Is a World? On Postcolonial Literature and World Literature*. Durham, NC: Duke University Press.
  2008. 'What Is a World? On World Literature as World-Making Activity". *Daedalus* 137 (3): 26–38.
Cheung, Kai-chong. 2003. 'The Haoqiu zhuan, the First Chinese Novel Translated in Europe: With Special Reference to Percy's and Davis's Renditions'. In *One Into Many: Translation and the Dissemination of Classical Chinese Literature*, edited by Leo Tak-hung Chan, pp. 29–37. Amsterdam: Rodopi.
Cheung, Martha P. Y. 2005. 'To translate' means 'to exchange'? A New Interpretation of the Earliest Chinese Attempts to Define Translation ('*fanyi*')'. *Target* 17 (1): 27–48.
Christakis, Nicholas A. and Hames H. Fowler. 2009. *Connected: The Surprising Power of Our Social Networks and How They Shape Our Lives*. New York: Little, Brown and Company.
Churchill, Caryl. 1990. *Plays 2*. London: Methuen.
Clarke, Kamari Maxine and Deborah A. Thomas, eds. 2006. *Globalization and Race: Transformations in the Cultural Production of Blackness*. Durham, NC: Duke University Press.

Cleary, Joe. 2012. 'Realism after Modernism and the Literary World-System'. *Modern Language Quarterly* 73 (3): 255–68.
Clover, Joshua and Juliana Spahr. 2014. *#Misanthropocene: 24 Theses*. Oakland, CA: Commune Editions.
Cohen, Walter. 2017: *A History of European Literature: The West and the World from Antiquity to the Present*. Oxford: Oxford University Press.
Coldiron, Anne E. B. 2015. *Printers Without Borders: Translation and Textuality in the Renaissance*. Cambridge: Cambridge University Press.
Cole, Peter. 2009. *The Dream of the Poem: Hebrew Poetry from Muslim and Christian Spain, 950–1492*. Princeton, NJ: Princeton University Press.
Collis, Stephen. 2013. *To the Barricades*. Vancouver: Talonbooks.
  2014. 'Notes Towards a Manifesto of the Biotariat.' *Beating the Bounds* (blog), 25 July. https://beatingthebounds.com/2014/07/25/notes-towards-a-manifesto-of-the-biotariat/
Collits, Terry. 2007. 'Conrad in the Time of Globalization: A Latin American *Nostromo*?' *Yearbook of Conrad Studies* 3: 165–80.
Connell, Liam and Nicky Marsh, eds. 2010. *Literature and Globalization: A Reader*. London: Routledge.
Conniff, Richard. 2019. 'The Last Resort'. *Scientific American* (January): 52–9.
Conrad, Joseph. 1923. *Chance: A Tale in Two Parts*. London: Dent.
  1924. *'Typhoon' and Other Stories*. London: Heinemann.
  1988. *Heart of Darkness*, edited by Robert Kimbrough. New York: W. W. Norton.
  2010. *Last Essays*, edited by Harold Ray Stevens and John H. Stape. Cambridge: Cambridge University Press.
  2012. *Lord Jim*, edited by John H. Stape and Ernest W. Sullivan II. Cambridge: Cambridge University Press.
  2017. *The Nigger of the 'Narcissus'*, edited by Allan H. Simmons. Cambridge: Cambridge University Press.
  2016. *An Outcast of the Islands*, edited by Allan H. Simmons. Cambridge: Cambridge University Press.
  2008. *A Personal Record*, edited by Zdzisław Najder and John H. Stape. Cambridge: Cambridge University Press.
  2007. *The Portable Conrad*. London and New York: Penguin.
  2010. *Youth, Heart of Darkness, The End of the Tether*, edited by Owen Knowles. Cambridge: Cambridge University Press.
Council on American-Islamic Relations-MA. 2015. 'CAIR-MA Publishes Report on Local Hate Group' Cairma.org. 29 July. www.cairma.org/cair-ma-publishes-report-on-local-hate-group/
Cowley, Abraham. 1694. *The Works of Abraham Cowley*. 8th ed. London: Kearsley.
Cox, Timothy. 2000. *Postmodern Tales of Slavery in the Americas from Alejo Carpentier to Charles Johnson*. London: Routledge.
Culler, Jonathan. 2015. *Theory of the Lyric*. Cambridge, MA: Harvard University Press.
Daly, Nicholas. 1999. *Modernism, Romance, and the Fin de Siècle*. Cambridge: Cambridge University Press.

Damrosch, David. 2009. *How to Read World Literature*. Malden, MA: Wiley-Blackwell.
David, Deirdre. 2005. 'Empire, Race, and the Victorian Novel'. In *A Companion to the Victorian Novel*, edited by Patrick Brantlinger and William B. Thesing, pp. 84–100. Oxford: Blackwell.
Davidproject.org. 'About Us'. Now redirects to Hillel International. https://hillel.org/about/news-views/news-views---blog/news-and-views/2019/09/24/hillel-international-launches-new-center-for-community-outreach
Davis, Mike. 2000. *Late Victorian Holocausts: El Niño Famines and the Making of the Third World*. London: Verso.
 2016. 'The Coming Desert: Kropotkin, Mars and the Pulse of Asia'. *New Left Review* 97: 23–43.
 2018. 'Taking the Temperature of History: Le Roy Ladurie's Adventures in the Little Ice Age'. *New Left Review* 110: 85–129.
Davies, Dominic. 2017. *Imperial Infrastructure and Spatial Resistance in Colonial Literature, 1880–1930*. Oxford: Peter Lang.
De Chardin, Pierre Tielhard. 1965a. 'Formation of the Noosphere'. *The Future of Man*. Translated by Norman Denny, pp. 149–78. London and New York: Doubleday.
 1965b. 'Life and the Planets'. *The Future of Man*. Translated by Norman Denny, pp. 90–116. London and New York: Doubleday.
De Loughry, Treasa. 2019. 'Polymeric Chains and Petrolic Imaginaries: World Literature, Plastic, and Negative Value'. *Green Letters* 23 (2): 179–93.
De Man, Paul. 1979. 'Shelley Disfigured'. In *Deconstruction and Criticism*, edited by Harold Bloom et al., pp. 39–73. New York: Continuum.
Demandt, Alexander. 1984. '210 Reasons for Decline of Roman Empire'. *Der Fall Roms: Die Auflösung des römischen Reiches im Urteil der Nachwelt*. Munich: C. H. Beck. Accessed 1 October 2021. https://courses.washington.edu/rome250/gallery/ROME%20250/210%20Reasons.htm
deMenocal, Peter D. 2001. 'Cultural Responses to Climate Change during the Late Holocene'. *Science* 292 (5517): 667–73.
Dean, Jodi. 2020. 'Communism or Neo-Feudalism'. *New Political Science* 42 (1): 1–17.
Deckard, Sharae. 2012. 'Editorial'. *Green Letters* 16 (1): 5–14. https://doi.org/10.1080/14688417.2012.10589096
Deckard, Sharae. 2012. 'Peripheral Realism, Millennial Capitalism, and Roberto Bolaño's *2666*'. *Modern Language Quarterly* 73 (3): 351–72.
 2019. 'Water Shocks: Neoliberal Hydrofiction and the Crisis of "Cheap Water."' *Atlantic Studies* 16 (1): 108–25.
Deleuze, Gilles and Felix Guattari. 1983. *Anti-Oedipus: Capitalism and Schizophrenia*. Translated by Robert Hurley, Mark Seem, and Helen R. Lane. MN: University of Minnesota Press.
 1987. *A Thousand Plateaus*. Translated by Brian Massumi. Minneapolis, MN: University of Minnesota Press.
DeLillo, Don. 1989. *The Names*. New York: Vintage.
'Demographics of China'. 2019. Wikipedia. https://en.wikipedia.org/wiki/Demographics_of_China#cite_note-Banister-4. Accessed 4 July.
'Demographics of India'. 2019. Wikipedia. https://en.wikipedia.org/wiki/Demographics_of_India#cite_note-chaf.lib.latrobe.edu.au-36. Accessed 4 July.

Deneire, Tom B. 2014. *Dynamics of Neo-Latin and the Vernacular: Language and Poetics, Translation and Transfer*. Bilingual edition. Leiden and Boston, MA: Brill.
Denning, Michael. 2004. *Culture in the Age of Three Worlds*. London and New York: Verso.
Derrida, Jacques. 1969. 'The Ends of Man'. *Philosophy and Phenomenological Research* 30 (1): 31–57.
  1974. *Of Grammatology*. Translated by Gayatri Chakravorty Spivak. Baltimore, MD: Johns Hopkins University Press.
  1978. *Writing and Difference*. Translated by Alan Bass. Chicago: University of Chicago Press.
  1989. *Edmund Husserl's 'Origin of Geometry': An Introduction*. Translated by John P. Leavey Jr. Lincoln: Nebraska University Press.
  1998. *Archive Fever: A Freudian Impression*. Translated by Eric Prenowitz. Chicago: University of Chicago Press.
  2005. *On Touching—Jean-Luc Nancy*. Translated by Christine Irizarry. Stanford: Stanford University Press.
D'Haen, Theo. 2012. *The Routledge Concise History of World Literature*. New York: Routledge.
Dickens, Charles. 1990. *David Copperfield*. London and New York: W. W. Norton.
  1999. *Great Expectations*. London and New York: W. W. Norton.
  2001. *Hard Times*. London and New York: W. W. Norton.
  2008. *Dombey and Son*. Oxford: Oxford University Press.
Dickinson, Adam. 2013. *The Polymers*. Toronto: House of Anansi Press.
Dilke, Charles. 2009. *Greater Britain, Volume 2*. Cambridge: Cambridge University Press.
Dillon, Sam. 2004. 'Columbia to Check Reports of Anti-Jewish Harassment'. *The New York Times*. www.nytimes.com/2004/10/29/nyregion/columbia-to-check-reports-of-antijewish-harassment.html
Donovan, Steven. 2005. *Joseph Conrad and Popular Culture*. Basingstoke: Palgrave.
Duncan-Jones, Richard P. 1996. 'The Impact of the Antonine Plague'. *Journal of Roman Archaeology* 9: 108–36.
Duso, Elena Maria. 2004. *Il Sonetto Latino e Semilatino in Italia Nel Medioevo e Nel Rinascimento*. Miscellanea Erudita; Nuova Ser., 69. Roma: Antenore.
Ea, Prince. 2015. '(1) Dear Future Generations: Sorry – YouTube'. www.youtube.com/watch?v=eRLJscAlk1M&t=55s
Earnest, David C. and James N. Rosenau. 2009. 'The Spy Who Loved Globalization'. *Foreign Policy* 120: 88–90.
Easterling, Keller. 2014. *Extrastatecraft: The Power of Infrastructure Space*. London: Verso.
ECCO: Eighteenth-Century Collections Online. Gale Group. www.gale.com/primary-sources/eighteenth-century-collections-online
Eisenstein, Elizabeth. 1980. *The Printing Press as Agent of Change*. Cambridge: Cambridge University Press.
Elias, Amy J. and Christian Moraru, eds. 2015. *The Planetary Turn: Relationality and Geoaesthetics in the Twenty-First Century*. Evanston: Northwestern University Press.

Eliot, Gregory. 2008. *Ends in Sight: Marx/Fukuyama/Hobsbawm/Anderson*. London: Pluto Press.
Eliot, Thomas S. 1963. *Collected Poems, 1909–1962*. New York: Harcourt, Brace & World.
   1964. *Selected Essays*. New York: Harcourt, Brace & World.
Ellis, Bret Easton. 1991. *American Psycho*. Basingstoke: Picador.
Emmerich, Karen. 2017. *Literary Translations and the Making of Originals*. New York: Bloomsbury.
Esty, Jed. 2012. *Unseasonable Youth: Modernism, Colonialism, and the Fiction of Development*. Oxford: Oxford University Press.
Evans, Joel. 2019. *Conceptualising the Global in the Wake of the Postmodern: Literature, Culture, Theory*. Cambridge: Cambridge University Press.
Evans, Nicholas P. et al. 2018. 'Quantification of Drought during the Collapse of the Classic Maya Civilization'. *Science* 361 (6401) (3 August): 498–501.
Fan, T. C. 1946. 'Percy's Hau Kiou Choaan'. *The Review of English Studies* 22 (86): 117–25.
Fanon, Frantz. 2008. *Black Skin, White Masks*. Translated by Charles Lam Markmann. London: Pluto Press.
   1967. *The Wretched of the Earth*. Translated by Constance Farrington. London: Penguin.
Featherstone, Michael. 1993. 'Global and Local Cutures'. In *Mapping the Futures: Local Cultures, Global Change*, edited by Jon Bird et al. London and New York: Routledge.
Felski, Rita. 2016. 'Comparison and Translation: A Perspective from Actor-Network Theory'. *Comparative Literature Studies* 53 (4): 747–65.
Fish, Stanley. 1980. *Is There a Text in This Class?* Cambridge, MA: Harvard University Press.
Fisher, Mark. 2008. *Capitalist Realism: Is There No Alternative?* Winchester: Zero Books.
Forster, Leonard. 1970. *The Poet's Tongues: Multilingualism in Literature*. Cambridge: Cambridge University Press.
Foucault, Michel. 1995. *Discipline and Punish: The Birth of the Prison*. Translated by Alan Sheridan. London: Vintage Books.
   1977. *Language, Counter-Memory and Practice: Selected Essays and Interviews*, edited by Donald F. Bouchard. Ithaca, NY: Cornell University Press.
   2002. *The Order of Things: An Archaeology of the Human Sciences*. London and New York: Routledge.
   2000. 'What Is an Author?' Vol. 2 of *The Essential Works of Foucault 1954–1984*, edited by James Faubion, pp. 205–22. London: Penguin.
Frank, Andre Gunder and Barry K. Gills. 1993. *The World System: Five Hundred Years or Five Thousand?* London and New York: Routledge.
Franke, Anselm, Ines Gleisner and Eyal Weizman. 2003. 'Islands: The Geography of Extraterritoriality'. *Archis* 6: n.p.
Freeman, Charles. 2004. *Egypt, Greece, and Rome: Civilizations of the Ancient Mediterranean*. 2nd ed. Oxford: Oxford University Press.
Friedman, Susan Stanford. 2015. *Planetary Modernisms: Provocations on Modernity across Time*. New York: Columbia University Press.

Fritsch, Matthias, Philippe Lynes and David Wood, eds. 2018. *Eco-Deconstruction: Derrida and Environmental Philosophy*. New York: Fordham University Press.
Fukuyama, Francis. 2016. 'America: The Failed State'. *Prospect*, 13 December. www.prospectmagazine.co.uk/magazine/america-the-failed-state-donald-trump
  1989. 'The End of History?' *The National Interest* 16: 3–18.
  1992. *The End of History and the Last Man*. London and New York: Penguin.
Gagnier, Regina. 2018. 'Dickens's Global Circulation'. In *The Oxford Handbook of Charles Dickens*, edited by John Jordan et al., pp. 722–37. Oxford: Oxford University Press.
Galleymore, Isobel. 2017. 'Posthuman Poetics'. *The London Magazine*, 5 October. www.thelondonmagazine.org/article/posthuman-poetics/
Garcia, Tiago Sousa. 2017. 'How *The Lusiad* Got English'd: Manuel Faria y Sousa, Richard Fanshawe and the First English Translation of Os Lusíadas'. *Literature Compass* 14 (4): 1–18.
Gaskill, Malcolm. 2018. 'The Natives Did a Bunk'. *London Review of Books* (19 July) 40 (14): 38–40.
Gibson, William. 2010. *Zero History*. London: Penguin.
  2011a. *Pattern Recognition*. London: Penguin.
  2011b. *Spook Country*. London: Penguin.
Gilroy, Paul. 1993. *The Black Atlantic*. London: Verso.
Glissant, Édouard. 1992. *Caribbean Discourse*. Translated by J. Michael Dash. Charlottesville, VA: University of Virginia Press.
  2020. *Treatise on the Whole-World*. Translated by Celia Britton. Liverpool: Liverpool University Press.
Goethe, Johann Wolfgang. 1998. *Conversations of Goethe with Johann Peter Eckermann*. Translated by J. Oxenford. [n.p.]: Da Capo.
  2014. 'Conversations with Eckermann on Weltliteratur'. In *World Literature in Theory*, edited by David Damrosch, pp. 15–21. Malden, MA: Wiley-Blackwell.
  2016. 'On German Architecture'. In *The Essential Goethe*, edited by Matthew Bell, pp. 867–72. Princeton, NJ: Princeton University Press.
Goodman, Sam. 2015. *British Spy Fiction and the End of Empire*. New York: Routledge.
Goodyear, Sarah Suleri. 2000. *Ravishing Disunities: Real Ghazals in English*. Middletown: Wesleyan University Press.
Gopinath, Praseeda. 2013. *Scarecrows of Chivalry: English Masculinities after Empire*. Charlottesville, VA: University of Virginia Press.
Goyal, Yogita. 2019. *Runaway Genres: The Global Afterlives of Slavery*. New York: New York University Press.
Graham, David A. 2015. 'Why the Muslim 'No-Go-Zone' Myth Won't Die'. *The Atlantic* (20 January). www.theatlantic.com/international/archive/2015/01/paris-mayor-to-sue-fox-over-no-go-zone-comments/384656/
Graham, Jorie. 2017. *Fast*. New York: HarperCollins.
Greig, David. 2002. *Plays 1*. London: Methuen.
Grocholski, Brent. 2019. 'Two Timelines for Extinction'. *Science* 363: 6429 (22 February): 831. http://science.sciencemag.org/content/363/6429/twis
Grossman, Jonathan H. 2012. *Charles Dickens's Networks: Public Transport and the Novel*. Oxford: Oxford University Press.

Guldi, Jo. 2012. *Roads to Power: Britain Invents the Infrastructure State*. Cambridge, MA: Harvard University Press.
Gutas, Dimitri. 2012. *Greek Thought, Arabic Culture: The Graeco-Arabic Translation Movement in Baghdad and Early'Abbasaid Society (2nd–4th/5th–10th c.)*. London and New York: Routledge.
Hage, Rawi. 2006. *DeNiro's Game*. London: Harper Perennial.
Halberstam, Jack. 2018. *Trans*: A Quick and Quirky Account of Gender Variability*. Oakland, CA: University of California Press.
Hall, Shyima and Lisa Wysocky. 2014. *Hidden Girl: The True Story of a Modern-Day Child Slave*. New York: Simon & Schuster.
Hampson, Robert. 2003. '"A Passion for Maps": Conrad, Africa, Australia, and South-East Asia'. *The Conradian* 28 (1): 34–56.
  2005. 'Conrad's Heterotopic Fiction: Composite Maps, Superimposed Sites, and Impossible Spaces'. In *Conrad in the Twenty-First Century: Contemporary Approaches and Perspectives*, edited by Carola M. Kaplan et al., pp. 121–36. New York: Routledge.
Hansen, James. 2011. *Storms of My Grandchildren: The Truth about the Coming Climate Catastrophe and Our Last Chance to Save Humanity*. London: Bloomsbury.
Harari, Yuval N. 2014. *Sapiens: A Brief History of Humankind*. London: Vintage.
Harper, Kyle. 2015. 'Pandemics and Passages to Late Antiquity: Rethinking the Plague of c. 249–270 Described by Cyprian'. *Journal of Roman Archaeology* 28: 223–60.
Harrison, Nicholas. 2014. 'World Literature: What Gets Lost in Translation?' *The Journal of Commonwealth Literature* 49 (3): 411–26.
Hardt, Michael and Antonio Negri. 2004. *Multitude: War and Democracy in the Age of Empire*. Cambridge, MA and London: Harvard University Press.
Hart, Matthew. 2015. 'Threshold to the Kingdom: The Airport Is a Border and the Border Is a Volume'. *Criticism* 57 (2): 173–89.
Hartman, Saidiya. 2008. 'Venus in Two Acts'. *Small Axe* 12 (2): 1–14.
Harvey, David. 1990. *The Condition of Postmodernity*. Cambridge and Oxford: Blackwell.
  2005. *A Brief History of Neoliberalism*. Oxford and New York: Oxford University Press.
  2011. *The Enigma of Capital and the Crises of Capitalism*. London: Profile Books.
  2012. *Rebel Cities: From the Right to the City to the Urban Revolution*. London and New York: Verso.
Hayot, Eric. 2012. *On Literary Worlds*. New York: Oxford University Press.
Head, Gretchen. 2015. '"The Sea Spits Out Corpses": Peripherality, Genre, and Affect in the Cosmopolitan Mediterranean'. *Global South* 9 (2): 38–59.
Headrick, Daniel. 1988. *Tentacles of Progress: Technology Transfer in the Age of Imperialism, 1850–1940*. Oxford: Oxford University Press.
Hegelsson, Stefan. 2018. 'Translation and the Circuits of World Literature'. In *The Cambridge Companion to World Literature*, edited by Ben Etherington and Jarad Zimbler, pp. 85–99. Cambridge: Cambridge University Press.
Heidegger, Martin. 1962. *Being and Time*. Translated by J. Macquarrie and E. Robinson. New York: Harper & Row.

1971. 'The Origin of a Work of Art'. In *Poetry, Language, Thought*. Translated by A. Hofstadter, pp. 17–87. New York: Harper & Row.

1977. *The Question Concerning Technology, and Other Essays*. Translated by William Lovitt. New York: Harper & Row.

1995. *The Fundamental Concepts of Metaphysics, World, Finitude, Solitude*. Bloomington: Indiana University Press.

2013. *The Question concerning Technology and Other Essays*. Translated and with an introduction by William Lovitt. New York: HarperCollins.

Heilbron, John. 1999. 'Towards a Sociology of Translation: Book Translations as a Cultural World System'. *European Journal of Social Theory* 2 (4): 429–44.

Hepburn, Allan. 2005. *Intrigue: Espionage and Culture*. New Haven, CT and London: Yale University Press.

Hexham, Henry. 1647–1648. *A Copious English and Netherdutch Dictionary Composed out of our Best English Authors*. Rotterdam. http://leme.library.utoronto.ca

Hirsch, Afua. 2019. 'What Is the Commonwealth If Not the British Empire 2.0?' *The Guardian*, 17 April. Accessed 3 September 2019. www.theguardian.com/commentisfree/2018/apr/17/commonwealth-british-empire-britain-black-brown-people

Hobson, John A. 1933. *Imperialism*. London: George Allen & Unwin.

Homer. 1962. *Iliad*. Translated by Richmond Lattimore. Chicago: University of Chicago Press.

Hoots, Anna Belle. 2019. 'Severing the Connection Between Sex Trafficking and U.S. Military Bases Overseas'. *Fordham Law Review* 88 (2): 733–59.

Hughes, J. Donald. 1994. *Environmental Problems of the Ancient Greeks and Romans*. Baltimore, MD: Johns Hopkins University Press.

Hughes, Langston. 2001. *The Collected Works of Langston Hughes: The Poems, 1921–1940*, edited by Arnold Rampersad. Columbia, MO: University of Missouri Press.

Human Rights Watch. 2003. 'Sudan, Oil, and Human Rights'. www.hrw.org/reports/2003/sudan1103/8.htm

Hunwick, Julie Scott. 1996. 'The Arabic Qasida in West Africa: Forms, Themes, and Contexts'. In *Qasida Poetry in Islamic Asia and Africa: Classical Traditions and Modern Meanings*, edited by Stefan Sperl and Christopher Shackle, pp. 137–82. Leiden and New York: Brill.

Husserl, Edmund. 1970. *The Crisis of the European Sciences and Transcendental Phenomenology: An Introduction to Phenomenological Philosophy*. Translated by David Carr. Evanston: Northwestern University Press.

Irigaray, Luce. 2003. *Between East and West: From Singularity to Community*. Translated by Stephen Pluhácek. New York: Columbia University Press.

Issar, Arie S. and Mattanyah Zohar. 2007. *Climate Change: Environment and History of the Middle East*. Berlin: Springer.

Izzo, Jean-Claude. 2005. *Total Chaos*. Translated by Howard Curtis. New York: Europa.

Jaffe, Alexandra. 2015. 'Bobby Jindal slams "no-go zones," pushes "assimilation."' *CNN Politics*. 21 January. www.cnn.com/2015/01/19/politics/jindal-no-go-zones-london/

James, Cyril L. R. 1938. *The Black Jacobins: Toussaint L'Ouverture and the San Domingo Revolution*. London: Secker and Warburg.

Jameson, Fredric. 1979. 'Reification and Utopia in Mass Culture'. *Social Text* 1: 130–48.
  1981. *The Political Unconscious: Narrative as a Socially Symbolic Act*. Ithaca, NY: Cornell University Press.
  1986. 'On Magic Realism in Film'. *Critical Inquiry* 12 (2): 301–25.
  1990. 'Modernism and Imperialism'. In *Nationalism, Colonialism and Literature*, edited by Seamus Deane. Minneapolis, MN: University of Minnesota Press.
  1991. *Postmodernism, or, the Cultural Logic of Late Capitalism*. London: Verso.
  2002. *A Singular Modernity: An Essay on the Ontology of the Present*. New York: Verso.
  2003. 'Fear and Loathing in Globalization'. *New Left Review* 23: 105–14.
  2007. *The Modernist Papers*. New York: Verso.
  2005. *Archaeologies of the Future: The Desire Called Utopia and Other Science Fictions*. London and New York: Verso.
  2009. *Valences of the Dialectic*. London and New York: Verso.
  2011. 'Fear and Loathing in Globalization'. In *Literature and Globalization: A Reader*, edited by Liam Connell and Nicky Marsh, pp. 244–51. London and New York: Routledge.
  2013. *The Antinomies of Realism*. London: Verso.
Jasanoff, Maya. 2017. *The Dawn Watch: Joseph Conrad in a Global World*. London: Collins.
Jetnil-Kijiner, Kathy. 2016. '1.5 to Stay Alive'. 13 January. https://jkijiner.wordpress.com/tag/1-5-to-stay-alive/
  2017. *IEP Jāltok: Poems from a Marshallese Daughter*. 3rd ed. Tucson: University of Arizona Press.
Johnson, Rebecca C. 2021. *Stranger Fictions: A History of the Novel in Arabic Translation, 1835–1913*. Ithaca, NY: Cornell University Press.
Johnson, Samuel. 1755. *A Dictionary of English Language*. 2 vols. London.
Johns-Putra, Adeline. 2019. *Climate Change and the Contemporary Novel*. Cambridge and New York: Cambridge University Press.
Jones, Philip D., T. J. Osborne and K. R. Briffa. 2001. 'The Evolution of Climate over the Last Millennium'. *Science* 292 (5517): 662–7.
Jordan, Chris. 2009. 'Midway'. www.chrisjordan.com/gallery/midway/#CF000313%2018x24
Joshi, Priti. 2011. 'The Middle Classes'. In *Charles Dickens in Context*, edited by Sally Ledger and Holly Furneaux, pp. 260–7. Cambridge: Cambridge University Press.
Joshi, Priya. 2002. *In Another Country: Colonialism, Culture, and the English Novel in India*. New York: Columbia University Press.
Joyce, James. 1990. *Ulysses*. New York: Vintage.
  1964. *A Portrait of the Artist as a Young Man*. New York: Viking Press.
  1989. *Critical Writings of James Joyce*, edited by Ellsworth Mason and Richard Ellmann. Ithaca, NY: Cornell University Press.
Kackman, Michael. 2005. *Citizen Spy: Television, Espionage, and Cold War Culture*. Minneapolis, MN: University of Minnesota Press.
Kaniewski, David et al. 2013. 'Environmental Roots of the Late Bronze Age Crisis'. *PLoS ONE* 8 (8): e71004. doi: 10.1371/journal.pone.0071004. http://journals.plos.org/plosone/article?id=10.1371/journal.pone.0071004

Kara, Siddharth. 2017. 'Modern Slavery: The 'Dark Underbelly' of Globalization'. *UN News*. https://news.un.org/en/audio/2017/10/634532
Karl, Frederick R. and Laurence Davies. 1983. *The Collected Letters of Joseph Conrad*, Vol. 1. Cambridge: Cambridge University Press.
  2007. *The Collected Letters of Joseph Conrad*, Vol. 8. Cambridge: Cambridge University Press.
Kassam, Raheem. 2017. *No Go Zones: How Sharia Law Is Coming to a Neighborhood Near You*. Washington, DC: Regnery Publishing.
Kathayat, Gayatri et al. 2017. 'The Indian Monsoon Variability and Civilization Changes in the Subcontinent'. *Science Advances* 3 (12) (13 December): e1701296.
Kaviraj, Sudipta. 2003. 'The Two Histories of Literary Culture in Bengal'. In *Literary Cultures in History: Reconstructions from South Asia*, edited by Sheldon Pollock, pp. 503–66. Berkeley, CA: University of California Press.
Kawano, Akira. 1983. 'Haiku and American Poetry: The Influence of Haiku upon American Poetry'. *Neohelicon* 10 (1): 115–22.
Keating, Peter. 1989. *The Haunted Study: A Social History of the English Novel, 1875–1914*. London: Secker and Warburg.
Keizer, Arlene R. 2004. *Black Subjects: Identity Formation in the Contemporary Narrative of Slavery*. Ithaca, NY: Cornell University Press.
Keown, Michelle. 2017. 'Children of Israel: US Military Imperialism and Marshallese Migration in the Poetry of Kathy Jetnil-Kijiner'. *Interventions* 19 (7): 930–47. https://doi.org/10.1080/1369801X.2017.1403944
  2018. 'Waves of Destruction: Nuclear Imperialism and Anti-Nuclear Protest in the Indigenous Literatures of the Pacific'. *Journal of Postcolonial Writing* 54 (5): 585–600. https://doi.org/10.1080/17449855.2018.1538660
Kersey, John. 1702. *A New English Dictionary*. London. http://leme.library.utoronto.ca
Keynes, John Maynard. 1920. *The Economic Consequences of the Peace*. London: Macmillan.
Khalaf, Farida. 2016. *The Girl Who Escaped ISIS: This Is My Story*. New York: Atria.
Khan, Maryam. 2017. 'The Oriental Tale and the Transformation of North Indian Prose Fiction'. *Modern Language Quarterly* 78 (1): 27–50.
Kiernan, Alvin. 1990. *The Death of Literature*. New Haven, CT: Yale University Press.
Kincaid, Jamaica. 1997. *A Small Place*. London: Vintage.
Kirkwood, Lucy. 2017. *The Children*. London: Nick Hern Books.
Klein, Naomi. 2015. *This Changes Everything: Capitalism vs. the Climate*. London and New York: Penguin.
Kleinhenz, Christopher. 1998. 'A Trio of Sonnets in Occitan: A Lyrical Duet and an Historic Solo'. *Tenso* 13 (2): 33–49.
Knight, Sarah, ed. 2018. *The Oxford Handbook of Neo-Latin*. Oxford: Oxford University Press.
Koch, Alexander et al. 2019. 'Earth System Impacts of the European Arrival and Great Dying in the Americas after 1492'. *Quaternary Science Reviews* 207 (March): 13–36.

Kohn, Eduardo. 2013. *How Forests Think: Toward an Anthropology beyond the Human*. Berkeley, CA: University of California Press.
Kojève, Alexandre. 1969. *Introduction to the Reading of Hegel: Lectures on the Phenomenology of Spirit*. Translated by James H. Nichols, Jr. London and New York: Basic Books.
Kolbert, Elizabeth. 2009. 'The Sixth Extinction?' *The New Yorker*, 25 May.
Konuk, Kader. 2010. *East West Mimesis: Auerbach in Turkey*. Stanford: Stanford University Press.
Koyré, Alexandre. 1968. *From the Closed World to the Infinite Universe*. Baltimore, MD: Johns Hopkins University Press.
Kubat, Premsyl. 2011. 'The Desiccation Theory Revisited'. *Les carnets de* l'Ifpo. 18 April. https://ifpo.hypotheses.org/1794
Kurzweil, Ray. 2009. *The Singularity Is Near: When Humans Transcend Biology*. London: Gerald Duckworth.
Kwarteng, Kwasi, Priti Patel, Dominic Raab, Chris Skidmore and Elizabeth Truss. 2012. *Britannia Unchained: Global Lessons for Growth and Prosperity*. New York: Palgrave Macmillan.
Latour, Bruno. 2017. *Facing Gaia: Eight Lectures on the New Climatic Regime*. Translated by Catherine Porter. Cambridge: Polity Press.
  2005. *Reassembling the Social: An Introduction to Actor-Network-Theory*. Oxford: Oxford University Press.
LeBaron, Genevieve. 2015. 'Unfree Labour Beyond Binaries'. *International Feminist Journal of Politics* 17 (1): 1–19.
Ledger, Sally. 1997. *The New Woman: Fiction and Feminism at the Fin de Siècle*. Bloomington: Indiana University Press.
Leonard, Philip. 2013. *Literature after Globalization: Textuality, Technology, and the Nation-State*. London: Bloomsbury.
  2019. *Orbital Poetics: Literature, Theory, World*. London: Bloomsbury.
Lewis, Paul. 1999. 'U.N. Criticism Angers Charities Buying Sudan Slaves' Release'. *The New York Times*, 12 March. www.nytimes.com/1999/03/12/world/un-criticism-angers-charities-buying-sudan-slaves-release.html
Lieberman, Victor B. 2009. *Strange Parallels: Mainland Mirrors: Europe, Japan, China, South Asia, and the Islands*. Cambridge: Cambridge University Press.
Lieu, Samuel N. C. 2012. *Medieval Christian and Manichaean Remains from Quanzhou (Zayton)*. Turnhout: Brepols.
Lindo, John et al. 2018. 'The Genetic Prehistory of the Andean Highlands 7000 Years BP through European Contact'. *Science Advances* 4 (11): eaau4921.
Little, Lester K. 2007. 'Life and Afterlife of the First Plague Pandemic'. In *Plague and the End of Antiquity: The Pandemic of 541–750*, edited by Lester K. Little, pp. 3–32. New York: Cambridge University Press.
Littman, Robert J. and Michael L. Littman. 1973. 'Galen and the Antonine Plague'. *American Journal of Philology* 94: 243–55.
Lovejoy, Paul E. 2011. '"Freedom Narratives" of Transatlantic Slavery'. *Slavery & Abolition* 32 (1): 91–107.
Löwith, Karl. 1949. *Meaning in History: The Theological Implications of the Philosophy of History*. Chicago: University of Chicago Press.

Lucretius. 1951. *On the Nature of the Universe*. Translated by R. E. Latham. London: Penguin.
Lyotard, Jean-François. 1992. 'An Answer to the Question: What Is the Postmodern?' In *The Postmodern Explained*. Translated by Don Barry et al. Minneapolis, MN: University of Minnesota Press.
    1984. *The Postmodern Condition: A Report on Knowledge*. Translated by Geoff Bennington and Brian Massumi. Manchester: Manchester University Press.
Macfarlane, Robert. 2016. 'Generation Anthropocene: How Humans Have Altered the Planet for Ever'. *The Guardian*, 1 April. www.theguardian.com/books/2016/apr/01/generation-anthropocene-altered-planet-for-ever
Mallette, Karla. 2011. *The Kingdom of Sicily, 1100–1250: A Literary History*. Philadelphia, PA: University of Pennsylvania Press.
Malpas, Simon. 2003. *Jean-François Lyotard*. London: Routledge.
Mam, Somaly. 2009. *The Road to Lost Innocence: The Story of a Cambodian Hero*. New York: Spiegel and Grau.
Mann, Charles C. 2011. *1491: New Revelations of the Americas before Columbus*. 2nd ed. New York: Vintage.
Mao, Douglas and Rebecca L. Walkowitz. 2009. 'The New Modernist Studies'. *PMLA* 123 (3): 737–48.
Markaris, Petros. 2004. *The Late-Night News*. Translated by David Conolly. London: Vintage.
Marriner, Nicholas et al. 2017. 'Tsunamis in the Geological Record: Making Waves with a Cautionary Tale from the Mediterranean'. *Science Advances* 3 (10): e1700485.
Marx, Karl. 1887. *Capital: A Critique of Political Economy*, Vol. I. Translated by Samuel Moore and Edward Aveling. Moscow: Progress.
Marx, Karl and Friedrich Engels. 2018. *The Manifesto of the Communist Party*. Minneapolis, MN: First Avenue Editions.
McCormick, Michael et al. 2012. 'Climate Change during and after the Roman Empire: Reconstructing the Past from Scientific and Historical Evidence'. *Journal of Interdisciplinary History* 43 (2): 169–220.
McElduff, Siobhán. 2013. *Roman Theories of Translation: Surpassing the Source*. New York: Routledge.
McIlroy, T. 2016. 'What the Big 5's Financial Reports Reveal About the State of Traditional Book Publishing'. *Book Business*, 5 August. www.bookbusinessmag.com/post/big-5-financial-reports-reveal-state-traditional-book-publishing/
McKay, Claude. 1970. *Banjo*. Boston, MA: Mariner Books.
    2008. *Complete Poems*. Champaign: University of Illinois Press.
McMichael, Anthony J. et al. 2017. *Climate Change and the Health of Nations: Famines, Fevers, and the Fate of Populations*. Oxford: Oxford University Press.
McMurry, Evan. 2016. 'Mediaite: Gov. Jindal Still Pushing Discredited Claim of "No-Go Zones"', *Newstex Trade & Industry Blogs*, 18 January. https://search.proquest.com/docview/1646324335?accountid=10226
McNeill, William H. 1998. *Plagues and Peoples*. New York: Anchor.
McNeill, John Robert and William H. McNeill. 2003. *The Human Web: A Bird's-Eye View of World History*. New York: W. W. Norton.

Meillassoux, Quentin. 2008. *After Finitude*. London: Continuum.
  2011. 'Potentiality and Virtuality'. In *The Speculative Turn: Continental Materialism and Realism*, edited by Levi Bryant, Nick Srnicek, and Graham Harman. London: re.press.
  2012. *The Number and the Siren: A Decipherment of Mallarmé's Coup de Dés*. Falmouth: Urbanomic.
Meisami, Julie Scott. 2014. *Medieval Persian Court Poetry*. Princeton, NJ: Princeton University Press.
Mezzadra, Sandro and Brett Neilson. 2013. *Border as Method, or, the Multiplication of Labor*. Durham, NC: Duke University Press.
Middle, Matthias and Katja Naumann. 2010. 'Global History and the Spatial Turn: From the Impact of Area Studies to the Study of Critical Junctures of Globalization'. *Journal of Global History* 5 (1): 149–70.
Miéville, China. 2007. 'Floating Utopias: Freedom and Unfreedom of the Seas'. In *Evil Paradises: Dreamworlds of Neoliberalism*, edited by Mike Davis and Daniel Bertrand Monk. New York and London: The New Press.
Miller, Gifford H. et al. 2012. 'Abrupt Onset of Little Ice Age Triggered by Volcanism and Sustained by Sea-Ice/Ocean Feedbacks'. *Geophysical Research Letters* 39 (2). https://agupubs.onlinelibrary.wiley.com/doi/full/10.1029/2011GL050168
Milton, John. 1959. *Complete Prose Works*, Volume 2: *1643–1648*, edited by Ernest Sirluck. New Haven, CT: Yale University Press.
Miniter, Richard. 1999. 'The False Promise of Slave Redemption'. *The Atlantic*. July. www.theatlantic.com/magazine/archive/1999/07/the-false-promise-of-slave-redemption/377679/
Mitchell-Boyask, Robin. 2007. *Plague and the Athenian Imagination*. Cambridge: Cambridge University Press.
Miyoshi, Masao. 2001. 'Turn to the Planet: Literature, Diversity, and Totality'. *Comparative Literature* 53 (4): 283–97.
Manuel Vázaquez Montalbán. 1986. *Southern Seas*. Translated by Patrick Camiller. London: Melville House.
Mattich, Alen. 2012. *Zagreb Cowboy*. Toronto: Anansi.
Mbembe, Achille. 2017. *A Critique of Black Reason*. Translated by Laurent Dubois. Durham, NC: Duke University Press.
Modiano, Patrick. 2017. *Sundays in August*. Translated by Damion Searls. New Haven, CT: Yale University Press.
Moody, Alys. 2018. 'Indifferent and Detached: Modernism and the Aesthetic Effect'. *Modernism/modernity Print Plus* 3.4. https://modernismmodernity.org/forums/posts/indifferent-and-detached
Moore, Grace. 2016. *Dickens and Empire: Discourses of Class, Race and Colonialism in the Works of Charles Dickens*. New York: Routledge.
Moore-Gilbert, Bart. 2003. 'Olive Schreiner's *Story of an African Farm*: Reconciling Feminism and Anti-Imperialism?' *Women: A Cultural Review* 14 (1): 85–103.
Morabia, A. 2009. 'Historical Review: Epidemic and population patterns in the Chinese Empire (243 B.C.E. to 1911 C.E.): Quantitative Analysis of a Unique but Neglected Epidemic Catalogue'. *Epidemiology and Infection* 137: 1361–8.

Moraru, Christian. 2011. *Cosmodernism: American Narrative, Late Globalization, and the New Cultural Imaginary*. Ann Arbor, MI: The University of Michigan Press.
 2015. *Reading for the Planet: Toward a Geomethodology*. Ann Arbor, MI: University of Michigan Press.
 2017. '"World," "Globe," "Planet": Comparative Literature, Planetary Studies, and Cultural Debt after the Global Turn." In *Futures of Comparative Literature: ACLA State of the Discipline Report*, edited by Ursula K. Heise, et al., pp. 124–33. New York: Routledge.
Morelli, Giovanna et al. 2010. '*Yersinia pestis* Genome Sequencing Identifies Patterns of Global Phylogenetic Diversity'. *Nature Genetics* 42 (December): 1140–3.
Moreton-Robinson, Aileen. 2015. *The White Possessive: Property, Power, and Indigenous Sovereignty*. Minneapolis, MN and London: University of Minnesota Press.
Moretti, Franco. 1991. *Atlas of the European Novel*. New York: Verso.
 2000. 'Conjectures on World Literature'. *New Left Review* 238 (1): 54–68.
Morrison, Toni. 1997. *Beloved*. London: Vintage.
 2009. *A Mercy*. London: Vintage.
Morson, Gary Saul. 1994. *Narrative and Freedom: The Shadows of Time*. New Haven, CT and London: Yale University Press.
Morton, Timothy. 2010. *The Ecological Thought*. Cambridge, MA: Harvard University Press.
 2013. *Hyperobjects: Philosophy and Ecology after the End of the World*. Minneapolis, MN and London. University of Minnesota Press.
 2019. *Humankind: Solidarity with Nonhuman People*. London: Verso.
Moul, Victoria, ed. 2017. *A Guide to Neo-Latin Literature*. Cambridge: Cambridge University Press.
Muhsen, Zana and Andrew Crofts. 1991. *Sold: One Woman's True Account of Modern Slavery*. London: Sphere.
Müller, Simone M. and Heidi J. S. Tworek. 2015. 'The Telegraph and the Bank: On the Interdependence of Global Communications and Capitalism, 1866–1914'. *Journal of Global History* 10: 259–83.
Mullett, Margaret. 2017. 'Performing Court Literature in Medieval Byzantium: Tales Told in Tents'. In *The Presence of Power: Court and Performance in the Pre-Modern Middle East*, edited by Maurice A. Pomerantz and Evelyn Birge Vitz, pp. 121–41. New York: New York University Press.
Murad, Nadia. 2017. *The Last Girl: My Story of Captivity, and My Fight Against the Islamic State*. New York: Tim Duggan.
Muravchick, Joshua. 1991. 'At Last, Pax Americana'. *The New York Times*, 24 January.
Murray, Cara. 2008. *Victorian Narrative Technologies in the Middle East*. London: Routledge.
Murphy, Laura T. 2019. *The New Slave Narrative: The Battle over Representations of Contemporary Slavery*. New York: Columbia University Press.
 ed. 2014. *Survivors of Slavery: Narratives of Modern-Day Slavery*. New York: Columbia University Press.

Muslim Arbitration Tribunal. 'The Gateway to Islamic and English Legal Services'. www.matribunal.com/faqs.php
Nandy, Ashis. 1983. *The Intimate Enemy: Loss and Recovery of Self under Colonialism*. London: Oxford University Press.
Navarro, José Enrique. 2017. 'Global Bolaño: Reading, Wrtiting, and Publishing in a Neoliberal World'. In *Roberto Bolaño as World Literature*, edited by Nicholas Birns and Juan E. De Castro, pp. 137–50. New York: Bloomsbury Academic.
Nazer, Mende. 2003. Slave: My True Story. *With Damien Lewis*. New York: Public Affairs.
Negri, Antonio. 2010. 'The Eclipse of Eschatology: Conversing with Taubes's Messianism and the Common Body'. *Political Theology* 11 (1): 35–41.
Nevel, Donna. 2013. 'How Pro-Israel Forces Drove Two Virulent Anti-Muslim Campaigns'. *Mondoweiss*, 22 September. https://mondoweiss.net/2013/09/how-pro-israel-forces-drove-two-virulent-anti-muslim-campaigns/
Newfield, Tim. 2016. 'The Global Cooling Event of the Sixth Century: Mystery No Longer?' *Historical Climatology*. www.historicalclimatology.com/features/something-cooled-the-world-in-the-sixth-century-what-was-it
Ngũgĩ wa, Thiong'o. 1986. *Decolonising the Mind: The Politics of Language in African Literature*. London: Heinemann.
Nickels, Joel. 2014. 'Claude McKay and Dissident Internationalism'. *Cultural Critique* 87 (Spring), 1–37.
Niland, Richard. 2017. 'Conrad, Capital and Globalization'. In *Conradology: A Celebration of the Work of Joseph Conrad*, edited by Becky Harrison and Magda Raczyńska, pp. 155–66. Manchester: Comma Press.
Nixon, Rob. 2011. *Slow Violence and the Environmentalism of the Poor*. Cambridge, MA: Harvard University Press.
2014. 'The Anthropocene: Promise and Pitfalls of an Epochal Idea'. *Edge Effects*, 6 November. http://edgeeffects.net/anthropocene-promise-and-pitfalls/
Norris, Christopher. 1992. *Uncritical Theory: Postmodernism, Intellectuals and the Gulf War*. London: Lawrence and Wishart.
'Northern Chinese Famine of 1876–1879'. 2019. Wikipedia. https://en.wikipedia.org/wiki/Northern_Chinese_Famine_of_1876%E2%80%9379. Retrieved 4 July.
Noyes, John K. 2015. 'Writing the Dialectical Nature of the Modern Subject: Goethe on World Literature and World Citizenship'. *Seminar* 51 (2): 100–14.
Nunokawa, Jeff. 1995. 'For Your Eyes Only: Private Property and the Oriental Body in Dombey and Son'. In *Macropolitics of Nineteenth-Century Literature*, edited by Jonathan Arac and Harriet Ritvo, pp. 138–58. Durham, NC and London: Duke University Press.
Olivelle, Patrick. 1999. *Pañcatantra: The Book of India's Folk Wisdom*. Oxford: Oxford University Press.
O'Neill, Joseph. 2014. *The Dog*. New York: Pantheon.
Orsini, Francesca. 2019. 'Between Qasbas and Cities: Language Shifts and Literary Continuities in North India in the Long Eighteenth Century'. *Comparative Studies of South Asia, Africa and the Middle East* 39 (1): 68–81.
Osterhammel, Jürgen. 2014. *The Transformation of the World: A Global History of the Nineteenth Century*. Translated by Patrick Camiller. Princeton, NJ and Oxford: Princeton University Press.

Pamuk, Orhan. 2005. *Snow*. Translated by Maureen Freely. New York: Vintage.
Parker, Geoffrey. 2014. *Global Crisis: War, Climate Change and Catastrophe in the Seventeenth Century*. Rev, edited by New Haven, CT: Yale University Press.
Parry, Benita. 1984. *Conrad and Imperialism: Ideological Boundaries and Visionary Frontiers*. Basingstoke: Palgrave Macmillan.
The Path of Islam Is Always the Same. *Google Images*. https://images.app.goo.gl/PxmUWzzRGVwk5Rkq9
Peksen, Dursun et al. 2017. 'Neoliberal Policies and Human Trafficking for Labor: Free Markets, Unfree Workers?' *Political Research Quarterly* 70 (3): 673–86.
Percy, Thomas, ed. 1761. *Hau Kiou Chooan or the Pleasing History*. London.
Perkin, Harold. 1989. *The Rise of Professional Society: England Since 1880*. New York: Routledge.
Petrowskaja, Katja. 2014. *Vielleicht Esther*. Berlin: Suhrkamp.
　2018. *Maybe Esther*. Translated by S. Frisch. London: Fourth Estate.
Petras, James and Henry Veltmeyer. 2001. *Globalization Unmasked: Imperialism in the 21st Century*. London: Zed Books.
Pettifor, Ann. 2019 *The Case for the Green New Deal*. London and New York: Verso.
Phillips, Caryl. 2005. *A Distant Shore*. New York: Vintage.
Philips, Katherine. 1705. *Letters from Orinda to Poliarchus*. London.
Pike Robert M. and Dwayne R. Winseck. 2007. *Communication and Empire: Media, Markets, and Globalization, 1860–1930*. Durham, NC: Duke University Press.
　2008. 'Communication and Empire: Media Markets, Power and Globalization, 1816–1910'. *Global Media and Communication* 4 (1): 7–36.
Pipes, Daniel. 2013. 'The 751 No-Go Zones of France'. Updated. www.danielpipes.org/blog/2006/11/the-751-no-go-zones-of-france
Pizer, John. 2006. *The Idea of World Literature*. Baton Rouge: Louisiana State University Press.
Plath, Sylvia. 2006. *Ariel*. London: Faber and Faber.
Pollard, Charles W. 2004. *New World Modernisms: T. S. Eliot, Derek Walcott, and Kamau Brathwaite*. Charlottesville, VA: University of Virginia Press.
Pollock, Sheldon. 2006. *The Language of the Gods in the World of Men: Sanskrit, Culture, and Power in Premodern India*. 1st ed. Berkeley, CA: University of California Press.
Pomeranz, Kenneth and Steven Topik. 2006. *The World That Trade Created: Society, Culture, and the World Economy*. London: M. E. Sharpe.
Potter, Simon. 2003. *News and the British World: The Emergence of an Imperial Press System*. Oxford: Clarendon Press.
Pound, Ezra. 1913. 'A Few Don'ts by an Imagiste'. *Poetry: A Magazine of Verse* 1 (6): 200–6.
　1968a. *The Spirit of Romance*. New York: New Directions, 1968. 1910.
　1968b. *Literary Essays of Ezra Pound*, edited by T. S. Eliot. New York: New Directions, 1968.
　1973. *Selected Prose: 1909–1965*, edited by William Cookson. New York: New Directions.

Powers, Richard. 2018. *The Overstory*. New York: W. W. Norton.
Pritchard, James B., ed. 2011. *The Ancient Near East: An Anthology of Texts and Pictures*. Princeton, NJ: Princeton University Press.
Putnam, Aaron et al. 2016. 'Little Ice Age Wetting of Interior Asian Deserts and the Rise of the Mongol Empire'. *Quaternary Science Reviews* 131. Part A (January): 33–50.
Quraishi, Muzammil. 2008. 'The Racial Construction of Urban Spaces in Britain and Pakistan'. *Asian Criminology* 3: 159–71.
Raddatz, F. 2015. *Jahre mit Ledig*. Reinbek: Rowohlt.
Rancière, Jacques. 2004. *The Politics of Aesthetics: The Distribution of the Sensible*. Translated by Gabriel Rockhill. London: Continuum.
Reynolds, Matthew, ed. 2020. *Prismatic Translation*. Cambridge: Legenda.
Richardson, Dorothy M. 1979. *Pilgrimage I: Pointed Roofs, Backwater, Honeycomb*. Chicago: University of Illinois Press.
Ricoeur, Paul. 1985. *Time and Narrative Volume 2*. Translated by Kathleen Blamey and David Pellauer. Chicago: University of Chicago Press.
Rigby, Kate. 2014. 'Confronting Catastrophe: Ecocriticism in a Warming World'. In *The Cambridge Companion to Literature and the Environment*, edited by Louise Westling, pp. 212–25. Cambridge: Cambridge University Press.
Robertson, Roland. 1998. *Globalization: Social Theory and Global Culture*. London: SAGE.
Robinson, Cedric. 2004. *Black Marxism: The Making of the Black Radical Tradition*. Chapel Hill, NC: University of North Carolina Press.
Rodríguez Martínez, María del Carmen, et al. 2006. 'Oldest Writing in the New World'. *Science* 313 (5793) (15 September): 1610–14.
Rodríguez, Sergio Gonzáles. 2012. *The Femicide Machine*. Translated by Michael Parker-Stainback. Cambridge, MA: MIT Press.
Rosenblatt, Roger. 2001. 'The Age of Irony Comes to an End'. *Time*, 185 (13) (24 September), http://content.time.com/time/subscriber/article/0,33009,1000893,00.html
Rubenstein, Michael. 2010. *Public Works: Infrastructure, Irish Modernism, and the Postcolonial*. Notre Dame: University of Notre Dame Press.
Rushdy, Ashraf H. A. 1999. *Neo-Slave Narratives: Studies in the Social Logic of a Literary Form*. New York: Oxford University Press.
Sage, Jesse and Liora Kasten, eds. 2006. *Enslaved: True Stories of Modern Day Slavery*. New York: Palgrave Macmillan.
Said, Edward. 1966. *Joseph Conrad and the Fiction of Autobiography*. Cambridge, MA: Harvard University Press.
  1975. *Beginnings: Intention and Method*. New York: Basic Books.
  1979. *Orientalism*. New York: Vintage Books.
  1984. *The World, the Text, and the Critic*. London: Faber and Faber.
  1989. 'Representing the Colonized: Anthropology's Interlocutors'. *Critical Inquiry* 15 (2): 205–25.
  1993. *Culture and Imperialism*. New York and London: Vintage/Cape.
  1999. *Out of Place*. London: Granta.
  2000. *Reflections on Exile*. Cambridge, MA: Harvard University Press.

2004. *Humanism and Democratic Criticism*. New York: Columbia University Press.
Saluzinsky, Imre. 2004. 'Criticism'. In *Power, Politics and Culture: Interviews with Edward Said*, edited by Gauri Viswanathan. London: Bloomsbury.
Sassen, Saskia. 2001. *The Global City*. Princeton, NJ: Princeton University Press.
  2007. *Territory, Authority, Rights: From Medieval to Global Assemblages*. Princeton, NJ: Princeton University Press.
Sasson, Theodore. 2013. *The New American Zionism*. New York: New York University Press.
Scanlon, Sean. 2016. 'Global Homesickness in William Gibson's Blue Ant Trilogy'. In *The City Since 9/11: Literature, Film, Television*, edited by Keith Wilhite, pp. 143–60. Lanham and London: Rowman and Littlefield.
Scheidel, Walter. 2017. *The Great Leveler: Violence and the History of Inequality from the Stone Age to the 21st Century*. Princeton, NJ: Princeton University Press.
Schmitt, Carl. 2007. *The Concept of the Political*. Translated by George Schwab. Chicago: University of Chicago Press.
Schreiner, Olive. 2003. *The Story of an African Farm*, edited by Patricia O'Neill. Ormskirk: Broadview Literary Texts.
Schwan, Anne. 2012. 'Crime'. In *Charles Dickens in Context*, edited by Sally Ledger and Holly Furneaux, pp. 301–9. Cambridge: Cambridge University Press.
Schwarz, Bill. 2011. *The White Man's World: Memories of Empire, Volume 1*. Oxford: Oxford University Press.
Scott, James C. 2009. *The Art of Not Being Governed: An Anarchist History of Upland Southeast Asia*. New Haven, CT and London: Yale University Press.
Seeley, John R. 1931. *The Expansion of England*. London: Macmillan.
  1971. *The Expansion of England*, edited by John Gross. Chicago: University of Chicago Press.
Segal, Rafi and Eyal Weizman. 2003. *A Civilian Occupation: The Politics of Israeli Architecture*. London: Verso/Babel.
Selden, Daniel L. 2012. 'Mapping the Alexander Romance'. In *The Alexander Romance in Persia and the East*, edited by Richard Stoneman et al., pp. 19–59. Groningen: Groningen University Library.
Sellars, Simon. 2005. 'J. G. Ballard Live in London'. *Ballardian.com*, 7 October. www.ballardian.com/jg-ballard-live-in-london
Selvon, Sam. 2006. *The Lonely Londoners*. London: Penguin.
Shackle, C. 1996. 'Settings of Panegyric: The Secular Qasida in Mughal and British India'. In *Qasida Poetry in Islamic Asia and Africa: Classical Traditions and Modern Meanings*, edited by Stefan Sperl and Christopher Shackle, pp. 206–52. New York and Leiden: Brill.
Shaikh, Fariha. 2018. *Nineteenth-century Settler Emigration in British Literature and Art*. Edinburgh: Edinburgh University Press.
Shakely, Farhad. 1996. 'The Kurdish Qasida'. In *Qasida Poetry in Islamic Asia and Africa: Classical Traditions and Modern Meanings*, edited by Stefan Sperl and Christopher Shackle, pp. 137–82. New York and Leiden: Brill.
Shapiro, Stephen. 2008a. *The Culture and Commerce of the North Atlantic: Reading the Atlantic World-System*. University Park: Pennsylvania State University Press.

2008b. 'Transvaal, Transylvania: *Dracula's* World-System and Gothic Periodicity'. *Gothic Studies* 10 (1): 29–47.
Shapiro, Stephen and Philip Barnard. 2017. *Pentecostal Modernism: Lovecraft, Los Angeles, and World-Systems Culture*. New York: Bloomsbury Academic.
Shapple, Deborah L. 2004. 'Artful Tales of Origination in Olive Schreiner's *The Story of an African Farm*'. *Nineteenth-Century Literature* 59 (1): 78–114.
Shilliam, Robbie. 2018. *Race and the Underserving Poor: From Abolition to Brexit*. Newcastle-upon-Tyne: Agenda Publishing.
Singh, Frances B. 1978. 'The Colonialistic Bias of Conrad's "Heart of Darkness."' *Conradiana* 10 (1): 41–54.
Skinner, Benjamin. 2008. *A Crime So Monstrous: Face-to-Face with Modern Slavery*. New York: Simon & Schuster.
Slobodian, Quinn. 2018. *Globalists: The End of Empire and the Birth of Neoliberalism*. Cambridge, MA and London: Harvard University Press.
Sloterdijk, Peter. 2014. *In the World Interior of Capital: For a Philosophical Theory of Globalization*. Translated by Wieland Hoban. Cambridge and Malden, MA: Polity Press.
Smith, Ali. 2017. *Autumn*. New York: Anchor.
    2018. *Winter*. London: Penguin.
Smith, John. 2016. *Imperialism in the Twenty-First Century: Globalization, Super-Exploitation, and Capitalism's Final Crisis*. New York: Monthly Review Press.
Solnick, Sam. 2016. *Poetry and the Anthropocene: Ecology, Biology and Technology in Contemporary British and Irish Poetry*. London: Routledge.
Spanos, William V. 1972. 'The Detective and the Boundary: Some Notes on the Postmodern Literary Imagination'. *Boundary* 21 (1): 147–60.
Spinner, Laura. 2017. *Pale Rider: The Spanish Flu of 1918 and How It Changed the World*. New York: Public Affairs.
Spitzer, Leo. 2016. *Linguistics and Literary History: Essays in Stylistics*. Princeton, NJ: Princeton University Press.
Spivak, Gayatri Chakravorty. 1985. 'Three Women's Texts and a Critique of Imperialism'. *Critical Inquiry*, 12 (1): 243–61.
    2003. *Death of a Discipline*. New York: Columbia University Press.
    2011. *An Aesthetic Education in the Era of Globalization*. Cambridge, MA: Harvard University Press.
St. André, James. 2003. 'Modern Translation Theory and Past Translation Practice: European Translations of Haoqiu zhuan'. In *One Into Many: Translation and the Dissemination of Classical Chinese Literature*, edited by Leo Tak-hung Chan, pp. 39–67. Amsterdam: Rodopi.
Stathakopoulos, Dionysios Ch. 2007. 'Crime and Punishment: The Plague in The Byzantine Empire, 541–749'. In *Plague and the End of Antiquity*, edited by Lester K. Little, pp. 99–118. Cambridge: Cambridge University Press.
Starnes, Dewitt. 1937. 'English Dictionaries of the Seventeenth Century'. *Studies in English* 17: 15–51.
Steel, David. 1981. 'Plague Writing from Boccaccio to Camus'. *Journal of European Studies* 11: 88–110.

Steger, Manfred B. 2007. 'Globalization and Ideology'. In *The Blackwell Companion to Globalization*, edited by George Ritzer. Oxford: Blackwell Publishing.

Stiegler, Bernard. 1998. *Technics and Time, 1: The Fault of Epimetheus*. Translated by Richard Beardsworth and George Collins. Stanford: Stanford University Press.

2009. *Technics and Time, 2: Disorientation*. Translated by Stephen Barker. Stanford: Stanford University Press.

2010. 'Memory'. *Critical Terms for Media Studies*, edited by Mark B. N. Hansen and W. J. T. Mitchell. Chicago: University of Chicago Press.

2015. *States of Shock: Stupidity and Knowledge in the 21st Century*. Translated by Daniel Ross. Cambridge: Polity Press.

2018. *The Neganthropocene*. Translated by Daniel Ross. London: Open Humanities Press.

2020. 'Elements for a General Organology'. Translated by Daniel Ross. *Derrida Today* 13 (1): 72–94.

Stiglitz, Joseph. 2002. *Globalization and Its Discontents*. London and New York: Penguin.

Stoler, Ann Laura. 2016. *Duress: Imperial Durabilities in Our Times*. Durham, NC and London: Duke University Press.

Szendy, Peter. 2017. *All Ears: The Aesthetics of Espionage*. Translated by Roland Végsö. New York: Fordham University Press.

Tarapata, Olga. 2019. 'Unique Mattering: A New Materialist Approach to William Gibson's Pattern Recognition'. In *The Matter of Disability: Materiality, Biopolitics, Crip Affect*, edited by David T. Mitchell, Susan Antebi and Sharon L. Snyder, pp. 67–87. Ann Arbor, MI: University of Michigan Press.

Taubes, Jacob. 2009. *Occidental Eschatology*. Translated by David Ratmoko. Stanford: Stanford University Press.

Taylor, Barry. 2013. 'Learning Style from the Spaniards in Sixteenth-Century England'. In *Renaissance Cultural Crossroads: Translation, Print and Culture in Britain, 1473–1640*, edited by Sarah K. Barker and Brenda Hosington, pp. 63–78. Boston, MA: Brill.

Teukolsky, Rachel. 2009. *The Literate Eye: Victorian Art Writing and Modernist Aesthetics*. New York: Oxford University Press.

Tiplady, Jonty. 2016. "Just Do It." Public Seminar. 12 February. https://publicseminar.org/2016/02/just-do-it/

Topham, Gwyn. 2015. 'One in Four Plane Stowaways Can Survive'. *Guardian*, 19 June.

Trivedi, Harish. 2019. 'Translation and World Literature: The Indian Context'. In *Translation and World Literature*, edited by Susan Bassnett, pp. 15–28. New York: Routledge.

Trollope, Anthony. 1848. *The Kellys and the O'Kellys*. London: Ward, Lock and Co.

Trotsky, Leon. 1967. *History of the Russian Revolution*. Translated by Max Eastman. London: Sphere Books.

Tsing, Anna. 2011. 'The Global Situation'. In *Literature and Globalization: A Reader*, pp. 49–60. London and New York: Routledge.

Turner, David. 1990. 'The Politics of Despair: The Plague of 746–747 and Iconoclasm in the Byzantine Empire'. *Annual of the British School at Athens* 85: 419–34.
Turner, Fred and Christine Larson. 2015. 'Network Celebrity: Entrepreneurship and the New Public Intellectuals. *Public Culture* 27 (1): 53–84.
Tymoczko, Maria. 2007. *Enlarging Translation, Empowering Translators*. Manchester: St Jerome.
UK Govt. 1996. Arbitration Act 1996. www.legislation.gov.uk/ukpga/1996/23/contents
Ümit, Ahmed. 2011. *A Memento for Istanbul*. Translated by Rakesh Jobanputra. Istanbul: Everest.
US Customs at Pearson. www.torontopearson.com/en/departures/us-customs-pearson
US General Accountability Office. 2009. 'Report to Congressional Requesters: Border Patrol'. www.gao.gov/new.items/d09824.pdf
Vågene, Åshild J. et al. 2018. '*Salmonella enterica* Genomes from Victims of a Major Sixteenth-Century Epidemic in Mexico'. *Nature Ecology & Evolution* 2: 520–8.
Van Deburg, William L., ed. 1996. *Modern Black Nationalism: From Marcus Garvey to Louis Farrakhan*. New York: New York University Press.
Venkatasubbia, A. 1966. 'A Javanese Version of the Pañcatantra'. *Annals of the Bhandarkar Oriental Research Institute* 47 (1): 59–100.
Venuti, Lawrence. 2019. *Contra Instrumentalism: A Translation Polemic*. Lincoln: University of Nebraska Press.
Vico, Giambattista. 2002. *The First New Science*, edited by and Translated by Leon Pompa. Cambridge and New York: Cambridge University Press.
Vitale, Francesco. 2018. *Biodeconstruction: Jacques Derrida and the Life Sciences*. Translated by Mauro Senatore. Albany: SUNY Press.
Vizenor, Gerald. 1998. *Fugitive Poses: Native American Indian Scenes of Absence and Presence*. Lincoln and London: University of Nebraska Press.
Voosen, Paul. 2018. 'Massive Drought or Myth? Scientists Spar over an Ancient Climate Event behind Our New Geological Age'. *Science Magazine*. n.p.
Wacks, David. 2007. *Framing Iberia: Maqamat and Frametale Narratives in Medieval Spain*. Leiden and New York: Brill.
Wainwright, John and John B. Thornes. 2004. *Environmental Issues in the Mediterranean: Processes and Perspectives from the Past and Present*. London and New York: Routledge.
Wallace, Alan B. 2009. *Contemplative Science: Where Buddhism and Neuroscience Converge*. New York: Columbia University Press.
Wallace-Wells, David. 2019. *The Uninhabitable Earth: Life after Warming*. New York: Tim Duggan Books.
Wallerstein, Immanuel. 1996. *Historical Capitalism with Capitalist Civilization*. London: Verso.
2007. *World-Systems Analysis: An Introduction*. Durham, NC: Duke University Press.

2011. *The Modern World-System I: Capitalist Agriculture and the Origins of the European World-Economy in the Sixteenth Century*. Berkeley, CA and Los Angeles: University of California Press.
Walk Free Foundation. 2018. *Global Slavery Index*. www.globalslaveryindex.org/
Wark, McKenzie. 2019. *Capital Is Dead: Is This Something Worse?* London and New York: Verso.
Warwick Research Collective, The. (WReC). 2015. *Combined and Uneven Development: Towards a New Theory of World-Literature*. Liverpool: Liverpool University Press.
Watts, Cedric. 1983. '"A Bloody Racist": About Achebe's View of Conrad'. *Yearbook of English Studies* 13: 196–209.
Weiss, Harvey et al. 1993. 'The Genesis and Collapse of Third Millennium North Mesopotamian Civilization'. *Science* 261 (5124): 995–1004.
Wells, Herbert George. 1928. *The Open Conspiracy: Blue Prints for a World Revolution*. London: Victor Gollancz.
  2005. *The Shape of Things to Come: The Ultimate Revolution*. London: Penguin.
  2016a. 'The Brain Organization of the Modern World'. In *World Brain*, pp. 49–53. London: Read Books.
  2016b. 'Idea for a Permanent World Encyclopaedia'. In *World Brain*, pp. 73–7. London: Read Books.
West, M. L. 1997. *The East Face of Helicon: West Asiatic Elements in Greek Poetry and Myth*. Oxford: Oxford University Press.
Westfahl, Gary. 2013. *William Gibson*. Urbana, Chicago and Springfield: University of Illinois Press.
WHO (World Health Organization). 2019. Global Health Observatory (GHO) Data: HIV/AIDS. www.who.int/gho/hiv/en/
Wilder, Gary. 2015. *Freedom Time: Negritude, Decolonization and the Future of the World*. Durham, NC: Duke University Press.
Wilkins, Ernest H. 1950. 'A General Survey of Renaissance Petrarchism'. *Comparative Literature* 2 (4): 327–42.
Williams, Raymond. 1973. *The Country and the City*. Oxford: Oxford University Press.
  1977. *Marxism and Literature*. New York: Oxford University Press.
  1983. *Writing in Society*. London and New York: Verso.
  2007. *The Politics of Modernism: Against the New Conformists*. New York: Verso.
Wolfe, Tom. 1988. *The Bonfire of the Vanities*. London: Cape.
Woods, Christopher. 2010. 'Introduction: Visible Language: The Earliest Writing Systems'. In *Visible Language: Inventions of Writing in the Ancient Middle East and Beyond*, edited by Christopher E. Woods et al., pp. 15–27. Chicago: Oriental Institute of the University of Chicago.
Woodard, Colin. 2011. 'Far from Border, US Detains Foreign Students'. *Chronicle of Higher Education*. http://chronicle.com/article/Far-From-Canada-Aggressive/125880/
Woolf, Virginia. 2008. *Jacob's Room*. Oxford: Oxford World Classics.
Wordsworth, William. 1984. *The Major Works: Including The Prelude*, edited by Stephen Gill. Oxford: Oxford University Press.
Wright, Richard. 1991. *The Outsider*. New York: Perennial.

Wylie, Alexander. 1964. *Notes on Chinese Literature: With Introductory Remarks on the Progressive Advancement of the Art; and a List of Translations from the Chinese Into Various European Languages*. Taipei, China: Literature House.

Yancheva, Gergana et al. 2007. 'Influence of the Intertropical Convergence Zone on the East Asian Monsoon'. *Nature* 445: 74–7.

Young, Paul. 2018. 'Dickens's World-System: Globalized Modernity as Combined and Uneven Development'. In *The Oxford Handbook of Charles Dickens*, edited by John Jordan et al., pp. 703–21. Oxford: Oxford University Press.

Zenz, Adrian. 2019. 'Beyond the Camps: Beijing's Grand Scheme of Forced Labor, Poverty Alleviation, and Social Control in Xinjiang'. https://doi.org/10.31235/osf.io/8tsk2

Zhang, David D. et al. 2006. 'Climate Change, Wars and Dynastic Cycles in China over the Last Millennium'. *Climatic Change* 76: 459–77. https://doi.org/10.1007/s10584-005-9024-z

  2011. 'Climate Change and Large-Scale Population Collapses in the Pre-Industrial Era'. *Global Geology and Biogeography* 20: 520–31.

  2005. 'Climate Change, Social Unrest and Dynastic Transition in Ancient China'. *Chinese Science Bulletin* 50 (2): 137–44.

Zhang, Zhibin. 2010. 'Periodic Climate Cooling Enhanced Natural Disasters and Wars in China during AD 10-1900'. *Proceedings of the Royal Society B* 277: 3745–53.

Zürcher, Erik. 2007. *The Buddhist Conquest of China: The Spread and Adaptation of Buddhism in Early Medieval China*. Vol. 11. New York and Leiden: Brill.

Žižek, Slavoj. 2006. *The Parallax View*. London and Cambridge: MIT Press.

Index

Achebe, Chinua, 103, 206
Actor Network Theory, 227–8
  and translation, 68–9
Africa, 258
  and Black political consciousness, 198
  and Chinese imperialism, 207
  and diaspora, 204
  and European colonialism, 220
  and *fin-de-siecle* literature, 221–2
  and Karl Marx, 196
  North, 266
African Fiction
  and the literary world-system, 206
Alexander Romance, 39
Alighieri, Dante, 29, 34, 46, 48, 50, 56, 58
Amazon, 161
America (United States of), 198, 199, 206, 214, 265
  and *A Mercy*, 209
  and cultural hegemony, 206
  and the world-literary system, 206
Amis, Martin, 9, 152, 154
Ancient Greek, 25, 28, 29, 41, 54
Anderson, Benedict, 89, 114
Anthropocene, 162–3, 165, 307, 313, 318–33
Anti-colonialism, 200, 269
Anti-semitism, 120–2
Arabic, 29, 38, 41, 68, 71, 74
Aristotle, 191
Ashbury, John, 318
Atwood, Margaret, 33
Auerbach, Erich, 5, 65, 127, 133–6
Augustine, St., 28, 55

Badiou, Alain, 183
Balibar, Étienne, 248
Ballard, J. G., 13, 253–5, 259, 260
Banks, Iain, 146
Barad, Karen, 165
Baudrillard, Jean, 150–2
Beck, Ulrich, 144–7

Benda, Christoph, 312
Berger, John, 247–8, 255
Bible, the, 22, 278
Bilal, Parker, 272
Black Lives Matter, 209
Bok, Francis, 14, 297–304
Bolaño, Roberto, 11, 212–19
Boltanski, Luc, 279, 289
Bond, James, 277
Borders, 248, 260, 282, 283
  lack of, 291, 322
Braudel, Fernand, 263
Buchan, John, 211
Bulawayo, NoViolet, 206
Bush, George H. W., 155

Camões', Luis de, 70
Camus, Albert, 265
Caribbean, the, 8, 98, 111, 198, 203, 213, 264
Carlotto, Massimo, 271
Casanova, Pascale, 204–6
Caxton, William, 69
Césaire, Aimé, 11, 200–2
Chaucer, Geoffrey, 29–30
China
  and Buddhist writings, 28, 30, 39
  and communism, 52
  and Conrad, 107
  and decolonization, 199
  and *Dombey and Son*, 92
  and early literacy, 25
  and early world-systems, 35
  and Ezra Pound, 112
  and neo-imperialism, 207
  and plague, 27
  and slavery, 294
  and Special Economic Zones, 250
  and territorial expansion, 326
  and the 1876–79 famine, 33
  and the Black Death, 30

362

and the Song Dynasty, 29
and the Tang Dynasty, 29
Chinese (language), 25
Chinese literature
   and translation, 78
Chinese novel, the, 72
Churchill, Caryl, 9, 150
Circulation, 3, 159
   and commodities, 147
   and postmodernity, 185
   and pre-modern poetry, 41–2
   and short pre-modern prose, 40
   and the *qasida*, 45
   and the sonnet, 46
   and translation, 5, 67
   and world-systems, 75
   economic and literary, 38
   Goethe on, 229
   of literary forms, 4
Cleary, Joe, 114, 117
Climate change
   and extinction, 53
   and global cooling, 22, 25, 30–2
   and global warming, 22, 33–4
   and messianic time, 329
   and peripheral poetry, 321–3
   and satellite technology, 310
   and the biotariat, 331
   and the Mediterranean, 275
   Intergovernmental Panels on, 318
Clover, Joshua, 326–9
Cold War, 52, 126, 154, 213, 262, 264, 277, 280, 306, 312, 313
Collis, Stephen, 16, 329–32
Colonialism
   and Blackness, 202
   and diaspora, 204
   and genre, 225
   and 'Greater Britain', 82, 222
   and mediterranean noir, 267
   and modernity, 117
   and neo-imperialism, 204
   and old European powers, 206
   and realism, 84
   and resource extraction, 87, 201
   and the Marshall Islands, 322
   and the other, 113
   and the United States, 208
   and the white male, 102
   and translation, 73
   and violence, 92
   and world literature studies, 67
Conrad, Joseph, 7, 8, 14, 82, 97–109, 112, 114, 127–8
Contingency, 10, 178–94

Cosmopolitanism
   and Ali Smith, 256
   and early Islam, 43
   and language, 40–2
   and modernism, 111, 116–20
   and Persian literature, 43
   and postmodernism, 147
   and socialism, 199
   and the Arabic *qasida*, 45
   and the Latin sonnet, 49
   and the *qasida*, 49
Coupland, Douglas, 65

Damrosch, David, 67
de Chardin, Pierre Tielhard, 64
Dean, Jodi, 292–3
Deconstruction, 6, 9, 139, 165, 166
Defoe, Daniel, 71
Deleuze, Gilles, 173–4
DeLillo, Don, 65
   The Names, 312
Derrida, Jacques, 159–63, 176, 188–9, 230, 306
Dickens, Charles, 6, 81–93
Dickinson, Adam, 332
Digital culture, 6, 175–6
Digital humanities, 76
Digital, the, 3, 10, 16, 160
   and grammatization, 167
   and life, 176
   and poetry, 329
   and temporality, 189
   and the analogue, 164, 168
   and the generalisation of Blackness, 197

Easton Ellis, Bret, 9, 153–4
Eckermann, J. P., 73, 228–9
Ecology, 24, 145, 202
Eliot, George, 87, 114
Eliot, T. S., 115–16, 120, 328
Emmerich, Karen, 75
Empire, 3, 6, 22
   Akkadian, 24
   and modernism, 113, 120
   and the country estate novel, 223
   and the *qasida*, 45
   and *The Wasteland*, 112
   and World War, 63
   and world-systems, 35
   British, 80–93
   critique of, 123
   end of, 277
   European, 70, 73, 204
   German, 227
   Mongol, 27
   Ottoman, 30, 74

Empire (cont.)
  remains of, 266, 268
  Roman, 27, 28, 146
Enclaves, 249–60, 308
End of history, the, 5, 51–65, 155
Engels, Friedrich, 184
Entropocene, 167
Eschatology, 5, 65
Eurafrasia, 4, 37, 40, 50
European Union, The, 256
Extinction, 21, 53, 65, 213, 306–7, 323, 326–9

Facebook, 161
Famine, 22, 30–3, 112
Fanon, Frantz, 11, 140, 202–3
  Black Skin, White Masks, 202
Fanshawe, Richard, 71
Finance, 7, 28, 145, 150, 204, 205, 218, 221, 250
fin-de-siècle, 12, 223
Forster, E. M., 106, 113
Foucault, Michel, 90, 127
  and anti-humanism, 134
  and authorship, 233
  and Edward Said, 127, 140
  and imperial infrastructure, 90
  The Order of Things, 281
Fukuyama, Francis, 54, 63, 155

Gaia, 331
Geist, 63, 132
Gibson, William, 14, 277–93
Gilroy, Paul, 11, 195–201, 207–9, 294
Global Britain, 82
Goethe, J. W., 12
  and *Hau kiou chooan*, 73
  and *weltliteratur*, 134
  and world literature, 228–33, 128
  end of world literature, 138
  in the twentieth century, 235
  statue of, 226
Google, 161, 326, 327
Google Maps, 312
Graham, Jorie, 318–20
Greece, 25, 38, 112, 265
Greig, David, 156–8
Guattari, Félix, 173

Hage, Rawi, 272
Haggard, H. Rider, 221–2, 225
Harari, Yuval Noah, 65
Harlem Renaissance, 110, 198
Harvey, David, 10, 178–94
Hebrew, 25, 29, 40, 43, 46
Hegel, G. W. F., 51, 52, 64, 133
Heidegger, Martin, 230, 235, 309, 311

Hobson, J. A., 113, 223
Hyper-reality, 9

Imperialism, 7–8, 11, 15, 33, 72, 75, 80, 83, 104, 111, 113–24, 146, 192, 198, 206, 223, 266
India, 5, 26, 29, 30, 68, 70, 74, 79, 98
  and Britain's second empire, 82
  and famine, 30–3
  and the *Shahnameh*, 38
  and world-systems, 36
  in *David Copperfield*, 91
Izzo, Jean-Claude, 267, 274

Jacobs, Charles, 298–301
James, C. L. R., 197, 201
James, Henry, 115
Jameson, Fredric
  and contemporary historical fiction, 33
  and critique, 157
  and cultural dominants, 132
  and empire, 113–14
  and genre, 218
  and global capitalism, 146
  and Joseph Conrad, 106
  and modernity, 117
  and post-fordism, 181
  and postmodernism, 9, 144, 148–50
  and the utopian, 59, 251
  and totality, 14, 192, 285–6
  and William Gibson, 279–80, 287
Jetñil-Kijiner, Kathy, 16, 321–5
Johnson, Samuel, 77
Joyce, James, 8, 112, 119–24, 126, 133
  Portrait of the Artist as a Young Man, 119, 216
  Ulysses, 57, 123

Keynes, John Maynard, 62
Kincaid, Jamaica, 205
Kojève, Alexandre, 52
Koyré, Alexandre, 159
Kurzweil, Ray, 65

Labour
  and frontiers, 108
  and platforms, 293
  and post-fordism, 181
  and slavery, 14, 196, 294–5, 303
  and the Panama Canal, 199
  and the world-system, 11
Larsson, Stieg, 264
Latin, 46, 54, 69, 71, 77
Latour, Bruno, 68, 162, 227, 331
Lebanon, 13, 265, 296
Linear B, 25

Index

Lucretius, 54
Lyotard, Jean-François, 152–3, 157, 280

Marana, Giovanni, 71
Markaris, Petros, 13, 270–2
Marshall Island, the, 321–5
Marx, Karl, 57, 119, 184, 196, 287
Marxism
  and critique, 59, 182
  and Edward Said, 127
  and Pan-Africanism, 198
  and penetration, 186
  and postmodernism, 147
  and world-systems critique, 218
Mattich, Alen, 274–5
Mbembe, Achille, 195–7, 200, 203, 205, 209
McKay, Claude, 110–1, 118, 199
McWorld, 9, 148
Meillassoux, Quentin, 183
Miéville, China, 248, 313
Mitchell, David, 313
  Cloud Atlas, 33, 213
Modernism, 31
  and absence, 103
  and Aimé Césaire, 202
  and Black history, 195
  and cosmopolitanism, 120
  and earlier aesthetic movements, 223
  and East Germany, 235
  and imperialism, 110–15
  and Joseph O'Neill, 251
  and nationalism, 124
  and realism, 58
  and Roberto Bolaño, 216
  and the past, 269
  and the random moment, 58
  and time, 60, 65
  and totality, 192
  and utopia, 59
Modernity
  and Black history, 195
  and Earth, 310
  and eschatology, 51
  and infinity, 159
  and modernism, 117
  and *négritude*, 200
  and Richard Wright, 200
  and slavery, 294
  and the sea, 105
  end of, 145
Montalbán, Manuel Vázquez, 267
Moretti, Franco, 84, 195, 218
Morrison, Toni, 208

Naipaul, V. S., 115
Nationalism
  and Black political consciousness, 198
  and Ireland, 121
  and James Joyce, 124
  and Paul Gilroy, 196
  and philology, 133
  in the nineteenth century, 81
  in the twentieth century, 8, 64, 156
  in the twenty-first century, 64, 257
Nation-state, the, 50, 80, 83, 92, 106, 120, 218, 249, 279, 322
  and Iain Banks, 146
  and the IMF, 156
  and the region, 112
  and the world market, 145
  and totality, 114
  and William Gibson, 290, 291
  in Ulysses, 122
Nazer, Mende, 296
Neganthropocene, 170
Negri, Antonio, 53, 60
Neo-feudalism, 13, 224, 292–3
Neoliberalism, 3, 145, 174, 184, 292
New Criticism, 126, 136, 138
North America, 210, 240, 314

Occitan, 46, 48, 50
Old Testament, 55, 56
O'Neill, Joseph, 250–1, 313
Orientalism, 8, 73–4, 126

Pamuk, Orhan, 315–16
Pan-Africanism, 198
Pañcatantra, 38–41
Pandemics, 22, 27–8, 32, 165, 166, 249, 312, 313
  and European colonisation, 30
  and The Black Death, 30
Percy, Thomas, 73
Persian (language), 29, 38, 39, 43
Petrarch, Francesco, 29–30, 46, 49
Petrowskaja, Katja, 12, 239–43
Phillips, Caryl, 13, 257–9
Plato
  and Prometheus, 190
  and the *kallipolis*, 252
Postmodernism
  and Bret Easton Ellis, 153–4
  and Caryl Churchill, 150
  and Fredric Jameson, 149
  and Jean Baudrillard, 150–1
  and Jean-François Lyotard, 152–3
  and Martin Amis, 152
  and modernism, 117
  and post-fordism, 186–7, 194
  and totality, 281
  and transnational capitalism, 147

Postmodernism (cont.)
　emergence of, 144
　end of, 158
Postmodernity
　and neoliberalism, 185
　and the end of history, 53
　and time, 60
Pound, Ezra, 7, 111, 117, 120, 251
Powers, Richard, 313–14

Rancière, Jacques, 211
Ricoeur, Paul, 193–4
Russia, 25, 52, 97, 199, 212, 240, 265, 280, 283, 286

Said, Edward, 8, 73, 82, 104, 126–43
Sanskrit, 4, 26, 78, 269
Sassen, Saskia, 248, 262
Schreiner, Olive, 6, 81–93
Sea, the, 98–100
　and *A Mercy*, 208
　and Conrad, 104–9
　and travel, 178
　and utopia, 265, 272–6
　level, 321
　South China, 326
Seeley, John, 80–3, 222
Selvon, Sam, 203–4
Shakespeare, William
　and male actors, 238
　and Spain, 29
　King Lear, 32
Slavery, 14
　and Blackness, 196–8
　and Chinese labour, 271
　and modernity, 294
　and neo-imperialism, 303
　and the canonical novel, 83
　in the contemporary world, 294–7
　the legacy of, 205–9
Smith, Ali, 13, 65, 256–7
Social media, 161, 166, 167, 172, 188, 320, 327
Sonnet, the, 41
　and Petrarch, 30
　origins of, 45–50
South Africa, 209
　and the Kingdom of Lesotho, 249
Soviet Union, 2, 52, 155, 156
Spahr, Juliana, 325–9
Spitzer, Leo, 63, 128, 133, 136
Spivak, Gayatri Chakravorty, 6, 83, 305, 314
Stiegler, Bernard, 10, 166–8, 187–91, 327
Stoke, Bram, 222
Stross, Charles, 65
Sudan, 265, 296–301

Sumeria, 25
Szendy, Peter, 278

Taubes, Jacob, 51
Technics, 160, 166, 167, 171–3, 179, 189
The Warwick Research Collective, 213
Thiong, Ngũgĩ wa, 204
Thousand and One Nights, 73
Time-space compression, 10, 178–94
Totality, 11, 53, 321, 331
　and Blackness, 10
　and humanity, 169
　and Joe Cleary, 114
　and Lyotard, 153
　and modernism, 8, 113
　and philology, 61
　and postmodernism, 149
　and spy fiction, 280–1
　and William Gibson, 14, 283–93
Tourism, 99, 161, 205, 263, 275
Turkey, 58, 265, 315
Twitter, 327

Ümit, Ahmet, 13, 268
Utopian, the, 12, 13, 61, 234–43, 249–56, 309
　and Conrad, 105
　and critique, 58
　and the sea, 266, 276

Vico, Giambattista, 127–8, 131–3, 141

Wallerstein, Immanuel, 11, 41, 140
　and geoculture, 210–1
　and translation, 75
　The Modern World-System, 35
Walrond, Eric, 11, 199
War on terror, 157, 248
Warwick Research Collective, 196
Wells, H. G., 64, 222, 224
Whitman, Walt, 106
Wikipedia, 167
Wilkinson, James, 72
Williams, Raymond, 80, 87–8, 93, 116–17, 218
Wolfe, Tom, 145
Woolf, Virginia
　Jacob's Room, 112
　To the Lighthouse, 57
Wordsworth, Dorothy, 323
Wordsworth, William, 159
World History, 2, 196, 243
World literature
　and decentralization, 75
　and difference, 159
　and European influence, 79
　and Goethe, 73, 229

and orientalism, 74
and philology, 134, 137
and postcolonial literature, 139
and Renaissance translation, 70
and scale, 35–8
and *The Black Atlantic*, 195
and translation, 69
and world authorship, 232–4
end of, 61
World-systems
and *2666*, 212–18
and actor network theory, 75
and African diaspora, 199
and alternatives, 307
and decline, 1, 64
and dysfunctionality, 313
and Eurafrasia, 40
and genre-systems, 218–25
and geoculture, 210–12
and new power structures, 291
and novelty, 97
and Paris, 114
and phenomenology, 212–18
and scale, 35–8
and spy fiction, 286
and the end of history, 63
and the periphery, 321–2
and theory, 3
and transformation, 262
and translation, 75